D0003469

Publisher's Note

Books purporting to reveal secret manufacturing methods and formulas were very popular in the late 1800s. With lawsuits far less common and class action suits unheard of, authors would blithely recommend everything from doubtful medical treatments to mixing potentially lethal concoctions. But at the same time, books contained a wealth of information on basic industrial practices, ranging from how to make your own lime to the various ways to treat metals to achieve desired surface effects.

It is all interesting even though some of it is alarming. Nuggets can be found throughout. A quick scan of "Jockey Tricks" on pages 284 to 285 provides insight into practices later refined by used car salesmen. An aging horse in the 19th century was the equivalent of a used car in the 20th century. A wealth of information can be gleaned from this book, but all advice should be taken with a grain of salt; the warning on the facing page should be heeded always.

Leonard G. Lee, Publisher
Ottawa
January, 1998

WARNING

This is a reprint of a book compiled in 1895. It describes what was done and what was recommended to be done in accordance with the knowledge of the day.

On the medical side, some of the proposed remedies would not only be considered inadequate today, but would also be considered potentially harmful.

ON ALL MEDICAL ADVICE, CONSULT YOUR PHYSICIAN. DO NOT TAKE THE ADVICE GIVEN HERE.

It would also be advisable to treat all corrosive, explosive and toxic materials with greater caution than is indicated here, particularly any materials that come in contact with the body.

LEE'S
Priceless Recipes

A VALUABLE COLLECTION OF

TRIED FORMULAS AND SIMPLE METHODS

FOR

Farmers, Housekeepers, Mechanics, Manufacturers, Druggists, Chemists, Perfumers, Barbers, Chiropodists, Renovators, Dyers, Bakers, Confectioners, Woodworkers, Decorators, Painters, Paper-hangers, Metal-workers, Hunters, Trappers, Tanners, Taxidermists, Stockmen, Etc., and all People in Every Department of Human Endeavor.

ALPHABETICALLY INDEXED

COMPILED BY

DR. N. T. OLIVER

CHICAGO
LAIRD & LEE, Publishers

CONTENTS

DEPARTMENT I.—THE DRUGGIST.

DEPARTMENT II.—THE CHEMIST.

DEPARTMENT III.—TOILET ARTICLES.

DEPARTMENT IV.—THE HOUSEHOLD.

DEPARTMENT V.—ALL TRADES.

DEPARTMENT VI.—THE FARM AND DAIRY.

DEPARTMENT VII.—GENERAL MISCELLANY.

EXPLANATORY

It is the aim of the compiler to present in as small a space as possible the **rules** and **processes,** together with the **formulas** and **recipes** for manufacturing many of those articles used by mechanics, artisans, families, and all people in every walk of life, and by so doing, not only furnish the knowledge as to the "way it is done," but also to place the reader in a position "to do it." As far as possible, ambiguous and technical terms have been refrained from. Occasionally some such phrase may be found, not generally understood, in which event a dictionary will soon explain.

The cardinal points of excellence, namely, "**Reliability, Usefulness, Brevity** and **Simplicity,**" have been closely followed, and if the searcher after information will carefully read the Table of Contents, then scan the pages of this work, study well the signs, abbreviations, processes, table of weights and measures, etc., and then closely follow the given rules, success must surely crown each and every effort.

The **various departments** are characteristically **classified,** divided under sub-heads, and the alphabetical index is so comprehensive that any special article can be found by referring to the index for that department. If the formula desired is not found under any particular class, search the Miscellaneous Department of each division, or the Department of General Miscellany, and if it is an article of general use it will be found.

In conclusion the author wishes to state that great care has been taken in compiling the work, which represents the result of **twenty years' conscientious collecting;** and that it may prove a never-failing friend and a means of saving and earning money for its possessor is the sincere hope of

THE AUTHOR.

MORTAR AND PESTLE.

FUNNEL.

GRADUATING GLASS.

RETORT.

CHEMICAL JAR.

FRUIT DRYING STOVE.

SCALES.

FILTER.

ALEMBIC.

HYDROMETER.

DEPARTMENT I.

THE DRUGGIST.

Abbreviations and Signs in general use in medical prescriptions and recipes are as follows:

Signs.	Derivations.	Meanings.
℞	Recipe	Take
aa.,	Ana	Of each
℔	Libra	Pound
℥ or oz	Uncia	Ounce
ℨ or dr	Drachma	Dram
℈ or Sc	Scrupulus	Scruple
Cong	Congius	Gallon
O. or pt	Octarius	Pint
f ℥ or F. oz	Fluid uncia	Fluid ounce
f ℨ F. dr	Fluid drachma	Fluid dram
M	Minimum	Minim
Chart	Chartula	Small paper
Coch	Cochlear	Spoonful
Collyr	Collyrium	Eye water
Decoct	Decoctum	Decoction
Ft	Fiat	Make
Garga	Gargarisnia	Gargle
Gr	Granum	Grain
Gtt	Gutta	Drop
Haust	Haustus	Draught
Infus	Infusum	Infusion
M—	Misce	Mix
Mass	Massa	Mass
Mist	Mistura	Mixture
Pulv	Pulvis	Powder
Q. S.	Quantum sufficit	Sufficient quantity
Sig. or S	Signa	Write
Ss.	Semis	Half

Useful Table of equivalents of measures in taking medicines or preparing them;

Teaspoonful..........	about 1 F. dram
Dessert spoonful.......................	about 2 F. drams
Tablespoonful........	about 4 F. drams
Wine glassful.........................	about 2 F. ounces
Teacupful.............................	about 4 F. ounces
Breakfast cupful.......................	about 8 F. ounces
Tumblerful...........................	about 8 F. ounces
Thimbleful...........................	about ¾ F. dram

NOTE.—In preparing or taking medicine exercise particularity in following directions.

TABLES OF WEIGHTS AND THEIR EQUIVALENTS.

Apothecaries Weight is used by druggists in compounding medicines, and is the official standard of the *United States Pharmacopœia*. In buying and selling medicines not ordered by prescription, avoirdupois weight is used. The denominations of apothecaries weight and their relative values are as follows:

Pound.	Ounces.	Drams.	Scruples.	Grains.
1..........	=12.........	=96.........	=228......	..=5,760
0.............	1.........	= 8.........	= 24.............	= 480
0.............	0.........	1.........	= 3.............	= 60
0.............	0.........	0.........	1.............	= 20

Or, giving the table in its usual form, we say:

20 grains................................	1 scruple
3 scruples..............................	1 dram
8 drams................................	1 ounce
12 ounces..............................	1 pound

Troy Weight is used by jewelers and at the mints. It is for the weighing of precious metals and stones. Its denominations and their relative values are:

Pound.	Ounces.	Pennyweights.	Grains.
1......	=12.........	=240........	=5,760
0.............	1.........	= 20........	= 480
0..........	0.........	1........	= 24

Or—

24 grains................................	1 pennyweight
20 pennyweights.......................	1 ounce
12 ounces..............................	1 pound

Avoirdupois Weight is used for weighing all goods except those for which troy and apothecaries weights are employed, and for compounding recipes for domestic purposes and for the mechanical arts. Its denominations and their relative values are as follows:

Ton.	Cwt. (hundredweight.)	Quarters. (Qrs.)	Pounds. (lbs.)	Ounces. (ozs.)	Drams. (drs.)
1	=20	=80	=2,240	=35,840	=573,440
0	1	= 4	= 112	= 1,799	= 28,672
0	0	1	= 28	= 448	= 7,168
0	0	0	1	= 16	= 258
0	0	0	0	1	= 16

Or—

16 drams...1 oz.
16 ounces ....1 ℔.
28 pounds...1 qr.
4 quarters...1 cwt.
20 hundredweight.......................................1 ton

The common standard weight by which the relative values of these systems are compared is the grain, which, for this purpose, may be regarded as the unit or beginning of weight. The pound troy and that of apothecaries weight have each 5,760 grains; the pound avoirdupois has 7,000 grains. The relative proportions and values are as follows:

Troy.		Avoirdupois.
	oz.	dr.
1 pound...................................	=13	2.65
1 ounce...................................	= 1	1.55
1 pennyweight (dwt)......................	= 0	0.877

		Apothecaries.			
	℔.	oz.	dr.	sc.	gr.
1 pound.......................	=1	0	0	0	0
1 ounce.......................	=0	1	0	0	0
1 pennyweight.................	=0	0	0	1	4
1 grain.......................	=0	0	0	0	1

Apothecaries.		Avoirdupois.
	oz.	dr.
1 pound...................................	=13	2.65
1 ounce...................................	= 1	1.55
1 dram....................................	= 0	2.19
1 scruple.................................	= 0	0.73

		Troy.		
	℔.	oz.	dwt.	gr.
1 pound.......................	=1	0	0	0
1 ounce.......................	=0	1	0	0
1 dram........................	=0	0	2	12
1 scruple.....................	=0	0	0	20

Avoirdupois.

	lb.	*oz.*	Troy. *dwt.*	*gr.*
1 ton...............=2,922	2	13	8	
1 hundredweight.. .. ..=	146	1	6	16
1 quarter..................=	34	0	6	16
1 pound...................=	1	2	11	16
1 ounce...................=	0	0	18	5½
1 dram....................=	0	0	1	3 11-32

	lb.	*oz.*	Apothecaries. *dr.*	*sc.*	*gr.*
1 pound.....................=1	2	4	2	0	
1 ounce............ ....=0	0	7	0	17½	
1 dram.....................=0	0	0	1	7 11-32	

Tables of Measure.—Most liquid substances are dispensed by measure instead of by weight. Apothecaries or wine measure is the official or standard system in use by the pharmacists of the United States. Its denominations are gallon, pint fluid ounce, fluid dram and minim, and the signs used to express them and their relative values, are as follows;

Cong.	*O.*	*F oz.*	*F dr.*	*Minims.*
1................=8.........=128.......=1,024.....=61,440				
0.........	1.........= 16......= 128......= 7,680			
0.........	0.........	1.......= 8.....= 780		
0.........	0.........	0......	1.....= 60	
0.........	0.........	0......	0.....	1

Or—

| 60 Minims...1 F dr. |
| 8 F drs. ....1 F oz. |
| 16 F ozs. ....1 O. |
| 8 O..1 Cong. |

Imperial Standard Measure is the system in use by British pharmacists. Its denominations and their relative values are as follows;

Gal.	*Qts.*	*Pts.*	*F oz.*	*F dr.*	*Minims.*
1 ....=4....=8...=160....=1,280.... =76,800					
0.	1....=2...= 40....= 320.... =19,200				
0.	0...	1....= 20....= 160....= 9,600			
0.	0...	0...	1....= 8....= 480		
0.	0...	0...	0....	1.... = 60	

Or—

| 60 minims...1 F dr. |
| 8 F drs...1 F oz. |
| 20 F ozs...1 pt. |
| 2 pints...1 qt. |
| 4 quarts...1 gal. |

This measure is in general use in all parts of the world, including the United States. The relative value of the United States apothecaries and British Imperial measures is as follows:

United States Apothecaries.			British Imperial.			
				Pt.	F oz.	F dr.	Drops.
1 gal.	=	.83311	Imperial gal. or	6	13	2	22.85
1 pint	=	.83311	Imperial pt. or	0	16	5	17.86
1 F oz	=	1.04139	Imperial F oz. or	0	1	0	19.76
1 F dr.	=	1.04139	Imperial F dr. or	0	0	1	2.48
1 minim	=	1.04139	Imperial min. or	0	0	0	1.04

APPARATUS.

The following are of great assistance in the making up of medical preparations, and although other articles can be used, it is by far the best plan to procure the tools of the trade if satisfactory results are expected:

Mortars.—These are among the articles of most frequent use in pharmaceutical processes. They are made of glass, wood, porcelain, iron, composition, marble and other substances, and vary in size from one ounce up. They are used for mixing ointments, cerates and soft pulverized substances; also for pulverizing barks, spices, etc.

The Pestle is the necessary assistant of the mortar, and is usually made in two pieces. This necessary piece of apparatus can be purchased of any drug supply house.

Scales are an absolute necessity, as the proper proportion of the materials cannot be ascertained without them. Two pairs should be used—one known as the prescription scale for weighing 1 drachm and under, and a larger pair for weighing over 2 drachms.

Graduates or graduating glasses are glass vessels marked with a scale, and are necessary for measuring liquids. They can be obtained in several sizes.

Spatulas are made of glass, ivory and steel, are a flat, flexible bladed knife, used for mixing. The steel spatula or palette is the best for ordinary purposes. They come in several sizes. A common case knife answers the purpose.

Percolator is a vessel made of tin, glass or wood, and is used for extracting the soluble principles from vegetable substances. (*See Percolation.*) Sometimes they are made of porcelain or earthenware. The tin is the most generally used. It is in the form of a tube about 8 inches long and 3½ inches in diameter, terminating at one end in a funnel, and contains easily removable loosely, fitting perforated plates. The instrument acts somewhat on the principle of a strainer. *See Processes, article on Percolation.*

Funnels, or tunnels, are made of glass, porcelain, hard rubber, tin or other metals. They are used in transferring liquids, and several sizes are necessary.

Retorts are made of glass or iron and are in several sizes. With them are needed stands or frames to support them, and funnels, filtering and displacement apparatus are necessary. Retorts are used in all processes of distillation. *See Distillation.*

Filter Rack.—A funnel-shaped framework of wire used to hold the filtering paper. *See Filtration.*

Lamps used in the process of distillation. The alcohol lamp is the best for the purpose, and should be provided with a frame or rack in which to place it. A cap is required to place over the wick of the alcohol lamp after using to prevent evaporation.

Baths are used for securing a more uniform and fixed degree of heat than are obtained from the open flame or an ordinary heating apparatus. They are of various kinds, but those most generally used are the Sand Bath, made of an iron or copper vessel containing ordinary clean sand, in which the vessel containing the material to be heated is so imbedded and surrounded as to prevent the two vessels coming in contact, and the Water Bath, which consists of one vessel within another, as an ordinary double glue pot, so arranged that they cannot come in contact at any point to which the heat is applied.

Sieves come in several sizes; are fitted with silk or brass wire gauze for fine purposes, or horse hair cloth or wire netting for coarser ones. Drum sieves are such as are furnished with covers, rendering loss and dust impossible. Sieves are used in preparing powders, mixing vegetable pulverizations, etc.

NOTE.—The above are the articles in most general use, and are the most needed in large laboratories. Test tubes, crucibles, drug mills, tincture presses and a host of others are made use of, but for all ordinary purposes the list as here given is all that will be required. We will now pass on to the various ways of compounding medicines.

PROCESSES.

Decocting.—A method for extracting the active or useful principle from animal or vegetable substances, where the same cannot be injured by heat. It consists of boiling for a certain length of time; where the proportions are not given, use one ounce of raw material to one pint of water.

Distillation.—The vaporization of a liquid in one vessel and conducting it in this condition to another, where it is condensed and collected. It is used for separating liquids from the solids with which they are mixed; for separating more volatile liquids, as ether, alcohol, etc., from others less so with which they are mixed, and for impregnating liquids with the volatile principles of plants, etc., as in the preparation of the aromatic spirits, cologne water, etc. It is performed with a retort and receiver. Apply the heat with a spirit or alcohol lamp under the bulb of the retort, and produce condensation by wrapping cloths wet with cold water around the retort. when the principle desired will be effected.

Filtration.—A process for separating insoluble matters, precipitates, etc., by means of *porous media*, or the medium of slow pouring or dripping, which allows the passage of the liquids only. and employed for rendering liquids, tinctures, etc., clear and transparent, and separating valuable precipitates. Tinctures and dilute spirits are usually filtered through a specially prepared paper called filtering paper, and which can be procured of any druggist. It is cut in a peculiar manner, made into the shape of a funnel and placed in a rack or funnel, where it cleanly separates the articles to be run through. The process of making the paper filter is as follows: Cut a circular disc of filtering paper in two through the line of its diameter; take either half and fold it across the line of the radius, bringing the edges close together; then turn down the double edge of the cut side and fold it several times; finally, run a smooth, hard surface along the seam thus produced, to compress it. and spread the finished filter into an appropriate rack or funnel, first moistening it with water before the liquid to be filtered is poured in.

A Cheap Filter is made by taking an ordinary, large-sized flower pot; plug the hole with a piece of sponge; then put a layer of powdered charcoal about 1 inch thick, the same of silver sand: then a layer of small stones and gravel about 2 inches thick. This makes an excellent filter for impure water.

Another method of purifying water is by placing in a tank of impure water a vessel so arranged that a sponge which it contains shall lap over the edge and dip into the water of the tank. The sponge gradually sucks up and purifies the water in the reservoir and allows it to drop into a smaller vessel or receiver, from which it can be drawn off by a tube. By placing a few lumps of charcoal in the receiver, filtration of the most perfect kind is effected.

Any Vessel open at both ends (one smaller at one end than the other is preferable) can be used as a filter by setting it in an upright position and putting straw, sand or charcoal in the bottom, and passing the liquid to be filtered through it.

Magnesia in small quantities placed in the paper filter greatly assists in clarifying tinctures. etc.

Clarification. The removal of impurities from liquids by the admixture of some substances, usually albumen in some form, as milk, the white of an egg. or a solution of gelatine, which, by being coagulated, entangles and precipitates the contained impurities, rendering the liquids clear. Vegetable acids will clarify the expressed juices of plants. The following composition is said to bleach all colored liquids: Albumen, 300 parts; neutral tartrate of Potash, 2; alum. 5; sal ammoniac, 700. The albumen must of course not be coagulated. The ingredients are first dissolved in a little water and then added to the liquid to be clarified.

Expression is required to separate the last portions of tinctures, infusion, etc.; also the juices of fresh plants, fruits, etc., after they are properly crushed. A screw press is generally used, but strong bags or cloths can be made use of.

Infusion.—When the principles to be extracted from any substance are soluble in water, and at the same time but slightly volatile, pour boiling water on it., cover the vessel carefully and allow the whole to remain untouched for several minutes or even hours, according to the greater or less penetrability of the substance. Tea is properly made by infusion. When the proportions are not given, it is to be generally understood that 1 ounce is to be used to 1 pint of boiling water.

Percolation. This is the most rapid process for extracting the soluble principles from vegetable substances. First reduce the material to a powder, then mix together by means of the sieve or mortar and pestle, according to the recipe for preparation. Moisten the mass thoroughly with alcohol, allow it to stand or macerate for 12 hours in a close covered vessel, then place in the percolator, pouring in more alcohol and water, if in the recipe, and permitting it to run through the percolator. If the liquor which first passes through is thick and turbid, introduce again into the instrument. Be very careful not to have the powder too coarse or loosely pressed or it will permit the liquid to run through too rapidly; on the other hand not too fine, or it will offer an undesired resistance. A simple percolator can be made by using a large funnel with a plug of carded cotton in the neck, or a fine sponge will answer the purpose; then fill the funnel with hay or straw, a piece of cotton cloth allowed to hang loosely over the edge, forming a sort of bag in the interior, completes the apparatus.

MEDICAL PREPARATIONS.

CORRECT CLASSIFICATIONS.

Antacids are remedies for acidity of the stomach. Their action is purely chemical and are simply palliatives, or a relief for the time being. Dyspepsia and diarrhœa are the principle affections for which they are employed. The alkalies are the principles antacids. Ammonia, carbonate of lime, washing soda and magnesia come under this head.

Antiseptics are medicines used for preventing putrifaction. Among them are boracic acid, carbolic acid, powdered charcoal, creosote, nitric acid and chloride of lime.

Anthelmintics are medicines which destroy or expel worms from the stomach and intestines. Among them are calomel, kousso, male fern, oil of turpentine, pink root, pumpkin seeds, santonin and worm seed.

Astringents.—These are substances which contract and strengthen the animal fibres. Alder alum, birch, blackberry root, sumach, tannic acid and wintergreen are valuable for this purpose.

Absorbents stimulate those vessels and glands which concur in the exercise of absorption. They carry off poisonous or irritant substances, are used in diarrhœa and vomiting and are chiefly included in antacids and cathartics.

Alteratives.—Medicines which change the morbid or unhealthy action of the system. This class is largely included in emetics and tonics.

Anodynes.—Preparations used for the relief of pain. Included under the head of cerebro-spinants.

Antiarthritics.—Medicines 'which subdue an influence in the blood which gives rise to rheumatism, gout, or diseases of the joints. They are classified under the head of antacids, cathartics and tonics.

Anticonvulsives correct convulsive disorders dependent upon blood deterioration and nervous debility. Embraced in tonics and cerebro-spinants.

Antiemetics.—Medicines which prevent vomiting. They will be found among stimulants and cerebro-spinants.

Antiperiodics have an influence over diseases which have a periodic tendency, such as malarial fevers. This class is largely included in tonics.

Antiphlogistics counteract all inflammatory processes; are used in inflammatory fevers, etc. Many medicines of this class will be found under the head of emetics, cathartics, diaphoretics, diuretics and refrigerants.

Antiscorbutics.—Medicines which counteract blood deteriorations caused by scurvy. These are embraced in tonics.

Antispasmodics antagonize spasms and allay nervous irritation. Included in emetics and cerebro-spinants.

Cathartics are medicines which exercise a strong action upon the bowels. They are divided into two kinds: the excessive and the moderate, or the purgative and the drastic. Among others are aloes, blue flag, calomel, castor oil, prunes, rhubarb, rochelle salts, senna sulphur and may apple or mandrakes.

Cerebro-Spinants are of that class which affect the brain and spinal cord. They are either paralysers, stupefacients or intoxicants, and care should be exercised in their use. Among them are to be found, aconite, alcohol, belladonna, bromide of potash, camphor, chloral, hydrate, chloroform, cocaine, hops, morphia, opium, strychnia, sulphuric ether, tobacco, valerian, etc.

Carminatives.—Medicines having a spicy smell, an agreeable odor and a soothing effect upon the bowels; used with purgatives, they prevent griping. They are mentioned among stimulants.

Chologogues stimulate the action of the liver and increase the flow of bile. They belong to the class entitled cathartics.

Deliriants.—Substances having a sedative effect over the heart and circulation. They are mentioned among the cerebrospinants.

Demulcents are a class of soothing medicines, used in colds or obstinate coughs, to shield the passages from the cold air, or to protect the coating of the stomach from the action of corrosive or irritating acids, poisons, etc. They are also used to save the mucous membrane of the urinary organs from the arid action of the water in certain affections of the kidneys and bladder; are used either by the mouth or in the form of an injection. Among them are included arrowroot, gum arabic or gum acacia, gum tragacanth, Iceland moss, Irish moss, licorice, marshmallow and slippery elm.

Diaphoretics.—These are medicines which exercise almost exclusive action on the skin, producing perspiration. The use of diaphoretics is indicated in nearly all diseases accompanied by fever and a dry skin, particularly in febrile and pectoral affections. Catnip, citrate of potash, sage, sassafras and sweet spirits of nitre are reliable medicines of this class.

Diluents.—These are preparations employed to quench thirst, dilute and make thin the thickened blood and cool the fevered system. Tea, barley water, water gruel and similar articles are the most common diluents after pure water. The copious use of diluents is recommended in all acute inflammatory diseases not of a congestive character.

Diuretics act upon the kidneys, and produce an increased flow of urine from the bladder. There are few diseases where medicines of this class are not of great benefit, and in dropsy they become paramount. Uva ursi, carrots, balsam of copaiba, cream of tartar, dandelion, juniper berries, onions, parsley, acetate of potassa, tar and the infusion of watermelon seeds are peculiarly adapted for diuretics.

Emetics are of that class of drugs which produce vomiting and are of vast benefit in cases of poisons. They should never be given to persons disposed to apoplexy or a tendency to rush of blood to the head; women in pregnancy should refrain from the use of them. Warm or tepid water is a reliable emetic; ipecac, lobelia, mustard and tartar emetic are others.　●

Emmenagogues will promote the menstrual discharge when either restrained or suspended, and are few in number, ergot and madder being the only drugs which exercise a direct influence on the uterus. There are a number, however, which act upon the general system, producing the effect by constitutional treatment. Cotton root, iron. mather root, saffron, pennyroyal and savine are among the articles in common use.

Emolients are medicines which soften the skin when applied externally. They diminish the pain of inflamed parts and aid the suppuration process. They owe their virtue to the moisture they contain. The mode of applying emolients is by poultice, oftenest made from flaxseed or meal. Most of the demulcents are emolients when applied externally, slippery elm being an instance of this character.

Epispastics are substances which produce blistering or irritating action on the skin. Principally used are cantharides, mustard and cayenne.

Escharotics.—These are caustic medicines used to eat off, as it is popularly called, fungoid growths or excessive granulations, or what is known as proud flesh. Burut. alum, iodine, lunar caustic, mercurial caustic, nitric acid caustic and zinc caustic are among the reliable escharotics.

Expectorants increase the secretion of the tracheal and bronchial mucous. Vapors are the only agents that can act directly upon the organs affected, those that are taken into the stomach acting only in an indirect manner. The inhaling of the vapor of warm water simply mixed with vinegar is very useful in this way. Ammonia, balsam of tolu, garlic and syrup of squills are used as expectorants.

Febrifuges have the power of checking fever. They are found principally among diaphoretics and diuretics; also to some extent among cathartics, emetics and refrigerants.

Hœmostatics, when taken internally, contract the blood vessels and check hemorrhage. They are included in astringents.

Hypnotics are medicines which produce sleep. They are included under cerebro-spinants.

Laxatives are similar to cathartics, but their action is milder.

Narcotics.—Poisonous substances acting principally upon the brain, either as a sedative or a stimulant. *See cerebro-spinants.*

Nervines.—Medicines which act upon the nerves, quieting nervous excitement. Embraced in cerebro-spinants.

Nutritives.—Medicines which possess the quality of nourishing. They are largely included in tonics and stimulants. ●

Refrigerants.—These are named from the cooling effects on the surface of the body produced by their use. They are employed in cases of high vascular action, as in fevers unaccompanied with typhoid symptoms. Although sedative in their general impression, some of them, as antimony, produce a local stimulant effect upon some of the organs. Acetic acid, vegetable acids, antimonial wine, borax, citric acid, muriatic acid and orange are all refrigerants.

Rubifacients.—These are medicines which produce inflammation of the skin when applied externally. The indications for their use and general application are much the same as in epispastics. The latter are preferred where a slow stimulant effect is to be produced, the former where the effect is to be quick and transitory. Cayenne, mustard and croton oil are well-known rubifacients.

Sialagogues are a class of medicines which produce a quick flow of saliva, principal among which is the extract of jaborandi.

Sedatives have a calming effect on the nervous system. Embraced in cerebro-spinants.

Stomachics.—Medicines which improve the stomach and appetite. They are included in stimulants and tonics.

Sudorifics produce a moist condition of the skin. Included in diaphoretics.

Stimulants.—These are agents which produce a quickly diffused and transient increase of vital energy and force of action in the heart and arterial system. Sesqui carbonate of ammonia, aniseed, benzoic acid, cayenne pepper, cod liver oil, coriander, corrosive sublimate, ginger, myrrh, pancreatin, valerian and Virginia snake root come under the head of stimulants.

Tonics.—These are a class of medicines which gradually and permanently increase the tonicity and general tone of the system; strengthening and invigorating it when weakened and debilitated, increasing the appetite, assisting the digestion and thus building up the entire system. Angelica, arsenic, black cohosh, boneset, burdock, chamomile, cinchona or peruvian bark, golden seal, elecampane, iron, pepsin, quinine, sarsaparilla and wild cherry are all in the class of tonics.'

HOW TO PREPARE DECOCTIONS AND INFUSIONS.

When the disease for which the preparations are intended is not mentioned refer to "Classification of Medical Preparations," where will be stated the class or character of the remedy.

Alder, Decoction of. Bark of common alder 1 ounce, water 20 ounces; boil to 16 ounces. Dose, 2 ounces to be taken every 4 hours.

Alkaline Infusion.—Hickory ashes 1 pound, wood soot ¼ pound boiling water ½ gallon. Let them stand 24 hours, then filter through a cotton cloth. Dose, wineglassful 3 times daily. A good remedy for dyspepsia with acidity. An antacid.

Arnica, Decoction of. Flowers of arnica montana 1 ounce, water 3 pints; boil to 1 quart, filter and add of syrup of ginger 3 ounces. Dose, 1 to 2 fluid ounces every 2 or 3 hours. In aphonia, paralysis of the voluntary muscles, rheumatism, ague, etc.

Barley, Decoction of. Pearl barley (washed clean) 1 ounce; boil for 20 minutes in 15 ounces of water, and strain. This is used as a demulcent in fevers, consumption, etc. It is slightly laxative. If this is objectionable, add a few drops of laudanum.

Blood Root, Infusion of. Blood root ½ ounce, boiling water 1 pint. Is used as a stimulant an emetic. Dose for stimulant or alterative, 1 teaspoonful 3 times daily; as an emetic 1 or 2 tablespoonfuls every hour until vomiting is produced.

Blue Flag, Infusion of. Pulverized root of blue flag ½ ounce, boiling water 1 pint; steep 2 hours and filter. Dose, teaspoonful with 10 drops of tincture of capsicum or cayenne once in 2 hours until its laxative or diuretic effects are experienced by the bowels or kidneys.

Boneset or Thoroughwort, infusion of. Boneset and sage of each ½ ounce, cascarilla 1 dram, boiling water 1½ pints, infuse until cold, then strain. In hectic fever a wineglass of this efficient remedy administered every hour until nausea and perspiration are indu⸱⸱⸱ s been highly recommended in influenza.

Buchu, Infusion of. Buchu 1 ounce, boiling water 1 pint; let stand for two hours in a tightly closed vessel, then strain. Used in affections of the kidneys and bladder. A superior diuretic. Dose, 1 to 2 ounces twice daily.

Bran, Decoction of. **1.** Bran ¼ pound, water 1¼ pints; boil to 1 pint. In diabetes; and sweetened with sugar as a demulcent and laxative drink for cough and sore throat. **2.** Bran 1 quart, water 1½ gallons; boil 5 minutes, and add cold water enough to bring to proper temperature. Use as an emollient foot bath.

Capsicum or Cayenne Pepper. Infusion of. Powdered capsicum ½ ounce, boiling water 1 pint. Dose, ½ fluid ounce.

Cascarilla, Infusion of. Cascarilla in coarse powder 1 ounce, boiling water (distilled) 10 ounces; infuse for 1 hour in a closed vessel, then strain. Dose, 1 to 2 ounces, usually combined with carbonate of soda and tincture of cascarilla 8 times daily. An excellent remedy for dyspepsia, debility and diarrhœa.

Chamomile, Infusion of. Chamomile flowers ½ ounce, boiling water 10 ounces; infuse for 15 minutes and strain. This is tonic, bitter, stomachic and emetic; drink cold. It is an emetic when warm. Dose as stomachic, 1 to 3 ounces; as an emetic, 5 to 10 ounces.

Coffee, Decoction of. Ten drams of raw coffee berries boiled in 8 ounces of water down to 5 ounces. Give in 3 doses during the intermission of intermittent fever.

Cotton Root, Decoction of. Inner part of the root of the cotton plant 4 ounces, water 1 quart; boil to 1 pint. Dose, 1 wineglassful occasionally as an emmenagogue, or every 30 or 40 minutes to produce uterine contraction, for which purpose it is said to be as effectual as ergot of rye.

Dandelion, Infusion of. Bruised root of dandelion 2 ounces, boiling water 1 pint; steep two hours and strain. Dose, a wineglassful 3 times a day. It is a tonic, resolvent and stimulant.

Elecampane, Decoction of. Elecampane root ½ ounce, water 1 pint; boil a few minutes and strain. Tonic and expectorant, and in some cases diuretic and diaphoretic. Dose, 1 wineglassful every hour or two.

Elm Bark, Infusion of· Steep 1 ounce of slippery elm bark bruised and sliced in 1 pint of boiling water for two hours in a closed vessel, then strain. Use freely as a drink in coughs and kidney affections, and in inflammatory diseases of the bowels.

Ergot, Decoction of. Ergot of rye 1 dram, water 6 fluid ounces; boil 10 minutes and strain. Dose, ⅓ every half hour until the whole is taken, as a parturifacient.

Fern Root, Decoction of. Dried fern root 1 ounce, water 1 pint; boil to 16 fluid ounces and strain. Dose, wineglassful, fasting until it excites slight nausea. As a vermifuge, more particularly for tape worm.

Figs, Decoction of. Figs chopped 1 ounce, water 1 pint; boil and strain. Demulcent and pectoral taken freely as a drink.

Flaxseed, Infusion of. Flaxseed 1 ounce, boiling water 1 pint; let it stand for 2 hours and then strain. Useful in inflammatory diseases of the lungs and affections of the kidneys. The addition of a tablespoonful of cream of tartar, sufficient lemon peel or of lemon juice, with sugar to sweeten to taste, improves this remedy, and increases its action upon the kidneys.

Hoarhound, Infusion of. The leaves 1 ounce, boiling water 1 pint, steep 2 hours, then strain. Given in wineglassful doses. Demulcent, pectoral, a popular remedy in coughs, colds, hoarseness, etc.; taken freely.

Hops, Infusion of. Hops 6 drams, boiling distilled water 1 pint, steep 4 hours in a covered vessel, then strain and press. Tonic and anodyne. Dose, 2 fluid ounces 3 times a day.

Iceland Moss, Decoction of. Iceland moss 1 ounce, water 1½ pints, boil for 10 minutes in a covered vessel and strain. Nutritious demulcent, pectoral and tonic. Dose, 1 to 4 fluid ounces every 3 or 4 hours, in chronic affections of the chest and stomach, especially pulmonary consumption, dyspepsia, old coughs, dysentery and chronic diarrhœa.

Irish Moss, Decoction of. Carrageen or Irish moss 1 ounce, steep in 1 pint of lukewarm water for 10 minutes, then take it out, drain and boil in water or milk 3 pints for 15 minutes, and strain through linen. If twice the above weight of moss is employed it forms a mucilage which, if sweetened, makes an excellent article of spoon diet. It is taken in the same cases as Iceland moss, and is often used for giving solidity in cooking blanc mange, etc.

Indian Sarsaparilla, Decoction of. Root of Indian sarsaparilla 2 ounces, water 1½ pints; boil to 1 pint. Diuretic, alterative and tonic.

Indian Sarsaparilla, Infusion of. Indian or scented sarsaparilla 2 ounces, boiling water 1 pint, steep 2 hours; uses same as decoction. Dose, tablespoonful 3 times daily, which if the same to be used for the decoction.

Juniper, Infusion of. **1.** From the berries alone. As a stimulant-diuretic in dropsy. Juniper berries 2½ ounces, boiling water 1 pint. **2.** To this add when cold 10 fluid drams compound spirit of juniper, bitartrate of potassa 1 dram.

Kino, Infusion of. Kino 5 drams, boiling water 1 pint. In diarrhœa; also, diluted in 5 times its bulk in water, as an injection for chronic gonorrhœ. Dose, 1 dessert spoonful.

Kousso, Infusion of. Kousso powdered fine ½ ounce, boiling distilled water 8 fluid ounces, steep in a covered vessel for 15 minutes, must not be strained. Dose, from 1 wineglassful to 1 tumblerful, for tapeworm.

Licorice, Decoction of. Sliced licorice root 1½ ounces, water 16 fluid ounces; boil 10 minutes and strain. A mild demulcent. Dose, wineglassful taken freely.

Marshmallow, Decoction of. Dried root and herb of marshmallow 4 ounces, stoned raisins 2 ounces, water 7 pints; boil down to 5 pints, strain, allow the sediment to settle and run off the clear liquid. Demulcent. Dose, a cupful at pleasure, in coughs, colds, calculus affections and diseases of the urinary organs.

Oak Bark, Decoction of. **1.** Bruised oak bark 10 drams, water 1 quart; boil down to 1 pint and strain. **2.** Oak bark 1½ ounces, water 1½ pints; boil 10 minutes and strain. It is an astringent, used as a gargle in ulcerated sore throat, relaxation of the uvala, etc.; as a wash and as an injection in piles, leucorrhœa, hemorrhages, prolapsusani, etc. **3.** Bruised oak bark 1½ ounces, distilled water 1 pint; boil for 10 minutes and strain.

Orange Peel, Infusion of. Dried bitter orange peel cut small 1 ounce, boiling water 20 ounces; infuse for 15 minutes, then strain. Bitter and stomachic; an excellent, effective remedy.

Parsley Root, Infusion of. Made from the root of the garden parsley, bruised, 2 ounces, boiling water 1 pint; steep 2 hours in a covered vessel, then strain. Dose, 2 fluid ounces. Aromatic, diuretic and slightly aperient. Recommended for dropsy.

Pennyroyal, Infusion of. Pennyroyal 1 ounce, boiling water 1 pint; steep 15 minutes and strain. A remedy for nausea, flatulence, colds, whooping cough, hysteria, obstructed men struations, etc. Should not be taken during pregnancy. Dose, tablespoonful 3 times daily.

Peppermint, Infusion of. Peppermint 3 drams, boiling water ½ pint; steep 15 minutes and strain. In flatulence, colic, griping and as a vehicle for other medicines.

Peruvian Bark, Decoction of. Yellow cinchona or calisaya bark, bruised, 1¼ onnces, distilled water 1 pint; boil for 10 minutes in a tightly-closed vessel, and when cold strain and pour on the bark sufficient water to make 1 pint. Dose, 1 to 2 fluid ounces 3 or 4 times daily. As a tonic, stomachic and febrifuge.

Pink Root, Infusion of. Made from Indian pink root. Is a vermifuge, and a good one. Pink root 1 ounce, boiling water 1 pint; steep 20 minutes, strain and give, combined with or followed by a purge, in 1 or 2 tablespoonsful doses to a child 3 to 5 years of age.

Pomegranate Root, Decoction of. A wonderful remedy for tapeworm. Bark of the root 2 ounces, water 1 pint; boil to ½ pint. This is the form used in India. Take a wineglassful half-hourly until the whole is taken; a light diet and a dose of castor oil having been taken the day previously. It usually expels the worm in 5 or 6 hours. Look for the head, and if it does not appear, repeat the dose in a day or so.

Sage, Infusion of. Made from the leaves of the common garden sage; ½ ounce of the leaves steeped in ½ pint boiling water for ½ hour, then strained, proves a fine remedy for hectic fever, in tablespoonful doses. Carminative and stomachic, for flatulence and dyspepsia; drank in water, it lessens night sweats.

Sarsaparilla, Decoction of. Sarsaparilla sliced and bruised 6 ounces, bark of sassafras root sliced, guaiacum wood rasped, licorice root bruised, of each 1 ounce, megereon sliced 3 drams; steep for 12 hours in 4 pints of water, then boil for 15 minutes and strain. Used in certain scrofulous and depraved conditions of the system. in syphilis, chronic rheumatism and a number of skin diseases. Use freely in wineglassful doses. The addition of one-fifth alcohol to this recipe makes it a valuable medicine.

Savine or Savin, Infusion of. Fresh leaves or herb 1 dram, boiling water 1 fluid ounce; infuse in a covered vessel. Stimulant, emmenagogue and vermifuge in chlorosis and suppressed menstruation, depending on torpid action of the uterine vessels; in chronic rheumatism, worms, etc. Dose, 1 to 2 tablespoonsful, cautiously administered. Should not be taken during pregnancy.

Senna, Infusion of. **1.** Senna 1 ounce, ginger sliced 30 grains, boiled distilled water 10 ounces; infuse 1 hour and strain. Dose, 1 to 2 ounces. **2.** Senna 15 drams, bruised ginger 4 scruples, boiling water 1 pint; steep for 1 hour in a covered vessel and strain. **3.** Senna 1½ ounce, ginger ½ dram, boiling water 1 pint. **4.** Senna ¼ ounce, ginger ½ dram, boiling water

½ pint. Purgative. It is usually given in doses of 1 to 1½ fluid ounces, combined with 3 to 6 drams of epsom salts or other saline purgative under the name of "black draught." Add 1 grain of nitrate of potassa to each ounce to prevent spoiling in warm weather.

Slippery Elm, Infusion of. Inner bark of slippery elm 1 ounce, boiling water 16 fluid ounces; infuse for 2 hours, then strain. Demulcent.

Squill, Decoction of. Squill 3 drams, juniper berries 4 ounces, snake root 3 ounces, water 4 pounds; boil to one-half, strain and add of sweet spirits of nitre 4 fluid ounces. In chronic coughs and other chest affections, unaccompanied with active inflammatory symptoms. Dose, 1 to 3 fluid ounces 2 or 3 times daily.

Sweet Flag, Infusion of. Sweet flag 1 ounce, boiling water 1 pint; steep 2 hours in a covered vessel and strain. Dose, 1 wineglassful. An aromatic, stimulant, tonic and stomachic.

Tansy, Infusion of. From the dried herb, or the green herb using twice the quantity. Tansy dried and bruised 1 ounce, boiling water 1 pint; steep 2 hours in a covered vessel and strain. Dose, 2 teaspoonsful every 4 hours. Aromatic, bitter, tonic and vermifuge.

Tar, Infusion of. Wood tar 1 quart, cold water 1 gallon; stir with a stick for 15 minutes, then let the tar subside, strain and keep in well-corked jars. Taken to the extent of 1 pint daily in chronic catarrhal and nephritic affections; also used as a lotion in chronic cutaneous diseases; especially those of the scalp in children.

Tobacco, Infusion of. Tobacco leaves 1 dram, boiling water 16 fluid ounces; steep for 1 hour. Used for enemas in strangulated hernia or rupture, obstinate colic, etc., observing not to administer more than ½ at a time.

Wild Cherry Bark, Infusion of. Dry wild cherry bark bruised ½ ounce (if green a small handful), cold water 1 pint; let it stand covered closely 24 hours and strain. Useful in nervous irritability with increased action of the heart, in debilitated conditions of the stomach, and in general debility following inflammatory diseases. Dose, 1 tablespoonful 3 times a day.

Wintergreen, Decoction of. Chimaphila (dried herb) 1 ounce, water 1½ pints; boil to 1 pint and then strain. Tonic, stomachic alterative and diuretic. Dose, 1 to 2 fluid ounces in dropsy, scrofula, debility, loss of appetite, etc., and in those affections of the urinary organs in which uva ursi is commonly given.

Waterdock, Decoction of. Root of common waterdock 1 ounce, water 1 pint; boil for 10 minutes and strain. Dose, 2 fluid ounces. This decoction is astringent and used as a remedy for scurvy and some other cutaneous diseases. It is the only remedy which proves efficacious for that disease when the ulcers are healed and the patient is attacked with asthma.

NOTE.—The decoctions and infusions herein mentioned form a cheap and reliable system of treatment for all diseases, can be easily prepared, and are always effectual. Look through them carefully. They will save you doctor's bills.

LINIMENTS, OINTMENTS. SALVES, CERATES, ETC.

Of these external remedies liniments are thicker than water, but more liquid than salves or ointments. Cerates have a a greater consistency than salves, but are not so pasty or as thick as poultices. Among those here given are many preparations well known to the general public; patent medicines that have been on sale for years. All of these formulas are of great value, having been tested and found effectual.

Aconite Ointment.—Alcoholic extract of aconite 1 dram, lard 2 drams; rub together carefully and thoroughly. For neuralgia.

Alum Ointment.—Alum, in very fine powder, 1 dram, lard 1½ ounces; mix thoroughly. For piles.

Belladonna Liniment.—Extract of belladonna 1 dram, olive oil 1 ounce; stir together. Useful in rheumatism, neuralgia, etc.

Benzoin Ointment.—Tincture of benzoin 2 ounces, lard 16 ounces; melt the lard, add the tincture, stirring well. For itch and skin diseases.

Black Liniment.—Sulphuric acid 1 dram, olive oil 1 ounce, turpentine ½ ounce; mix the acid with the oil slowly. When cold add the turpentine. A fine counter irritant. Effectual in swelling of the joints. Apply twice a day on lint.

Calomel Cerate.—Calomel 1 dram, spermaceti cerate 7 drams. In herpes and other skin diseases.

Camphor Liniment.—Camphor ½ ounce, olive oil, 2 fluid ounce; dissolve the camphor in the oil. For rheumatism and neuralgia.

Carbolic Acid Ointment.—Camphor 1 ounce, carbolic acid in crystals 1 ounce, simple cerate 14 ounces; mix. Antiseptic, stimulant and detergent.

Centaur Liniment.—Oil spike 1 ounce, oil wormwood 1 ounce, oil sassafras 1 ounce, oil organum 1 ounce, oil cinnamon 1 ounce, oil cloves 1 dram, oil cedar 1 dram, sulphuric ether 1 ounce, aqua ammonia 1 ounce, tincture opium 1 ounce, alcohol 1 gallon; mix. This is an excellent liniment, and good whenever a liniment is needed.

Cucumber Ointment.—Oil of sweet almonds 7 fluid ounces, spermaceti 18 drams, white wax 5 drams, glycerine 1 fluid ounce, green cucumbers 4 pounds; cut the cucumbers in small pieces, mash in a mortar (wooden), let them stand in their own liquor for 12 hours, press and strain; melt the almond oil, spermaceti and wax together, add to it the strained liquor of the cucumbers, stirring constantly, so as to incorporate the whole together; set aside in a cool place until it becomes hard, then beat with a wooden spoon, so as to separate the watery portions of the cucumbers from the ointment; pour off the liquor thus obtained and mix the glycerine with the ointment without the aid of heat, by working it with the hands until all are thoroughly mixed: put up in 4-ounce jars, cover with a layer of rose water and set aside in a cool place. This ointment is one of the finest preparations for the skin known to medical science, and thus prepared will keep for 12 months.

Davis' Pain Killer.—Proof alcohol 1 quart, chloroform 1 dram, oil sassafras 1 ounce, gum champhor 1 ounce, spirits of ammonia 1 dram, oil cayenne 2 drams; mix well, and let stand 24 hours before using.

Downers' Salve.—Beeswax 4 ounces, opium ¼ ounce, sugar of lead 1 ounce; melt the beeswax and rub the lead up in the wax, then the opium, then add 1 gill of sweet oil: mix all thoroughly together and spread lightly on cloth. Good for burns, piles, etc.

Emollient Liniment.—Camphor 1 dram, peruvian balsam ½ dram, oil of almonds 1 fluid ounce; dissolve by heat, add of glycerine ½ fluid ounce, agitate well, and when cold further add of oil of nutmeg 15 drops. Good for chapped hands, lips, nipples, etc.

Eye Ointments (the best in use).—**1.** Nitric oxide of mercury, carbonate of zinc, acetate of lead and dried alum, of each 1 dram, corrosive sublimate 10 grains, rose ointment 1 ounce. Used in chronic aphthalmia, profuse discharges, etc., usually diluted. **2.** Nitrate of silver 10 grains, zinc ointment 2 drams, balsam of peru ½ dram. Used in ulceration of the cornea and in acute, purulent and chronic aphthalmia; great caution should be employed in its use. **3.** Spermaceti ointment 1 dram, solution of diacetate of lead 15 drams, nitrate of silver 2 to 10 grains. Use as the last and in cases where direct caustic action is desired; the stronger ointment often occasions intense pain. **4.** Black oxide of mercury 2 grains, spermaceti cerate and walnut oil, of each 1 dram. Used in chronic affections of the eye and eyelids, particularly in those of a syphilitic character. **5** (Petit's). White wax 4 ounces, spermaceti 12 ounces, olive oil 2 pounds, white precipitate 3 ounces, oxide of zinc 4 ounces, benzoic acid 2 drams, sulphate of morphia 48 grains, oil of rosemary 20 drops; melt the spermaceti, wax and olive oil together, rub the precipitate, zinc and benzoic acid in a portion of the warm mixture, add together, lastly add the rosemary, stir till cool. This is the finest preparation of its kind known.

Flagg's Instant Relief.—Oil of cloves 1 fluid dram, oil of sassafras 2 fluid drams, spirit of camphor 1½ fluid ounces; mix well.

Green Mountain Salve.—Powdered verdigris 1 ounce, oil of wormwood ½ ounce, venice turpentine ½ ounce, oil of red cedar, organum, hemlock and balsam of fir, each 1 ounce, mutton tallow, beeswax and burgundy pitch, each 4 ounces, resin 5 pounds; melt the resin, pitch, beeswax, tallow and balsam together, add the oils with the verdigris and other ingredients; mix well. Used for all sores, excoriations, chilblains, etc.; very fine.

Good Samaritan Liniment.—Take 98 per cent alcohol 2 quarts, and add to it the following articles: Oils of sassafras, hemlock, spirits of turpentine, tincture of cayenne, catechu, guaic (guac) and laudanum, of each 1 ounce, tincture of myrrh 4 ounces, oil of organum 2 ounces, oil of wintergreen ½ ounce, gum camphor 2 ounces, chloroform 1½ ounces. This is one of the best applications for internal pains.

Hamlin's Wizard Oil.—Oil of sassafras 2 ounces, oil of cedar 1 ounce, gum camphor 1 ounce, sulphuric ether 2 ounces, chloroform 2 ounces, tincture of capsicum 1 ounce, aqua ammonia 2 ounces, oil of turpentine 1 ounce, tincture of quassia, 3 ounces, alcohol ½ gallon; mix, and you have a fine liniment.

Hops Ointment.—Hops 2 ounces, lard 10 ounces. Useful in painful piles and cancerine sores.

Indian Oil (Healy & Bigelow's).—Oil of sassafras 2 ounces, oil of cloves 1½ ounces, gum camphor 4 ounces, tincture of myrrh 4 ounces, tincture opium (laudanum) 4 ounces, tincture capsicum 4 ounces, spirits of ether 4 ounces, alcohol 2 gallons, water 1⅔ gallons; mix. The above will fill 240 2-ounce vials. The addition of ⅛ ounce of menthol to every gallon greatly improves this excellent remedy.

Iodide of Mercury Ointment.—1. White wax 2 ounces, lard 6 ounces; melt them together, add of iodide of mercury 1 ounce and rub them well together. **2.** Green iodide of mercury 23 grains, lard 1½ ounces. Useful in tubercular skin diseases, as a friction in scrofulous swellings and indolent granular tumors, and as a dressing for ill-conditioned ulcers, especially those of scrofulous character.

Iodoform Ointment.—Iodoform 1 dram, vaseline 1 ounce; reduce the iodoform to a powder and add to the vaseline, heat until dissolved. Antiseptic; healing for all sores.

Itch Ointment.—1. Unsalted butter 1 pound, burgundy pitch 2 ounces, spirits of turpentine 2 ounces, red precipitate, pulverized, 1¼ ounces; melt the pitch and add the butter, stirring well together, then remove from the fire and when a little cool add the spirits of turpentine and lastly the precipitate; stir until cold. **2.** Alum, nitre and sulphate of zinc, of each in very fine powder 1¼ ounces, vermillion ½ ounce; mix, add gradually of sweet oil ¾ pint; triturate, or mix together until well mixed, then add of lard 1 pound, with oils of anise, lavender and organum quantity sufficient to perfume. **3.** Chloride of lime 1 dram. rectified spirits 2 fluid drams, sweet oil ½ fluid ounce, common salt and sulphur, of each 1 ounce, soft soap 2 ounces, oil of lemon 20 drops. Cheap, effectual and inoffensive.

King of Pain.—Alcohol 1 pint, tincture of capsicum 1 dram, spirits of turpentine 1 dram, gum camphor 1 ounce, sulphuric ether 1 ounce; mix.

Kickapoo Buffalo Salve.—Vaseline 1 pound, tallow 1 pound, white wax 3 ounces, oxide of zinc 1¾ ounces, red precipitate 1½ ounces, oil of cedar ¾ ounce; melt and stir together until cold, then box.

Magnetic Ointment.—Elder bark 1 pound, spikenard root 1 pound, yellow dock root 1 pound; boil in 2 gallons of water down to 1, then press the strength out of the bark and roots and boil the liquid down to ½ gallon; add best resin 8 pounds, beeswax 1 pound and tallow enough to soften. Apply to the sores, etc., by spreading on linen cloth.

Magic Oil.—Sweet oil 1 gallon, oil of hemlock 2 ounces, oil of organum 2 ounces, chloroform 2 ounces, spirits of ammonia 4 ounces; mix, let it stand 24 hours and it is ready for use. Dose, internally, 1 teaspoonful for adults. Bathe the affected parts well. This is a great remedy for aches and pains, rheumatism, neuralgia, and all nervous and inflammatory diseases.

Magnetic Toothache Drops.—Take equal parts of camphor, sulphuric ether, ammonia, laudanum, tincture of cayenne and ⅛ part oil of cloves; mix well together. Saturate with the liquid a small piece of cotton and apply to the cavity of the diseased tooth, and the pain will cease immediately.

My Own Liniment.—Take oil of cajeput 2 ounces, oil of spike 1 ounce, oil of sassafras 1 ounce, oil of cloves 1 ounce, oil of organum 1 ounce, oil of mustard ½ ounce, tincture of capsicum 1 ounce, gum camphor 2 ounces, alcohol ½ gallon. Use as other liniments for any ache or pain. For sore throat or hoarseness, saturate a towel with the liniment, place it over the mouth, let it remain so for 4 or 5 hours and you will be cured. For croup, bathe throat and chest with the liniment. Give ¼ teaspoonful of liniment in one teaspoonful of warm water every 5 to 10 minutes until relieved.

Mustang Liniment.—Linseed oil 14 ounces, aqua ammonia 2 ounces, tincture of capsicum ¼ ounce, oil of organum ¼ ounce, turpentine 1 ounce, oil of mustard ¼ ounce; mix.

Mustard Ointment.—1. Flour of mustard ¾ ounce, water 1 fluid ounce; mix, and add of resin cerate 2 ounces, oil of turpentine ½ ounce. Rubifacient and stimulant, as a friction in rheumatism, etc. **2.** Flour of mustard 3 ounces, oil of almonds ½ fluid ounce, lemon juice quantity sufficient. Used in freckles, sunburn. etc.; a fine preparation.

Pile Ointment.—1. Burnt alum and oxide of zinc, of each ¼ dram, lard 7 drams. **2.** Morphia 8 grains, melted spermaceti ointment 1 ounce; mix together until complete, then add of finely powdered galls ½ dram, essential oil of almonds 12 to 15 drops and stir until the mass becomes hard. This is useful in painful piles, prolapsus, etc.; it does not soil the linen as most other liniments.

Radway's Ready Relief, or R. R. R.—Alcohol 2 pints, oil of sassafras 2 ounces, oil of organum 2 ounces, spirits of camphor ½ ounce, tincture of opium 1 ounce. chloroform, 1 ounce; mix.

St. Jacob's Oil.—Gum camphor 1 ounce, chloral hydrate 1 ounce, chloroform 1 ounce. sulphate of ether 1 ounce, tincture of opium (non-aqueous) ½ ounce, oil of organum ½ ounce. oil of sassafras ⅓ ounce, alcohol ½ gallon: dissolve gum camphor with alcohol and then add the oil, then the other ingredients.

Tar Ointments.—1. Tar and suet, of each 1 pound; melt them together and press the mixture through a linen cloth. **2.** Tar 5 ounces, beeswax 2 ounces, melt together and stir the mixture briskly until it concretes. **3.** Tar ½ pint, yellow wax 4 ounces. A detergent application in ringworm, scald heads, scabby eruptions, foul ulcers. etc.; at first dilute with one-half its weight of lard or sweet oil.

LOZENGES, TROCHES, TABLETS, COUGH DROPS, WORM WAFERS, ETC.

Are made of finely-powdered ingredients, mixed with gum or something of like character to make them firm. Great care must be taken to have the ingredients finely powdered and carefully mixed. They can be rolled out the same as bread or pastry dough and cut into shape with a thimble having the small end open. This is the simplest method.

Brown's Bronchial Troches.—Take ½ pound of pulverized extract of licorice. ¾ pound of pulverized sugar, 2 ounces each of pulverized cubebs and gum arabic, and ½ ounce of pulverized extract of conium.

Caffeine Lozenges.—Each lozenge contains ¼ grain of caffeine and ½ grain of citric acid. Useful in hemicrania, hypochondriasis, etc.

Calomel Lozenges.—Each lozenge contains 1 grain of calomel. Alterative. etc.; they afford a simple way of introducing mercury into the system. During their use salt food and acid liquors should be avoided. When given for worms, they should be followed in a few hours by a purge.

Carbolic Acid Lozenges.—Carbolic acid 350 grains, gum arabic 220 grains, refined sugar 12½ ounces, mucilage 1 ounce, distilled water sufficient quantity to make 1 pound; divide into 350 lozenges, and finish as with benzoic acid lozenges.

Catechu Lozenges.—1. Extract of catechu 4 ounces, sugar 16 ounces, mucilage of gum tragacanth sufficient quantity; make into 10-grain lozenges. **2.** Magnesia 2 ounces, powdered catechu 1 ounce, sugar 13 ounces, mucilage of gum tragacanth (made with cinnamon water) sufficient quantity to mix. These are taken in diarrhœa, in relaxation of the uvula, in irritation of the larynx and to disguise a fetid breath; the one containing magnesia is also sucked in dyspepsia, acidity and heartburn.

Charcoal Lozenges.—Prepared charcoal 4 ounces, white sugar 12 ounces, mucilage sufficient quantity to mix. Used in diarrhœa, cholera, dyspepsia, etc.

Ching's Yellow Worm Lozenges.—Fine sugar 28 pounds, calomel, washed with spirits of wine, 1 pound, saffron 4 drams; dissolve gum tragacanth sufficient to make a paste, make decoction of the saffron in 1 pint of water, strain and mix with it. Each lozenge should contain 1 grain of mercury.

Chlorate of Potassa Lozenges.—1. Each lozenge contains 1½ grains of chlorate of potassa. Used in phthisis, sore throat, etc. Dose, 6 to 12 a day. **2.** Chlorate of potassa, in powder, 3,600 grains (8¼ ounces). refined sugar, in powder, 25 ounces, gum acacia, in powder, 1 ounce, mucilage 2 ounces, distilled water 1 ounce, or a sufficiency; mix the powders, and add the mucilage and water to form a proper mass; divide into 720 lozenges.

Chloride of Gold Lozenges.—Each lozenge contains 1-40 grain of neutral chloride of gold. Dose, 2 to 4 daily, in scrofula, cancer, etc.

Clove Lozenges.—Cloves, powdered along with sugar, 2 ounces, or essential oil 1 fluid dram to each pound of sugar. Carminative and stomachic, also used as a restorative after fatigue; added to chocolate to improve its flavor and sucked to sweeten the breath.

Cough Lozenges.—Dissolve licorice in water to the consistency of thin molasses, add to the dough, made of gum water and sugar, and work it well; also work in at the same time 2 ounces of ipecacuanha, 1 dram acetate of morphia (morphine). 1 ounce oil of aniseed, 1 ounce powdered tartaric acid; mix thoroughly, roll out and cut.

Croton Oil Lozenges.—Croton oil 5 drops, powdered starch 40 grains, white sugar 1 dram, chocolate 2 drams; divide into 30 lozenges: 5 or 6 generally prove cathartic.

Cubebs Lozenges.—Cubebs 2 drams, balsam of tulu, 6 grains; mix. and add extract of licorice 1 ounce, syrup of tulu 1 dram, powdered gum sufficient quantity; divide into 10-grain lozenges. One of these allowed to melt gradually in the mouth, is said to alleviate the obstruction in the nose in coryza.

● Ginger Lozenges.—Best unbleached jamaica ginger and gum arabic, of each, in very fine powder, 1½ ounces, double refined lump sugar 1 pound, rose water, tinged with saffron, sufficient quantity. A still finer quality may be made by using an equivalent proportion of essence of ginger instead of the powder; inferior qualities are prepared with coarser sugar, to which some starch is often added. Ginger lozenges are carminative and stomachic, and are useful in flatulency, loss of appetite, etc.

Hemlock Confection.—Fresh hemlock leaves beaten up with an equal weight of sugar. Dose, 10 to 20 grains, as a pill, 2 or 3 times daily, where the use of hemlock is indicated. The confection of other narcotic plants may be made in the same way.

Iceland Moss Chocolate.—Simple chocolate 32 parts, sugar 29 parts, dried jelly of Iceland moss 11 parts; mix.

Indian Worm Killer (Healy & Bigelow's).—Kousso flowers ¾ pound, scammony 4 ounces, santonin 4 ounces, pulverized jalap 4 ounces, pulverized sugar 12 pounds, oil of anise 2 ounces, cornstarch 4 pounds, gum tragacanth 8 ounces; dissolve the gum in water of sufficient quantity to make thick mucilage, make an infusion of the kousso flowers, then mix the other ingredients with the gum, adding the kousso infusion, making a stiff mass; mix with the cornstarch and knead thoroughly; when well mixed roll out into sheets and cut with a round die or thimble about the size of 1 cent coin; the sheets should be quite thin. Dose, ½ to 1 lozenge twice daily.

Opium Lozenges.—1. Opium 2 drams, tincture of tulu ½ ounce; triturate together; add of powdered sugar 6 ounces, extract licorice and powdered gum acacia of each 5 ounces; mix and divide into 10 grain lozenges. Each lozenge contains 1-6 to 1-7 opium. Used to allay tickling cough and irritation of the fauces, and as an anodyne and hypnotic. **2.** Opium in fine powder 2 drams. extract of licorice, gum arabic and sugar. of each 5 ounces, oil of aniseed, ½ fluid dram, water sufficient quantity; divide into 6 grain lozenges.

⋅Pomegranate Electuary.—1. From the root bark 1 dram, asafœtida ½ dram, croton oil 6 drops, consene of roses 1 ounce. Dose, 1 teaspoonful night and morning. **2.** Extract of the root bark 6 drams, lemon juice 2 fluid drams, linden water 3 fluid drams. gum tragacanth, sufficient quantity to make an electuary. Take ½ at once; the remainder in an hour. Both are given in tapeworm.

Squill Honey.—1. Thick clarified honey 3 pounds, tincture of squill 2 pounds; mix. **2.** Dried squill 1 ounce, boiling water ¾ pint; infuse 2 hours, strain and add of honey 12 ounces, and evaporate to a proper consistence.

↓Tannic Acid Lozenges.—Tannic acid 360 grains; tincture of tulu, ½ ounce, refined sugar 25 ounces, gum acacia 1 ounce, mucilage 2 ounces, distilled water 1 ounce; dissolve the tannic acid in the water; add first the tincture of tulu, previously mixed with the mucilage, then the gum and the sugar, also previously well mixed: form the whole into a proper mass and divide into 720 lozenges, and dry them in a hot-air chamber with a moderate heat. Dose, 1 to 6 lozenges.

Tulu Lozenges.—1. Sugar 4 pounds, balsam of tulu 3 drams, or the tincture of the balsam 1 fluid ounce, cream of tartar 6 ounces, or tartaric acid 1 dram; dissolve gum sufficient to make a paste. These may also be flavored by adding ¼ ounce of vanilla and 60 drops of the essence of amber. The articles must be reduced to a fine powder with the sugar; they are pectoral and balsamic. **2.** Balsam of tulu and rectified spirit of each 1 ounce; dissolve and add of water 2 fluid ounces, heat the mixture in a water-bath and filter. Make a mucilage with the filtered liquor and gum tragacanth 80 grains, add of sugar 16 ounces; make a mass and cut it into lozenges.

Vermifuge Lozenges.—Santonin 60 grains, pulverized sugar 5 ounces, mucilage of gum tragacanth sufficient to make into thick paste, worked carefully together, that the santonin shall be evenly mixed throughout the whole mass; then, if not in too great a hurry, cover up the mortar in which you have rubbed them, and let them stand from 12 to 24 hours to temper, at which time they will roll out better than if done immediately: divide into 120 lozenges. Dose, for a child 1 year old, 1 lozenge night and morning; of 2 years, 2 lozenges; of 4 years, 3 lozenges; of 8 years, 4 lozenges; of 10 years or more, 5 to 7 lozenges. In all cases to be taken twice daily, and continuing until the worms are discharged.

Wistar's Cough Lozenges.—Gum arabic, extract of licorice and sugar, of each 2½ ounces, powdered opium 1 dram, oil of aniseed 40 drops; for 60 lozenges. Dose, 1 three or four times a day.

Worm Lozenges.—Most of the advertised nostrums under this name have a basis of calomel, and require to be followed by a purge a few hours afterwards. **1.** Ethereal extract of wormseed 1 dram, jalap, starch and sugar, of each 2 drams, mucilage of gum tragacanth sufficient quantity; divide in 60 lozenges. **2.** Wormseed 1 ounce, ethiops mineral and jalap, of each 3 drams, cinnamon 2 drams, sugar 7 ounces, rose water sufficient quantity.

PLASTERS AND POULTICES.

Alum Poultice.—Powdered alum 1 dram, whites of two eggs; shake them together until they form a coagulum. Applied between the folds of soft linen for chilblains, sore nipples, inflamed eyes, etc.

Antiseptic Poultice.—Barley flour 6 ounces, powdered peruvian bark 1 ounce, water sufficient quantity; boil and when cool add powdered camphor 1 dram.

Boynton's Adhesive Plaster.—Yellow resin 1 ounce, lead plaster 1 pound; melted together. Recommended for bad legs and other like affections.

Belladonna Plaster.—Soap plaster 3 ounces; melt it by the heat of a water bath; add extract of belladonna 3 ounces and keep constantly stirring the mixture until it acquires a proper consistence.

Cancer Plasters.—1. Wax plaster 1 ounce, extract of hemlock 1 dram, levigated arsenious acid ½ dram. 2. Extract of hemlock 1 ounce, extract of henbane ½ ounce powdered belladonna 1 dram, acetate of ammonia of sufficient quantity to form a plaster. Should be used with great caution

Cantharides Plaster.—Melt together yellow wax and suet each 7½ pounds, lard 6 ounces, and resin 3 ounces; while cooling sprinkle in and mix thoroughly 1 pound very finely powdered Spanish flies.

Court Plaster.—This plaster is a kind of varnished silk, and its manufacture is very easy. Bruise a sufficient quantity of isinglass, and let it soak in a little warm water for 24 hours. Expose it to heat over the fire until the greater part of the water is dissipated, and supply its place by proof spirits of wine, which will combine with the isinglass. Strain the whole through a piece of open linen, taking care that the consistence of the mixture shall be such that when cool it may form a trembling jelly. Extend a piece of black or flesh-colored silk on a wooden frame. and fix it in that position by means of tacks or twine. Then apply the isinglass, after it has been rendered liquid by a gentle heat, to the silk with a brush of fine hair (badger's is the best). As soon as this coating is dried, which will not be long, apply a second, and afterward, if the article is to be very superior, a third. When the whole is dry, cover it with two or three coatings of the balsam of peru. This is the genuine court plaster. It is pliable and never breaks, which is far from being the case with spurious articles sold under the same name.

Lead Plaster.—Take 1¼ pounds of very finely powdered semivitrified oxide of lead, 1 quart of olive oil and ½ pint of water; boil together over a gentle fire, stirring constantly till the oil and litharge unite and form a plaster; if the water nearly all evaporates before the process is completed, add a little boiling water. This is a useful plaster for ulcers, burns, etc.

Linseed Meal Poultice.—To boiling water ½ pint, add gradually, constantly stirring, 4½ ounces of linseed or flaxseed meal, or a sufficient quantity to thicken. Used to promote the ripening or suppuration of boils, tumors, etc. A little oil or fresh lard should be added and some smeared over the surface as well to prevent the poultice hardening.

Pitch Plaster.—Burgundy pitch 6 parts, yellow resin 8 parts, yellow wax 3 parts, lard 7 parts, turpentine 1 part, palm oil 1 part, linseed oil 1 part; melt together.

Poorman's Plaster.—Melt together, beeswax 1 ounce, tar 3 ounces, resin 3 ounces; spread on paper or muslin.

Spice Plaster.—Take of powdered cloves 1 ounce, ground

cinnamon 1 ounce, ground allspice 1 ounce, ground black pepper 2 ounces, flour 3 or 4 ounces, or enough to mix; mix in a paste with vinegar and spread on muslin. This is a stimulating plaster; if a more powerful one is desired, substitute cayenne for black pepper.

Strengthening Plaster.—Lead plaster 24 parts, white resin 6 parts, yellow wax and olive oil, of each 3 parts, red oxide of iron 8 parts; let the oxide be rubbed with the oil and the other ingredients added, melted; mix the whole well together. This plaster, after being spread over leather, should be cut into strips 2 inches wide and strapped firmly around the joint.

Warming Plaster.—Take of any blistering plaster 1 part, burgundy pitch 14 parts; mix them by means of moderate heat. This plaster is a stimulant, slightly irritating the skin, and is useful in coughs, colds, whooping cough, sciatica and other local pains.

SYRUPS.

Syrups are saturated solutions of sugar in water, or sugar dissolved in a quantity of water sufficient to make the substance a mass; are used as a vehicle for many medicines, most cough medicines being prepared in this form, also many other preparations. The proper quantity of sugar for making syrups is 2 pounds avoirdupois to every pint of water. Only the very best sugar should be used, and either distilled water or filtered rain water made the agent for dissolving same. The process should be accomplished over a gentle fire, too much heat producing decomposition; do not keep on fire any longer than is necessary to make a clear, transparent syrup. All ingredients to be added in the preparation of any medicine should be first filtered and made perfectly clear.

Almond.—1. Sweet almonds 1 pound, bitter almonds 1 ounce; blanch, beat them to a smooth paste and make an emulsion with barley water 1 quart, strain; to each pint add of sugar 2 pounds and a tablespoonful of orange flower water, put the mixture in small bottles and keep in a cool place; a little brandy assists in the preservation. **2.** Sweet almonds 8 ounces, bitter almonds 2 ounces; blanch, beat in a marble mortar with a wooden pestle to a paste, adding gradually of water 16 fluid ounces, of orange flower water 3 fluid ounces; after straining through a flannel, dissolve 3 pounds of sugar in each pint of the mixture.

Cathartic Syrup.—Best senna leaf 1 ounce, butternut (the inner bark of the root, dried and bruised) 2 ounces, peppermint leaf ½ ounce, fennel seed ½ ounce, alcohol ½ pint, water 1½ pints, sugar 2 pounds; put all into the spirit and water except the sugar and let stand for 2 weeks, then strain, pressing out from the dregs, adding the sugar and simmering over a gentle fire a few minutes only to dissolve the sugar. For chronic constipation, sick headache, etc.; a superior remedy. Dose, 1 tablespoonful once a day or less often if the bowels become too loose; if griping is caused, increase the fennel seed and peppermint leaf.

Fuller's Cough Syrup.—Take 6 ounces comfrey root and .12 handsful plantain leaves; cut and beat them together well, strain out the juice, then with an equal weight of loaf sugar boil to a syrup. Dose, 1 to 2 tablespoonsful 3 or 4 times per day.

Gum Syrup.—Dissolve pale and picked gum arabic in an equal weight of water by a gentle heat, add the solution to 4 times its weight of simple syrup, simmer for 2 or 3 minutes, remove the scum and cool. This is a pleasant demulcent; the addition of 1 or 2 fluid ounces of orange flower water to each pint greatly improves it.

Gum Traganth.—Gum traganth 1 ounce, water 32 ounces; macerate for 48 hours, press through a linen cloth and mix the mucilage with 8 pounds of syrup heated to 176° Fahrenheit; strain through a coarse cloth.

Hall's Balsam for the Lungs.—Fluid extract of ipecac ½ ounce. fluid extract of squills 1 ounce, chloroform ¼ ounce, wine of tar 1 ounce, tincture of opium 1-5 ounce, fluid extract of mullen 1 ounce, syrup enough to make 1 pint.

Hall's Honey of Hoarhound and Tar.—Wine of tar 1 ounce, fluid extract of hoarhound 1 ounce, tincture of opium 1 dram, syrup of orange peel ½ ounce, honey 3 ounces, syrup enough to make 1 pint.

Hive Syrup.—Put 1 ounce each of squills and seneca snake root into 1 pint of water; boil down to one-half, then strain; then add ⅓ pound of clarified honey containing 12 grains of tartrate of antimony. Dose, for a child, 10 drops to 1 teaspoonful according to age. This is an excellent remedy for croup.

Hoarhound.—1. Dried hoarhound 1 ounce, hoarhound water 2 pounds; digest in a water bath for 2 hours, strain and add of white sugar 4 pounds. **2.** White hoarhound 1 pound, boiling water 1 gallon; infuse for 2 hours, press out the liquor, filter and add of sugar a sufficient quantity. This is a fine remedy for coughs and diseases of the lungs. Dose, a tablespoonful at pleasure.

Horseradish.—Scraped horseradish 1 ounce, hot water 8 fluid ounces; mix, let stand until cold, strain and dissolve in the liquor twice its weight of sugar. Dose, 1 dram frequently in hoarseness.

Ipecac.—1. Mix 2 ounces of fluid extract of ipecac in 30 ounces of simple syrup. **2.** Fluid extract of ipecac 1 fluid ounce, glycerine 1 fluid ounce. simple syrup 14 fluid ounces; first mix the glycerine with the fluid extract and then add the syrup.

Orange Peel.—1. Tincture of orange peel 1 part, syrup 7 parts; mix. Dose, 1 to 2 drams. **2.** Fresh orange peel 1 8 ounces, sugar 18 pounds, water of sufficient quantity to make syrup.

Piso's Consumption Cure.—Tartar emetic 4 grains, tincture tolu ½ ounce, sulphate morphia 4 grains, fluid extract lobelia 2 drams, chloroform 1 dram, fluid extract cannabes indica 2 drams, essence spearmint 10 drops, hot water 8 ounces, sugar 4 ounces; dissolve the morphia and tartar emetic in hot water and add the rest.

Rhubarb.—Take 1½ ounces of bruised rhubard, ½ ounce each of bruised cloves and cinnamon, 2 drams bruised nutmeg, 2 pints diluted alcohol, 6 pints of syrup; macerate the rhubarb and aromatics in the alcohol for 14 days and strain; then by gentle heat evaporate the liquor to 1 pint, and while hot mix with it the syrup previously heated.

Rose.—**1,** Dried leaves of provence roses 8 ounces, double rose leaves 6 ounces, water 1 pint, sugar 4 pounds; pour the water on the leaves when nearly boiling into a glazed earthenware vessel; cover it quite close and let it remain in a warm place for 1 day, then strain. The leaves of the damask rose are purgative. **2.** Dried petals of the damask rose 7 ounces, boiling water 3 pints; macerate for 12 hours; filter and evaporate to 1 quart, and add white sugar 6 pounds, and when cool add rectified spirits 5½ fluid ounces.

Sarsaparilla.—Sarsaparilla 15 ounces, boiling water 1 gallon; macerate for 24 hours; boil to 2 quarts and strain; add of sugar 15 ounces and boil to a syrup.

Senna.—**1.** Take of Senna 3½ ounces, bruised fennel seed 10 drams, boiling water 1 pint; macerate for 6 hours with a gentle heat, then pour out the liquid through a linen cloth and dissolve in it of manna 3 ounces; next add this solution to molasses 3 pounds, which has been boiled almost to the consistency of candy; stir them well together. **2.** Senna 4 ounces, boiling water 24 fluid ounces; infuse, strain, add of molasses 48 ounces, and evaporate to a proper consistency. This is an aperient. Dose, 1 to 4 drams.

Squills.—**1.** Dissolve 24 Troy ounces of sugar in 1 pint of vinegar of squills with gentle heat, and strain while hot. **2.** Vinegar of squills 3 pints, white powdered sugar 7 pounds; dissolve by gentle heat.

Tar (Boschee's German Syrup).—Wine of tar 2 ounces, fluid extract squills 1 ounce, tincture opium 2 drams. fluid extract sanguinarie 2 drams, syrup of sugar 8 ounces. Mix.

Wild Cherry.—Moisten 5 ounces of wild cherry bark, coarsely powdered, with water, and let it stand for 24 hours closely covered; then pack it firmly in a glass percolator and gradually pour water on it until 1 pint has passed through, and dissolve in this 28 Troy ounces of crushed sugar.

TINCTURES, ESSENCES AND ELIXIRS.

Tinctures are alcoholic solutions of the active medicinal properties of the substances from which they are prepared. They are generally used in liniments and other medicines, and are obtained by percolation and filtration. *See Percolation and Filtration.*

Essences are somewhat similar, while Elixirs are compounds of various medicinal substances, being mixtures of aromatic wines and tinctures mixed with sugar. They are popular, because palatable. Dose, 1 to 2 teaspoonfuls.

Among the following formulas will be found many superior remedies, including beef, iron and wine, and many others:

Aconite Tincture.—1. Powdered root 1 part, alcohol to percolate 8 parts; macerate for 48 hours with three-quarters of the alcohol agitating occasionally; pack in a percolator and let it drain, then pour on the remaining spirits. When it ceases to drop press the marc and add alcohol to make up 8 quarts. Dose, 5 to 15 minims 2 or 3 times a day. **2.** Take of aconite root, coarsely powdered, 15 ounces, rectified spirits 1 quart; macerate for 7 days, press and filter.

Aloes Tincture.—Socotrine aloes 1 part, extract of licorice 3 parts, proof spirits (alcohol) 4o parts; macerate 7 days, press and wash the marc with spirits to make 40 parts. Dose, 1 to 2 drams.

Angelica Tincture.—Dried angelica root 1 ounce, proof spirits 6 ounces; digest and filter. Dose, 1 dram.

Aniseed Essence.—Oil of anise 1 part, rectified spirits 4 parts; mix. Use as a stimulant, aromatic and carminative. Dose, 10 to 20 minims. Used also to flavor liquors and to make aniseed water.

Arnica Tincture.—Flowers of arnica montana 1½ ounces, spirits, specific gravity 900, 1 pound; digest for 8 days and strain with expression. Dose, 10 to 30 drops. Used in diarrhœa, dysentery, gout, rheumatism. paralysis. etc.

Aromatic Elixir.—Orange peel 4 drams, coriander seed 2 drams, angelica seed 2½ drams, cochineal 1 dram, alcohol 12 ounces, water 10 ounces, glycerine 5 ounces, syrup 6 ounces; reduce the solid ingredients to a moderately fine powder and pack firmly in a percolator, mix the other ingredients and percolate 2 pints, adding water enough to make this amount.

Aromatic Tincture.—Cinnamon 4 ounces, cardamon 1 ounce, cloves 1 ounce, galangal root 1 ounce, ginger 1 ounce, all in coarse powder; proof spirits 3 lbs. 2 ozs.; macerate 8 days and strain.

Bark and Protoxide of Iron Elixir.—Elixir of calisaya 15 ounces, crystalized sulphate of iron 128 grains, ammonia and nitric acid, of each sufficient; dissolve the sulphate of iron in boiling water and add to it enough ammonia to precipitate the oxide of iron, wash the precipitate thoroughly with boiling water, collect it on a muslin strainer and press it thoroughly to expel the moisture; then add to it cautiously and by portions enough nitric acid mixed with 3 times its volume of water to redissolve the precipitate; a slight excess of acid is desired; lastly, filter the solution and mix it with sufficient elixir of calisaya to complete 1 pint.

Beef and Iron Wine.—Sherry wine 14 ounces, simple syrup 2 ounces, extract of beef 4 drams, ammonia-citrate of iron 123 grains, tincture of fresh orange peel 30 minims; mix and filter.

Belladonna Tincture.—1. The dried leaves, in coarse powder, 1 part, proof spirits 20 parts; macerate 48 hours in 15 parts of the spirits, agitating occasionally; pack in a percolator, and when it ceases to drop add the remaining spirits, let it drain, wash and press the marc, filter and make up 2 parts. Dose, from 5 to 20 minims. **2.** Dried leaves of belladonna 4 ounces, proof spirits 1 quart; macerate for 7 days, press and filter.

Benzoin Tincture.—1. Benzoin 2 ounces, rectified spirits 10 ounces; digest for 8 days, frequently shaking, then filter. **2.** Benzoin 8 parts, prepared storax 6 parts, balsam of tulu 2 parts, socotrine aloes 1½ parts, rectified spirits 80 parts; macerate 7 days, filter, and wash the marc with spirits to make up 80 parts. Dose, ½ to 1 dram, triturated with mucilage or yolk of egg. **3.** Gum benzoin, coarsely powdered, 3½ ounces, prepared storax 2½ ounces, balsam of tulu 10 drams, socotrine or hepatic aloes, in coarse powder, 5 drams, rectified spirits 1 quart; macerate with frequent agitation for 7 days, and strain.

Bitter Elixir.—Extract of buckbean, extract of orange peel, of each 2 parts, peppermint water and alcohol (68 per cent), of each 16 parts, spirits of ether (made of 3 parts alcohol and 1 part ether) 1 part; dissolve and mix.

Buchu Tincture.—Buchu, bruised, 1 part, proof spirits 8 parts; macerate for 48 hours with ¾ parts of the spirits; pack in a percolator and let it drain, then pour on the rest of the spirits; when it ceases to drop, press and wash the marc, filter and make up in 8 parts. Dose, 1 to 2 drams.

Calisaya Bark Elixir.—Take 8 ounces of calisaya bark, 4 ounces each of orange peel, cinnamon and coriander seed, ½ ounce each anise seed, caraway seed, and cardamons; reduce all to a moderate powder, and percolate with 4 pints of alcohol, diluted with 12 pints of water, and add 2 pints of simple syrup.

Camphorated Tincture of Opium.—1. Opium, in coarse powder, 40 grains, benzoic acid 40 grains, camphor 30 grains, oil of anise ½ dram, proof spirits 20 ounces: macerate 7 days, strain, wash the marc with spirits and filter 20 ounces. Dose, 15 to 16 minims. **2.** Camphor 50 grains, powdered opium and benzoic acid of each 72 grains, oil of aniseed 1 fluid dram, proof spirits 1 quart; macerate for 7 days and filter.

Cantharides Tincture.—Cantharides, in coarse powder, 1 part, proof spirits 80 parts; macerate, agitating occasionally, for 7 days in a closed vessel; strain, press, filter, and add sufficient proof spirits to make up 80 parts, Dose, 5 to 20 minims.

Capsicum Tincture.—1. Capsicum, bruised, 1 part, rectified spirits 27 parts; macerate 48 hours with ¾ of the spirits, agitating occasionally: pack in a percolator and let it drain, then pour on the remaining spirits; as soon as it ceases to drop, wash the marc with spirits to make up 27 parts. Dose, 10 to 20 minims. **2.** Capsicum, bruised, 10 drams, proof spirits 1 quart; digest 14 days. Dose, 10 to 60 drops in atonic dyspepsia, scarlet fever, ulcerated sore throat, etc., it is also made into a gargle.

Capsicum and Cantharides Tincture.—Cantharides, in fine powder, 10 drams, capsicum 1 dram, diluted alcohol 1 pint; mix and digest for 10 days, and filter. This is a stimulant and rubefacient. Used as a counter irritant in deep-seated, painful affections.

Capsicum and Veratria Tincture.—Dissolve 4 grains of veratria in 1 ounce of concentrated tincture of capsicum.

Cascarilla Essence.—Cascarilla 12 ounces, proof spirits 1 pint; proceed either by digestion or percolation; the product is 8 times the strength of the infusion of cascarilla.

Catechu Wine.—Tincture of catechu 1 part, red wine 12½ parts; mix, and after a few days filter.

Catechu Tincture.—Pale catechu in coarse powder 2½ parts, cinnamon bruised 1 part, proof spirits 20 parts; macerate for 7 days with agitation, strain, press and filter, and add spirits to make 20 parts. Dose, ½ to 2 drams.

Celery Elixir (Celery Compound).—For increasing, preserving and producing virility; a cure for sexual debility or loss of manhood. Juniper berries, angelica root, lovage root, of each 1 part, alcohol 12 parts, orange flower water and rose water, of each 4 parts, spring water of sufficient quantity; distill 20 parts, and mix the distillate with 12 parts of clarified honey. Dose, 1 to 2 drams.

Celery Essence.—Very fine; used for flavoring. **1.** Celery seed, bruised or ground, 4½ ounces, alcohol 1 pint, digest 14 days and strain. **2.** Celery seed 7 ounces, alcohol 1 pint; digest as before.

Centaury Wine.—Centaury, orange peel, extract of blessed thistle gentian, myrrh and cascarilla, of each 1 dram, sherry wine 2 parts.

Chloroform Tincture.—Mix 2 fluid ounces of chloroform with 8 fluid ounces of alcohol and 10 fluid ounces of compound tincture of cardamons. Dose, 10 to 20 minims.

Cinnamon Tincture.—Cinnamon, bruised, 1 ounce, cardamon seed (bruised without the shells) ½ ounce, long pepper and ginger, of each 2½ drams, alcohol 1 quart; digest for 7 days. Cordial, aromatic and stomachic.

Clove Essence.—Cloves 3½ ounces, proof spirits ¾ pint, water ¼ pint; digest 1 week and strain.

Colchicum Tincture.—1. Colchicum seeds, bruised 5 ounces, aromatic spirits of ammonia 1 quart: digest for 7 days, then press and filter. Dose, 20 drops to 1 fluid dram, in gout, etc. **2.** Colchicum seeds, bruised, 1 part, proof spirits 8 parts; macerate 48 hours with 6 parts of the spirits, agitating occasionally; pack in a percolator and let it drain, then pour on the remainder of the spirits; when it ceases to drop, wash the marc with spirits to make 8 parts. Dose, 15 to 30 minims.

Colchicum Wine.—An excellent remedy for acute rheumatism, gout and other inflammatory diseases. **1.** Colchicum corns, dried and sliced, 4 parts, sherry wine 20 parts; macerate 7 days and strain. Dose, 20 to 30 minims. **2.** Dried corns of meadow saffron 8 ounces, sherry wine 1 quart; macerate 7 days and strain. This is a powerful sedative and purgative. Dose, ½ to 1 fluid dram.

Cough Elixir.—Extracts of blessed thistle and dulcamara, of each 1 dram, cherry laurel water 1 fluid dram, fennel water 1 fluid ounce. Dose, 1 to 2 teaspoonsful 3 or 4 times a day; a most useful remedy in nervous coughs.

Cubebs Tincture.—Cubebs, in powder, 1 part, rectified spirits 8 parts; macerate 48 hours with 6 parts of the spirits, agitating occasionally; pack in a percolator and let it drain, pour on the remaining spirits, and when it ceases to drop, wash the marc with spirits to make up 8 parts. Dose, 1 to 2 drams.

Digitalis Tincture.—Digitalis, recently dried and in fine powder, 4 ounces, diluted alcohol a sufficient quantity; moisten the powder with 2 fluid ounces of the alcohol, pack it firmly in a conical percolator and gradually pour diluted alcohol over it until 2 parts of tincture are obtained. It is stimulant, but afterwards sedative, diuretic and narcotic. In overdoses it occasions vomiting, purging, vertigo, delirium and death. Used in inflammatory diseases, phthisis, dropsies, palpitation of the heart, etc.; in mania, epilepsy and asthma. Dose, 10 to 20 drops.

Elecampane Tincture.—Powdered elecampane 4 ounces, proof spirits 1 pint; macerate for 15 days. Tonic, deobstruent and expectorant. Dose, ½ to 2 fluid drams, in dyspepsia, palsy, uterine obstructions, etc.

Ergot Tincture.—Ergot (ground in a coffee mill) 2½ ounces, proof spirits 1 pint; digest for 7 days, strain and filter. Dose, 1 teaspoonful. Used to excite the action of the uterus in labor.

Iodine Tincture.—Iodine ½ dram, iodide of potassium ¼ dram, rectified spirits 20 drams: dissolve and filter through filter paper. Dose, 5 to 20 minims. An excellent application for the throat in diphtheria.

Iron Wine.—Ammonia, tartrate of iron 1½ drams, sherry 1 pint; dissolve. Dose, 1 to 5 fluid drams, as a mild chalybeate.

Lavender Tincture.—English oil of lavender 90 minims, English oil of rosemary 10 minims, cinnamon, bruised, 150 grains, nutmeg 150 grains, red sandalwood 800 grains, rectified spirits 40 ounces: macerate the cinnamon, nutmeg and red sandalwood in the spirits for 7 days, then press out and strain: dissolve the oils in the strained tincture and add sufficient spirits to make 40 ounces. Dose, ½ to 2 drams.

Lobelia Tincture.—Lobelia, dried and bruised, 1 part, spirits of ether 8 parts; macerate 7 days, press and strain. Dose, 10 to 30 minims, as an antispasmodic.

Myrrh Tincture.—Gum myrrh 2 ounces, alcohol 1 quart; steep 4 days, then filter.

Opium Tincture (Laudanum).—Powdered opium 3 ounces, alcohol 1 quart; macerate 7 days, filter.

Pepsin, Bismuth and Strychnia Elixir.—For dyspepsia, gastralgia, general debility and lack of tone in the general system. Citrate of bismuth and ammonia 256 grains, Hall's solution of strychnia 2 ounces, warm water 1 ounce, elixir of pepsin 13 ounces; dissolve the bismuth in the water by the aid of a few drops of aqua ammonia. Dose, 1 teaspoonful.

Quinine Elixir.—Sulphate of quinine 128 grains, citric acid 20 grains, aqua ammonia of sufficient quantity: simple elixir to make 1 pint. Take 2 portions of elixir: in one dissolve the citric acid, in the other dissolve the quinine by rubbing in the mortar; mix the solutions and add the balance of the elixir: lastly, add aqua ammonia, a few drops at a time, until the mixture is clear: take care to add no more ammonia than is necessary to clarify the solution, else the ammonia will precipitate the quinine. Used in febrile diseases and intermittent and remittent fevers. Dose, 1 to 2 teaspoonsful.

Squill Tincture.—Dried squill, bruised, 1 part, proof spirits 8 parts; macerate 48 hours with 6 parts of the spirits, agitating occasionally: pack in a percolator, when it ceases to drop, press, filter and add spirits to make 8 parts. Dose, 15 to 30 minims.

Tolu Tincture.—Balsam of tolu 1 part, rectified spirits 8 parts: dissolve, filter and make up to 8 parts. Dose, 15 to 30 minims, in syrup, for coughs and colds.

Tonic Tincture.—Excellent. Peruvian bark, bruised, 3 ounces, orange peel, bruised, 2 ounces, brandy 2 pints; infuse 10 days, shake the bottle every day, pour off the liquor and strain. Dose, 1 teaspoonful in a wineglass of water, when languid.

Valerian Tincture.—Valerian, in moderately fine powder, 4 troy ounces, diluted alcohol of sufficient quantity; moisten the powder with 1 fluid ounce of the alcohol, macerate for 7 days, strain and filter, using 1 fluid ounce of alcohol to make up quantity needed. This is stimulant and antispasmodic; used in hysteria, etc.

Wild Cherry Bark Tincture.—Wild cherry bark, bruised, 2 ounces, proof spirits 1 pint; digest 14 days, press and filter. Dose, 1 tablespoonful.

POPULAR PATENT MEDICINES.

TONICS, ALTERATIVES, CARMINATIVES, BITTERS, DIURETICS, STOMACHICS, ETC.

In this list will be found the correct formulas for the principal patent medicines now on the market. The formulas are guaranteed genuine, and the list is a good one. Please read carefully and follow directions closely.

Ayer's Cherry Pectoral.—Take 4 grains of acetate of morphia, 2 fluid drams of tincture of bloodroot, 3 fluid drams each of antimonial wine and wine of ipecacuanha, and 3 fluid ounces syrup of wild cherry. Mix.

August Flower.—Powdered rhubarb 1 ounce, golden seal ¼ ounce, aloes 1 dram, peppermint leaves 2 drams, carbonate of potash 2 drams, capsicum 5 grains, sugar 5 ounces, alcohol 3 ounces, water 10 ounces, essence of peppermint, 20 drops; powder the drugs and let stand covered with alcohol and water, equal parts, for 7 days; filter and add through the filter enough diluted alcohol to make 1 pint.

Blood Purifier—B. B. B.—Fluid extract burdock 1 ounce fluid extract of sarsaparilla 1 ounce, fluid extract yellow dock 1 ounce, fluid extract senna 1 oz., syrup 8 ozs., alcohol 2 ozs.; mix.

Castoria.—Pumpkin seed 1 ounce, cenria leaves 1 ounce, rochelle salts 1 ounce, anise seed ½ ounce, bicarbonate soda 1 ounce, worm seed ½ ounce; mix and thoroughly rub together in an earthen vessel, then put into a bottle and pour over it 4 ounces water and 1 ounce alcohol, and let stand 4 days, then strain off and add syrup made of white sugar, quantity to make 1 pint, then add ½ ounce alcohol drops, and 5 drops wintergreen. Mix thoroughly, and add to the contents of the bottle, and take as directed.

Canada Catarrh Cure.—Carbolic acid 10 to 20 drops, vaseline 1 to 2 ounces; mix, and use with an atomizer 3 or 4 times per day. Try this, it is excellent.

Cough Drops.—Tincture of aconite 5 drops, tincture of ascelpias 1 dram, glycerine 2 ounces, syrup of wild cherry; mix, and take a teaspoonful every 40 minutes until relieved.

Drops of Life.—Gum opium 1 ounce, gum kino, 1 dram,

gum camphor 40 grains, nutmeg, powdered, ½ ounce, French brandy 1 pint; let stand from 1 to 10 days. Dose, from 30 to 40 drops for an adult; children, half dose. This is one of the most valuable preparations in the *Materia Medica*, and will in some dangerous hours, when all hope is fled, and the system is racked with pain, be the soothing balm which cures the most dangerous diseases to which the human body is liable—flux, dysentery and all summer complaints.

Godfrey's Cordial.—Tincture of opium 6 ounces, molasses 4 pints, alcohol 8 ounces, water 6 pints, carbonate of potash 4 drams, oil of sassafras cut with alcohol 1 dram; dissolve the potash in water, add the molasses, heat over a gentle fire till it simmers, remove the scum, add the other ingredients, the oil dissolved in the alcohol.

Harter's Iron Tonic.—Calisaya bark 2 ounces, citrate of iron 2 ounces, gentian 2 ounces, cardamon seed 2 ounces, syrup 2 ounces, alcohol 2 ounces, water 8 ounces; mix.

Hood's Sarsaparilla.—Fluid extract of sarsaparilla 1 ounce, fluid extract of yellow dock 1 ounce, fluid extract of poke root ½ ounce, iodide of potash ½ ounce, syrup of orange peel 1 ounce, alcohol 4 ounces, syrup enough to make 1 pint.

Hop Bitters.—Hops 4 ounces, orange peel 2 ounces, cardamon 2 drams, cinnamon 1 dram, cloves ½ dram, alcohol 8 ounces, sherry wine 2 pints, simple syrup 1 pint, water sufficient; grind the drugs, macerate in the alcohol and wine for 1 week, percolate and add enough syrup and water to make 1 gallon.

Hostetter's Bitters.—Gentian root, ground, ½ ounce, cinnamon bark ½ ounce, cinchona bark, ground, ½ ounce, anise seed ½ ounce, coriander seed, ground, ½ ounce, cardamon seed ⅛ ounce, gum kino ¼ ounce, alcohol 1 pint, water 4 quarts, sugar 1 pound; mix and let stand for 1 week, pour off the fluid, boil the drug for a few minutes in 1 quart of water, strain off and add first the fluid and then the sugar and water.

Indian Sagwa.—Gentian ½ pound, seneca ¼ pound, cubebs ½ pound, rhei ¼ pound, salts ½ pound, aloes ⅛ pound, bicarbonate of soda 2¼ pounds, senna ⅓ pound, anise ¼ pound, coriander ¼ pound, pareivabrava ⅝ pound, guaiac ⅝ pound, licorice 1¼ pounds, alcohol 3 quarts, water 6 gallons; steep 10 days, percolate and bottle. The above will fill 65 12-ounce bottles.

Injection Brou.—Water 4 ounces, nitrate of silver 20 grains, tincture of opium ½ ounce, sulphate of bismuth and hydrastis, 2 ounces; mix.

Jayne's Expectorant.—Syrup of squills 2 ounces, tincture of tolu 1 ounce, spirits of camphor 1 dram, tincture of digitalis 1 dram, tincture of lobelia 1 dram, wine of ipecac 2 drams, tincture of opium 2 drams, antimonia 2 grains; mix.

Jayne's Tonic Vermifuge.—Santonine 20 grains, fluid extract of pink root 3 drams, fluid extract of senna 2 drams, simple elixir 2 ounces, syrup 2 ounces; mix. Dose, 1 table-spoonful night and morning.

S. S. S. Fluid.—Extract of phytolacca 1 ounce, fluid extract of sarsaparilla 1 ounce, iodide of potash 1 ounce. fluid extract of xanthoxylon ½ ounce, fluid extract of Culiver's root 1 ounce, acetate of potash 1 ounce, tincture of cinnamon ¼ ounce, tincture of cardamon seed 1 ounce, alcohol 4 ounces, sugar ½ pound, water 36 ounces; mix.

Smith's Tonic Syrup.—Fowler's solution of arsenic 2 drams, Culiver's root 1 ounce, syrup of orange peel 4 ounces, simple syrup 12 ounces; mix, then add cinchona 40 grains, dissolved in aromatic sulphuric acid; shake to mix well.

Sozodont Fragrant.—Tincture of soap bark 2 ounces, tincture of myrrh 1 dram, glycerine ½ ounce, water 1½ ounces, essence of cloves 10 drops, essence of wintergreen 10 drops, tincture of cochineal enough to color; mix. Accompanying the above is a powder composed of prepared chalk, orris root, carbonate magnesia, of equal parts; mix.

Shaker's Extract of Herbs.—Fluid extract of blue flag 20 drops, fluid extract of Culiver's root 20 drops, fluid extract of stalinga 20 drops, fluid extract of poke root 20 drops, fluid extract of butternut 20 drops, fluid extract of dandelion 20 drops, fluid extract of prince pine 10 drops, fluid extract of mandrake 5 drops, fluid extract of gentian 5 drops, fluid extract of calcium 5 drops, fluid extract of black cohose 30 drops, tincture of aloes 30 drops, tincture of capsicum 10 drops, tincture of sassafras 30 drops, borax 1 dram, salt ¾ drams, syrup 3 ounces, water 8 ounces.

Succus Alterns (McDade's).—Fluid extract of stillingia 1 ounce, fluid extract of sarsaparilla 1 ounce, fluid extract of phytolacca decandra ½ ounce, fluid extract of lappa minor 1 ounce, fluid extract of xanthoxylon ½ ounce, syrup 14 ounces; mix. Dose, 1 teaspoonful 3 times a day.

Seven Seals of Golden Wonder.—Oil of cajeput 2 drams, oil of sassafras ½ ounce, oil of organum 1 dram, oil of hemlock 1 dram. oil of cedar 1 dram, tincture of capsicum ¼ ounce, alcohol enough to make 1 pint.

Swain's Vermifuge.—Wormseed 2 ounces, valerian, rhubarb, pink root, white agaric, of each 1¼ ounces; boil in sufficient water to yield 3 quarts of decoction and add to it 30 drops of oil of tansy and 45 drops of oil of cloves; dissolve in a quart of rectified spirits. Dose, 1 tablespoonful at night.

Warner's Tippecanoe Bitters.—Cardamon seed 2 ounces, nutmeg 1 dram, grains of paradise 1 dram, cloves 1 ounce, cinnamon 2 ounces, ginger 1 ounce, orange peel 1 ounce, lemon peel 1 ounce alcohol 1 gallon, water 1 gallon, sugar 3 pounds; mix and let stand 6 or 7 days and filter. Then add enough water to make 4 gallons.

Warner's Safe Cure.—Take of smart weed 4 pounds, boil for 1 hour with 1 gallon of soft water, adding warm water to supply waste by evaporation; then strain off and add acetate potash 4 ounces, sugar 4 pounds. Boil again till sugar is dissolved, then add alcohol 8 ounces, and flavor with oil of wintergreen cut with alcohol.

Wakefield's Blackberry Balsam.—Blackberries crushed 2 pounds, boiling water 4 ounces, sugar 4 ounces, Jamaica ginger 4 grains, alcohol 2 ounces; mix and add syrup enough to make 16 ounces.

TRIED REMEDIES.

These remedies are not classified, but are efficient for the various troubles for which they are recommended. In this list will be found a little bit of everything, such as corn cures, tapeworm expellers, cough drops, salves, liniments, ointments, pile remedies, pills, etc. Read the list over carefully.

Eye Water.—Table salt and white vitriol, each 1 teaspoonful; heat them on earthen dish until dry; now add to them soft water ½ pint, white sugar 1 teaspoonful, blue vitriol, a piece as large as a common pea. Should this be too strong add a little more water. Apply to the eye 3 or 4 times a day.

To Remove Tapeworm.—Let the patient miss 2 meals. give 2 teaspoonfuls powdered kamala. Should the bowels not move within 2½ hours give another teaspoonful of the kamala. You may follow this in 2 hours by from ½ to 1 ounce of castor oil. This is a positive cure for tapeworm, it will not make the patient sick. In buying the drug be sure and get kamala, not camellea. Kamala is in appearance like quite red brick dust, and is nearly tasteless, whereas camellea is of a yellowish color.

A Sure Cure for Smallpox.—It is claimed that the following is a sure and never-failing cure for smallpox: One ounce cream of tartar dissolved in a pint of boiling water, to be drank when cold, at intervals. It can be taken at any time, and is a preventative as well as a curative. It is known to have cured in thousands of cases without a failure.

For Itch.—Calamine (precipitated) 2 drams, oxide of zinc 2 drams, carbolic acid 30 drops, lime water to make 8 ounces. Wash and apply with muslin.

For Leucorrhoea.—Tannic acid 1 ounce, glycerine 4 ounces. Dissolve tannic acid in glycerine with gentle heat. One teaspoonful to a pint of tepid water, and inject twice a day.

Sure Cure for Diphtheria.—Sulpho-calcine and glycerine 1 ounce of each; mix. Apply to throat with a mop every 3 or 4 hours.

Onanism.—Fluid extract salix nigra (aments). Teaspoonful 3 times daily.

Tetter Ointment.—One ounce spirits of turpentine, 1 ounce red percipitate in powder, 1 ounce burgundy pitch in powder, 1 pound hog's lard; melt all these ingredients over a slow fire until the ointment is formed; stir until cold. Spread on a linen rag and apply to the parts affected.

A Sure Cure for Piles,—Confection of senna 2 ounces, cream of tartar 1 ounce, sulphur 1 ounce, syrup of ginger enough to make a stiff paste; mix. A piece as large as a nut is to be taken as often as necessary to keep the bowels open. One of the best remedies known.

Healing Salve.—Lard 1 pound, resin ½ pound, sweet elder bark ½ pound; simmer over a slow fire 4 hours, or until it forms a hard, brown salve. This is for the cure of cuts, bruises, boils, old sores and all like ailments; spread on cotton cloth and apply to the parts affected.

Specific Inflammatory Rheumatism.—Saltpetre, pulverized, 1 ounce, sweet oil 1 pint; bathe the parts affected 3 times a day with this mixture and a speedy cure will be the result.

Another Salve.—Sheep's tallow 1 ounce, beeswax 1 ounce, sweet oil ½ ounce, red lead ⅓ ounce, gum camphor 2 ounces; fry all these together in a stone dish, continue to simmer for 4 hours, spread on green basswood leaves or paper and apply to the sore.

Cough Drops.—Tincture of aconite 5 drops, tincture of ascelpias 1 dram, glycerine 2 ounces, syrup of wild cherry; mix, and take 1 teaspoonful every 40 minutes until relieved.

Cure for Sore Throat in All Its Different Forms.—Cayenne pepper 2 ounces, common salt 1 ounce, vinegar ½ pint; warm over a slow fire and gargle the throat and mouth every hour. Garlic and onion poultice applied to the outside. Castor oil 1 spoonful, to keep the bowels open.

Ointment of Stramonium.—Stramonium leaves 1 pound, lard 3 pounds, yellow wax ½ pound; boil the stramonium leaves in the lard until they become pliable, then strain through linen; lastly, add the wax previously melted and stir until they are cold. This is a useful anodyne application in irritable ulcers, painful hemorrhoids and in cutaneous eruptions.

Cathartic Pills.—Extract of colacinth, in powder, ½ ounce, jalap, in powder, 3 drams, calomel 3 drams, gamboge, in powder, 2 scruples; mix these together and with water form into mass and roll into 180 pills. Dose, 1 pill as a mild laxative, 2 in vigorous operations. Use in all billious diseases when purges are necessary.

Lozenges for Heartburn.—Gum arabic 1 ounce, licorice root, pulverized, 1 ounce, magnesia ¼ ounce, add water to make into lozenges; let dissolve in mouth and swallow.

Another Cough Cure.—Good. Take the white of an egg

and pulverized sugar; beat to a froth. Take 1 tablespoonful every hour for 3 or 4 hours.

Warts and Corns.—To cure in 10 minutes. Take a small piece of potash and let it stand in the open air until it slacks, then thicken it to a paste with pulverized gum arabic, which prevents it from spreading where it is not wanted.

Tetter Ointment.—Spirits of turpentine 1 ounce, red precipitate, in powder, 1 ounce, burgundy pitch, in powder, 1 ounce, hog's lard 1 pound; melt all these ingredients over a slow fire until the ointment is formed; stir until cold; spread on a linen rag and apply to the parts affected.

Diphtheria.—Take a clean clay tobacco pipe, put a live coal in it, then put common tar on the fire and smoke it, inhaling and breathing back through the nostrils.

Said to Be Good for Grip.—Peroxide of hydrogen (medicinal) is a marvelous remedy in the treatment of grip or influenza. This medicine should be diluted with water and administered internally, and by sniffing through the nostrils or by spraying the nostrils and throat. The good results from this treatment, which has never been known to fail of producing a speedy cure, are due to the destruction of the microbe upon which this disease depends. The remedy is simple and within the reach of everybody, and can easily be tested.

Lung Medicine.—Take black cohosh ½ ounce, lobelia ¼ ounce, canker root ¾ ounce, blackberry root ¼ ounce, sarsaparilla 1 ounce, pleurisy root ½ ounce; steeped in 3 pints of water. Dose, 1 tablespoonful 3 times a day, before eating. Sure cure for spitting blood.

Toothache Drops.—Four ounces pulverized alum, 14 ounces sweet spirits of nitre. Put up in 1 ounce bottles. Retails readily at 25 cents per bottle. This is the most effective remedy for toothache that was ever discovered, and is a fortune to anyone who will push its sale. It sells at every house.

A Certain Cure for Drunkenness.—Sulphate of iron 5 grains, magnesia 10 grains, peppermint water 11 drams, spirits of nutmeg 1 dram, twice a day. This preparation acts as a tonic and stimulant, and so partially supplies the place of the accustomed liquor and prevents that absolute physical and mental prostration that follows a sudden breaking off from the use of stimulating drinks.

Fever and Ague.—Quinine 1 scruple, elixir vitriol 1 dram; dissolve the quinine in the elixir and tincture of black cohosh 14 drops. Dose, 20 drops in a little water once an hour.

Corns, a Sure Cure and Painless Eradication.—Extract of cannabis indicus 10 grains, salicylic acid 6 grains, colodion 1 ounce; mix and apply with a camel's hair pencil so as to form a thick covering over the corn for 3 or 4 nights. Take a hot foot bath and the corn can easily be removed by the aid of a knife.

Plain Court Plaster that will not stick and remains flexible. Soak isinglass in a little warm water for 24 hours, then evaporate nearly all the water by a gentle heat; dissolve the residue with a little proof spirits of wine, and strain the whole through a piece of open linen. The strained mass should be a stiff jelly when cool. Stitch a piece of silk or sarcenet on a wooden frame with tacks or thread. Melt the jelly and apply it to the silk thinly and evenly with a badger hair brush. A second coating must be applied when the first has dried. When both are dry apply over the whole surface two or three coatings of balsam of peru. This plaster remains quite pliable, and never breaks.

A Cure for Cancer.—The following has been used by a New York physician with great success: Take red oak bark and boil it to the thickness of molasses, then mix with sheep's tallow of equal proportion; spread it on leaves of linnwood, green, and keep the plaster over the ulcer. Change once in 8 hours.

To Strengthen and Invigorate the System.—Two drams essential salt of the round leaf cornel, 1 scruple extract rhubarb, 1 scruple ginger powder. Make into pills, and take for a dose 2 or 3 times a day.

Chilblains.—We glean these two prescriptions from the *British Medical Journal*. They are now being used in this country, and with good results, **1.** Belledonna liniment 2 drams, aconite liniment 1 dram, carbolic acid 5 minims, flexible colodion 1 ounce. Mix and apply every night with a camel's hair pencil. **2.** Flexible colodion 4 drams, castor oil 4 drams, spirits of turpentine 4 drams. Use 3 times daily with camel's hair brush.

How to Remove Pain and Soreness from Wounds.—The value of the smoke from burned wool to remove the pain and soreness from wounds of all kinds, or from sores is great, and it will give immediate relief from the intense pain caused by a gathering. The easiest way to prepare this is to cut all-wool flannel—if you haven't the wool—into narrow strips; take some hot ashes with a few small live coals on a shovel, sprinkle some of the flannel strips on it, and hold the injured member in the smoke for five or ten minutes, using plenty of flannel to make a thick smoke. Repeat as often as seems necessary, though one smoking is usually enough.

Dropsy, Cure for.—Take of bruised juniper berries, mustard seed, and ginger, ½ ounce each, bruised horseradish and parsley root, 1 ounce each, sound old cider, 1 quart; infuse. Dose, a wineglassful 3 times a day.

Catarrh, A Simple Remedy for.—Catarrh is an inflammation of the mucous membrane, especially of the air passages of the head and throat, with an exudation on its free surface. Treatment: Simple but effective. Take 1 ounce each of fine salt, pulverized borax and baking soda, mix thoroughly together and dissolve in ½ pint of water. To use take 1 tablespoonful of the solution to 2 or 3 of warm water, and snuff up the head at bed-time. The salt stimulates, the borax cleanses and heals, and the soda soothes; use soft water.

Influenza or "Grippe," Treatment for.—It is reported as having been quite fatal in France in 1311 and 1403. In 1570 it also prevailed, and in 1557 spread over Europe, and extended to America. It occurred again in 1729, 1743, 1775, 1782, 1833, 1837, with notable violence. In the United States, one of the most remarkable epidemics for extent, was that of 1843. Another was that of 1872, following nearly the course of the epizootic among horses of the latter part of that year. The last epidemic (1890) has been a remarkable one for its extent, invading all Europe and the United States. Mild cases require housing and little more. The following prescriptions will be found excellent: Take of antipyrine 18 grains, Dover's powder 12 grains, powdered extract valerian 3 grains; mix, and divide into 6 capsules. Take one every 2 hours. If there be a tight cough, take the following: Take of muriate of ammonia 30 grains, deodorized tincture of opium 1 dram, syrup of senega snakeroot ½ ounce, distilled water 1 ounce, syrup of balsam tolu enough to make 3 fluid ounces; mix, and take a teaspoonful every 2 hours.

Eczema Ointment.—Salicylic acid 20 grains, oxide of zinc 20 grains, finely powdered starch 60 grains, vaseline 1 ounce; mix thoroughly; apply to parts effected.

Tonic.—Peruvian bark 1 ounce, gentian root 1 ounce, orange peel 1 ounce, dandelion root 1 ounce. Infuse for 4 hours with 2 pints of water, and evaporate to 13 ounces; add 3 ounces of alcohol. Dose, 1 teaspoonful in sweetened water after meals.

For Indigestion.—Scale pepsin 1 dram, tincture of nux vomica 2 drams, dilute muriatic acid (chemically pure) 2 drams, compound tincture of gentian 2 ounces, syrup of ginger to make 4 ounces. Powder the scale pepsin, then rub with 1 ounce of the syrup of ginger; then add tincture of gentian, muriatic acid and tincture nux vomica; then add syrup of ginger to make the 4 ounces. Dose, 1 teaspoonful after meals.

Cholera Mixture.—Tincture of opium ½ ounce, tincture of capsicum ½ ounce, spirits of camphor ½ ounce, chloroform 1½ drams, alchhol 2½ ounces, syrup sufficient to make 8 ounces. Dose, 2 teaspoonfuls in water after each discharge, or when in pain.

Cough Mixture.—Ground senega root 1 ounce, ground wild cherry bark 1 ounce, extract licorice 1 ounce, balsam tolu 1 ounce, ground henbane 1 dram. Infuse all together for 4 or 5 hours, slowly with one pint of water. Then add 1 pound of sugar. When dissolved, strain through a cloth with enough water added to make a pint. Then add 2 drams of granular sal ammoniac. It is improved by adding 15 drops of chloroform. Dose, 1 teaspoonful every 2 or 3 hours.

DEPARTMENT II.

THE CHEMIST.

In this department is included—under sub-heads—inks, gold and silver imitations, preparations made from acids, pharmaceutical chemistry, fireworks and explosives, freezing mixtures, plating fluids and many recipes requiring chemical manipulation. Some valuable secrets are herein given.

INKS—ANY COLOR, FOR EVERY PURPOSE—INK ERASERS, ETC.

Buchner's Carmine Ink.—Pure carmine 12 grains, water of ammonia 3 ounces; dissolve, then add powdered gum 18 grains; ½ dram of powdered drop lake may be substituted for the carmine, where expense is an object.

Black Copying Ink, or Writing Fluid.—Take 2 gallons of rain water and put into it gum arabic ¼ pound, brown sugar ¼ pound, clean copperas ¼ pound, powdered nutgalls ¾ pound: mix, and shake occasionally for 10 days, and strain; if needed sooner let it stand in an iron kettle until the strength is obtained. The ink will stand the action of the atmosphere for centuries if required.

Brown Ink.—A strong decoction of catechu. The shade may be varied by the cautious addition of a little weak solution of bichromate of potash.

Beautiful Blue Writing Fluid.—Dissolve basic or soluble prussian blue in pure water. This is the most permanent and beautiful blue ink known.

Black Ink.—Shellac 4 ounces. borax 2 ounces, water 1 quart; boil till dissolved, and add 2 ounces gum arabic, dissolved in a little hot water: boil, add enough of a well triturated mixture of equal parts of indigo and lamp-black to produce a proper color; after standing several hours. draw off and bottle.

Black Ink.—Extract of logwood 1 ounce, bichromate of potash ¼ ounce; pulverize and mix in a quart of soft hot water.

51

This makes a beautiful jet black ink, which will not spoil by freezing.

Black Ink.—Perchloride of mercury, the wash is hydro-chloric of tin.

Blue Ink.—Persian blue 6 parts, oxalic acid 1 part; triturate with a little water to smooth paste, add gum arabic and the necessary quantity of water.

Brilliant Red Ink.—Brazil wood 2 ounces, muriate of tin ¼ dram. gum arabic 1 dram; boil down in 32 ounces of water to one-half, and strain.

Common Ink.—To 1 gallon boiling soft water add ¾ ounce extract of logwood; boil 2 minutes, remove from the fire and stir in 48 grains bichromate of potash and 8 grains prussiate of potash; for 10 gallons, use 6½ ounces extract of logwood, 1 ounce bichromate of potash and 80 grains prussiate of potash; strain. Six cents should buy the former and 25 cents the latter.

Copying Ink.—Soft water ½ gallon, gum arabic 1 ounce, brown sugar 1 ounce, clean copperas 1 ounce, powdered nut-galls 3 ounces; mix, and shake occasionally from 7 to 10 days and strain. The best copying ink made.

Commercial Writing Ink.—Galls 1 ounce, gum ½ ounce, cloves ½ ounce, sulphate of iron ½ ounce, water 8 ounces; digest by frequent shaking till it has sufficient color. This is a good, durable ink, and will bear diluting.

Gold Ink.—Honey and gold leaf equal parts, turpentine until the gold is reduced to the finest possible state of division; agitate with 30 parts hot water, and allow it to settle; decant the water and repeat the washing several times, finally dry the gold and mix it with a little gum water for use.

Green Ink.—Dissolve 180 grains bichromate of potash in 1 fluid ounce of water; add while warm ½ ounce spirits of wine; then decompose the mixture with concentrated sulphuric acid until it assumes a brown color; evaporate this liquid until its quantity is reduced one-half, dilute it with 2 ounces of distilled water, filter it, add ½ ounce alcohol, followed by a few drops of strong sulphuric acid; it is now allowed to rest, and after a time it assumes a beautiful green color; add a small quantity of gum arabic and it is ready for use.

Horticultural Ink.—Copper 1 part, dissolve in nitric acid 10 parts, add water 10 parts; used to write on zinc or tin labels.

"Handy" Water Pens.—Take best quality violet aniline, reduce to a thick paste with water, then add mucilage and mix thoroughly; apply the paste thus made to the pen, and let it dry 12 hours. Any steel pen may be prepared in this way. Directions for using: Start action by dipping in water up to filling. If pen should be greasy, wet point with the tongue. To make the ink flow thick, dip to the filling, if wanted thin or pale, dip only to the eye of pen after starting. After using throw the water off, but don't wipe it, for it will dry in a minute.

Ink Powder.—Powdered nutgalls 4 ounces, copperas 3 ounces, logwood 1 ounce, gum arabic ½ ounce; sufficient for 1 quart of water.

Invisible Ink.—Sulphuric acid 1 part, water 20 parts; mix together and write with a quill pen, which writing can be read only after heating it.

Invisible Ink (New).—To make the writing or drawing appear which has been made upon paper it is sufficient to dip it in water. On drying, the traces disappear again, and reappear again at each succeeding immersion. The ink is made by intimately mixing linseed oil 1 part, water of ammonia 20 parts, water 100 parts. The mixture must be agitated each time before the pen is dipped into it, as a little of the oil may separate and float on top, which would, of course, leave an oily stain upon the paper.

Indelible Ink to Mark Linen.—Nitrate of silver 1½ ounces, dissolved in 6 ounces of liquor ammonia fortis, archill 1 ounce for coloring, gum arabic ½ ounce; mix.

Indelible Marking Ink without a Preparation.—Dissolve separately 1 ounce of nitrate of silver and 1½ ounces of sup-carbonate of soda (best washing soda) in rain water; mix the solutions and collect and wash the precipitate in a filter; while still moist rub it up in a marble or hardwood mortar with 8 drams of tartaric acid, and 2 ounces of rain water, mix 6 drams white sugar and 10 drams powdered gum arabic ½ ounce archil and water to make up 6 ounces in measure. It should be put up in short dram bottles and sold at 25 cents. This is the best ink for marking clothes that has ever been discovered. There is a fortune in this recipe, as a good marking ink is very salable

Indelible Ink for Glass or Metal.—Borax 1 ounce, shellac 2 ounces, water 18 fluid ounces; boil in a covered vessel; add of thick mucilage 1 ounce; triturate it with levigated indigo and lamp-black q. s. to give it a good color; after two hours' repose decant from the dregs and bottle for use. It may be bronzed after being applied. Resists moisture, chlorine, and acids.

Indelible Ink for Marking Linen.—Add caustic alkali to a saturated solution of corpous chloride until no further precipitate forms; allow the precipitate to settle, draw off the supernatant liquor with a siphon and dissolve the hydrated copper oxide in the smallest quantity of ammonia; it may be mixed with about 6 per cent of gum dextrine for use.

Luminous Ink.—Shines in the dark. Phosphorous ½ dram, oil cinnamon ½ ounce; mix in a vial, cork tightly, heat it slowly until mixed. A letter written in this ink can only be read in a dark room, when the writing will have the appearance of a fire.

Purple.—Solution of gold and muriate of tin.

Red Ink.—Two ounces cochineal bruised, pour over it 1 quart boiling water, let it stand eight hours; boil 2 ounces brazil wood in 1 pint of water, let it stand eight hours and then add the two together; dissolve ½ ounce gum arabic in ½ pint hot water; add all together and let it stand four days; strain and bottle for use.

Silver Ink.—For silver ink the process is the same as gold, substituting silver leaf for the gold leaf.

Ticketing Ink for Grocers, Etc.—Dissolve 1 ounce of gum arabic in 6 ounces of water and strain, this is the mucilage; for a black color, use drop black, powdered and ground with the mucilage to extreme fineness; for blue, ultra-marine is used in the same manner; for green, emerald green; for white, flake white; for red, vermilion, lake, or carmine; for yellow, chrome yellow. When ground too thick they are thinned with a little water. Apply to the cards with a small brush. The cards may be sized with a thin glue, afterwards varnished, if it is desired to preserve them.

The Lightning Ink Eraser.—The great lightning ink eraser may be used instead of a knife or scraper for erasing in order to rectify a mistake or clean off a blot without injury to the paper, leaving the paper as clean and good to write upon as it was before the blot or mistake was made, and without injury to the printer's ink upon any printed form or ruling upon any first-class paper. Take of chloride of lime 1 pound, thoroughly pulverized, and 4 quarts of soft water; the above must be thoroughly shaken when first put together; it is required to stand twenty-four hours to dissolve the chloride of lime: then strain through a cotton cloth, after which add a tablespoonful of acetic acid (No. 8 commercial) to every ounce of chloride of lime water. The eraser is used by reversing the penholder in the hand, dipping the end in the fluid, and applying it, without rubbing, to the blot to be erased. When the ink has disappeared absorb the fluid into a blotter, and the paper is immediately ready to write upon.

Sympathetic Ink.—One of the best known kinds of sympathetic ink consists of a weak solution of chloride or nitrate of cobalt. Writing executed with such a solution is invisible until warm, when it appears green or bluish, disappearing on exposure to moist air.

Indelible Ink.—An indelible ink that cannot be erased, even with acids, can be obtained from the following recipe: To good gall ink add a strong solution of Prussian blue dissolved in distilled water. This will form a writing fluid which cannot be erased without destruction of the paper. The ink will be greenish blue, but afterward will turn black.

Traveler's Ink.—White blotting paper is saturated with aniline black, and several sheets are pasted together, so as to form a thick pad. When required for use a small piece is torn off and covered with a little water. The black liquid which dissolves out is a good writing ink. A square inch of paper will produce enough ink to last for a considerable writing, and a few pads would be all that an exploring party need carry with them. As water is always available, the ink is readily made. This is a perfectly original and new recipe. Any enterprising man can make a large income out of its manufacture.

To Write Secret Letters.—Put 5 cents' worth of citrate of potassa in an ounce vial of clear cold water. This forms an invisible fluid. Let it dissolve and you can use on paper of any color. Use quill pen in writing. ⟩When you wish the writing to become visible hold it to a red-hot stove.

To Make Rubber Stamp Ink.—Dissolve aniline in hot glycerine and strain while hot or warm.

Violet Copying Ink.—For blue violet, dissolve in 300 parts of water, methyl violet 5 B., Hofman's violet 3 B., or gentiana violet B. For reddish violet, dissolve in a similar quantity of water, methyl violet BR. A small quantity of sugar added to these inks improves their copying qualities. If the writing, when dry, retains a bronzy appearance more water must be added.

White Ink.—Mix pure freshly precipitated barium sulphate or flake white with water containing enough gum arabic to prevent the immediate precipitation of the substance. ·Starch or magnesium carbonate may be used in a similar way. They must be reduced to palpable powders.

Yellow.—Subacetate of lead, wash with hydrochloric acid.

Zodiac Branding Ink,—A waterproof branding ink, good for marking sheep Shellac 2 ounces, borax 2 ounces, water 24 ounces, gum arabic 2 ounces, lampblack sufficient; boil the borax and shellac in the water till they are dissolved and withdraw them from the fire; when the solution becomes cold complete 25 ounces with water and add lampblack enough to bring the preparation to a suitable consistency. When it is to be used with a stencil it must be made thicker than when it is used with a brush. The above gives black ink. For red ink, substitute venetian red for lamp black; for blue, ultramarine, and for green, a mixture of ultramine and chrome yellow.

SOME ADDITIONAL FORMULAS.

Gilding Writing.—For illustrating the covers of books, cards, etc. A little size is mixed with the ink and the letters are made as usual; when they are dry, a slight degree of stickiness is produced by breathing upon them, when gold leaf is immediately applied, and by a little pressure is made to adhere.

To Restore Faded Black Ink.—**1.** Cover the letters with a solution of ferrocyanide of potassium, with the addition of diluted muriatic acid, upon the application of which the letters will turn to a deep blue color. To prevent the color from spreading, the ferrocyanide should be put on first, the diluted acid next. **2.** Dampen a piece of soft white paper, lay it on the faded writing, press it down closely, put a tablespoonful of spirits of hartshorn in a tin vessel with a candle or lamp under it, hold the soft damp paper over it, so that it may receive the fumes of the hartshorn; if the writing is not exhibited on the soft paper plain enough, dampen again and repeat the process until satisfactory results reward the effort. **3.** Faded writing on old parchments or paper may be made perfectly legible by dampening same with water and then passing over the lines a brush moistened with sulphide of ammonia. The writing will immediately appear quite dark in color, and this color, in parchment, it will preserve; on paper, the color gradually fades away, but can be reproduced by an application at any time.

Waterproof Ink.—Suitable for inscriptions on stone, tombs, or any place where dampness may attack. Pitch 11 pounds, lampblack 1 pound, turpentine sufficient to make soluble; mix with heat.

Vanishing Inks.—**1.** A piece of sal ammoniac is placed 4 or 5 days in nitric acid, and then powder of touchstone, such as jewelers use to test gold and silver, is mixed with the liquid. This gives a fluid which bleaches in 6 or 8 days. **2.** A still better ink of this kind may be obtained as follows: Boil 4 ounces of powdered or crushed nutgalls in diluted nitric acid and add 2 ounces of sulphate of iron and some chloride of ammonia. Writing done with this mixture will disappear in a few days, leaving no trace.

Ink Eraser.—Blotting paper or a similar material is immersed in a hot concentrated solution of citric acid, then rolled into a pencil and the larger portion of it coated with paper or lacquer. For use the eraser is moistened with the tongue or water and rubbed over the ink to be removed. A drop of water containing chloride of lime is then dropped upon the ink spot, whereby the ink immediately disappears.

Copying Pad.—Put 1 ounce of glue to soak in cold water until pliable and soft. Drain off the surplus water and place the dish in another dish containing hot water. When the glue is thoroughly melted, add 6 ounces of glycerine, which has been previously heated, and mix the two, adding a few drops of carbolic acid to prevent molding. Pour out this mixture into a shallow pan (9x12 inches) and set away to cool, taking care that the surface is free from blisters. After standing 12 hours it is ready for use. To use, write on a sheet of paper what you wish to duplicate with a sharp steel pen and strong aniline ink. When dry, lay the paper face down on the pad, pressing it lightly, and allow it to remain for a moment. On removing the paper an impression will be found on the face of the pad, and if another paper is placed upon it, it will receive a similar impression.

When enough impressions have been taken, the face of the pad should be immediately washed with a sponge and cold water until the ink impression is wholly removed. If the surface of the pad becomes dry, wipe it with a moist sponge, and, if uneven, melt over a slow fire.

GOLD AND SILVER.

IMITATIONS—PLATING POWDERS FOR CLEANING, ALSO PREPARATIONS FOR CLEANING OTHER METALS.

Gold, to Imitate.—1. One hundred parts, by weight, pure copper, 14 parts zinc or tin, 6 parts magnesia, 3 6-10 parts sal ammoniac, limestone and cream of tartar. The copper is melted, then the magnesia, sal amoniac, limestone and cream of tartar added, in powder, separately and gradually, the mass stirred ⅓ hour, the zinc or tin dropped in piece by piece, and the stirring kept until they melt; finally, the crucible is covered and the mass kept in fusion for 35 minutes, the scum removed and the metal poured into molds, when it is ready for use. This makes a metal susceptible to high polish, and will not easily oxidize. **2.** Platina 2 parts, silver 1 part, copper 3 parts. **3.** Take the following metals and melt them in a covered crucible: 'Virgin platina 16 ounces, pure copper 24 ounces.

Artificial Gold.—Virgin platina 16 parts, copper 7 parts, zinc 1 part; put these in a crucible with powdered charcoal, and melt them together till the whole forms a mass and are thoroughly incorporated together. This also makes a gold of extraordinary beauty and value. It is not possible, by any tests that chemists know of, to distinguish it from pure virgin gold. All I ask of men is to use it for good and lawful purposes, for the knowledge that I here give will bring you a rich and permanent reward without using for unlawful purposes.

Manheim, or Jeweler's Gold.—Copper 3 parts, zinc 1 part, block tin 1 part. If these are pure and melted in a covered crucible containing charcoal, the resemblance will be so good that the best judges cannot tell it from pure gold without analyzing it.

Best Pinchblack Gold.—Pure copper 5 ounces, zinc 1 ounce. This makes gold so good in appearance that a great deal of deception by its use in the way of watches and jewelry has been successfully practiced for several hundred years back.

Imitation Gold.—Platina 4 ounces, silver 3 ounces, copper 1 ounce.

Oroide Gold.—The best article is made by compounding pure copper 4 parts, pure zinc 1¾ parts, magnesia ¼ part, sal ammoniac 1-10 part, quicklime 1-12 part, cream of tartar 1 part;

melt the copper first, then add as rapidly as possible the other articles in the order named.

How to Increase the Weight of Gold.—Take your bar of gold and rub it long and carefully with thin silver, until the gold absorbs the quantity of silver that you require. Then prepare a strong solution of brimstone and quicklime. Now put the gold into a vessel with a wide mouth. Now let them boil until the gold attains the right color, and you have it.

Imitation Silver.—Refined nickel 11 ounces, metallic bismuth 2 ounce; melt the composition 3 times, and pour them out in ley. The third time, when melting, add 2 ounces of pure silver.

Silver.—Nickel 40 ounces, copper 20 ounces, block tin 30 ounces.

Still Other Methods.—1. Combine by fusion 1 part pure copper, 24 parts block-tin, 1½ parts pure antimony, ¼ part pure bismuth, and 2 parts clear glass; the glass may be omitted, save in such cases where it is an object to have the metal sonorous. **2.** Pure copper 750 parts, nickel 140 parts, black oxide of cobalt 20 parts, tin in stick 18 parts, zinc 72 parts. **3.** Melt 4 pounds pure copper with 3 ounces of tin. This closely resembles and rings like sterling silver, and is valuable where pure silver would be too expensive.

Silver Fluid.—For silvering brass and copper articles of every description.—Take 1 ounce of precipitated silver to ½ an ounce cyanate of potash and ¼ of an ounce of hypersulphate of soda; put all into a quart of water, add a little whitening and shake before using. Apply with a soft rag.

Original and Genuine Silver Plating Fluid.—Galvanism Simplified.—Dissolve 1 ounce of nitrate of silver in Crystal in 12 ounces of soft water; then dissolve in the water 2 ounces of cyanwret of potash; shake the whole together and let it stand until it becomes clear; have ready some ½-ounce vials, and fill them half full with Paris white or fine whiting, then fill up the bottles with the liquid and it is ready for use. The whiting does not increase the coating power, it only helps to clean the articles and to save the silver fluid by half filling the bottles. The above quantity of materials will only cost about $1,50, so that the fluid will only cost about 3 cents a bottle.

Silver Polish for Tin, Brass, and Metallic Articles.—Quicksilver, tinfoil,,or rotten-stone equal parts, all pulverized together.

The Housekeeper's Friend or Electric Powder.—This is one of the most salable articles of the day and staple as flour—something that every housekeeper will buy. It is used for gold and silver plated ware, German silver, brass, copper, glass, tin, steel, or any material where a brilliant luster is required. To 4 pounds of the best quality of whiting add ½ pound cream of tartar, and 3 ounces calcined magnesia mix thoroughly together, box, and label. Directions: Use the polish dry with a piece of chamois skin or canton flannel, previously moistened with water or alcohol, and finish with the polish dry. A few moments' rubbing will develop a surprising luster, different from the polish produced by any other substance.

Silver Powder.—Nitrate of silver and common salt each 30 grains, cream of tartar 3½ drams; pulverize finely, mix thoroughly, and bottle for use. Unequalled for polishing copper and plated goods.

To Clean Brittania Ware.—Brittania ware should be washed with a woolen cloth and sweet oil, then washed in water and suds, and rubbed with soft leather and whiting. Thus treated it will retain its beauty to the last.

A Gold Plate for Small Articles Without a Battery. Digest a small fragment of gold with about ten times its weight of mercury until it is dissolved; shake the amalgam together in a bottle and, after cleansing the articles, coat them uniformly with the amalgam; then expose them on an iron tray heated to low redness for a few minutes; the mercury volatilizes, leaving the gold attached as a thin coating to the article. The heating should be done in a stove, so that the poisonous mercurial fumes may pass up the chimney.

Crucibles.—The best crucibles are made of a pure fire clay, mixed with finely-ground cement of old crucibles, and a portion of black lead or graphite; some pounded coke may be mixed with the plumbago; the clay should be prepared in a similar way as for making pottery-ware. The vessels after being formed must be slowly dried and then properly baked in a kiln. Black lead crucibles are made of 2 parts of graphite and 1 of fire clay, mixed with water into a paste, pressed in molds, and well dried, but not baked hard in the kiln. This compound forms excellent small or portable furnaces.

FIREWORKS AND EXPLOSIVES.

EXPLOSIVES.

Dynamite.—Mix infusorial silica with about 75 per cent of nitro-glycerine, which it readily absorbs; exploded by percussion priming.

Fulminate of Mercury.—Mercury 100 parts, nitric acid 1,000 parts; dissolve by a gentle heat, when the solution has acquired the temperature of 130 degrees Fahrenheit, slowly pour it through a glass funnel tube into alcohol 830 parts; as soon as the effervescence is over and the white fumes cease to be evolved, filter through double paper, wash with cold water and dry by steam or hot water; then pack in 100 grain paper parcels and store in a tight box or corked bottle.

Fulminate of Silver.—Digest oxide of silver (recently precipitated and dried by pressure between bibulous papers) in concentrated liquor of ammonia for 12 or 15 hours; pour off the liquid and cautiously dry the black powder in the air, in divided portions; the decanted ammoniacal liquor, when gently heated, yields, on cooling, small crystals, which possess a still more formidable power of detonation than the black powder, and will scarcely bear touching even when under the liquid.

Fulminating Powder.—**1.** Mix together in a warm mortar 3 parts of pulverized nitre, 2 parts of dry carbonate of potash, 1 part of sulphur; a small quantity heated on an iron shovel or ladle until it fuses will explode with great violence. **2.** Sulphur 1 part, chlorate of potash 3 parts.

Greek Fire.—A solution of phosphorus in bisulphide of carbon; not strictly an explosive, but an agent of ancient warfare which burns on water.

Gun Cotton.—Mix 4½ ounces of pure dry nitrate of potash with 30 fluid drams of sulphuric acid; after cooling thoroughly, stir with this mixture carefully 30 drams of best carded cotton; as soon as saturation is complete, throw the cotton into a tubful of clear rain water and change the water repeatedly until testing with litmus paper fails to show the existence of acid; then squeeze it in a cloth, and after being well pulled out, dry it cautiously in a temperature not to exceed 140 degrees Fahrenheit. It is now an explosive, and too much caution cannot be exercised in handling it.

Gunpowder (blasting).—Saltpetre 62 parts, sulphur 20 parts, charcoal, powdered, 15 parts.

Gunpowder (sporting).—Saltpetre 79 1-6 parts, sulphur 9 1-6 parts, charcoal 13 1-5.

Nitro-Glycerine.—This is prepared by the action of strong nitric and sulphuric acids on glycerine at a low temperature. Sulphuric acid 4¾ pounds, nitric acid 2¼ pounds, glycerine 1 pound; nitro-glycerine collects at the bottom of the vessel and is freed from the acids by carefully washing in a copious supply of water; the explosion is caused by the rapid transformation from the liquid to the gaseous state.

Nitroline.—From 5 to 20 parts of sugar or syrup are mixed with from 25 to 30 parts of nitric acid in a wooden or gutta percha vessel; of this compound, 25 to 30 parts are mixed with from 13 to 35 parts of nitrate of potassa and from 13 to 15 parts of cellulose.

FIREWORKS.

The three prime materials in the art of pyrotechny are niter, sulphur, and clear coal, along with filings of iron, steel, copper zinc, and resin, camphor, shellac, lycopodium, etc. Gunpowder is used either in grain or crushed, as may best answer the purpose. As fireworks can be more easily purchased than manufactured, a few formulas only will be given, principally for colored fires and easily made pieces.

Colored Fires.—The ingredients for these must be dry, not too finely powdered, and mixed together uniformly. Each should be reduced to a powder separately and mixed very lightly with the other powders; the whole must then be passed through a sieve once or twice. Great care must be exercised in handling chlorate of potash. The following compositions form the different fires:

Blue Fire.—1. Sulphur 4 ounces, mealed powder 4 ounces, antimony 2 ounces, lampblack 16 ounces. **2.** Sulphur, sulphate of potassa, and ammonia, sulphate of copper, of each 15 parts, niter 27 parts, chlorate of potassa 28 parts. **2.** Realgar 2 parts, charcoal 3 parts, chlorate of potassa 5 parts, sulphur 13 parts, nitrate of baryta 77 parts.

Crimson Fire.—Charcoal 4½ parts, sulphuret of antimony 5½ parts, chlorate of potassa 17¼ parts, sulphur 18 parts, nitrate of strontia 55 parts.

Green Fire.—1. Nitrate of baryta 80 parts, chlorate of potash 32 parts, sulphur 24 parts, calomel 16 parts, fine clear coal 3 parts, shellac 2 parts. **2.** Chlorate of baryta 2 ounces, nitrate of baryta 3 ounces, sulphur 1 ounce. **3.** Metallic arsenic 2 parts, charcoal 3 parts, chlorate of potash 5 parts, sulphur 13 parts, nitrate of baryta 77 parts. **4.** Nitrate of baryta 10 ounces, chlorate potash 4 ounces, gum shellac 2 ounces.

Lilac Fire.—1. Black oxide of copper 6 parts, dry chalk 20 parts, sulphur 25 parts, chlorate of potassa 49 parts. **2.** Black oxide of copper 3 parts, dried chalk 22 parts, sulphur 25 parts, chlorate of potassa 50 parts.

Orange Fire. Sulphur 14 parts, chalk 34 parts, chlorate of potassa 52 parts.

Pink Fire.—1. Charcoal 1 part, chalk and sulphur of each 2 parts, chlorate of potassa 27 parts, niter 32 parts. **2.** Chlorate of potassa 12 ounces, saltpeter 5 ounces, milk sugar 4 ounces, lycopodium 1 ounce, axalate of strontia 1 ounce.

Purple Fire.—1. Chlorate of potash 5 parts, nitrate of strontia 16 parts, realgar 1 part, sulphur 2 parts, lampblack 1 part. **2.** Chlorate of potash 2 ounces, sulphur 1 dram, oxide of copper 1 ounce. **3.** Sulphuret of antimony 2¾ parts, black oxide of copper 10 parts, sulphur and nitrate of potassa of each 22¾ parts, chlorate of potassa 42 parts.

Red Fire.—1. Nitrate of strontia 37½ parts, flowers of sulphur 10 parts, charcoal 1¼ parts, powdered chlorate of potash 5 parts, black sulphur of antimony 3⅛ parts. **2.** Sulphur, sulphuret of antimony and nitre, of each 1 part, dried nitrate of strontia 5 parts. **3.** Chlorate of potash 32 parts, nitrate of strontia 48 parts, calomel 20 parts, shellac 12 parts, chertier's copper 4 parts, fine charcoal 1 part. **4.** Nitrate of strontia 10 ounces, potash 4 ounces, gum shellac 2 ounces, all powdered.

Violet Fire.—1. Charcoal 8 parts, sulphur 10 parts, metallic copper 15 parts, chlorate of potassa 30 parts. **2.** Alum and carbonate of potassa, of each 12 parts, sulphur 16 parts, chlorate of potassa 60 parts. **3.** Sulphur 14 parts, alum and carbonate of potassa 16 parts, chlorate of potassa 54 parts.

White Fire.—1. From nitre 60 parts, sulphur 20 parts, black antimony 10 parts, meal powder 6 parts, powdered camphor 4 parts. **2.** Niter 16 ounces, mealed powder 4 ounces, sulphur 8 ounces.

Yellow Fire.—1. Niter 2 ounces, sulphur 4 ounces, nitrate of soda 20 ounces, lampblack 1 ounce. **2.** From sulphur 16 parts, dried carbonate of soda 23 parts, chlorate of potassa 61 parts.

Colored Flames (green).—Mix chloride of copper or boracic acid with alcohol.

Red Flame.—Mix alcohol with nitrate of strontium, nitrate of iron or nitrate of lime.

Yellow Flame.—Mix alcohol with nitrate of soda.

Flame or Electric Paper.—1. Soak Swedish filtering paper for 10 minutes in a mixture of 4 parts of oil of vitriol with 5 parts of strong nitric acid, both by measure; when the strips are removed from the acid they must be thoroughly washed, first with cold, then with hot rain or distilled water, till the washings cease to be acid; then make different solutions, not too strong, of such of the chlorates of the metals as give the desired flame reactions; make them slightly warm, and saturate the papers separately with them; dry the papers before the fire previous to lighting them; they show to best advantage when a slip is loosely crumpled up into a pellet, lighted quickly at one corner and thrown into the air against a dark background; by briskly rubbing these papers on a woolen surface they become highly magnetic, and interesting experiments may be made with them. **2.** Dry 1,000 grains of pure niter at a moderate heat, place it in a dry retort, pour on it 10 drams, by measure, of strong sulphuric acid; distill until 6 drams of nitric acid have passed over into the receiver; dry some thin unsized paper, such as filter paper, and weigh out 60 grains of it; mix 5 measured drams of the nitric acid with an equal volume of strong sulphuric acid in a small glass vessel; allow the mixture to cool; immerse the paper; press it down with a glass rod; cover the vessel with a glass plate; set it aside for 15 or 20 minutes; lift the paper out with a glass rod; throw it into a bucket of water; wash it thoroughly in a stream of water till it no longer tastes acid or reddens blue litmus paper; dry it by exposure to the air, or at a very gentle heat.

Flyers, with Brilliant Fire.—1. Meal powder 8 parts

sulphur 1 part, iron filings 2 parts. **2.** Meal powder 36 parts, sulphur 1 part, steel filings 8 parts. **3.** Meal powder 18 parts, sulphur 1 part, litharge 2 part, steel filings 3 parts.

Golden Rain.—Procure a piece of brass rod the diameter of which is 3-16 of an inch, or rather less, the length from 6 to 8 inches: cut thin brown paper into short strips about 2 inches wide, and long enough, when wrapped around the former, to make a case whose external diameter should be ¼ inch, or rather more: the former should have a small cup-shaped hollow cut in one of its ends, into which the paper may be turned, to form a closed end to the cases; paste the strips of paper all over; rub some paste on the former; then roll the paper round the former and draw it out so as to leave its cupped end ¼ of an inch inside one of the ends of the case; pinch in the paper that projects beyond the former, and drive it down with a tap upon the pasting slab, so that the twisted end is pressed into the cup of the former; dip this into warm size of glue; if a little red lead is mixed with the size it will solidify much more rapidly; dipping the ends of the cases into size should not be done until they are dry from the paste; for filling the cases a tin funnel is used that will exactly fit into the mouth of the golden rain cases: when the case is charged the funnel must be removed, and the space that was occupied by its nozzle filled with gunpowder or meal powder, moistened with gum water; take care that this paste is pressed well into the mouth of the cases, and fills them. The compositions used are: **1.** Niter 16 ounces, sulphur 11 ounces, mealed powder 4 ozs., lampblack 3 ozs., flowers of zinc 1 oz., gum arabic 1 oz : materials used must be in the state of fine powders and perfectly dry. **2.** Saltpetre 16 parts, sulphur 8 parts, fine charcoal 2 parts, pen soot 2 parts, meal powder 4 parts. **3.** Saltpetre 4 parts, sulphur 2 parts, fine charcoal 4 parts, meal powder 16 parts.

Japanese Matches (Scintellettes).—Lampblack 5 parts, sulphur 11 parts, gunpowder from 26 to 30 parts, this last proportion varying with the quality of the powder; grind very fine; make the material into a paste with alcohol, form it into dice about ¼ inch square with a knife as a spatula, let them dry rather gradually on a warm mantelpiece, not too near a fire: when dry fix one of the little squares into a cleft made at the end of a lavender stalk or, what is better, the straw-like material of which housemade carpet-brooms are made, light the material at a candle, hold the stem downward, after the first blazing off a ball of molten lava will form, from which the curious corruscations will soon appear.

Pharoah's Serpents' Eggs.—Take mercury and dissolve it in moderately diluted nitric acid by means of heat, take care, however, that there be always an excess of metallic mercury remaining: decant the solution and pour it in a solution of sulphocyanide of ammonia or potassium, which may be bought at a good drug store or of a dealer in chemicals; equal weights of both will answer; a precipitate will fall to the bottom of the beaker or jar, which is to collected on a filter and washed two or three times with water, when it is put in a warm place to dry; take for every pound of this material 1 ounce of gum tragacanth which has been soaked in hot water; when the gum is completely softened it is to be transferred to a mortar, and then pulverized and dried precipitate gradually mixed with it by means of a little water, so as to present a somewhat dried pill mass, from which, by hand, pellets of the desired size are formed. put on a piece of glass, and dried again. They are then ready for use.

Pin or Scroll Wheels.—A long wire about 3-16 inch in diameter is the former; on this wire are formed the pipes which, being filled with composition, are afterward wound around a small circle of wood so as to form a helix or spiral line; the cases are generally made of double-crown paper (yellow wove) and cut into strips, so as to give the greatest length, and of width sufficient to roll about four times around the wire, and paste at the edge, so as to bite firmly at the end of the last turn; when a number of pipes are made and perfectly dry they are filled with composition; these cases are not driven for filling, but are filled by means of a tin funnel with a tube ¾ inch long, made to press easily into the mouth of the case, which is done gradually by lifting a wire up and down in this tube, the dry composition being placed in the funnel, the moment an action of the wire takes place the composition begins to fall into the case, which the charging wire compresses by continuous motion until you have filled the pipe to within ¾ inch of the top; the pipe is then removed and the mouth neatly twisted, which will be the point for lighting. When a number of pipes are ready place them on a damp floor, or in any damp situation, until they become very pliant, but by no means wet; then commence winding them round a circle of wood whose substance must be equal to the thickness of the diameter of the pipe; either close together or openly in the form of a scroll; when wound, secure the end with sealing wax to prevent its springing open; after winding the required quantity let them dry; cut some strips of crimson or purple paper 3-16 inch wide and in length twice the diameter of the wheel; then paste all over thoroughly; take a strip and paste it across the wheel diametrically; rub it down, then turn the wheel over and place the ends down to correspond with the opposite side; when dry the wheel will be ready for firing; they may be fired on a large pin or held in the hand, but it is preferable to drive the pin into the end of a stick, which will prevent any accident, should a section of the wheel burst. The following are the compositions used:

BRILLIANT: Niter 1 part. sulphur 1 part, mealed powder 16 parts, and steel filings 7 parts.

CHINESE; Niter 1 part, sulphur 1 part, mealed powder 7 parts, and cast-iron filings 7 parts.

COMMON: Niter 6 parts, sulphur 1 part, mealed powder 16 parts, charcoal 6 parts.

WHITE; Niter 6 parts, sulphur 7 parts, and mealed powder 16 parts.

Rockets.—Make the cases of any kind of thick stiff paper, either cartridge paper, or what is equally as good and much cheaper, common bag paper; roll up the cases with a smooth, round ruler, exactly the size of the cavity of the rocket and 10 or 12 times as long; lay a sheet of paper on a slate or slab, marble or glass, and paste 4 or 5 inches along the end of it, leaving the rest of sheet of paper without paste; roll it smoothly over the ruler, dry end first, until the whole is rolled up, when, of course, the paste will stick and a thin case be formed; keep rolling it along the slab with the hands, in the same way as a rolling pin is used, for 2 or 3 minutes, until the various folds of the paper set close and tight to each other; put on another sheet in the same way, and so on, till the case is thick enough, that is, until the sides are a trifle more than ⅙ the thickness of the ruler; the size of the rocket case, and consequently the width that the sheets of brown paper are to be cut before pasting,.varies with the size of the rockets; in small rockets the length of the case may be 6 times the diameter; in larger rockets 4 or 5 times is sufficient; now choke the case; then fasten a thin cord at one end to a staple in the wall, and the other tied around the waist of the operator; as he may lean back, of course the cord would be tightened and the sides of the case brought together until they nearly touch; when the case is sufficiently compressed, tie it with 2 or 3 turns of strong string; put the cases in the mould (as elsewhere described) with the piercer in it, and put enough composition in it to fill about 1 inch of the case; take the rammer, ram it down with 3 or 4 strong blows with a mallet; put in the same quantity of composition again and ram that down in the same manner, and so on till the case is filled to the top of the piercer and 1 diameter above it; separate some of the central folds of the paper, which, it has been observed. is not pasted, and turn them down upon the composition, ramming them down hard upon it; or, what will do as well, put in a piece of paper as wadding; when this is rammed down, and firm, bore with a brass brad awl 3 or 4 holes through it; these holes serve to make the requisite communication between the rocket and the head. The rocket being charged, the head or pot must be fixed; this is a paper case made upon a wooden former, turned cylindrical, about 4 inches in length and a shade larger in diameter than the exterior of the rocket case; take some thick brown paper and cut it in strips large enough to go twice around the former; paste and roll as for the case; pinch one end, and a cylinder of paper will be thus made which should fit nicely over the lay end of the rocket; now fix upon the pinched end a conical cap made upon a former of like shape; trim the end which was choked, which is still open, and which has a hole passing up it, which the piercer occupied; fill up the hole with loose gunpowder made into a stiff paste with very weak gum water. and paste a piece of touch paper over it. The composition used is: Niter 26 ounces, sulphur 5½ ounces, charcoal 1·9 ounces. The sticks are fastened on to the case by means of wires or strings, and are of the following size: Two-pound rockets require sticks

9 feet 4 inches long, 1 inch square at the top and rather more than ½ inch square at the bottom; 1-pound rocket sticks are 8 feet 2 inches long, ¾ inch square at top and ⅜ inch at bottom; 8-ounce rocket sticks are 6 feet 2 inches long, ¾ inch square at top and ⅜ inch at bottom; 4-ounce rocket sticks are 5 feet 3 inches long, ⅜x½ inch at top and ¼ inch square at bottom; 2-ounce rocket sticks are 5 feet 1 inch long, 3-10x½ inch at top and 4-10 inch at bottom; 1-ounce rocket sticks are 3 feet 6 inches long, and so on for other various sizes. The weight and the length of the stick must be such as that, when tied on, the rocket shall balance on the finger, at a point about 1 inch from the part choked.

Rockets, Mold for.—This consists of a solid foot of wood; upon the center of this stands a short cylinder about ½ inch high and exactly of the size of a mold, to be placed over it, as afterward described; this short cylinder has a shoulder above, and terminates in a round top; out of the middle of the top is a tapering, thick brass wire, projecting some inches upward; the whole is so arranged that, when one of the newly-made cases is put upon the wire and forced down, the wire fills up the choke hole, the round top fits into the small parts of the case below the choke, the shoulder of the cylinder bears the extreme end of the case and the short cylinder agrees in size with the outsides of the case; then fit over this a strong woolen or metal tube, so that it is seen that there is no cavity anywhere, except the inside of the rocket case, and even in this a thick wire runs up nearly to the top of that part of the case where the composition is rammed, or nearly ⅜ of the whole case form the choke upwards; all rockets must be placed in the mold to be filled, as well as to smooth and consolidate the part choked.

Roman Candles.—Have a composition to burn in the intervals between the stars, which will throw a jet of fire uniformly good throughout, to have stars of tolerably rapid combustion (otherwise they will not be ignited before they are blown into the air), and to have the charges of powder for blowing the stars regulated to a great nicety, the former of the case must be ⅝ of an inch in diameter and 18 inches long. The cases require rather a large amount of strawboard for their manufacture, but otherwise they are made similar to rocket cases. The following are the compositions used between the stars: **1.** Niter 18 parts, sulphur 6 parts, fine charcoal 7 parts, meal powder 4 parts. **2.** Niter 16 parts, meal powder 8 parts, fine charcoal 6 parts, sulphur 6 parts. **3.** Niter 16 parts, meal powder 11 parts, sulphur 6 parts, antimony 4 parts. The next thing is to fill the case. Before charging, tamp a little clay in the bottom of the case to prevent blowing out; ram down as much composition as will fill the case 1-6 of its height; over this put a small piece of paper covering about ⅜ of the diameter; then a little rifle powder and upon that a star, observing that the star is rather smaller than the diameter of the case; over this first ball more of the composition must be put and rammed lightly down to prevent breaking the ball, till the case is ⅓ full then a little powder and another ball as before, till the case is filled with balls and composition; take care to place composition above the highest ball; when the case is thus filled cap it with tough paper by pasting it round the orifice, and add a little priming of powder.

Silver Rain.—1. Saltpeter 4 ounces, sulphur, mealed powder and antimony, of each 2 ounces, salprunella ½ ounce. **2.** Saltpeter 8 ounces, sulphur 2 ounces, charcoal 4 ounces. **3.** Saltpeter 1 pound, antimony 6 ounces, sulphur 4 ounces. **4.** Saltpeter 4 ounces, sulphur 1 ounce, powder 2 ounces, steel-dust ¾ ounce; used in similar cases and treated in the same way as golden rain.

Stars.—These are made as follows: Moisten the composition very slightly, and the mold in which stars are shaped is a brass tube of a size proportioned to the dimension required. The drift with which the composition is pressed into the tube is made of boxwood or metal and fits easily into the tubular mold; at one of its ends there is a wire point; place the end having the point in the mold as far as it will go; it will leave a space at the end of the mold unoccupied by the drift; press this empty end of the tube into the slightly moistened composition until it is filled by it, so that the drift being driven down upon the composition will compress it into a firm cylindrical mass, into the center of which the point projects; when the star is thus formed in the mold the drift must be withdrawn, reversed, its long plain end inserted, and the star pushed out and placed separately upon the tray to dry. The following compositions are used;

BLUE.—**1.** Chlorate of potash 8 parts, sulphide of copper 6 parts; Chertier's copper 5 parts, sulphur 4 parts. 2. Chlorate of potash 16 parts, Chertier's copper 12 parts, calomel 8 parts, stearine 2 parts, sulphur 2 parts, shellac 1 part. 3. Niter 12 parts, sulphuret of antimony 2 parts, sulphur 4 parts, lampblack 2 parts.

BRILLIANT.—**1.** Mealed powder ¾ ounce, saltpeter 3½ ounces, sulphur 1½ ounces, spirits of wine 1¼ ounce. 2. Niter 16 parts, sulphur 8 parts, sulphuret of antimony 4 parts, meal powder 3 parts.

CRIMSON.—**1.** Chlorate of potash 24 parts, nitrate of strontia 32 parts, calomel 12 parts, sulphur 6 parts, shellac, in fine powder, 6 parts, sulphide of copper 2 parts, fine charcoal 2 parts. 2. Chlorate of potash 12 parts, nitrate of strontia 20 parts, sulphur 11 parts, charcoal 2 parts, antimony 2 parts, mastic 1 part.

GREEN.—**1.** Chlorate of potash 20 parts, nitrate of baryta 40 parts, calomel 10 parts, sulphur 8 parts, shellac 3 parts, fine charcoal 1 part, fused sulphide of copper 1 part. 2. Nitrate of baryta 42 parts, realgar 2 parts, sulphur 8 parts, lampblack 1 part. 3. Chlorate of potash 28 parts, nitrate of baryta 12 parts, sulphur 15 parts, mastic 1 part.

LILAC.—Potash 50 parts, sulphur 25 parts, chalk 22 parts, black oxide of copper 3 parts.

ROSE.—Chlorate of potash 20 parts, carbonate of strontia 8

parts, calomel 10 parts, shellac 2 parts, sulphur 3 parts, fine charcoal 1 part.

VIOLET.—Chlorate of potash 9 parts, nitrate of strontia 4 parts, sulphur 6 parts, carbonate of copper 1 part, calomel 1 part, mastic 1 part.

WHITE.—Mealed powder 4 ounces, saltpeter 12 ounces, sulphur 6½ ounces, oil of spike 2 ounces, camphor 5 ounces.

YELLOW.—1. Chlorate of potash 20 parts, bicarbonate of soda 10 parts, sulphur 5 parts, mastic 1 part. 2. Nitrate of soda 74½ parts, sulphur 19½ parts, charcoal 6 parts.

Torpedoes (Toy).—Are made by inclosing a small quantity of fulminate of silver with a little common gravel, washed free from dirt, in a piece of paper twisted together; the gravel is to make weight; the torpedo explodes by concussion on being dropped upon the floor.

Triangles and Vertical Wheels.—Are made by using three or more driving cases arranged on a frame to be pivoted in the center, so that as the cases are discharged they will cause the frame to revolve, thereby forming a wheel or circle of fire. The driving cases are made similar to a rocket case, but without the pot or head; the cases are to be connected together with a quick-match, so that the fire will communicate from one to another.

DEPARTMENT III.

PERFUMES, COSMETICS, TOILET ARTICLES

Including distilled waters and oils, toilet soaps, preparations for the skin, hair, teeth, and nails; in fact, all these artices sold by druggists and perfumers as necessary for the care of the person.

DISTILLED WATERS AND OILS.

Perfumes can be distilled by the use of a glass retort. A napkin wet with cold water should be placed about the tube and a receiver placed upon the table. A lamp should be kept burning under the retort, removed far enough away to prevent the liquid running. It should pass drop by drop into the receiver, and when inclined to run the lamp should be moved farther from the retort. Stills for manufacturing perfumes can be purchased without difficulty, and are superior to the above contrivance. All waters prepared for perfumeries should be distilled.

Aromatic Water.—1. Coriander seed ground 5 ounces, star anise and cinnamon, of each, 5 ounces, cloves, nutmeg, and fresh orange peel, of each, 2½ ounces; mix in a still with 12 pints of water and distill 8 pints. **2.** Oil of star anise, cinnamon, and coriander, of each 10 drops, oil of cloves, nutmeg, and orange, of each 5 drops, carbonate of magnesia 120 grains, water 2 pints; triturate the oil with the magnesia; add the whole quantity of water and filter, adding enough water through the filter to make the filtrate measure 2 pints.

Cinnamon Water.—Powdered cinnamon 20 ounces, water 2 gallons; distill 1 gallon.

Orange Flower Water.—Orange flowers 12 pounds, water 36 pounds; place the flowers in the water when it has nearly reached the boiling point in the still.

Rose Water.—Roses 15 pounds, water 40 pounds; distil.

Strawberry Water.—Bruised strawberries 4 pounds, water gallon; macerate for 12 hours. Distil 6 pints.

69

To Extract Ottar of Roses and Other Flowers.—Procure a quantity of the petals of any flowers which have an agreeable fragrance, card thin layers of cotton, which dip into the finest Florence or Lucca oil; sprinkle a small quantity of fine salt on the flowers alternately until an earthen vessel or wide mouthed glass bottle is full; tie the top close with a bladder, parchment, or rubber cloth; then lay the vessel in the heat of the sun, and in 15 days a fragrant oil may be squeezed away equal to the high-priced essences.

PERFUMES.

Ambergris Tincture.—Ambergris 30 grains, orris powder 1 dram, alcohol 8 ounces; powder the ambergris and orris together; add the alcohol; macerate 30 days; filter.

Benzoin Tincture.—Benzoin 2 ounces, alcohol 1 pint; mix.

Civet Tincture.—Civet 30 grains, orris root powder 1 dram, alcohol 8 ounces; macerate 30 days; strain; filter.

Cologne.—Take 1 gallon 95 per cent alcohol or cologne spirits, 2 ounces oil of bergamot, ½ ounce orange, ½ ounce oil of cedar, ⅓ dram oil of nevio, ½ dram oil of rosemary; mix well and it is fit for use. A nice article.

Cologne Water.—Oils of lemon and cedrat. of each 2 drams, oil of rosemary 1 dram, oil of bergamot 1 ounce, spirts of neroli 2 fluid ounces. purest alcohol 5 fluid ounces.

Cologne Water.—1. Oil of lavender 1 dram, oil of bergamot 1 dram, oil of lemon 2 drams, oil of rosemary 2 drams, tincture of musk 50 drops, oil of cinnamon 8 drops, oil of cloves 8 drops, alcohol 1 pint. **2.** Take essences of bergamot and citron, of each 5 drams, essence of lemon 4 drams, essence of rosemary 2½ drams, essence of orange flower 3 drops, alcohol 1 quart; mix together. Those who prefer a fuller perfume may add 5 drams of lavender.

Floral Bouquet.—Musk tincture 2 ounces, orris, tonka and vanilla tinctures, of each 6 drams, ambergris tincture 1 ounce, rose spirits 4 ounces; mix.

Florida Water.—Dissolve ½ ounce of each of the oils of lemon, lavender and bergamot, ½ dram each of the oils of cinnamon and cloves in 1 quart of the best deodorized alcohol; add 2 quarts of filtered water and bottle.

Frangipanni.—Essence of vetiver 3 ounces, oil of neroli 15 minims, oil of sandalwood ½ dram, attar of roses 40 minims. essence of musk 3 drams. esprit de violette 3 ounces, essence of ambergris 6 drams, rectified spirits to make up 20 ounces,

Frozen Perfume.—Take 2 ounces oil of lemon grass, ½ ounce oil of cloves and ¼ ounce oil of lavender flowers; mix them well together; for this amount of perfume you require about 4 quarts of melted paraffine: pour the oils into the melted paraffine while warm, stirring it while pouring. This perfume is in a solid, transparent form, and by rubbing on the handkerchief it imparts an exquisite perfume; by carrying it in the pocket it perfumes the entire wearing apparel; by keeping in a drawer or box all articles therein obtain the benefits of this perfume.

Geranium Water.—Oil of rose geranium and tincture of orris root, of each 1 ounce, tincture of musk 2 drams, alcohol 2 pints, rose water 4 ounces.

Genuine Royal Essence (for the handkerchief).—**1.** Ambergris 25 parts, musk 12 parts, civet 5 parts, oil of rose 2 parts, oil of cinnamon 3 parts, oil of wood of Rhodes 2 parts, oil of orange flowers 2 parts, carbonate of potash 6 parts, 90 degrees alcohol 860 parts; macerate 15 days and filter. **2.** Oil of lavender 3 fluid drams, oil of bergamot 3 fluid drams, extract of ambergris 6 minims, camphor 1 grain, alcohol 1 pint; mix, shake well every day for 12 days; filter. **3.** Oils of rosemary and lemon, of each ½ ounce, bergamot and lavender, of each ½ dram, cinnamon 4 drops, cloves and rose, of each 10 drops, alcohol 1 quart; mix, and let stand 1 week.

'Heliotrope.—Orange flower essence and rose spirits, of each 1 ounce, vetiver spirits 2 ounces, vanilla tincture 1 ounce, orris tincture 2 ounces, tonka tincture and orange flower spirits, of each 1 ounce, ambergris tincture 4 drams, sandalwood attar 10 minims, clove attar 4 minims; mix.

Jockey Club.—Spirits of wine 5 gallons, orange flower water 1 gallon, balsam of Peru 4 ounces, essence of bergamot 8 ounces, essence of musk 8 ounces, essence of cloves 4 ounces, essence of neroli 2 ounces; mix.

Kiss-Me-Quick.—Spirits 1 gallon, essence of thyme ¼ ounce, essence of orange flowers 2 ounces, essence of neroli ½ ounce, attar of roses 30 drops, essence of jasmine 1 ounce, essence of balm mint ½ ounce, petals of roses 4 ounces, oil of lemon 20 drops, calorous aromaticus ½ ounce, essence of neroli ¼ ounce; mix and strain.

Ladies' Own.—Spirits of wine 1 gallon, attar of roses 20 drops, essence of thyme ½ ounce, essence of neroli ¼ ounce, essence of vanilla ½ ounce, essence of bergamot ¼ ounce, orange flower water 6 ounces.

Lavender Water.—Oils of lavender and bergamot, of each 3 drams, attar of roses and oil of cloves, of each 6 drops, oil of rosemary and essence of musk, of each ¾ dram, benzoic acid ½ dram, honey 1 ounce, alcohol 1 pint, esprit de roses 2 ounces; mix well, and keep till old.

' Lavender Water.—Take spirits of wine 1 pint, oil of lavender ½ ounce, oil of bergamot ½ ounce, musk 12½ cents' worth; mix all together in a bottle, and shake it occasionally. The longer it is kept the better it becomes.

Lemon Essence.—Alcohol ½ pint, fresh lemon peel 4 ounces; let it stand 1 month, strain and bottle.

Moss Rose.—Rose spirits 3 ounces. orange flower essence 1 ounce, ambergris tincture ⅛ ounce, musk tincture 2 drams; mix.

Musk Extract.—Musk and civet tinctures, of each 2 ounces, attar of roses 10 minims, alcohol 1 ounce; mix.

Musk Tincture.—Tonquin grain musk 1 dram, hot water 4 drams, alcohol 1 pint; digest the musk in the hot water for 3 or 4 hours, then add the alcohol and macerate for 30 days with occasional agitating; filter.

New Mown Hay Extract.—Moss rose extract 1 ounce, benzoin tincture 1 ounce, tonka tincture 4 ounces, musk tincture 1 ounce, attar of rose geranium 40 minims, ottar of bergamot 40 minims, alcohol 1 ounce; mix,

Orris Tincture.—Orris root powder 2 ounces, alcohol 4 ounces; macerate the orris root for 7 days and filter, then percolate the orris root with the alcohol sufficient to make 4 fluid ounces.

Patchouli Extract.—Attar of patchouli 2 drams, attar of roses 20 minims, alcohol 15 ounces; mix.

Rose Water (spirituous).—Procure a glass bottle with a wide mouth and ground glass stopper, fill ⅔ full with deodorized alcohol, add rose leaves until no more can be forced into the bottle, let it stand several months, keeping it air-tight; strain. White roses are the best.

Rose Water.—Attar of roses 12 drops, rub it up with ½ ounce of white sugar and 2 drams of carbonate of magnesia, then add gradually 1 quart of water and 2 ounces of proof spirits, and filter through paper. Preferable to the distilled for a perfume, or for culinary purpose.

Rose Water (artificial).—Attar of roses 25 drops, rub in with it 1 ounce of white sugar, powdered, and 4 drams carbonate of magnesia, add gradually ½ gallon of water and 4 ounces of proof spirits.

Superior Cologne Water.—Oil of lavender 2 drams, oil of rosemary 1½ drams, oils of orange, lemon and bergamot, of each 1 dram, essence of musk 2 drams, attar of roses 10 drops, proof spirits 1 pint; shake all together thoroughly 3 times a day for 1 week.

Tuberose Extract.—Essence of tuberose 4 ounces, orris and ambergris tinctures, of each ½ ounce; mix.

Upper Ten.—Spirits of wine 4 quarts, essence of cedrat 2 drams, essence of violets ¼ ounce, essence of neroli ½ ounce, attar of roses 20 drops, orange flower essence 1 ounce, oil of rosemary 30 drops, oils of bergamot and neroli, of each ½ ounce.

Vanilla Tincture.—Vanilla bean 6 Troy drams, alcohol 1 pint; beat the vanilla to a coarse powder, macerate with gentle heat for 4 hours, filter, while macerating keep a wet towel over the mouth of the bottle using a water bath.

Verbena Extract.—True attar of verbena 1 dram, attar of lemon 1 dram, alcohol 8 ounces; mix.

Vetiver Essence.—Two pounds of the root of vetever (cut small), moisten with a little water, macerate for 24 hours, then beat in a marble mortar, macerate in sufficient alcohol to cover for 8 or 10 days, and strain with pressure; filter through paper and in a fortnight repeat the filtration.

Violet Extract.—Violet essence 4 ounces, cassia essence 1 ounce, rose essence 3 drams, orris tincture 1 ounce, ambergris and civet tinctures, of each, 2 drams, almond spirits 20 minims; mix.

West End.—Rose spirit 3 ounces, benzoin and musk tinctures of each 1 ounce, verbena extract and civet tincture, of each ½ ounce, sandalwood attar 10 minims; mix.

White Rose Extract.—Rose spirit 4 ounces, violet and jessamine essence, of each 2 ounces, patchouly extract ½ ounce; mix.

Ylang Ylang Extracts.—**1.** Extract of jessamine 8 ounces, extract of rose 16 ounces, tincture of orris root 8 ounces, tincture of civet 4 ounces, oil of ylang ylang 4 drams, alcohol 2 pints. **2.** Tincture of tonka beans 3 ounces, tincture of musk and extract of tuberose and cassia, of each 4 ounces, tincture of orris root 8 ounces, oil of orange (fresh) 2 dram neroli ½ dram, alcohol q. s. to make 4 pints.

DRY PERFUMES, SACHET POWDERS, ETC.

Frangipanni.—Powdered violet root 3 pounds, powdered sandalwood ¼ pound, orange oil, rose oil, oil of sandalwood, of each 1 dram, pulverized musk 1 ounce, pulverized civet 2 drams.

Incense.—**1.** Olibanum 2 or 3 parts, gum benzoin 1 part. **2.** Olibanum 7 parts. gum benzoin 2 parts, cascarilla 1 part; on a hot plate or burned it exhales an agreeable perfume. **3.** Styrax 2½ ounces, benzoin 12 ounces, musk 15 grains, burnt sugar ½ ounce, frankincense 2½ ounces, gum tragacanth 1½ ounces, rose-water sufficient to form a mass to be divided into small tablets.

Pastels for Burning, Deodorizing, Etc.—**1.** Benzoin 4 ounces, cascarilla ½ ounce, niter and gum arabic, of each 3 drams, myrrh 1 dram, oils of nutmegs and cloves, of each 25 drops, charcoal 7 ounces. all in fine powder; beat to a smooth ductile mass; with cold water form into small cones with a tripod base and dry in the air or dip thin sticks of pine into the mass and permit to dry. **2.** Yellow sanders 3 ounces, styrax 4 ounces, benzoin 3 ounces, olibanum 6 ounces, cascarilla 6 ounces. ambergris 1 dram. peruvian balsam 2 drams, myrrh 1½ ounce, niter 1½ ounces, oil of cinnamon 20 drops, oil of cloves ½ dram, attar 30 to 60 drops, oil of lavender 1½ drams, balsam of tolu 1½ ounces, camphor ½ ounce, strong acetic acid 2 ounces, charcoal 3 pounds; mix; beat into a paste with a mucilage of tragacanth and form into conical pastels. This is the finest deodorizer known.

Rose Powder.—Pulverized rose leaves 1 pound, pulverized sandalwood ½ pound, rose oil 2 drams.

Sachet Powder, Cassia.—Flowers of acacia farnesiana and powdered orris root equal parts; mix.

Sachet, Heliotrope.—Take of powdered orris root 2,000 parts, rosa centifolia 1,000 parts, tonka bean 500 parts, cut vanilla bean 250 parts, powdered musk 10 parts, essential oil of bitter almonds 1 part; pound the musk and vanilla bean together and add the rest; pass through a not too close sieve. An excellent imitation of heliotrope.

Satchet Lavender.—Take of powdered lavender 75 parts, powdered benzoin 20 parts, oil of lavender 1 part.

Satchet a la Mareschale.—Take of sandalwood and orris root, of each 280 parts, rosa centifolia, cloves and cassia bark (laurus cassia), of each 140 parts, musk 1 part; powder coarsely.

Satthet Millefleurs.—Lavender flowers, ground orris root, rose leaves and benzoin, of each 1 pound, tonka beans, vanilla, sandalwood and ground cloves, of each ¼ pound, cinnamon and allspice, of each 2 ounces, mustard and civet, of each 2 drams.

Satchet for Perfuming Linen.—Orris root and rosa centifolia, of each 125 parts, nutmegs 8 parts, granular musk 15 parts; powder coarsely and mix.

Inexhaustible Smelling Salts.—Sal tartar 3 drams, muriate of ammonia, granulated, 6 drams, oil of neroli 5 minims, oil of lavender flowers 5 minims, oil of rose 3 minims, spirits of ammonia 15 minims; put into the pungent a small piece of sponge filling about ¼ the space, and pour on it a due proportion of the oils, then put in the mixed salts until the bottle is ¾ full, and pour on the spirits of ammonia in proper proportion and close the bottle.

Violet Powder.—Wheat starch 6 parts, orris root powder 2 parts; having reduced the starch to an impalpable powder, mix thoroughly with the orris root and then perfume with attar of lemon, attar of bergamot and attar of cloves, using twice as much of the lemon as of each of the other attars.

Volatile Salts for Pungents.—1. Liquor of ammonia fort 1 pint, oil of lavender flowers 1 dram, oil of rosemary, fine, 1 dram, oil of bergamot ½ dram, oil of peppermint 10 minims; mix thoroughly and fill pungents or keep in well-stoppered bottle. **2.** Sesqui-carbonate of ammonia, small pieces, 10 ounces, concentrated liquor of ammonia 5 ounces; put the sesqui-carbonate in a wide mouth jar with air-tight stopper, perfume the liquor of ammonia to suit and pour over the carbonate, close tightly the lid and place in a cool place, stir with a stiff spatula every other day for 1 week, and then keep it closed for 2 weeks, or until it becomes hard, when it is ready for use.

Excellent Scent Powder.—Coriander, orris root, rose leaves and aromatic calamus, of each 1 ounce, lavender flowers 10 ounces, rhodium ¼ dram, musk 5 grains; these are to be mixed and reduced to a coarse powder. This is one of the cheapest, most durable and satisfactory dry perfumes made; it scents clothes as though flowers had been pressed in their folds.

SKIN PREPARATIONS.

These preparations include pastes, washes, powders and ointments for the face and hands. The best known, harmless and effectual.

Almond Paste.—Bleached almonds 4 ounces; add the white of 1 egg; beat the almonds to a smooth paste in a mortar, then add the white of egg, and enough rose water mixed with its weight of alcohol to give the proper consistence. Used as a cosmetic to beautify the complexion, and is also a remedy for chapped hands, etc.

Almond Paste for the Hands.—Beat 4 ounces of bitter almonds, add 3 ounces of lemon juice, 3 ounces oil of almonds, and enough of alcohol and ether diluted to make a paste. Apply on retiring.

Black Spots on the Face.—These are sometimes called Fleshworms. Squeeze out the spot, then wash the part affected with diluted alcohol several times a day. If the trouble comes from fleshworms take some blood purifier. (*See Draughts and Infusion.*)

Blotched Face, Wash For.—Rose water 3 ounces, sulphate of zinc 1 dram; mix and wet the face; gently dry it, and then couch it over with cold cream, which also dry off gently.

Chapped Hands, Ointments and Liniments For.—1. Borax 2 scruples, glycerine ½ ounce, water 7½ ounces; mix and apply as a lotion twice a day. **2.** Glycerine 1 ounce; spermaceti 2 drams; olive oil 2 ounces; mix with heat and apply every night and morning. **3.** Take ¼ pound unsalted hog's lard, work it well through clear, cold water, drain and work again in a wineglass of rose water, the yolks of 2 fresh eggs and 1 tablespoonful of honey; mix gradually as much finely powdered oatmeal as will make a paste about the consistency of new butter; spread on the hands at night; cover with kid gloves, and in the morning wash off. **4.** Lard 16 parts, coca oil 24 parts, spermaceti 8 parts; yellow wax 3 parts, alkanet root 1 part; melt and keep at a gentle heat 15 minutes; strain through a cloth and mix with oil of lemon and oil of bergamot each 1-6 parts, oil of bitter almonds 1 to 15 parts; pour into suitable vessels and cork.

Chapped Lips, Liniments and Ointments for.—1. Two spoonfuls of clarified honey, a few drops of any perfume;

mix and anoint the lips frequently. **2.** Cut 4 ounces fresh unsalted butter into small pieces, place in an earthen vessel, cover with rose water, cover the vessel closely and stand aside for 5 days in cool place, then drain off any remaining liquid and put the earthen jar in a saucepan of warm water, add 1 ounce of grated spermaceti, 1 ounce of grated beeswax, ½ ounce of alkanet root, 2 drams of pulverized gum benzoin, 1 ounce of pulverized borax, ½ ounce of powdered white sugar and 1 tablespoonful of clear lemon juice; beat all well together and place over a slow fire, stirring until it reaches the boiling point, remove from the fire before it boils and when coal put in jars.

Cold Cream.—1. White wax ½ ounce, put in small basin with 2 ounces of almond oil; when quite melted add 2 ounce of rosewater: this must be done very slowly, little by little, and as you pour it in beat the mixture smartly with a fork to make the rose water incorporate; when all this is incorporated the cold cream is complete. **2.** Spermaceti 10 drams, white wax 10 drams, prepared lard 8 ounces, subcarbonate potash 15 grains, rosewater 4 ounces, spirits of wine 2 ounces, attar of roses 10 drops. **3.** Take of the oil of almonds 2 ounces, spermaceti ½ ounce, and white wax ½ ounce; put them in a close vessel and set the vessel in a skillet of boiling water; when melted beat the ingredients with rosewater until cold. Keep it in a tight box or wide-mouthed bottle, corkèd up close.

● Complexion Paste,—The following is the recipe for the paste by the use of which Madame Vestris is said to have preserved her beauty until very late in life; it is applied to the face on retiring for the night: The white of 4 eggs boiled in rosewater, ½ ounce alum, ½ ounce of sweet almonds; beat the whole together till it assumes the consistence of a paste.

To Remove Fleshworms.—Sometimes little black specks appear about the base of the nose, or on the forehead, or in the hollow of the chin, which are called fleshworms; are occasioned by coagulated secretion that obstructs the pores of the skin; they may be squeezed out by gentle pressing; they are permanently removed by washing with warm water and severe friction with a towel, and then applying a little of the following preparation: Liquor of potassa 1 ounce, cologne 2 ounces, white brandy 4 ounces The warm water and friction alone are sometimes sufficient.

Freckle Compound.—The so-called "Unctión de Maintenon," after the celebrated Madame de Maintenon, mistress and wife of Louis XIV., is made as follows: Venice soap 1 ounce, lemon juice ½ ounce, oil of bitter almonds ¼ ounce, deliquidated oil of tartar ¼ ounce, oil of rhodium 3 drops.

Freckle Wash.—One dram of muriatic acid, half pint of rainwater, half teaspoonful of spirit lavender; mix them well together and apply 2 or 3 times a day to the freckles with a camel's-hair brush.

Celebrated Moth and Freckle Lotion.—For the skin

and complexion. Distill 2 handsful of jessamine flowers in a quart of rose water and a quart of orange water; strain through porous paper and add a scruple of musk and a scruple of ambergris; bottle and label. Splendid wash for the skin.

Freckles, To Remove.—**1.** Ox gall 6 ounces, camphor 1¼ scruples, burned alum 1½ scruples, borax 1 dram, rock salt 2 ounces, rock candy 2 ounces. **2.** Take grated horseradish and put in very sour milk; let it stand 4 hours, then wash the face night and morning. **3.** Rectified spirits 1 ounce, water 8 ounces, orange-flower water ½ ounce or rosewater 1 ounce, distilled muriatic acid 1 teaspoonful; mix To be used after washing. **4.** Lemon juice 1 ounce, powdered borax ¼ dram, sugar ½ dram; mix and let stand in a glass bottle for a few days, then rub on face and hands night and morning. Two teaspoonsful of lemon juice equal 1 ounce. **5.** Sulpho-carbolate of zinc 2 drams, glycerine 3 fluid ounces, alcohol ½ fluid ounce, rosewater q. s. for 8 fluid ounces.

Mask, To Remove.—This frightful discoloration can be removed by a wash made from 30 grains of chlorate of potash in 8 ounces of rose water.

Moles, To Remove.—The common mole is situated in the middle layer of the skin, the coloring matter is probably some chemical combination of iron; they are often elevated above the surface and then the natural down of the skin over them is changed into a tuft of hair; the less they are trifled with the better, and avoid particularly the use of depilatories to remove the hair from them, as it often causes a foetid, suppurating wound; when slight, they may be removed by touching them every day with a little concentrated acetic acid by means of a hair pencil, observing due care to prevent the application from spreading to the surrounding parts; the application of lunar caustic is also effective, but it turns the spot temporarily black; when other means fail, the hair may be safely removed by surgical means; they can also be removed with a sunglass: seat the patient in a clear, strong sunlight, bring the concentrated rays of the sun to bear on the mole 5 or 10 minutes, in 3 or 4 weeks the mole will scale off and new skin form.

Mottle Patches, To Remove.—Wash with a solution of common bicarbonate of soda and water several times during the day until the patches are removed; after the process wash with some nice toilet soap and the skin will be kept nice, clean and free from patches; lemon juice is good rubbed on the skin.

Pimples, To Remove.—**1.** Barley meal 1 ounce, powdered bitter almonds 1 ounce, honey q. s. to make a smooth paste. **2.** White vinegar 4 ounces, sulphur water 2 ounces, acetated liquor of ammonia ½ ounce, liquor or potassa 2 grains, distilled water 4 ounces; mix and apply twice a day. **3.** Beat a quantity of houseleek in a marble mortar, squeeze out the juice and clarify it, pour a few drops of rectified spirits on the juice and it will instantly turn milky.

Pitting, To Remove.—Simple oil, pomade or ointment medicated with croton oil and of a strength sufficient to raise a very slight postular eruption is probably the safest and most effective of all preparations employed for the purpose; apply at intervals extending over several weeks.

POWDERS, PAINTS AND WASHES FOR THE COMPLEXION.

Powder for the Complexion.—1. Tincture of elder blossoms ½ ounce, beef marrow ½ ounce, orange flower water ½ pint, cassia buds 1 ounce, bitter almonds 2 ounces, spirits of oriental roses 4 drams; mix, and apply it in the evening and wash it off in the morning. **2.** Rice powder 1 pound, lake carmine 2 drams, essence of rose 9 grains, essence of santal 9 grains; mix well.

Malorrisine.—Pulverized marshmallow root 4 ounces, pulverized starch 2 ounces, pulverized orris root 3 drams, essence jasmine 20 drops; mix well, and sift through muslin. This elegant compound is excellent for softening and whitening the skin, and will prevent chapping. It may be used on the most sensitive and delicate complexions without fear of injury, and is one of the best cosmetics made.

Rose Powder.—Sifted starch, 1 ounce, rose pink, ½ dram, essence jasmine 10 drops, attar of roses 3 drops. This powder is better liked than rouge for imparting a delicate coloring to the skin, and as it is perfectly harmless, it may be used as often as necessary.

Paste for Oily Complexions.—1. Cold cream, 1 ounce, acetate of zinc 2 grains; perfume as preferred. **2.** Bicarbonate of soda 18 grains, aqua desillata 8 ounces, essence of roses quantity sufficient. **3.** A good cosmetic for a fine, delicate complexion which cannot bear greasy pomades, is the following preparation: Milk of almonds 8 ounces, ammonia chlorhydrate 2 grains, bichloride hydrargyri, 2 grains.

Milk of Roses.—Blanched almonds 2 ounces, rosewater 12 ounces, rectified spirits, 3 ounces, Windsor soap, white wax, oil of almonds, of each 2 drams, oil of bergamot, 1 dram, oil of lavender 15 drops, attar of roses 8 drops. To prepare this compound beat the almonds well, add rosewater for an emulsion; mix the soap, wax and oils together, rub the mixture in a mortar, and strain through fine muslin. A reliable druggist will prepare this recipe properly, if thought too difficult for home manufacture.

Color for Lips.—Color for the lips is nothing more than cold cream with a larger quantity of wax than usual melted in it with a few drams of carmine for vermillion tint. Use a strong infusion of alkanet; keep the chippings for 1 week in the almond oil of which the cold cream is made, and afterwards incorporate with wax and spermaceti; always tie alkanet in a muslin bag when it is needed for coloring.

Lip Salve.—1. Spermaceti ointment ½ pound, alkanet root ½ ounce; melt together until colored; strain and, when cooled a little, add balsam of peru 3 drams; stir well, and in a few minutes pour off the clear portion from the drugs; lastly stir in oil of cloves 20 to 30 drops. **2.** Oil of almonds 3 ounces, spermaceti ½ ounce, virgin rice ½ ounce; melt over a slow fire, mixing with them a little powder of alkanet root to color it; stir till cold and add a few drops of oil of rhodium. **3.** Dissolve a small lump of white sugar in a tablespoonful of rosewater (common water will do, but is not so good); mix it with a couple of large spoonsful of sweet oil, a piece of spermaceti of the size of half a butternut; simmer the whole well together 8 or 10 minutes, then turn into a small box.

Pearl Powder.—The best white is literally pearl powder; that is, made from pearls, and this is as safe as its effects are natural and beautiful. A most dangerous compound of bismuth is, however, sold under this name. The following is a good recipe: Pure pearl white and French chalk (scraped fine) equal parts, triturated together. Some add more French chalk.

Pearl Water for the Complexion.—Castile soap 1 pound, water 1 gallon; dissolve them; add alcohol 1 quart, oil of rosemary and oil of lavender, of each 2 drams; mix well.

Remove Pimples.—There are many kinds of pimples, some of which partake almost of the nature of ulcers, which require medical treatment, but the small red pimple, which is the most common, may be removed by applying the following twice a day: Sulphur water 1 ounce, acetated liquor of ammonia ½ ounce, solution of potassa ½ ounce, white wine vinegar 2 ounces, distilled water 2 ounces. These pimples are sometimes cured by frequent washing in warm water and prolonged friction with a coarse towel. The cause of these pimples is obstruction of the skin and imperfect circulation.

Rouge.—1. Mix vermilion with enough gum tragacanth dissolved in water to form a thin paste; add a few drops of almond oil, place in rouge pots, and dry by very gentle heat. **2.** (Turkish.) Alcohol ½ pint, alkanet 1 ounce; macerate 10 days, pour off the liquid and bottle. **3.** (Vinegar.) Acetic acid 4 drams, alum 30 grains, rosewater 12 ounces, alcohol 26 ounces, balsam of peru 50 grains, carmine No. 40 2 drams, water of ammonia 1 dram; dissolve the balsam of peru in the alcohol and the alum in the rosewater; mix the two solutions; add the acetic acid and macerate for a few hours; add to it the carmine dissolved in the ammonia; shake well and after 10 minutes decant the bottle.

Skin Pomades.—1. When the skin is dry, rough, and spotted the following pomades will be found excellent: Spermaceti 1 dram and 1 scruple, oil of bitter almonds 1 scruple, galien cerate 1 ounce. **2.** Mutton suet 2 drams, fresh butter 4 drams, lard 4 drams, oil of bitter almonds 1 dram; wash in rosewater and add enough white wax to make a paste.

Preventive Wash for Sunburn.—Borax 2 drams, Roman

alum 1 dram, camphor 1 dram, sugar ½ ounce, ox-gall 1 pound; mix and stir well together, and repeat the stirring 3 or 4 times a day until the mixture becomes transparent, then strain it through filtering paper, and it is fit for use.

Lemon Cream for Sunburn, Etc.—Put 2 spoonfuls of fresh cream into ½ pint of new milk, squeeze into it the juice of a lemon, and half a glass of brandy, a little alum and loaf sugar; boil the whole, skim it well, and when cool it is fit for use.

SPECIAL PREPARATIONS OF GREAT MERIT.

Bloom of Roses.—1. Dried red rose leaves 1½ ounces, boiling water 1 pint: infuse in earthenware vessel for 2 hours, press out the liquor and add juice of 3 lemons, the next day filter the clear portions, keep in a cool place; a little alcohol, 3 or 4 fluid ounces to the pint, is sometimes added, and improves it. **2.** Carmine ¼ ounce, strong liquor of ammonia, not weaker than 900, 1 ounce; put them into a stoppered bottle, set in a cool place and occasionally agitate for 2 or 3 days to effect a solution; then add rose water 1 pint, and after admixture add of esprit de rose ½ fluid ounce, pure rectified spirits 1 fluid ounce; agitate well and set aside for a week; lastly, decant the clear portion from the dregs for use.

Balm of Beauty.—Pure soft water 1 quart, pulverized castile soap 4 ounces, emulsion of bitter almonds 6 ounces, rose and orange flower waters, of each 8 ounces, tincture of benzoin 2 drams, borax 1 dram, add 5 grains bichloride of mercury to every 8 ounces of the mixture; to use, apply on a linen or cotton cloth to the face; an excellent preparation.

Bloom of Youth.—Boil 1 ounce Brazil wood in 3 pints of water 15 minutes, strain; then add ¾ ounce isinglass, ¼ ounce cochineal, 1 ounce alum, ½ ounce borax; dissolve by heat and strain.

Lemon Juice Lotion.—Fresh lemon juice 2 ounces, glycerine 1 ounce, rose water or rain water, with 3 or 4 drops of attar of roses added, 1 pint; anoint the hands and face 3 or 4 times daily, allow to remain on several minutes before wiping.

Wrinkles, To Remove.—1. Sulphate of alumine 1 scruple 16 grains, pure water ½ pint; mix, and bathe the face 3 times a day. **2.** Fresh butter 2 drams, essence of turpentine 2 drams, mastic 1 dram.

PREPARATIONS FOR THE HANDS, NAILS AND FEET.

If the use of soaps irritates the skin and produces roughness and cracks, use honey instead. Rub it on when the skin is dry. Moisten a little, rub it in well, then wash thoroughly and your hands will be perfectly clean.

To Soften the Hands.—To soften the hands fill a wash

basin half full of fine white sand and soap suds as hot as can be borne; wash the hands in this 5 minutes at a time, washing and rubbing them in the sand. The best is the flint sand or the white powdered quartz sold for filters. It may be used repeatedly by pouring the water away after each washing and adding fresh to keep it from blowing about; rinse in warm lather of fine soap, and after drying rub the hands with dry bran or cornmeal, dust them and finish with rubbing cold cream well into the skin. This effectually removes the roughness caused by housework, and should be used every day, first removing ink or vegetable stains with some one of the following preparations:

Stains, To Remove.—1. Fruit and ink stains may be taken out by immersing the hands in water slightly acidulated with oxalic acid or a few drops of oil of vitriol, or to which a little pearlash or chloride of lime has been added; afterwards rinse them well in warm, clean water, and do not touch soap for some hours, as any alkline matter will bring back the stains after their apparent removal by all of the above substances except the last. **2.** Wash the hands in clear water, wipe them lightly, and while moist strike a match, closing the hands above it so as to catch the smoke; the stains will disappear. **3.** Rubbing the hands with a slice of raw potato will remove vegetable stains. **4.** Damp the hands first in water, then rub them with tartaric acid as you would with soap, rinse them and rub dry.

Soften the Hands.—2. Keep a dish of Indian meal on the toilet stand near the soap and rub the meal freely on the hands after soaping them for washing. It will surprise you if you have not tried it, to find how it will cleanse and soften the skin.

Soften the Hands.—3. Before retiring take a large pair of gloves and spread mutton tallow inside, also all over the hands; wear the gloves all night and wash the hands with olive oil and white castile soap in the morning; after cleansing the hands with soap rub them well with oatmeal while still wet; honey is also very good used in the same way as lemon juice, well rubbed in at night.

Paste to Whiten the Hands, Used With Gloves.—1. Take ½ pound soft soap, a gill of salad oil, an ounce of mutton tallow, and boil them until thoroughly mixed; before the mixture is cold add 1 gill of spirits of wine and 1 grain of musk. **2.** Half ounce white wax, ½ ounce of spermaceti, ¼ ounce powdered camphor; mix them with as much olive oil as will form them into a very stiff paste. Use whenever the hands are washed. **3.** Mixture of 2 parts glycerine, 1 part ammonia, and a little rosewater whiten and soften the hands.

For Chapped and Rough Hands.— The following wash will prove of great benefit, and will remedy the trouble if used long enough: Lemon juice 3 ounces, white wine vinegar 3 ounces, white brandy ½ pint. Another remedy for chapped hands in the form of an ointment is made by melting together gum camphor 3 drams, white beeswax 3 drams, olive oil 2 ounces; apply before going to bed and wear gloves. Many women are annoyed by red, dry, and rough hands, with surfaces that are continually made worse by exposure and the use of soap and water. Bran water and almond paste are good for such skins. Always use warm water and mild soap, taking care to dry thoroughly. Chapped and cracked hands may be cured by anointing them with the following mixture and wearing gloves while sleeping; White wax 4 drams, olive oil 2 drams, spermaceti 18 grains.

Nails, Wash for.—1. Tincture myrrh 1 dram, diluted sulphuric acid 2 drams, spring water 4 ounces; mix. Cleanse the nails with white soap, then dip into wash. **2.** When the nails are stained and discolored a little lemon juice or vinegar and water is a good application; occasionally a little pumice stone in powder or a little putty powder may be used with water and a little piece of soft leather or flannel; the frequent employment of these substance is injurious to the healthy growth of the nails.

To Color the Nails.—Fine color may be given to the nails after washing with scented soap, by rubbing them with a mixture of equal parts of cinnabar and emery, followed by oil of bitter almonds. White specks may be removed by applying equal parts of pitch and turpentine melted together in a cup, adding powdered sulphur and vinegar; pitch and myrrh will effect the same result. Do not cut the nails too short; they should be polished by rubbing with a sponge dipped into cinnabar and emery. Many persons are obliged to cut their nails often, because of brittleness and breaking. The nails may be toughened by anointing them at night with this compound: Tar 18 grains, lard 1 ounce, mix. Wear gloves over night, and wash thoroughly with warm water and soap on arising.

Offensive Feet, Wash For.—1. Wash the feet in warm water to which a little hydrochloric acid or chloride of lime has been added. **2.** Bathe every night or oftener in a strong solution of borax. **3.** Bathe in a weak solution of permanganate of potash, 1 scruple of salt to 8 ounces of water. **4.** Common kitchen soda dissolved in water.

Powder for Feet.—1. A good deodorizer for unpleasant smelling feet is the following: A mixture of equal parts salicylic acid, soap, talc, and starch, to be applied in the form of powder. **2.** For excessive perspiration of the hands and feet the following is recommended; Carbolic acid 1 part, burnt alum 4 parts, starch 200 parts, French chalk 50 parts, oil of lemon 2 parts; make into a fine powder to apply to the hands or feet, or to be sprinkled inside the gloves or stockings.

Corns.—For several reliable medicines see "Tested Remedies" in Department I. The following is as good as anything that can be used: Salicylic acid 1 dram; cut the corn with a sharp knife; apply the acid; cover with a piece of court plaster. In 3 days remove the plaster and the corn will come with it. They may also be removed by the following preparation: White diachylon plaster plaster 4 ounces, shoemaker's wax 4 ounces, muriatic acid 60 drops; boil a few minutes in an earthenware vessel; when cold roll the mass by hand and apply a little on a piece of soft, thin leather. Soft corns may be cured by wrapping the afflicted toe with a soft linen rag, which has been saturated with turpentine, night and morning; in a few days the corn will disappear; relief, however, will be instantaneous. Care should always be taken to have the shoes sufficiently wide, but equal care should be exercised not to have them too loose.

PREPARATIONS FOR THE HAIR AND BEARD.

OILS, TONICS, DYES, RESTORATIVES AND WASHES.

Preparations for the hair are classified under the heads of tonics, restoratives, and washes to promote the growth and keep clean; depilatories for removing superfluous hair; dyes and bleaches, oils, pomades, and fluid for curling, etc. Included under the department for beards will be found some excellent recipes for forcing the growth, soaps for shaving, with some hints on the proper use and care of the razor and strap, pomades and articles used in the toilet.

OILS.

Baldness, For.—Boil ½ pound green Southern wood in 1½ pints sweet oil, add ½ pint port wine; strain through a fine linen bag 3 times, each time adding fresh Southern wood; then add 2 ounces bear's grease and replace near the fire in a covered vessel until the bear's grease is dissolved; mix and bottle close.

Bear's.—Cotton-seed oil 15 gals., oil of fennel 3 ozs., oil of lavender 2 ozs., oil of citronella 3 ozs., oil of cloves 3 ozs.

Brilliantine.—castor oil in eau de cologne 1 part in 4. or glycerine and eau de cologne, each 1 part, honey 2 parts, rectified spirits 4 parts,

Cocoanut.—Cocoanut fat 2½ pounds, castor oil 1 gallon, alcohol 1 ounce, oil of lavender 4 ounces. oil of cloves 2 ounces, oil of cinnamon 2½ ounces, oil of rose geranium 2 drams, melt the cocoanut fat at a gentle heat; add castor oil, mix thoroughly; add alcohol and perfume.

Colorings for Oil.—A red tinge is given to oils by allowing the oil to stand for a few hours over a little alkanet root, 2 drams to 1 pint; before scenting apply a gentle heat to facilitate the process. Yellow and orange are given by a little annatto or palm oil, and green by steeping a little green parsley or lavender in them for a few days, or by dissolving 2 or 3 drams of gum guaiacum in each pint by the aid of heat, and when cold desanting.

French Lustral.—Take castor oil 3 ounces, alcohol 1½ ounces, ammonia 1-16 ounce; well shaken and mixed together; perfume to suit—bergamot or any other perfume; splendid hair dressing.

Glycerine.—New rum 1 quart, concentrated spirits of ammonia 15 drops, glycerine oil 1 ounce, lac. sulphur 5½ drams, sugar of lead 5½ drams; put the liquor into a bottle, add the ammonia, then the other components; shake occasionally for 4 or 5 days.

Hair Oil.—Cologne spirits, 90 per cent proof, 1 gallon, castor oil 1 ounce, oil of cinnamon 1 ounce; mix well and it is fit for use.

Lyons' Kathairon.—Castor oil 2 gallons, alcohol 3 gallons; mix; tincture of cantharide (officinal) 10 ounces, bergamot 12 ounces; dissolve in alcohol; tincture of red sanders (strength 1 pound to 5 gallons 95 per cent alcohol) 4 ounces to 30 gallons.

Macassar.—Olive oil 1 quart, alcohol 2½ ounces, rose oil 1½ ounces; then tie 1 ounce of chipped alkanet root in a muslin bag and put it in the oil; let stand some days until it turns red, then remove; do not press.

Marrow.—1. Simple marrow oil scented to suit taste. **2.** Marrow oil 4 ounces, spirits of rosemary 4½ ounces, oil of nutmeg 12 drops. **3.** Cold drawn nut oil and marrow oil equal parts; scent.

New York Barber's Star Hair Oil.—Castor oil 6½ pints, alcohol 1½ pints, oil of citronella ½ ounce, lavender ¼ ounce; mix well.

To Make the Hair Soft and Glossy.—Alcohol 1 pint, castor oil 4 ounces; mix and flavor with bergamot; apply frequently with the hands.

HAIR RESTORATIVES, TONICS AND WASHES.

Ammonia.—1. When the hair has been neglected, cut it to an even length and wash the scalp nightly with soft water into which ammonia has been poured; this may be strong, so it does not burn the skin; afterward put 3 large spoonfuls of ammonia to a basin of water, apply with a brush, stirring the hair well; dry thoroughly, comb and shake out the tresses until nearly dry, then it may be done up loosely. One teaspoonful of ammonia to 1 pint of warm water makes a wash that may be used on a child's head daily. **2.** To wash the head thoroughly, drop about 2 ounces of ammonia into a basin of lukewarm water and soap; if the hair is long, braid it in 6 or 7 loose braids, some coming to the top of the head, and tie firmly; take a raw egg and rub vigorously into the scalp in every part. This is one of the best remedies for removal of dandruff. After rubbing in the egg wash the head in the water and ammonia with a little castile soap, wring the braids out and dry with a towel; then after the hair is dry, comb out and brush. Care should be taken to go in no draughts while the hair is wet; the ammonia helps it to dry quickly.

Dry and Brittle Hair may be made soft and brilliant by the use of the following formula: Oil of roses 2 ounces, oil of tuberoses 2 drams, oil of orange flower 2 drams, oil of jessamine 2 drams, oil of vanilla 1 ounce. essence of almonds 1 drop.

Dandruff is increased by the use of pomades, and those whose hair is naturally oily should abstain from their use. To remove dandruff: **1.** Water 8 ounces, carbonate of soda 1 dram; dissolve, and add yolks of 2 eggs well beaten. **2.** Chlorate of potash 2 scruples, rose water 8 ounces. Dandruff may be entirely removed by the use of the following mixture: Take a thimbleful of powdered refined borax, let it dissolve in a teacupful of water; first brush the head well, and then wet a brush with the solution, and rub the scalp well with it. Do this every day for a week, and twice a week, until no trace of dandruff is found.

Falling Out, To Prevent.—1. Sherry wine ½ pint, elder water ½ pint, tincture of arnica ½ ounce, spirits hartshorn 1 teaspoonful; apply with a sponge every night. **2.** Mix 1 ounce gum camphor and 2 ounces pulverized borax; pour over it 2 quarts boiling water: when cold, bottle and keep tightly corked; apply night and morning, rubbing it briskly into the scalp.

Gray Hair, To Prevent.—Hulls of butternuts 4 ounces; infuse in 1 quart of water 1 hour; add ½ ounce copperas; apply with a soft brush every 2 or 3 days. When sea air turns hair gray, it should be kept oiled with some vegetable oil; not glycerine, as that combines with water too readily. The water that potatoes have been boiled in applied to the hair prevents grayness.

Hair Restoratives.—1. An excellent stimulant and restorative for the hair is the following: Add ½ ounce of the oil of mace to ¾ of a pint of deodorized alcohol; pour a spoonful or two into a saucer, dip a small, stiff brush into it, and brush the hair smoothly, rubbing the tincture well into the roots. **2.** On bald spots, if hair will start at all, it may be stimulated by rubbing the scalp with a piece of flannel till the skin looks red, and anointing it with the above tincture. This process must be repeated 3 or 4 times a day for weeks, then the hair begins to grow; apply the tincture once a day till the growth is well established, bathing the head in cold water every morning. **3.** Bathing the head in a strong solution of rock salt is said to benefit gray hair in some cases. Pour boiling water on rock salt, in the proportion of 2 heaping tablespoonfuls to a quart of water, and let it stand till cold before using. **4.** A good wash for the hair is 1 teaspoonful of ammonia to a quart of warm water.

Hair Restorative.—Sugar of lead, borax and lac sulphur each 1 ounce, aqua ammonia ½ ounce, alcohol 1 gill: mix and let stand 20 hours, then add bay rum 1 gill, fine table salt 1 tablespoonful, soft water 3 pints, essence of bergamot ½ ounce.

Hair Restorative and Invigorator.—Sugar of lead, borax and lac sulphur of each 1 ounce. aqua ammonia ½ ounce, alcohol 1 gill; mix and let stand for 14 hours; then add bay rum 1 gill, fine table salt 1 tablespoonful, soft water 3 pints, essence of bergamot 1 ounce. This preparation not only gives a beautiful gloss. but will cause hair to grow upon bald heads arising from all common causes, and turning gray hair to a dark color. Manner of application: When the hair is thin or bald, make 2 applications daily until this amount is used up. Work it into the roots of the hair with a soft brush or the ends of the fingers, rubbing well each time. For gray hair 1 application daily is sufficient.

Hair Tonic.—Sugar of lead 5 grains, sulphate quinine 2 grains. muriat of ammonia 1 dram, glycerine 6 ounces, distilled water 6 ounces; mix, and apply 2 or three times a day.

Cure for Baldness.—Water 1 pint, pearl ash ¼ ounce, onion juice, 1 gill.

Hall's Restorative.—Glycerine 2 ounces, bay rum 8 ounces, salt 2½ ounces, Jamaica rum 4 ounces. lac sulphur and sugar of lead, each 1 dram and 15 grains, rain or distilled water 16 ounces; mix; digest 12 hours. Shake well before using.

Shampooing Liquids.—An excellent shampoo is made of salts of tartar, white castle soap, bay rum, and lukewarm water. The salts will remove all dandruff, the soap will soften the hair and clean it thoroughly, and the bay rum will prevent taking cold. **2.** (Dry). Sulphuric ether 1 ounce, alcohol 1 ounce, glycerine 1 ounce. aqua ammonia 1 dram, sliced castile soap 2 ounces, rain water 2 pints; mix.

Wilson's Lotion.—**1.** Eau de cologne (strongest) 8 fluid ounces, tincture cantharides 1 fluid ounce, oils of lavender and rosemary. each ½ fluid dram. **2.** Water of ammonia, almond oil and chloroform 1 part each; dilute with 5 parts alcohol or spirits of rosemary; add 1 dram oil of lemon. Use after a thorough friction with the hair brush.

Bay Rum Restorative.—Oil of bay 1 dram, oil of nutmeg 5 drops, oil of oranges ½ dram, Jamaica rum 4 ounces, alcohol 2 pints, water to make 4 pints; cut oils in alcohol, add rum and water, let stand 2 or 3 weeks and filter through magnesia and charcoal.

Eyebrows and Eyelashes. To Improve.—The eyelashes will increase in length if occasionally clipped. and anointed with a salve of 2 drams of ointment of nitric oxide of mercury and 1 dram of lard. Apply the mixture to the edges of the eyelids night and morning, washing afterward with warm milk and water. A good prescription for stimulating their growth: Sulphate of quinine 5 grains, sweet almond oil 1 ounce; apply with fine sable brush.

Eyebrows, To Make Grow.—Sulphate of quinine 5 grains, alcohol 1 ounce; apply after combing.

Eyebrows, Brown Dye For.—Lead filings 1 ounce, iron dust 1 ounce, vinegar 1 pint; boil all together to ½ pint, shake well when cool, and apply with small brush.

HAIR DYES AND BLEACHES.

Dyeing the hair is not all advisable, many evil results having accrued from the practice. All dyes are dangerous, so great care should be exercised in their use. The following list is of the best dyes in use at the present time.

Hair Dye, Black.—**1.** Distilled water 6 ounces, alcohol 1 ounce, pyrogalic acid 1 dram; the acid must be dissolved in the alcohol before the water is added. **2.** Aqua ammonia 1 ounce, water 1 ounce, nitrate of silver 2 drams; dissolve the silver in water and add the ammonia. Cork tight and keep in a cool place. **3.** Water 4 ounces, sulphate of potash ½ ounce; mix. To dye the hair or whiskers have them free from dirt or soapsuds; they should be a little damp; add carefully No. 1, using care not to allow the dye to touch the skin. When somewhat dry apply No. 2; in about 3 minutes apply No. 3. Use care not to allow any of these preparations to touch the skin.

Blonde Bleach.—White wine 3 gills, rhubarb (dry) 5 ounces; boil to half quantity and strain; wash the hair and let it dry. Peroxide of hydrogen is an effective bleach.

Brown.—Dissolve permanganate of potash ½ oz. in 1 pint of rosewater, and after having cleansed the hair with a solution of hartshorn, a teaspoonful to 1 quart of water, and dry it well with a towel, apply. It takes effect immediately, and the desired shade may be obtained by applying more or less of the solution.

Brown, Dark.—**1.** Pyrogallic acid 4 grains, distilled water 2 ounces. **2.** Crystalized nitrate of silver 1 dram, gum arabic 1 dram, distilled water 2 ounces.

Brown, For Red Hair.—Oils of nutmeg and rosemary, of each 1 dram, castor oil 1 ounce, tincture of cantharides 2 drams, strong brandy 7 ounces; mix. Use a small portion once a day, and brush the hair with a stiff brush half an hour.

Chestnut.—Permanganate of potash 1 dram, powdered gum arabic 2 drams, rose water 3 ounces; mix. Apply carefully with a toothbrush.

Golden.—**1.** Crystalized caustic baryta 7 parts, potassium chlorate 3 parts; mix in fine powder, melt by gentle heat; the mass must be washed in cold water to remove the chlorate of potassium, and the residue shaken in the cold with a solution of 8 parts of glacial phosphoric acid in 25 parts of water, the whole cooled with ice; when the peroxide of barium is decomposed, the fluid should be decanted. **2.** Moisten the hair, previously washed and dried, with a solution of acetate or nitrate of lead, and followed with a mordant of yellow chromate of potash.

Walnut Hair Dye.—The simplest form is the pressed juice of the bark or shell of green walnuts; to preserve this juice a little rectified alcohol may be added to it, with a few bruised cloves, and the whole digested together with occasional agitation for a week or two, when the clear portion is decanted and, if necessary, filtered. Sometimes only a little common salt is added to preserve the juice; it should be kept in a cool place.

CURLING FLUIDS AND FIXATURES.

Curloline, For Making the Hair Curl.—1. Olive oil 1 pound, oil of origanum 1 dram, oil of rosemary 1½ drams; mix well, bottle and label. Apply 2 or 3 times weekly; will curl the straightest hair if not cut too short. 2. Scrapings of lead 2 ounces, litharge ½ ounce, gum camphor ¼ ounce; boil all in 1 pint of soft water for 30 minutes; let it cool; pour off liquid and add 1 dram rosemary flowers; boil all again and strain, when it is ready for use. Apply about once a week.

Curling Fluid.—Put 2 pounds common soap, cut small, into 3 pints spirits of wine; melt together, stirring with clean piece of wood, add essence of ambergris, citron and neroli, of each ¼ ounce.

French Curlique.—Oil of sweet almonds 1 ounce, spermaceti 1 dram, tincture of mastic 3 drams; dissolve the spermaceti (white wax is as good) in the oil with a slow heat, then add the tincture. Apply a small quantity.

Gum Arabic.—1. To common gum arabic add enough alcohol to make thin; let stand all night, then bottle to prevent evaporating; put on the hair after it is done up in paper. 2. Pale gum arabic, picked, 1½ ounces, rose water 2 fluid ounces, pure water 3 fluid ounces; dissolve. 3. Gum arabic 3¼ ounces, water ½ pint; dissolve, and then drop in cologne gradually until the cloudiness ceases to be removed by agitation; the next day decant.

Gum Tragacanth.—1. Gum tragacanth 1½ dram, water 7 ounces, proof spirits 3 ounces, attar of roses 10 drops; macerate 24 hours and strain. 2. Gum tragacanth ¼ ounce, rose water 1 pint, glycerine 5 drops; mix and let stand over night; if the tragacanth is not dissolved, let it be 12 hours longer; if too thick, add more rose water, and let stand some hours; when it is a smooth solution it is fit for use. 3. Finest gum tragacanth, reduced to powder, 1 ounce, rose water 1 pint; put into a wide-mouthed vessel and shake daily 2 or 3 days, then strain; if required to be colored, infuse cochineal in the water employed before making.

POMADES.

Baldness, For.—1. Macerate 1 dram powdered cantharides in 1 ounce spirits wine; shake frequently during a fortnight, and then filter; rub together 10 parts of this tincture with 90 parts of cold lard; add any perfume. Rub well into the head night and morning. **2.** Extract yellow Peruvian bark 14 grains, extract rhatany root 8 grains, extract burdock root and oil nutmeg (fixed), each 2 drams, camphor (dissolved with spirits of wine) 15 grains, beef marrow 2 ounces, best olive oil 1 ounce, citron juice ½ dram, aromatic essential oil to render fragrant; mix and make into an ointment.

Balsam of Tolu.—Prepared lard 2 ounces, white wax 3 ounces, melt together; remove from the fire, and when they are beginning to thicken add, with constant stirring, balsam of tolu 2 drams, essence of bergamot 30 drops.

Circassian Cream.—Two flasks oil, 3 ounces white wax, 1 ounce spermaceti, ½ ounce alkanet root; digest the oil with the alkanet until colored; strain; melt the wax and spermaceti with the oil; when cool add 2½ drams English oil of lavender and ⅓ dram essence of ambergris.

Black Pomade.—Melt together in a bowl set in boiling water 4 ounces white wax in 9 ounces olive oil, stirring in, when melted and mixed, 2 ounces burned cork in powder; this gives a lustrous blackness to the hair. Apply like pomade, brushing it well and in through the hair, it changes the color instantly.

German Pomade.—Eight ounces purified marrow; melt in a glass or stoneware vessel; add 1½ ounces fresh bay leaves, 1 ounce orange leaves, 1 ounce bitter almonds, ½ ounce nutmeg, ½ ounce cloves, 1 dram vanilla, all bruised; cover the vessel and digest 24 hours with a gentle heat; strain while warm through linen and stir it as it cools.

Hard Pomade.—1. Purified suet 1 pound, white wax 1 pound, jasmine pomatum ½ pound, tuberose pomatum ½ pound, attar of roses 1 dram. **2.** White; Suet 1 pound, wax ½ pound, attar of bergamot 1 ounce, attar of cassia 1 dram. Brown and black are made in the same way, but colored with fine ivory black or umber ground in oil.

Hungarian or Mustache Wax.—White wax 4 ounces, lard 2 ounces, Canada balsam ¼ ounce, oil of bergamot 1 dram, oil of lavender 15 drops; add the balsam to the wax and lard, previously heated; when nearly cold, add the essential oils, and mold. It may be colored black or brown.

Oil of Almond.—Melt together with gentle heat 2 ounces purified beef marrow, 2 drams yellow wax, 1 ounce spermaceti, oil of almonds; stir until almost cold, and add essence bergamot ½ ounce, attar of roses 10 drops, and oil of nutmeg 10 drops.

Rose Pomade.—Prepared lard 16 ounces, prepared suet 2 ounces; melt with gentle heat; add 2 ounces rose water, 6 drops attar of roses; beat well together and pour into pots. For making jasmine, violet and orange pomade, put the same quantity of water, and 1 dram of essence.

Transparent Pomade.—Spermaceti 2 ounces, castor oil 5 ounces, alcohol 5 ounces, oil of bergamot ½ dram, oil of portugal ⅓ dram.

White Pomade.—Benzoinated suet 1 pound, white wax 1 pound, jasmine pomatum 8 ounces, tuberoses pomatum 8 ounces, attar of roses 1 dram: melt at a gentle heat and cast in molds.

DEPILATORIES.

The following are for removing superfluous hair; care should be exercised in their use:

Arsenical—1. Nitre and sulphur each 1 part, arpiment 3 parts, quicklime 8 parts, soap lees, 32 parts: boil to the consistence of cream. **2.** Quicklime 30 parts, arpiment 4 parts, powdered gum arabic 60 parts; mix and keep in a tightly corked bottle; when used, form a paste with water, apply, and let remain 5 or 10 minutes, when the superfluous hair can be removed with the back of a knife.

Boettger's.—Powdered sulphydrate of sodium 1 part, washed chalk 3 parts: make into a thick paste with a little water; let a layer about the thickness of the back of a knife be spread upon the surface; in 2 or 3 minutes the hair is transformed into a soft mass, which may be removed by water. A more prolonged action would attack the skin.

Chinese.—Crystallized hydrosulphate of soda 3 parts; quicklime in powder 10 parts, starch 10 parts; mix with water and apply to the skin; scrape off in 2 or 3 minutes with a wooden knife.

Electric.—A moistened sponge electrode from the positive pool of the battery, having previously been placed on the back of the neck, or fixed at some other convenient spot; a three-cornered needle, with sharp cutting edges, set in a handle and attached to the negative pole of the battery, is made to enter the hair follicle alongside the hair, care being taken to make the needle penetrate to the depth of the follicle. The action of the current causes a few bubbles of viscid froth to be observed; as soon as this manifests itself, the needle should be rotated a few times to cause the sharp corners to scrape away the debris and allow electrical contact with a fresh surface. The operation is continued until the hair becomes loose and comes away with the slightest traction. The operator then proceeds with the next hair in like manner, and so on.

Plaster.—Spread equal parts of resin and pitch on a piece of thin leather, and apply; let it remain 3 minutes, and pull off suddenly, when it brings the hair with it; if the plaster were left on longer, it would be apt to bring the skin.

THE BEARD

Bay Rum, Equal to the Best Imported.—Oil of bay fine, 1½ drams, oil of neroli (bigard) 10 drops, ether acetic 7 drams, alcohol, deodorized (strong) 3 pints, water 2¼ pints, caramel sufficient to tinge; let it stand 2 weeks and filter.

Imperial Onguent, For Forcing Whiskers and Mustache to Grow.—Benzoin composition 2 drams, tincture of cantharides 2 drams, castor oil 6 ounces, alcohol 9¼ ounces, oil of bergamot 1 dram; mix well, bottle and label. Apply the on guent night and morning; circulation should be stimulated with a rough towel.

Paste, To Produce Whiskers.—Oil of paricada 1 ounce, southern wood bark 2 ounces, dog's lard 1 ounce; fry over a slow fire until it forms a paste. Apply to the face once a day until the whiskers begin to grow.

Shaving Soap.—1. Good white soap, in fine shavings, 3 pounds, balm soap 1 pound, soft water ¾ pound, soda 1 ounce; melt carefully over a slow fire in an earthen vessel, then add oil of lavender 60 drops. oil of lemon 40 drops; mix well and make into forms. **2.** Castile soap, in shavings. 4 ounces, proof spirits 1 pint; dissolve, and add a little perfume. **3.** Venetian soap ¾ pound, salts of tartar 1 ounce, benzoin ½ ounce, alcohol 1 gallon. (*See Soaps.*)

Mustache Grower.—Simple cerate 1 ounce, oil of bergamot 10 minims, saturated tincture of cantharides 15 minims; rub them together thoroughly, or melt the cerate and stir in the tincture while hot, and the oil as soon as it is nearly cold, then run into molds or rolls. To be applied as a pomade, rubbing in at the roots of the hair; care must be used not to inflame the skin by too frequent application.

Razor-strop Paste.—Wet the strop with a little sweet oil and apply a little flour of emery evenly over the surface.

Shaving Compound.—Plain white soap ½ pound, dissolved in a small quantity of alcohol, as little as can be used; add a tablespoonful of pulverized borax; shave the soap and put it in a small tin basin or cup; place it on the fire in a dish of boiling water; when melted, add the alcohol, and remove from the fire; stir in oil of bergamot sufficient to perfume it.

Shaving Cream.—1. White soap 3 ounces, proof spirit 8 ounces, water 4 ounces, carbonate of potassa 1 dram. oil of lemon 10 drops; mix. add the potassa and oil of lemon last. **2.** White wax. spermaceti, almond oil each ¼ ounce; melt and while warm beat in 2 squares Windsor soap previously reduced to a paste with rose water.

To Make a Razor Strap.— Select a piece of maple or rosewood 12 inches long, 1¾ inches wide, and ⅜ inch thick. allow 3½ inches for length of handle; ½ inch from where the handle begins notch out the thickness of the leather, so that the same can fit smoothly in the wood: select a fine piece of calfskin, fasten securely to the wood, and on the other side secure a piece of coarse canvas. The razor should be strapped first on the canvas and then on the leather.

Razor Paste.—1. Mix fine emery with fat or wax until of proper consistency and then rub it well into the leather strap: prepare the emery by pounding it in a mortar. **2.** The grit from a fine grindstone is excellent for a razor paste. **3.** Levigated oxalic acid ¼ ounce, powdered gum 20 grains; make into a stiff paste with water and spread it thinly over the strap; this gives a fine edge to the razor and its efficiency is increased by moistening it.

TOOTH POWDERS, WASHES, ETC.

PASTES.

Camphor.—One ounce saliammoniac, 4 drams camphor; powder and mix with sufficient honey to make a smooth paste: triturate until perfectly smooth.

Charcoal Paste.--Chlorate of potassa 1 dram, mint water 1 fluid ounce: triturate until dissolved; add of powdered charcoal 2 ounces, honey 1 ounce. **2.** Suds of castile soap and spirits of camphor equal parts; make into a thick paste with pulverized chalk and charcoal equal parts.

Honey Paste.—1. One ounce myrrh in fine powder, a little green sage, two spoonsful white honey. **2.** Two scruples myrrh in fine powder, 18 scruples juniper gum, 10 grains rock alum; mix in honey. Apply frequently.

Magic Paste.—White marble dust 4 ounces, pumice stone (in impalpable powder) 3 ounces, rose pink 1 ounce, honey ½ pound, attar of roses 15 drops. Whitens the teeth, but should not be used too freely nor too frequently.

Violet Paste.—Prepared chalk and cuttle-fish bone, each 3 ounces, powdered white sugar 2 ounces, orris root 1 ounce, smalts ½ ounce, syrup of violets q. s. to mix.

POWDERS AND WASHES.

To Beautify the Teeth and Make the Breath Smell Sweet and Pleasant.—Chlorate of lime 1 ounce in 1 pint of soft water, and let it stand 24 hours; then pour off the clear water and add 40 drops of essence of rose.

To Clean the Teeth.—Castile soap and cigar ashes applied with a soft rag is one of the best tooth preparations known.

Powders.—1. Borax powder 2 ounces precipitate chalk 4

ounces, myrrh 1 ounce. iris 1 ounce **2.** Precipitate chalk ½ pound, powdered starch ¼ pound, iris powder ¼ pound, sulphate of quinine ½ scruple; put mixture through a sieve. **3.** Peruvian bark 2 drams, charcoal 2 drams, iris powder 1 scruple. **4.** Prepared chalk 1½ ounces, peruvian bark ½ ounce. camphor ¼ ounce.

Sozodont Fragrant.—Tincture of soap bark 2 ounces, tincture of myrrh 1 dram, glycerine ½ ounce, water 1½ ounces, essence of cloves 10 drops, essence of wintergreen 10 drops, tincture of cochineal enough to color; mix. Accompanying the above is a powder composed of prepared chalk, orris root, carbonate of magnesia, of equal parts; mix.

Camphorated Powders.—1. Camphor, pulverized by the acid of a few drops of spirits, 1 ounce, prepared or precipitated chalk 3 ounces. **2.** Camphor 1 ounce, precipitated chalk 2 ounces, cuttlefish bone ½ ounce, myrrh 2 drams, borax 2 drams, lake or rose pink 1 dram, or of sufficient quantity. **3.** Prepared chalk 8 ounces, powdered cuttlefish bone 4 ounces, camphor 1 dram, oil of cloves 1 dram; dissolve the camphor with alcohol, add the remaining ingredients and mix.

Myrrh.—1. Myrrh ½ ounce, cuttlefish bone, prepared chalk, orris, of each 1 ounce, cassia ½ ounce; mix. **2.** Bole 1 ounce, myrrh, bark and orris, of each ½ ounce; mix.

Myrrh, Washes,—1. Turkey myrrh 3 ounces, eau de cologne 1 quart; digest for 7 days and filter. **2.** Borax 1 ounce, shellac ½ ounce. water 8 ounces; boil together to 4 ounces, and add spirits of scurvy grass 1 pint, camphor ½ ounce, myrrh 2 ounces; digest and filter. **3.** Mix ½ pint of Jamaica spirits, ½ teaspoonful each of powdered alum and pulverized saltpeter and 1 ounce pulverized myrrh. **4.** Tincture of myrrh ½ ounce, tincture of peruvian bark 2 ounces; a few drops in water when brushing the teeth.

Mouth Pastel to Sweeten the Breath.—1. Extract of licorice 3 ounces, oil of cloves 1½ drams, oil of cinnamon 15 drops; mix and divide into 1 grain pills and silver them. **2.** Chocolate powder and ground coffee, of each 1½ ounces. prepared charcoal 1 ounce, sugar 1 ounce, vanilla (pulverized with the sugar) 1 ounce, enough mucilage; make into lozenges to suit the taste. of which 6 or 8 may be used daily to disinfect the breath. **3.** (Bologna Cachous.) Extract of licorice 3 ounces, water 3 ounces; dissolve by heat in a water bath and add catechu 1 ounce, gum arabic ½ ounce; evaporate to the consistence of an extract, and add (in powders) ½ dram each of mastic, cascarilla, charcoal, and orris: remove from the fire and add oil of peppermint ½ dram, essence of ambergris and essence musk, each 5 drops; roll flat on an oiled marble slab and cut into small lozenges. Used by smokers..

To Sweeten the Breath.—From 6 to 10 drops of the concentrated solution of chloride of soda in a wineglassful of spring water. taken immediately after the ablutions of the morning, will sweeten the breath by disinfecting the stomach, which far from being injured will be benefited by its use. If necessary this may be repeated in the middle of the day. In some cases the odor from carious teeth is combined with that of the stomach; if the mouth is well rinsed with a teaspoonful of the chloride in a tumbler of water the bad odor from the teeth will be removed.

Violet Mouth Wash.—Tincture of orris ½ pint, spirit of rose ½ pint, alcohol ½ pint, attar of almonds 5 drops; shake thoroughly and rinse the mouth after eating.

TOILET AND MEDICINAL SOAPS.

An Excellent Toilet Soap.—Take 2 pounds pure beef tallow, 2 pounds sal soda, 1 pound salt, 1 ounce gum camphor, 1 ounce oil of bergamot, 1 ounce borax; boil slowly an hour; stir often; let it stand till cool, then warm it over so it will run easily, and turn into cups or molds dipped in cold water. This is very nice for all toilet purposes and is greatly improved by age.

A Celebrated French Toilet Compound which is far better than soap is made of 8 ozs. of bitter almonds, oil of same 12 ounces, savon vert of the perfumes 8 ounces, spermaceti 4 ounces, cinnabar 2 drams, essence of rose 1 dram; melt the soap and spermaceti with the oil in a water bath, add the powder and mix the whole in a mortar. It forms a paste and may be used as desired.

Almond.—Oil of almonds 7 pounds, soda 1½ pounds; water sufficient; the soda must be rendered caustic before adding it to the oil and heat then applied; an easy way of preparing the soda is to treat it in a solution with powdered quicklime

Antimonial Soap.—Prepared by dissolving 1 part golden sulphuret of antimony of 2 parts of a saturated solution of caustic potash, to this add of caustic soap, in powder, 4 parts; triturate till the whole assumes a proper consistency.

Bouquet Soap.—**1.** White curd soap, finest, 17½ pounds, olive oil soap 2½ pounds, oil of bergamot 1 ounce, oils of cassia, cloves, sassafras and thyme, of each 1½ drams, oil of neroli 1 dram, brown ocher, levigated, 2 ounces; proceed as for almond soap; it may be varied by substituting oil of lavender for the neroli. **2.** White curd soap 20 pounds, oil of bergamot 2⅔ ounces, oil of cloves ½ dram, oil of neroli ½ dram, oil of sassafras ⅓ dram, oil of thyme ⅓ dram, colored with 2½ ounces of brown ocher. **3.** Good tallow soap 30 pounds, essence of bergamot 4 ounces, oils of cloves, sassafras and thyme, of each 1 ounce, color brown ocher 7 ounces. **4** (Palmer's). White castile soap 10 pounds, oil of English lavender 2 drams, oil of citronella 2½ drams, oils of lemon and bergamot, of each 4 drams, palm oil 2 pounds; melt the soap and palm oil together by a gentle heat, and when nearly cold, add the perfumes, previously dissolved in sufficient alcohol.

Carbolic Acid Soap.—Take freshly prepared cocoanut oil soap 75 parts, and fuse; then add a solution of alcohol 5 parts, carbolic acid 3 parts, caustic potassa 1 part, oil of lemon 1 part; mix, with stirring; to be poured into molds.

Castile Soap.—**1.** Made like almond soap, only using olive oil; it is mottled by adding a solution of sulphate of iron while in the liquid state. **2.** Boil common soft soap in lamp oil 3½ hours.

Cinnamon Soap.—Tallow soap 14 pounds, palm oil soap 7 pounds, oil of cinnamon (cassia) 3 ounces, oil of sassafras and essence of bergamot, of each ½ ounce, levigated yellow ochre ¼ pound.

Cocoanut Oil Soap.—Put 50 pounds cocoanut oil and 50 pounds caustic soda lye of 27° Baumé into a soap kettle; boil and mix for 1 or 2 hours until the paste thickens; then diminish the heat, but continue stirring till the cooling paste assumes a white, half-solid mass, then transfer quickly to the frames.

Coloring.—For coloring ordinary fancy soaps mineral colors are employed; for superior toilet and transparent soaps organic pigments are used, generally the red coloring matter is derived from vermillion or chrome red, the violet from fuchsine solved in glycerine, the red-brown and brown from cameral and the various kinds of umber, for green chrome green is used; a beautiful vegetable green is obtained by stirring in the soap, saponified with 7 to 10 per cent of palm oil, some smalts or ultramarine, for blue, smalts or ultramarine; yellow is obtained by mixing palm butter with the fat to be saponified; for black common lampblack is used. Fine toilet soaps and transparent soaps may be colored as follows: For red color, tincture of dragon's blood or liquid carmine: rose, tincture of carthamine or of archil; yellow and orange, tincture of annatto or saffron; blue and violet, tincture of litmus, or of alkanet root, or soluble Prussian blue, basic, or a very little indigo in impalpable powder; green, a mixture of blue and yellow.

Cream Wash Balls.—White curd soap 7 pounds, powdered starch 1 pound, water or rose water quantity sufficient: beat the whole together, and form into balls.

English Bath.—Tallow oil 4 pounds, palm oil 4 pounds, cocoanut oil 2 pounds, alcohol 4 pints, soda lye, at 36°, 5 pounds, oil of sassafras ½ ounce, oil of peppermint ⅓ ounce, oil of lemon ½ ounce, oil of cinnamon ⅓ ounce, oil of lavender ⅓ ounce; mix and proceed as in the directions for transparent soap, omitting the glycerine.

Floating Soap.—Fine soda oil soap (in shavings) 9 parts, water 1 part; put them in a clean copper kettle, place it in a water bath; melt, then agitate the mixture until its volume is doubled, or until it becomes wholly composed of froth, then pour it out to cool and cut into cakes.

Glycerine Soap.—**1.** Take toilet soap, slice and melt with gentle heat, and add to 1 pound soap 1 ounce pure glycerine; when sufficiently cool make into balls. **2.** Take 100 parts oleine of commerce (winter strained lard oil will answer), and add 314 parts heavy glycerine; heat to 50° and then add 56 parts aqueous solution of caustic potassa, specific gravity 1.34, and stir the mixture well. This soap exhibits the consistency of honey, in which state it remains.

Glycerine Balls.—To any recently made toilet soap, sliced and melted by a gentle heat, without water if possible, add glycerine 1 ounce to the pound; thoroughly incorporate by stirring until the mass has cooled considerably, when it should be made into balls.

Honey Soap.—Cut 2 pounds common bar soap into shavings and put in a tin pail with barely hot water enough to cover, place the pail in a kettle of boiling water, and when its contents are melted, stir thoroughly, and add ¼ pound each of honey, almond oil and powdered borax; mix together by stirring for 10 minutes, then add oil of cinnamon or bergamot, a few drops, or any scent preferred; mix well, and turn the soap into a deep dish to cool, then cut into squares. It can be made into sand balls by adding equal quantities of white sand and Indian meal until it is so stiff that you can roll it in the hands. There is no soap that will whiten the hands like this. **2.** Some of the finer kinds are made of olive oil soap and palm oil soap, of each 1 part, white cured soap 3 parts, deepened in color, while in a liquid state, with a little palm oil or annatto, and scented with 1 to 1½ ounces essential oils to each ¼ pound, or 1 to 1½ pounds to each hundredweight.

Iodine Soap.—Make a solution of 1 part iodine potassium in 3 parts of water; to this add of powdered castile soap 16 parts; melt in a porcelain vessel by the aid of water bath.

Lavender Soap.—The basis of Windsor soap. scented with oil of lavender, 1 to 1½ fluid ounces per 7 pounds, supported with a little oil of bergamot and the essence of musk and ambergris. It is often colored with a little tincture of litmus or corresponding mineral pigments.

Marine Soap.—This is made by substituting cocoanut oil for fats and oils used in the manufacture of common soap. It has the advantage of forming a lather with salt water.

Mercurial Soap.—Beat into a homogeneous mass in a wedgewood mortar castile soap 1 pound; protochloride of mercury ½ ounce, dissolved in 4 ounces of alcohol.

Oatmeal Soap.—make a saturated solution of borax (the pulverized is the best), cut into it bits of fancy castile or glycerine soap; let the mixture boil until the soap is dissolved; make it as thick as cream by boiling or by adding more if too thick; then stir into the mass oatmeal enough to make a soft paste, stir until it cools and hardens; a little sulphur, also pulverized camphor of sulphur, may be mangled with the meal;

while warm and soft place in a box, so that when hard it may be turned out and cut into squares. This soap softens the skin.

Perfuming.—Perfuming is generally done when the paste is in the frame, as, if added in the pan when the soap is hot, most of the essential oils would be volatilized. It is best to mix the colors and the perfumes together with some alcohol or glycerine and stir in well.

Rose Soap.—1.—Palm oil soap in shavings 3 pounds, finest white curd soap in shavings 2 pounds, soft water ¼ pint; melt together in a bright copper pan and set in a water bath; add levigated vermilion ¼ ounce; and when the mixture is cooled a little stir in finest attar of roses 2 drams, oil of bergamot 1½ drams, oil of cinnamon and oil of cloves of each ¾ drams, oil of rose geranium ½ dram; mix well and pour the mass into an open bottomed wooden frame set on a polished marble slab. Sometimes it is colored with tincture of dragon blood or of archil instead of with vermilion. **2.** White curd soap 20 pounds, essence of rose 1¼ ounces, oil of cloves ½ dram, oil of cinnamon ⅛ dram, oil of bergamot 1 dram, oil of neroli ½ dram; colored with 2 ounces of vermilion.

Sand Soap.—Prepared soap 8 pounds, marine soap 7 pounds, sifted silver sand 25 pounds; oil of French lavender thyme, caraway and cassia of each 2 ounces; mix the usual way.

Shaving Soap.—1. Take 4 pounds white bar soap, 1 quart of rain water, ½ pint beef gall, and 1 gill spirits of turpentine; put the whole over the fire and boil until dissolved, stirring meanwhile. **2.** A nice soap for shaving may be made by mixing ¼ pound castile soap, 1 cake old Windsor soap, 1 gill each of lavender and cologne water, and a little alcohol; boil all together until mixed. **3.** Good white soap (in thin shavings) 3 pounds, palm soap 1 pound, soft water ¾ pounds, soda 1 ounce, melt carefully over a slow fire in an earthen vessel, then add oil of lavender, 60 drops oil of lemon 40 drops, bergamot 50 drops; mix well and make it into forms. **4.** Take 3 pounds white bar soap, 1 pound castile soap, 1 quart rain water, ½ pint beef gall, 1 gill spirits turpentine; cut the soap into thin slices and boil 5 minutes after the soap is dissolved; stir while boiling; scent with oil of rose or almonds; to color it use ½ ounce vermilion.

Transparent Soap.—Slice 6 pounds nice yellow bar soap into shavings; put into a brass, tin or copper kettle, with alcohol ½ gallon, heating gradually over a slow fire, stirring until dissolved; then add 1 ounce sassafras essence; stir until mixed and pour into pans about 1½ inches deep, and when cold cut into square bars.

Violet Soaps.—Any white toilet soap strongly scented with essence of orris root, either colored or not, with tincture of litmus or a little levigated smalts, ultra marine or indigo.

White Toilet Soap.—Ten pounds refined tallow, boiled in lye made from 5 pounds soda, ½ as much fresh lime, boiled ¼ hour in 7 gallons of water. When the lye is cold it is drained from the soda and lime and boiled with the grease 1 hour until clear; then pour into a tub to cool. The soap floats on the top and may be cut into bars. 2. To 15 pounds lard or tallow made hot add slowly 6 gallons hot lye or solution of potash that will bear up an egg high enough to leave a piece as big as a dime bare. Take out a little and cool it; if no grease rises, it is done, if any grease appears add lye and boil until no grease appears; add 3 quarts fine salt and boil again; if this does not harden on cooling add more salt. If it is to be perfumed melt it next day, add the perfume and run it into molds or cut into cakes.

Windsor Soap, Brown.—Prepared soap 40 pounds, burnt umber 4 ounces, English vermilion 1 ounce, lampblack ½ ounce, oils of cinnamon and bergamot each 2 ounces, oils of thyme, peppermint, carraway seed and cloves, each 1½ ounces, lavender 2 ounces; mix according to the usual way.

Windsor Soap, White.—Curd soap 50 pounds, marine soap 10 pounds, oil soap 14 pounds, oils of cassia and cloves each 2 ounces, oil of carraway seed 4 ounces, oil of thyme 3½ ounces, rosemary 4 ounces; mix in the usual way.

Face Cosmetic.—Oxide of zinc ½ ounce, prepared chalk ½ ounce, glycerine 2 drams, rose water sufficient to make 6 ounces. Apply with small sponge. When dried, smooth off with dry hands.

Hand Lotion.—Quince seed 2 drams, hot water 16 ounces. Let stand for a few days; strain and add 4 ounces of glycerine, 8 ounces of alcohol, 3 drops of oil of rose geranium, 2 drams of tincture of benzoin, and water enough to make 1 quart.

Breath Purifier.—Carbolic acid 16 drops, oil of wintergreen 10 drops, glycerine 1 ounce, water 1 ounce. Dose, 1 teaspoonful when required.

Hair Tonic.—Tincture of Spanish fly 3 drams, castor oil 2 drams, oil of rosemary 1 dram, oil of rose geranium 3 drops, alcohol sufficient to make 4 ounces. Apply to scalp with fingers every 3 days.

Shampoo, or Scalp Cleaner.—Carbonate of potash 1 ounce, water of ammonia ¼ ounce, alcohol 4 ounces, water sufficient to make 8 ounces. Wet the head and pour sufficient of the solution to raise a good lather when rubbed. Then rinse with luke-warm water and dry.

VEGETABLES.

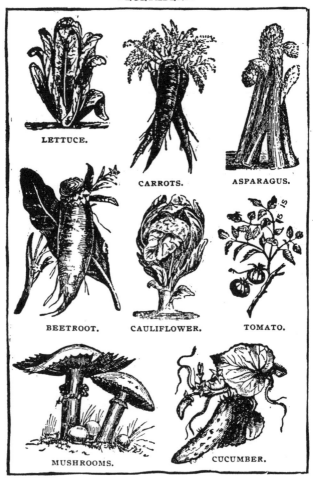

LETTUCE.

CARROTS.

ASPARAGUS.

BEETROOT.

CAULIFLOWER.

TOMATO.

MUSHROOMS.

CUCUMBER.

DEPARTMENT IV.

RECIPES FOR THE HOUSEHOLD.

RENOVATING RECIPES.

Cleaning Compound.—Mix 1 ounce of borax and 1 ounce gum camphor with 1 quart boiling water; when cool add 1 pint of alcohol, bottle and cork tightly. When wanted for use, shake well and sponge the garments to be cleaned. This is an excellent mixture for cleaning soiled black cashmere and woolen dresses, coat collars, and black felt hats.

Cream.—One-half pound white castile soap, ½ pound lump ammonia, 2 ounces alcohol, 2 ounces ether; cut the soap up fine and dissolve in 1 quart of hot water; then take off the fire and add 4 quarts cold water and the other ingredients. Bottle at once and cork tightly.

Coal Oil, To Remove.—Cover the spot with finely powdered chalk or cornmeal; lay a paper over it and rub it over with a moderately heated iron. To or three applications are all that is necessary.

Cloth, To Clean.—You need dry Fuller's earth moistened with lemon juice and a small quantity of powdered pearl ash; mix the Fuller's earth and pearl ash into balls with sufficient lemon juice to moisten; scour the cloth with the balls.

Cleaning Lace.—Fill a large bottle with cold water, and sew around it some clean, old white muslin. Tack one end of the lace to the muslin, and wrap the lace around the bottle, taking care to have no wrinkles; with a clean sponge and pure sweet oil saturate the lace thoroughly through the wrappings to the bottle, which is to be fastened by strings in a wash-kettle. Pour in a strong, cold lather of white castile soap and boil the suds until the lace is white and clean. Dry the bottle in the sun, remove the lace and wrap it around a ribbon block or press.

Cleaning Picture Frames.—Dingy or rusty gilt picture frames may be improved by simply washing them with a small sponge moistened with spirits of wine or oil of turpentine, the sponge only to be sufficiently wet to take off the dirt and fly marks. They should not be wiped afterward, but left to dry of themselves.

Cleaning Stains, Spots and Mildew from Furniture. —Take ½ pint of 98 per cent alcohol, ¼ ounce each of pulverized resin and gum shellac, add ½ pint of linseed oil, shake well and apply with a brush or sponge. Sweet oil will remove finger marks from varnished furniture, and kerosene from oiled furniture.

Cleaning Gilt Frames. —Gilt frames may be revived by carefully dusting them, and then washing with 1 ounce of soda beaten up with the whites of three eggs. Scraped patches should be touched up with gold paint. Castile soap and water, with proper care, may be used to clean oil paintings. Other methods should not be employed without some skill.

Corsets, To Clean. —Take out the steels at front and sides, then scour thoroughly with tepid or cold lather of white castile soap; using a small scrubbing brush; do not lay them in water; when quite clean let cold water run off them quite freely from the spigot to rinse out the soap thoroughly. Dry without ironing (after pulling lengthwise to make them straight and shapely) in a cool place.

Coffee Stains, To Remove. —Mix the yolk of an egg with a little milk warm water, and use it as soap on the stain. For stains that have been on the material for some time add a few drops of alcohol to the egg and water.

Color, To Restore. —1. If the color is taken out by acids wet the spots with liquid ammonia to kill the acid, and then wet with chloroform to restore the color. If the color is destroyed by alkalies, wet with acid to destroy the alkali and then use chloroform to restore the color. 2. If discoloration from any acid the color may be restored by rubbing a solution of carbonate of soda or magnesia on the part. In this case avoid the use of soap with water, as the former will restore the red appearance.

Crape, To Renew. —1. Rinse it with ox gall and water to remove the dirt; afterward in clear water to remove the gall, and lastly in a little gum water to stiffen and crisp it. It is then clapped between the hands until dry. 2. Skimmed milk and water, with a little bit of glue in it, made scalding hot, restores rusty Italian crape. If clapped and pulled dry like muslin it will look as good as new.

Feathers, To Bleach. —To bleach black, brown or gray feathers. First thoroughly wash with soap and water to free from any oil they may contain; next transfer to bath composed of bichromate of potash dissolved in water, to which has been added a few drops of nitric or sulphuric acid. In this bath they readily lose their color and become almost white. On being removed from this bath they should be well rinsed in water, and are then fit to be dyed, even the most delicate color. Great care is required in the process, as the flue of the feather is apt to be destroyed if kept too long in the bath. A bleached feather may be readily known by the yellow color of its stem.

Freshening Crape.—Brush the crape well with a soft brush, and hold tightly over a wide-mouthed jug of boiling water, gradually stretching it over the jug. If a stripe of crape, it is very easily held tightly over the water, letting the portion done fall over the jug until it is all completed. The crape will become firm and fit for use, every mark and fold being removed. White or colored crape may be washed and pinned over a newspaper, or towel, on the outside of a bed, until dry. Crape that has been exposed to rain or damp—veils especially—may be saved from spoiling by being stretched tightly on the outside of the bed with pins, until dry; and no crape should be left to dry without having been pulled into proper shape. If black crape, lace, or net, is faded or turned brown, it may be dipped into water, colored with the blue-bag, adding a lump of loaf sugar to stiffen, and pinned to a newspaper on a bed.

For Bleaching Cotton Cloth.—One pound chloride of lime, dissolved and strained; put in 2 or 3 pails of water; thoroughly wet the cloth and leave it over night: then rinse well in two waters. This will also take out mildew, and is equally good for brown cotton or white that has become yellow from any cause, and will not injure the fabric.

For Cleaning Merino or Any Woolen Stuff.—Purchase at a drug store 2 cents worth of carbonate of ammonia. Place it in a clean quart basin, and pour upon it a pint of boiling water; cover it with a clean plate, and let it stand till cold. Then proceed the same as directed for cleaning black silks. Gentlemen's clothes can thus be cleaned without taking to pieces, or ironing, unless quite convenient. Vests and coat collars are thus easily renovated, the color is revived, grease spots and white seams removed.

Freshen Marble.—Mix a bullock's gall with 4 ounces of soap lees and 2 ounces of turpentine, add pipe clay and make it into a paste. Apply it to the marble, and let it remain 24 hours; rub it off, and if not clean, repeat it till it is.

Feathers, To Clean.—Cut some white curd soap in small pieces; pour boiling water on them and add a little pearlash. When the soap is dissolved and the mixture cool enough for the hand to bear, plunge the feathers into it and draw them through the hand till the dirt appears to be squeezed out of them. Pass them through a clean lather with some blueing in it; then rinse them in cold water with blue, to give them a good color; beat them against the hand to shake off the water, and dry by shaking them near a fire. Black feathers may be cleaned with some water and gall, proceeding as above.

Feathers, to Curl.—When they are nearly dry draw each fibre or flue over the edge of a blunt knife, turning it around in the direction you wish the curl to take: thus, if the feather is to be flat, place it between the leaves of a book and press it.

Feathers, To Restore.—Take a little salt and sprinkle it on the hot stove, and hold the plume over the smoke a few minutes.

Gloves, Kid, To Clean.—1. After thoroughly cleansing the hands, put on the gloves and wash them, as though washing the hands, in a bowl of spirits of turpentine. Naphtha may be used instead of turpentine, with equally good results. After washing hang the gloves in a current of air, or in a warm room, taking care that no dust settles on them. **2.** Go over them with a clean towel dipped in skim milk, wearing them during the process and until they are quite dry. **3.** Dissolve 3 ounces of soap by heat in 2 ounces of water, and when nearly cold add 2 ounces of eau-de-javelle and 1 dram of water of ammonia; form a paste, which is to be rubbed over the gloves with flannel until sufficiently clean.

Genuine Cleaning Fluid.—Take 1½ ounces alcohol, ¼ ounce bay rum, ½ ounce oil wintergreen, ⅛ ounce aqua ammonia, ¼ ounce chloroform, 1 ounce sulphuric ether; let stand 6 hours in a tightly corked bottle; then add 1 ounce pulverized borax and 1 gallon deodorized gasoline.

Magic Annihilator.—To make 1 gross 8-ounce bottles; Aqua ammonia 1 gallon, soft water 8 gallons, best white soap 4 pounds, saltpetre 8 ounces; shave the soap fine, add the water, boil until the soap is dissolved, let it get cold, then add the saltpetre, stirring until dissolved. Now strain, let the suds settle, skim off the dry suds, add the ammonia, bottle and cork at once.

WHAT IT WILL DO.—It will remove all kinds of grease and oil spots from every variety of wearing apparel, such as coats, pants, vests, dress goods, carpets, etc., without injury to the finest silks or laces. It will shampoo like a charm, raising the lather in proportion to the amount of dandruff and grease in the hair. A cloth wet with it will remove all grease from door knobs, window sills, etc., handled by kitchen domestics in their daily routine of kitchen work. It will remove paint from a board, I care not how hard or dry it is, if oil is used in the paint, yet it will not injure the finest textures. Its chemical action is such that it turns any oil or grease into soap, which is easily washed out with clear, cold water. For cleaning silver, brass and copper ware it can't be beat. It is certain death to bed bugs, for they will never stop after they have encountered the Magic Annihilator.

DIRECTIONS FOR USE.—For grease spots, pour upon the article to be cleaned a sufficient quantity of the Magic Annihilator, rubbing well with a clean sponge, and applying to both sides of the article you are cleaning. Upon carpets and coarse goods, where the grease is hard and dry, use a stiff brush and wash out with clear, cold water. Apply again if necessary. One application is all that is needed for any fresh grease spots, but for old or dried a second may be required. For shampooing take a small quantity of the Magic Annihilator with an equal quantity of water, apply to the hair with a stiff brush, brushing into the pores of the scalp, and wash out with clear water. You will be surprised at the silk gloss of your hair. For cleaning silverware, etc., buy

5 cents worth of whitening, mix a small quantity with the Magic Annihilator and apply with a rag, rubbing briskly. For killing bed bugs, apply to the places they frequent, and they will leave in short order. You will find it useful in many other ways.

Nitrate of Silver or Nitric Acid Stains, To Remove.— **1.** Apply iodine, and afterwards rub briskly with strong water of ammonia. **2.** Apply diluted solutions of permanganate of potassa and hydrochloric acid, followed by washing with hyposulphite of soda solution, rinsing in plenty of fresh water.

Paint, To Remove.—When fresh, make repeated applications of spirits of turpentine or alcohol, rub down with a soft rag or flannel; ether also will answer if applied immediately. When neither turpentine nor benzine will remove paint spots from garments, try chloroform; it will remove paint which has been on for 6 months.

Ribbons, To Clean.—Gin ½ pint, honey ½ pound, soft soap ½ pound, water ⅛ pint; mix the above, then lay each breadth of silk upon a clean table and scrub well on the solid side with the mixture; have ready 3 vessels of cold water, take each piece of silk at two corners and dip it up and down in each vessel, but do not wring it, and take care that each piece has one vessel of quite clean water for the last dip; hanging it up dripping for a minute or two, then dab in a cloth and iron quickly with a very hot iron.

Sealing Wax, To Remove.—Dissolve the spots with alcohol or naptha; apply with a camel's-hair brush.

Spots and Stains from Dresses, To Remove.—To remove grease spots from cotton or woolen materials absorbent paste, purified bullock's blood and even common soap are used; apply to the spot when dry. When the colors are not fast, use fuller's earth or pulverized potter's clay; lay in a layer over the spot and press it with a very hot iron; from silks, moires and plain or brocade satins, begin by pouring over the spot 2 drops of rectified spirits, cover it over with a linen cloth instantly; the spot will look tarnished, for a portion of the grease still remains; this will be removed entirely by a little sulphuric ether dropped on the spot and a very little rubbing. If neatly done, no perceptible mark or circle will remain, nor will the luster of the richest silk be changed, the union of the two liquors operating with no injurious effects from rubbing; eau de cologne will also remove grease from cloth and silk.

Fruit Spots are removed from white and fast-colored cottons by the use of chloride of soda; commence by cold soaping the article, then touch the spot with a hair pencil or feather, dipped in the chloride, dipping it immediately in cold water to prevent the texture of the article being injured.

Ink Spots are removed by a few drops of hot water being applied immediately when fresh; by the same process, iron mold in linen or calico may be removed, dipping immediately in cold water to prevent injury to the fabric.

WAX dropped on a shawl, table cover or cloth dress is easily discharged by applying alcohol.

SYRUP AND PRESERVES.—By washing in lukewarm water with a dry cloth and pressing the spot between two folds of clean linen. Essence of lemon will remove grease, but it will make a spot itself in a few days.

To Remove Iron Rust from muslins or white goods, thoroughly saturate the spots with lemon juice and salt, and expose to the sun; usually more than one application is necessary. To prevent its reappearance, enclose in a muslin bag when being boiled.

To Renovate Black Goods.—Dissolve 4 ounces of castile soap shavings in a quart of boiling water; when cold add 4 ounces of ammonia, 2 ounces each of ether, alcohol and glycerine, and a gallon of clear, cold water; mix thoroughly and bottle. For men's clothing, he vy cloth, etc., dilute a small quantity in an equal amount of water, and, following the nap of the goods, sponge the stains with a piece of similar goods or a small sponge. The grease that gathers upon the collars of coats will immediately disappear, and the undiluted fluid will remove the more obstinate spots. When clean dry with another cloth, and press the underside with a warm iron This fluid is also useful when painted walls and woodwork need scouring, a cupful to a pail of warm water being the proper proportions.

To Restore Scorched Linen.—Slice 2 onions and extract the juice, to which add ½ ounce of white soap, 2 ounces of fuller's earth and ½ pint of vinegar; boil well, and spread it over the scorched places, leaving it to dry; wash the article.

To Remove Ink Stains.—1. Cream of tartar 1 ounce, salts of sorrel 1 ounce; mix well, and keep well corked. **2.** Wash carefully with clean water, and apply oxalic acid; if the latter changes the dye to a red tinge, restore the color with diluted water of ammonia.

To Wash Silk.—For a dress to be washed, the seams of a skirt do not require to be ripped apart, though it must be removed from the band at the waist and the lining taken from the bottom; trimmings or drapings, where there are deep folds, the bottom of which is very difficult to reach, should be undone so as to remain flat. A black silk dress, without being previously washed, may be refreshed by being soaked during 24 hours in soft clear water, clearness in the water being indispensable; if dirty, the black dress may be previously washed; when very old and rusty, a pint of gin or whisky should be mixed with each gallon of water; this addition is an improvement under any circumstances, whether the silk be previously washed or not. After soaking, the dress should be hung up to drain dry without being wrung. The mode of washing silk is as follows: The article should be laid upon a smooth, clean table, the flannel should be well soaped, just made wet with lukewarm water, and the surface of the silk rubbed one way with it, care being taken that this rubbing is quite even; when the dirt has disappeared, the soap must be washed off with a sponge and plenty of cold water, of which the sponge must be made to absorb as much as possible; as soon as one side is finished, the other must be washed in precisely the same manner. Let it be understood that not more of either surface must be done at a time than can be spread perfectly flat upon the table, and the hand conveniently reach; likewise, the soap must be quite sponged off one portion before application is made to another. Silks, when washed, should be dried in the shade on a horse and alone; if black or dark blue, they will be improved if, when dry, they are placed on a table and well sponged with gin or whisky and dried again. Either of these liquors alone will remove, without washing, the dirt or grease from a black necktie or handkerchief of the same color, which will be so renovated by the application as to appear almost new.

Tar, To Remove.—Scrape off as much as possible, then wet the place thoroughly with good salad oil or melted lard and let it remain for 24 hours; if linen or cotton, wash it out in strong, warm soap suds; if woolen or silk, take out the grease with ether or spirits of wine.

Velveteen, To Clean.—To wash velveteen use cold water, and do not wring, but shake thoroughly; spread on the line as much as possible; when partly dry, take down and shake again.

Velvets, To Restore.—1. The best mode of cleaning any kind of velvet is to sponge it with benzoline, and apply a weak solution of gum arabic to the back; then sew it in a frame (an embroidery frame will do) and iron it on the wrong side with a damp rag placed between. If the nap requires raising, hold it with the wrong side downward over a basin of hot water; if there are any grease spots, pour turpentine on the place and rub it till dry with a flannel. **2.** Strain it tightly over a board and sponge with pure Holland gin, the sponge being squeezed out very hard, that it may be damp, not wet; then hold near a fire, the wrong side to the heat, until the pile begins to rise; iron by pressing the wrong side over the edge of a warm flat iron, as no pressure must come on the right side.

RECIPES FOR THE LAUNDRY.

Including blueing, washing powders, soaps and enamels, with general hints and instructions as to the best methods of washing particular fabrics. Some valuable formulas will also be found in renovating recipes.

Blankets, To Wash.—Put 2 large tablespoonfuls of borax and 1 pint bowl of soft soap into a tub of cold water; when dissolved, put in a pair of blankets and let them remain over night;

next rub them out and rinse thoroughly in 2 waters and hang them to dry; do not wring them. This recipe will also apply to the washing of all kinds of flannels and woolen goods.

Bleaching Cotton.—Thirty yards of cotton cloth may be bleached in 15 minutes by 1 large spoonful of sal soda and 1 pound of chloride of lime dissolved in soft water. After taking out the cloth, rinse it in soft cold water, so that it may not rot; the color of French linen may be preserved by a bath of strong tea or common hay; calicos, with pink or green colors, will be brightened if vinegar is put in the rinsing water; while soda is used for purple and blue. If it is desired to set colors previous to washing, put a spoonful of ox galls to a gallon of water, and soak the fabrics in the liquid; colored napkins are put in lye before washing to set the color: the color of black cloth is freshened if it is put in a pail of water containing a teaspoonful of lye.

Bleaching Linen.—Linen may be bleached in a similar way to cotton, but the process is made more troublesome and tedious owing to its greater affinity for the coloring matter existing in it in the raw state.

Bluing, For Clothes.—Take 1 ounce of soft Prussian blue, powder it and put in a bottle with a quart of clear rainwater, and add ¼ ounce of oxalic acid; a teaspoonful is sufficient for a large washing.

Chemical Compound.—Aqua ammonia 2 ounces, soft water 1 quart, saltpeter 1 teaspoonful, shaving soap, in shavings, 1 ounce; mix all together; dissolve the soap well, and any grease or dirt that cannot be removed with this preparation, nothing else need be tried for it.

Iron Rust, To Remove.—*See Renovating Recipes.*

Ink Stains, To Remove.—*See Renovating Recipes.*

Improved Troy Starch Enamel.—Melt 5 pounds of refined paraffine wax in a tin boiler or pan over a slow fire; use care in melting. When melted, remove the vessel from the fire and add 200 drops of oil of citronelli. Take some new round tin pie pans, and oil them with sweet oil as you would for pie baking, but do not use lard. Put these pans on a level table, and pour in enough of the hot wax to make a depth in each pan equal to about the thickness of one-eighth of an inch. While hot, glance over the pans to see that they are level. As this is very essential, please remember it. If the pans are not level, the cakes will be all thickness, which should not be so. Then let them cool, but not too fast. Watch them closely, and have a tin stamp ready to stamp the cakes out about the size of an ordinary lozenge. This stamp should be about 8 inches long, larger at the top than at the bottom, so that the cakes can pass up through the stamp as you are cutting them out of the pans. Lay the cakes in another pan to cool. Before they become very hard, separate them from each other; if not, it will be difficult to do so when they become very hard; do not neglect this.

Direction for Use.—To a pint of boiling starch stir in 1 cake or tablet. This gives an excellent luster to linen or muslin, and imparts a splendid perfume to the clothes, and makes the iron pass very smoothly over the surface. It requires but half the ordinary labor to do an ironing. It is admired by every lady. It prevents the iron from adhering to the surface, and the clothes remain clean and neat much longer than by any other method.

Mildew, From Linen.—1. To extract from linen, put strong soap and salt on the mildew spots, keep them moist and expose to the sun; repeat the process several times. The soap used should be soft, such as is home-made from the lye of wood ashes. 2. Mix soft soap and powdered starch, half as much salt and juice of a lemon, put it on both sides with a brush, let it lay on the grass for a day and a night until the stains come out.

New England Soap.—Take 3 pounds hard white soap, shave it up fine, dissolve it in 10 quarts boiling water; add 1 ounce salts of tartar, 3 ounces borax; then take the same from the fire and set it away to cool; as soon as it becomes cool enough to bear your hand in, add 1 ounce liquid ammonia; stir each article as you put it in.

Patent Soap.—Half pint turpentine, 3 pints sal soda, 3 pounds grease, 2 pounds resin soap, 40 gallons water; boil 1 hour and it is fit for use. This is a great soap.

Soaps, Soft.—1. Put 1½ pails lye that will bear an egg in the soap barrel and add 8 pounds of melted grease free from sediment; thin with weak lye as it is obtained from the leach; stir occasionally. It should thicken and be ready for use in 2 or 3 days, providing the weather is warm or the barrel stands in a warm place. 2. Three-quarters pound washing soda and 1 pound brown soap (cut in small pieces); put into a large stone jar on the back of the range when not very hot and pour over it a pailful of cold water; stir occasionally and when dissolved put it away to cool. It forms a sort of jelly, and is excellent to remove grease from floors and shelves.

Soaps, Hard.—1. Three pounds grease, 1 pound Babbitt's potash, 10 quarts water. ½ pound borax; boil 4 or 5 hours; pour into a square wooden box, and when cold cut into blocks and set away to dry. 2. Five pounds grease, 1 pound concentrated potash, and 2 quarts water; put the potash into the water, and when dissolved heat the grease and add to it; let it stand over night and in the morning add 4 quarts of water and boil; turn out and set aside to dry.

To Glaze Linen.—The gloss or enamel, as it is sometimes called, is produced mainly by friction with a warm iron and may be put on linen by almost any person. The linen to be glazed to receive as much strong starch as it is possible for it to take up; then it is dried. To each pound of starch a piece of sperm or white wax about the size of a walnut is usually added; when ready to be ironed the linen is laid upon the table and moistened very lightly on the surface with a clean wet cloth; it is then ironed in the usual way with a flatiron, and is then ready for the glossing operation. For this purpose a flatiron weighing about 6 pounds is used; the heel of the iron is knocked off and made round and smooth; it should be heated as hot as possible, and the gloss is made by ironing across the fabric, instead of lengthways, as in the usual, the heel of the iron, or the rounded part, being used, not the face of the iron. "Elbow-grease" is the principal secret in the art of glossing linen.

To Soften Hard Water.—Boil it and expose to the air; add a little soda.

Washing Fluid.—Two pounds crude potash, 1 ounce sal ammoniac ½ ounce saltpeter, 2 gallons rain water, 1 pint for 8 gallons of water and 1 pound soap; put the clothes to soak over night and rinse in the morning.

Washing Powder.—Mix any quantity of soda ash with an equal portion of carbonate of soda (ordinary soda) crushed into coarse grains. Have a thin solution of glue or decoction of linseed oil ready, into which pour the soda until quite thick. Spread it out on boards in a warm apartment to dry.

RECIPES FOR CLEANING AND REPAIRING.

In every department of household work these valuable recipes will be found of untold worth. Read carefully.

Barrels, To Clean.—**1.** Scald well with boiling water, and let the water stand until cold; then fill with cold water and throw in a large quantity of live coals from a wood fire, leaving the cask uncovered; by repeating this the casks may be made perfectly sweet, providing they have not at any time contained fish. **2.** Fill with meal or bran and water and let stand until fermentation takes place. It will thoroughly cleanse them, and the mixture will afterwards do for food for hogs.

Brass, To Clean.—See Silver Powders, etc., in *The Chemist Department*-

Brass or Copper Kettles, To Clean.—A brass bell metal or copper kettle should be cleaned immediately after it is used. Even when not used it requires occasional cleaning, otherwise it will collect rust or verdigris, which is a strong poison. After washing the kettle with warm water; put into it a teacupful of vinegar and a tablespoonful of salt; place it over the fire, and when hot rub the kettle thoroughly with a cloth, taking care that the salt and vinegar touches every part, then wash with warm water; next take some wood ashes or fine sand and scour well; afterward wash with hot soap suds and finish by rinsing and wiping dry.

Brilliant Self-Shining Stove Polish.—This is one of the greatest inventions of the age. It has been the result of a large amount of study on the part of the inventor to perfect a polish that would work easily and satisfactorily in a perfectly dry state, thereby obviating the disagreeable task of mixing and preparing. A good stove polish is an absolute necessity in every family. It is only a question, then, of offering the best to make a sale. To prove that this polish is the best is an easy task. All you have to do is to have a box open and a piece of rag to begin operations. You now approach the stove and apply the polish. The result will be so startlingly beautiful that no further words will be necessary. If the stove is not convenient, anything will do to experiment with. You can produce on a piece of wood, a scrap of paper or a potato, a lustre equal to a burnished mirror.

RECIPE.—Take plumbago (black lead) finely pulverized and put in 2-ounce wood boxes, nicely labeled, and sell for 10 or 15 cents a box. Wholesale to stores and agents at $6 a hundred. Costs less than 3 cents a box to manufacture.

DIRECTIONS FOR USE.—Use a damp woolen rag, dip in the box, and apply to the stove Then polish with a dry cloth, and a most beautiful polish will appear.

Brittannia, To Clean.—Recipes for cleaning Brittannia, Silver, etc., will be found in *Department II.*, under the sub-head of "Gold and Silver Powders, etc."

Brushes, To Clean.—Hair brushes may be cleaned as follows: Dissolve a piece of soda in some hot water, allowing a piece the size of a walnut to a quart of water. Put the water into a basin, and after combing out the hair from the brushes, dip them, bristles downward, into the water and out again, keeping the backs and handles as free from the water as possible. Repeat this until the bristles look clean; then rinse the brushes in a little cold water; shake well, and wipe the handles and backs with a towel, but not the bristles, and set the brushes to dry in the sun, or near the fire; but take care not to put them too close to it. Wiping the bristles of a brush makes them soft, as does also the use of soap.

Combs, To Clean.—If it can be avoided, never wash combs, as the water often makes the teeth split, and the tortoise shell or horn of which they are made, rough. Small brushes, manufactured purposely for cleaning combs, may be purchased at a trifling cost; with this the comb should be well brushed, and afterward wiped with a cloth or towel.

Carpets, To Clean.–1. Shake and beat well, lay upon the floor and tack down firmly; then with a clean flannel cloth wash over with 1 quart of bullock's gall, mixed with 3 quarts of cold soft water, then rub it off with a clean flannel or linen cloth. Any very dirty spots should be rubbed with pure gall. **2.** If the carpets are so much soiled as to require cleaning all over, after the dirt has been shaken out, spread on a clean floor and rub on them with a new broom grated raw potatoes; let the carpets remain until dry before walking on them. **3.** Half a bar of castile soap, 2 ounces borax, 2 ounces washing soda: boil in ½ gallon of water until dissolved then add 2 gallons of tepid water and boil 10 minutes; when cold add ½ pint of alcohol: rub on with clean piece of flannel.

Carpets and Floor Cloths, To Remove Grease From.—1. Aqua ammonia 2 ounces, soft water 1 quart, saltpeter 1 teaspoonful, soap shavings 1 ounce; mix well; shake and let it stand 24 hours before using to dissolve the soap; when used pour on enough to cover any grease or oil that has been spilled, spraying and rubbing well, and apply again if necessary; then wash off with clean cold water.

Carpets, To Remove Ink From.—As soon as the ink has been spilled take up as much as you can with a sponge, and then pour on cold water repeatedly, still taking up the liquid; next rub the place with a little oxalic acid dissolved in cold water; then rub on some hartshorn.

Ceilings, To Clean.—See Wall Papers to Clean.

Floors, To Clean.—Take ¼ pound of Fuller's earth and ¼ pound pearlash; make them into a paste with about a quart of boiling water; spread a thick coating of this over the grease-stains and leave it for 10 or 12 hours; then wash it off with clean water, using sand if necessary. If the grease stains are very numerous and the floor very dirty a coating may be spread all over the floor and left for 24 hours before it is washed off. In washing boards never wash crossways, but always up and down with the grain.

Furniture, To Clean.—1. To improve the appearance of furniture, take a soft sponge wet with clean cold water and wash over the article, then take a soft chamois skin and wipe; dry the skin by wringing, and wipe the furniture, being careful to wipe only one way; never use a dry chamois on varnish work. In deeply-carved work the dust cannot be removed with a sponge; use a stiff-haired paint brush instead; for unpolished furniture, linseed oil is the best for cleaning; rub it thoroughly. **2.** Kerosene is excellent for cleaning furniture, either walnut or oak. **3.** The following is excellent for cleaning and polishing old furniture: Make a mixture of a quart of cold beer or vinegar, with a handful of common salt and a tablespoonful of muriatic acid and boil for 15 minutes; put it in a bottle and warm when wanted for use; wash the furniture with soft hot water, so as to remove the dirt, then apply the mixture, then polish with a soft flannel rag.

NOTE.—For complete list of polishes see "Polishes," *All Trades Department.*

Furniture Polish.—1. Beeswax ½ pound, alkanet ¼ ounce; melt together in a pipkin until the former is well colored; then add linseed oil and spirits of turpentine, of each ½ gill; strain through a piece of coarse muslin. **2.** Equal parts of sweet oil and vinegar and a pint of gum arabic finely powdered; shake the bottle and apply with a rag. It will make furniture look as good as new.—**3** (French Furniture Polish). Alcohol 98 per cent 1 pint, gum copal and shellac, of each 1 ounce, dragon's blood; mix and dissolve by setting in a warm place. **4.** Best vinegar 1 pint, turpentine ½ pint; mix and apply with a brush. **5.** One pint of boiled oil, 4 ounces of vinegar, 2 ounces of spirits of camphor, 1 ounce of ammonia, ½ ounce of antimony; shake and let stand 2 or 3 days before using. **6.** Rectified spirits of wine ¼ pint, gum shellac ½ ounce, pulverized rozum ½ ounce, raw linseed oil ½ pint; put gums into rectified wine and, when thoroughly dissolved, mix with linseed oil; shake well before using **7.** For French polishing cabinet-makers use: Pale shellac ½ pound, mastic 1 2-5 ounces; alcohol of 90 per cent standard 1 to 1 1-5 pints; dissolve cold, with frequent stirring.

Gilt Frames, To Brighten.—Take sufficient flour of sulphur to give a golden tinge to about 1½ pints of water, and in this boil 4 or 5 bruised onions, or garlic, which will answer the same purpose; strain off the liquid, and with it, when cold, wash with a soft brush, any gilding which requires restoring, and when dry it will come out as bright as new work. They may also be brightened in the following manner: Beat up the white of eggs with chloride of potassa or soda, in the proportion of 3 ounces of eggs to 1 ounce of chloride of potassa or soda; blow off as much dust as possible from the frames, and paint them over with a soft brush dipped in the above mixture; they will immediately come out fresh and bright.

How to Polish Horns.—First boil the horn to remove the pith, if it has been freshly taken from the animal. If it is an old, dry horn, the pith may be dried out, and boiling is not necessary; but it may be laid in hot water for a short time to make it soft. Then scrape off all the roughness with a coarse file, a knife or a piece of glass. When the rough spots are removed rub around the horn with coarse sandpaper, then with a finer kind. After this, rub the horn lengthwise with a flannel cloth which has been dipped in powdered pumice stone or rotten stone, and moistened in linseed oil. This rubbing should continue till all the sandpaper marks are removed, then give a final rubbing with a clean flannel cloth, and lastly, with a piece of tissue paper.

Liquid Stove Polish.—Mix 2 parts of copperas, 1 of bone black, 1 of pulverized graphite, with sufficient water to form a creamy paste. This stove polish is as nearly odorless as possible.

Mahogany Furniture Varnish.—Take of proof alcohol 1 quart, cut therein all the gum shellac it will take, add 2 ounces of Venice turpentine, and coloring to suit. This makes a beautiful polish and will wear for years.

To Take Stains Out of Mahogany.—Mix spirits of salts 6 parts, salt of lemons 1 part, then drop a little on the stains, and rub them till they disappear.

Piano Polish.—Take equal proportions of turpentine, linseed oil and vinegar; mix; rub in well with a piece of flannel cloth. Then polish with a piece of chamois skin. This treatment will entirely remove the dingy appearance that age gives to fine woods.

Polish for Removing Stains, Spots and Mildew from Furniture.—Take of 98 per cent alcohol ½ pint, pulverized resin and gum shellac, of each ¼ ounce. Let these cut in the alcohol; then add linseed oil ½ pint; shake well, and apply with a sponge, brush, or cotton flannel, or an old newspaper, rubbing it well after the application, which gives a nice polish.

To Renew Old Oil Paintings.—The blackened lights of old pictures may be instantly restored to their original hue by touching them with deutoxide of hydrogen diluted with 6 or 8 times its weight of water. The part must be afterward washed with a clean sponge and water.

To Get ⸬ Broken Cork Out of a Bottle.—If in drawing a cork, it breaks, and the lower part falls down into the liquid, tie a long loop in a bit of twine, or small cord, and put it in, holding the bottle so as to bring the piece of cork near to the lower part of the neck. Catch it in the loop, so as to hold it stationary. You can then easily extract it with a corkscrew.

A Wash for Cleaning Silver.—Mix together ½ ounce of fine salt, ½ ounce of powdered alum, ½ ounce of cream of tartar; put them into a large whiteware pitcher, and pour on 2 quarts of water, and stir them frequently, till entirely dissolved. Then transfer the mixture to clean bottles. and cork them closely. Before using it, shake the bottles well. Pour some of the liquid into a bowl, and wash the silver all over with it, using an old. soft, fine linen cloth. Let it stand about 10 minutes, and then rub it dry, with a buckskin. It will make the silver look like new.

Glass, To Clean.—1. Soda in water will clean glass. **2.** Take powdered indigo, dip into it a moistened linen rag, smear over the glass with it, and then wipe it off with a perfectly dry cloth or finely-sifted wood ashes applied bp a rag dipped in alcohol or ammonia will answer just as well.

Glass Windows, To Prevent Steaming.—Clean the glass occasionally with a cloth moistened with pure glycerine, wiping it so as to leave only a trace of the glycerine adhering to the surface—this on the inside.

Ivory, To Clean.—To clean and preserve the color of ivory ornaments, brooches, card-cases, bracelets, chains, etc., place the articles to be cleansed in a basin of cold water and allow them to stand for 24 hours. Take them out of the water and lay them on a clean, soft towel, but do not wipe them, they must dry by the air, and any water that remains in the carving of the ivory should be blown out; if allowed to settle on the ivory it would destroy tne color.

Lamp Chimneys, To Clean.—Rub lamp chimneys with

newspapers on which has been poured a little kerosene. This will make them much clearer than if soap is used; they will also be less liable to crack.

Lamp Burners, To Clean.—Wash them in ashes and water, and they will come out clean and bright.

Looking Glasses, To Clean.—Remove with a damp sponge fly stains and other soils (the sponge may be damped with water or spirits of wine). After this dust the surface with the finest sifted whiting or powder-blue and polish it with a silk handkerchief or soft cloth. Snuff of candle, if quite free from grease, is an excellent polish for looking glasses.

Marble, To Clean.—**1.** Take 2 parts of soda, 1 of pumice stone, and 1 of finely-powdered chalk: sift these through a fine sieve and mix them into a paste with water; rub this well all over the marble and the stains will be removed; then wash it in soap and water and a beautiful bright polish will be produced. **2.** Muriatic acid 2 pounds, acetic acid ½ pound, verdigris ¼ ounce; mix and apply with a brush; wash the stone after with sponge and water; after the stone is clean rub it smooth with pumice stone, keeping it wet with water: after some little practice you can clean an old, dirty tombstone so that a marble cutter cannot detect it from being new work.

Paint, To Clean.—See Magic Annihilator in Renovating Recipes, also To Renovate Black Goods. Either of these recipes is excellent for paint. Royal Washing Powder in Laundry Recipes is also good.

Paint, Glue Paint for Kitchen Floors.—To 3 pounds spruce yellow add 1 pound, or 2 if desired, of dry white lead, and mix well together; dissolve 2 ounces of glue in 1 quart of water, stirring often until smooth and nearly boiling; thicken the gum water after the manner of mush, until it will spread smoothly upon the floor. Use a common paint brush and apply hot.

Rust, To Remove From Steel.—**1.** Every particle of iron rust when the iron is not eaten into may be removed by softening it with petroleum (kerosene), and then rubbing well with coarse sandpaper. **2.** Rub well with sweet oil and in 48 hours use unslacked lime powdered very fine; rub until the rust disappears.

Rust on Tin,—If tinware is well rubbed with lard and then with common unslaked lime before being put away it will never rust: this is also the best plan to remove rust. **2.** Rub fresh lard on every part, then put it in an oven and heat it thoroughly; thus treated any tinware may be used in water constantly and remain bright and free from rust indefinitely.

Silver, To Clean.—**1.** Silver-plate can be beautifully cleaned and made to look like new by dipping a soft cloth or chamois-skin in a weak preparation of ammonia water and rubbing the articles with it. **2.** Wash in hot water containing a quantity of concentrated lye, or if very black boil for some time in soft water with a considerable amount of washing soda added; then wash in a good suds; rinse in clear water, and rub with a flannel cloth or, better, soft chamois-skin.

Silvers, Powders and Liquids for Plating and Polishing.—(*See Chemical Department.*)

Sponges, To Clean.—The following is a very simple and certain way of cleaning sponges from grease or any other impurities: Take some soda and break it up; measure about 3 tablespoonsful, put it (as much as you can) into the holes of the sponge, and keep the rest; then fill a large jug with boiling water and immediately put in your sponge and all your soda; cover over and leave it standing for about 12 hours; after you rinse it well you will see the sponge look almost like a new one.

Gilt Jewelry, To Clean.—Wash the brooch, earrings, etc., with soap and water; rinse, and with a small, soft brush wash the article with spirits of hartshorn.

Tight Ring, To Remove.—If the finger on which the ring has been placed has swollen, and there seems to be a difficulty of removing the ring, pass a needle and cotton under it, pull the cotton up toward the hand and twist the remaining cotton round the finger several times until it reaches the nail. By taking hold of the end nearest the hand it is generally an easy matter to slide the ring off the finger, however much difficulty there may have appeared in doing so before the experiment was tried.

Grease Eraser.—Benzine, alcohol, ether, equal parts: mix; apply with sponge (patting the spot); put a piece of blotting paper on each side and iron with a hot flatiron.

Gold Chains, To Clean.—Let the article required to be cleaned stand for some time in a solution of caustic potash until all the adhering dirt is removed.

White Silk Lace, To Clean.—The lace is stretched over small clean strips of wood to keep it evenly spread out, laid over night in warm milk, to which a little soap has been added, and rinsed in fresh water, laid for the same length of time in warm soap-lye, and finally rinsed without any friction. Linen lace is best cleaned by covering the outside of a large glass bottle smoothly with stout linen or white flannel, upon which the lace is sewn in a number of coils, and over the whole some coarse open tissue is secured. The bottle thus dressed is allowed to soak for a time in lukewarm soft water, and the outside wrapping is then rubbed with soap and a piece of flannel. After this the bottle is laid to steep for some hours in clean soft water. It is then rolled between dry towels, dipped in rice water, and rolled again. Finally the damp lace is unfastened from the bottle and ironed between linen cloths.

To Destroy the Effects of Acid on Clothes.—Dampen as soon as possible after exposure to the acid with spirits of ammonia; it will destroy the effect immediately.

Rendering Textiles Fireproof.—Dr. Doremus recommends phosphate of ammonia as a highly effective agent in rendering textiles uninflammable The fabrics are dipped in a watery solution of the salt, wrung out and dried, when, it is said, they will be found completely uninflammable. They will blacken, of course, and be destroyed where the flame touches them, but the flame will not spread, neither will there be any residue of red-hot cinders.

To Clean Brassware.—Mix 1 ounce of oxalic acid, 6 ounces of rotten stone, all in powder, 1 ounce of sweet oil, and sufficient water to make a paste; apply a small proportion and rub dry with a flannel or leather. The liquid dip most generally used consists of nitric and sulphuric acids, but this is more corrosive.

Stove Polish, To Make.—**1.** See "Brilliant Self-Shining Stove Polish" at beginning of this department. **2.** One-half pound black lead finely powdered, the whites of 3 eggs well beaten: dilute with sour beer until it becomes as thin as shoe blacking: after stirring, set over hot coals to simmer for 20 minutes; when cold, it may be kept for use. **3.** Polish for Grates: One pound of common asphaltum, ½ pint of linseed oil, 1 quart of oil of turpentine. Melt the asphaltum, and add gradually to it the other two ingredients. Apply this with a small painter's brush. and leave it to become perfectly dry. The grate will need no other cleaning, but will merely require dusting every day. and occasionally bru hing with a dry black lead brush. This is. of course. when no fires are used. When they are required, the bars, che ks and back of grate will need black-leading in the usual manner.

To Polish Tortoise Shell.—When by wear tortoise shell articles have lost their luster, the polished surface may be restored to its original condition by carefully rubbing with powdered rottenstone and oil. The rottenstone should be carefully sifted through the finest muslin. When all scratches on the surface of a tortoise shell are thus removed, a brilliant polish may be given to it by applying gentle friction with a piece of soft leather, to which some jeweler's rouge has been applied.

Treasury Department Whitewash.—The best in use. This wash is equally good on wood, brick or stone; is nearly as durable as paint and much cheaper. Slack ½ bushel of unslacked lime with boiling water. keeping it covered during the process; strain it and add a peck of salt dissolved in warm water; **3** pounds ground rice, put in boiling water and boiled to a thin paste: ½ pound powdered Spanish whiting and 1 pound of clear glue dissolved in hot water; mix these well together and let the mixture stand for several days. Keep the wash thus prepared in a kettle or portable furnace. and when used put it on as hot as possible with painter's or whitewash brushes.

To Paper Whitewashed Walls.—Make a flour starch as you would for starching calico clothes. and with a whitewash brush wet with the starch the wall you wish to paper. Let it dry; then, when it is wanted to apply the paper wet both the wall and paper with the starch, and apply the paper in the ordinary way.

To Clean Wall Paper.—The following is a most excellent and simple method of cleaning wallpaper, and can be used with confidence in every house: Take 1 quart of flour and stir in 5 cents' worth of ammonia and enough water to make a stiff dough; work and knead until smooth, then wipe the paper with this batch of dough, working it so that a clean surface will be presented with every stroke. Go over the paper in this way and your wall paper will be clean.

PESTS.

Recipes for the destruction of roaches, bugs, flies and other household pests.

Ants, Black.—1. A strong solution of carbolic acid and water poured into holes kills all ants it touches, and the survivors immediately take themselves off. **2.** A few leaves of green wormwood scattered among the haunts of these troublesome insects is said to be effective in dislodging them.

Ants, Red.—1. Set a quantity of cracked walnuts or shellbarks on plates, and put them in the closets and other places where the ants congregate. They are very fond of these and will collect on them in myriads; when they have collected, turn nuts and ants together into the fire, and then replenish the plates with fresh nuts. After they have become thinned out, powder some camphor and put in the holes and crevices. **2.** Grease a plate with lard and set it where the ants are troublesome; place a few sticks around the plate for the ants to climb upon; occasionally turn the plate over a fire where there is no smoke, and the pests will drop off into it; continue the operation until they are all caught; they will trouble nothing else while lard is near them.

Bed Bugs.—1. (See "Magic Annihilator" in Renovating Recipes.) **2.** Take the furniture in which they harbor to pieces and wash all the joints with soap and boiling water, carefully exploring all the cracks and openings with a stiff piece of wire; when the wood is dry, saturate the joints with kerosene oil, using a small paint brush; fill up the cracks with a mixture of plaster and linseed oil. If the rooms are papered, saturate the places where the paper joins the baseboards with benzine, using a brush or sponge, and carefully avoiding the presence of artificial light; do the same with linings of trunks. If the floor cracks are infested, fill them with plaster and linseed oil. **3.** Two ounces of red arsenic, ¼ pound of white soap, ½ ounce of camphor dissolved in a teaspoonful of alcohol, made into a paste of the consistency of cream; place this mixture in the openings and cracks of the bedstead.

Bees.—Place 2 or 3 shallow vessels half filled with water on the floors where they assemble, with strips of cardboard running from the edge of the vessel to the floor; they will eagerly ascend and find a watery grave.

Carpet Bugs.—Make a solution of 1 tablespoonful of corrosive sublimate in a quart of hot water, and saturate the floors and cracks of walls or closets; a weaker solution can be used to sponge the carpets: it is a sure cure.

Crickets.—Sprinkle a little quicklime near the cracks through which they enter the room; the lime may be laid down over night and swept away in the morning.

Cockroaches.—Mix together thoroughly 1 pound of powdered sugar, 1 pound of powdered borax and 10 cents' worth of paris green; put in all places which they infest with a puffer or blower.

Croton Bugs.—They attack the starch or sizing in the cloth covers of books, and often destroy the gold to secure the little albumen used in the work. Take a plentiful supply of powder in which pyrethrum is the principal ingredient; with a small bellows throw this powder among the books on the shelves and allow it to remain. This operation performed once a year will be sufficient to kill them out.

Fleas.—**1.** The oil of pennyroyal will drive these insects off, but a cheaper method, where the herb grows, is to throw the cat or dog whom they infest into a decoction of it once a week; when the herb cannot be obtained the oil can be used. Saturate cloths with it and tie around the necks of the dogs and cats. These applications should be repeated every 12 or 15 days. **2.** Oil of cloves 2½ drams, carbolic acid ½ dram, cologne 3 ounces, diluted alcohol 2 ounces; sprinkle bedding, beds, etc.

Flies.—See Sticky Fly Paper in Household Miscellany.

Fly Poison.—Sugar ½ ounce, ½ ounce thoroughly ground black pepper; make it to thin paste and place it on paper where the flies congregate.

Gnats.—The best preventative against gnats, as well as the best cure for their stings, is camphor.

Insect Powders, Persian.—The powder is the pulverized flowers of pyrethrum, carneum, and roseum, growing on the Caucasian mountains; it is not poisonous to man unless inhaled or swallowed in large quantities, but it is sure death to insect life in all its forms, first stupifying and then killing; scattered over the bedding and clothing or person it destroys bed bugs, lice, etc., for flies and mosquitoes the best way of application is by burning it; take a teaspoonful of the powder in a dish of any kind and set fire to it; a dense smoke arises which destroys the insects. A tincture prepared by placing 1 part of the powder in 4 of alcohol distilled with 10 times its bulk of water and applied to the body is said to be a perfect protection against vermin of all kinds, while hellebore answers the same purpose and is cheaper.

How to Destroy Insects.—The Bureau of Entomology, Department of Agriculture, Washington, sends out the following, for use as insecticides on or about plants. etc.: London Purple: To 20 pounds of flour from ¼ to ½ pound is added and well mixed. This is applied with a sifter or blower. With 40 gallons of water ¼ to ½ pound is mixed for spraying. Paris Green; With 20 pounds of flour from ¾ to 1 pound is mixed and applied by sifting or by a blower. The same amount of insecticide to 40 gallons of water is used as a spray. Bisulphate of Carbon: For use in the ground a quantity is poured or injected among the roots that are being infected. Against insects damaging stored grain or museum material a small quantity is used in an air-tight vessel. Carbolic Acid; A solution of 1 part in 100 of water is used against parasites on domestic animals and their barns and sheds; also on the surface of plants and among the roots in the ground. Helebore: The powder is sifted on alone or mixed 1 part to 20 of flour. With 1 gallon of water ¼ pound is mixed for spraying. Kerosene-Milk Emulsion: To 1 part of milk add 2 parts of kerosene, and churn by force pump or other agitator. The butter-like emulsion is diluted ad libitum with water. An easier method is to simply mix 1 part of kerosene with 8 of milk. Soap Elmusion: In 1 gallon of hot water ½ pound of whale oil soap is dissolved. This, instead of milk, is mixed to an emulsion with kerosene in the same manner and proportion as above. Pyrethrum, Persian Insect Powder; Is blown or sifted on dry, also applied in water 1 gallon to a tablespoonful of the powder. well stirred and then sprayed. Tobacco Decoction: This is used as strong as possible as a wash or spray to kill insect pests on animals and plants.

Lice.—Wash with a simple decoction of stavesacre or with a lotion made of the bruised seed in vinegar, or with the tincture, or rub in a salve made with the seeds and 4 times their weight of lard. very carefully beaten together. The acid solution and the tincture are the cleanest and most agreeable preparation; but all will destroy both the vermin and their eggs, and relieve the intolerable itching which their casual presence leaves behind on many sensitive skins. White precipitate ointment is also effective.

Mosquitoes.—1. Three ounces sweet oil, 1 ounce carbolic acid thoroughly applied upon the hands, face, and all exposed parts, carefully avoiding the eyes, once every half hour when they are troublesome, or for the first two or three days until the skin is filled with it, and after this its application will be necessary only at times. 2. Six parts sweet oil, 1 part creosote, 1 part pennyroyal; oil of pennyroyal alone is very effectual, pennyroyal and oil of peppermint is also used.

Moths.—1. Steep ¼ pound of cayenne pepper in 1 gallon of water; add 2 drams of strychnia powder; strain and pour this tea into a shallow vessel. Before unrolling a new carpet set the roll on each end alternately in this poisoned tea for 10 minutes, or long enough to wet its edges for at least an inch. After beating an old carpet. roll and treat its seams and edges to the same bath: let the carpet dry thoroughly before tacking it down in order to avoid the accidental poisoning of the tacker's fingers by the liquid. If preserved for future use, carefully label "poison." This preparation will not stain or disfigure carpets or corrode metals in contact with the carpet. **2.** If fine-cut tobacco be sprinkled under the edges of carpets and under places where bureaus, bookcases and the like may make it dark. the moths will be prevented from laying their eggs there, as it will drive them away. **3.** Tarred paper. the same as is used for covering roofs, when cut into slips and placed in convenient situations under carpets and behind sofas and chairs in a room will repel the moth miller from depositing its eggs. If similar strips are placed inside the backs and seats of parlor suits, it will render the furniture moth proof. **4.** Sprinkle furs or woolen stuffs, and the drawers or boxes in which they are kept, with spirits of turpentine, the unpleasant smell of which will evaporate on exposure of the goods to the air. Camphor gum is also a preventative for moths. Goods packed in a cedar chest are moth proof. If clothing is exposed to the air and well beaten occasionally it will prevent moths from depositing their eggs. Light and fresh air are the sworn foes of moths.

Rat, Mouse and Roach Exterminator.—One pint of alcohol, ¼ oz. cayenne pepper, 1 oz. powdered anise seod, ¼ oz. saltpeter, ¼ oz. white lead, 4 ozs. essence of hops; steam this slowly for an hour. then add 30 drops quassia; let stand 48 hours, and add 1 gallon of water; bottle for use. To use, saturate bread, meat etc.. and lay it in their frequented places. In two nights not one will be seen.

HOUSEHOLD MISCELLANY.

Beds, Dampness In.—After the bed is warmed put a glass globe in between the sheets, and if the bed be damp a few drops of wet will appear on the inside of the glass.

Bread, To Keep Moist.—Keep a large earthen jar (a cover of the same material is better than a wooden one) and have it aired and fresh: let the bread be well covered after it is taken from the oven; then place it in the jar and cover closely.

Butter, Rancid, To Sweeten.—Put 15 drops of chloride of lime to 1 pint of cold water, and wash the butter with it until every particle has come in contact with the water; then work it over in pure cold water.

Candle, To Burn Slowly.—Put finely powdered salt on the candle till i reaches the black portion of the wick; it will give a dull light, suitable for the sick room, and be sure to last the entire night.

Cellars, Freezing In.—Paste the wall and ceiling over with 4 or 5 thicknesses of newspapers, make a curtain of the same material, paste over the window at the top of the cellar; paste the papers to the base joist overhead, leaving an air space between them and the floor; it is better to use a coarse brown paper; whatever paper is employed sweep down the walls thoroughly, and use a very strong size to hold the paper to the stones; it is not necessary to press the paper down into all the depressions of the wall; every air space beneath it is an additional defense against the cold.

Cisterns, Waterproofing.—To make cisterns and tanks waterproof paint thickly on the inside with a mixture composed of 8 parts of melted glue and 4 parts of linseed oil, boiled with litharge; in 48 hours after application it will have hardened so that the cistern or tank can be filled with water.

Cistern Water, To Clear.—**1.** Never allow a mudhole to remain about a well. If the water is muddy and impure throw in a peck of lime to purify it; if animaculæ appear in the water throw in ½ gallon of salt to make them settle to the bottom. **2.** Add 2 ounces powdered alum and 2 ounces borax to a 20-barrel cistern of rain water that is blackened or oily and in a few hours the sediment will settle and the water be clarified and fit for washing.

Cistern Water, To Keep Sweet.—**1.** To prevent cistern water from becoming impure, have the supply pipe run nearly to the bottom of the well, where the purest water is always to be obtained. **2.** First collect the water in a tank, and filter it into the cistern below the surface; this will remove the organic matters and prevent fermentation. Care should be taken to prevent surface drainage into it. **3.** The spout from the roof should have a joint in it which can be drawn aside so as to prevent any water falling on the roof from reaching the cistern; it should be kept drawn aside during dry weather; when rain comes on allow the roof to get thoroughly washed off before replacing the joint; if this be done the water will always be clear and fit to drink. **4.** Drop into the cistern a large piece of common charcoal.

Clinkers in Stoves, To Remove.—When the firebricks have become covered with clinkers which have fused and adhered they may be cleaned by throwing oyster or clam shells in the firebox when the fire is very hot and allowing the fire to go out. The clinkers will generally cleave off without the use of much force the next morning. From 1 quart to a peck will be sufficient for most stoves, and the operation can be repeated if some of the clinkers still adhere. Salt sprinkled on clinkers adhering to firebrick will also loosen them.

Clothes, Burning, To Extinguish.—The clothes of females and children, when on fire, may be most readily extinguished by rolling the sufferer in the carpet, hearthrug, table cover, or any other woolen article at hand: if this be expertly done, the flames may be rapidly put out, unless the skirt of the dress be distended by hoops or crinoline, when there is great difficulty in staying the progress of the flames; should assistance not be at hand, the person whose clothes are on fire should throw herself on the ground and roll the carpet round her; or, if such a thing is not in the room, she should endeavor to extinguish the flames with her hands, and by rapidly rolling over and over on the floor; in this way the fire will be stifled, or the combustion will proceed so slowly that less personal injury will be experienced before assistance arrives.

Coal, Artificial.—1. Sifted peat 125 parts, river mud 10 parts, anthracite dust 1,000 parts, residues of schist oil 100 parts, or dry coal pitch 120 parts; mix. **2.** Small coal, charcoal or sawdust 1 part. clay, loam or marl 1 part, sand or ashes 2 parts, water of sufficient quantity to mix up wet into balls for use; these balls are piled on an ordinary fire to a little above the top bar; they are said to produce a heat considerably more intense than that of common fuel. and insures a saving of one-half the quantity of coals, while a fire thus made up will require no stirring, nor fresh fuel for 10 hours. The quantity of the combustible ingredient in them should be doubled when they are intended to be used with a very little foundation of coal.

Coal Oil, To Test.—In a small cup or glass place a small quantity of oil to be tested; immerse in the oil the bulb of a good thermometer; suspend the cup containing the oil in a vessel of water; move about close to the surface of the oil a lighted taper, and note the degree on the thermometer at which the oil begins to emit inflammable vapor (the flashing point), and again that at which the oil inflames; oil to be used in lamps should not take fire below 112 degrees Fahrenheit. In applying the lighted taper the flame must be kept away from the glass of the thermometer.

Coal, To Protect.—Soft coal should be kept protected from the frost, rain or snow; if allowed to become wet and subjected to alternate heat and cold, it will crumble and become difficult to handle and hard to burn: dry coal is tolerably clean to handle, while it kindles easily and produces comparatively little smoke.

Corkscrews, Substitutes For.—A convenient substitute for a corkscrew may be found in the use of a common screw, with an attached string to pull the cork: or, stick two steel forks vertically into the cork on opposite sides, not too near the edge, run the blade of a knife through the two, and give a twist.

Corks, To Remove.—With a stout string projected into the bottle, turn the bottle around until the cork is caught in the loop of the string, and with force pull out the cork.

Cream, To Keep.—Cream already skimmed may be kept 24 hours if scalded without sugar, and, by adding to it as much powder_ _ump sugar as will make it sweet, it will keep good 2 days in a cool place.

Doors, Creaking.—Rub a little soap or a mixture of tallow and black lead on the hinges; or apply to them with a feather a little sweet or sperm oil once or twice a year.

Fabrics, To Make Fireproof.—Eighty parts pure sulphate of ammonia, 25 parts carbonate of ammonia, 30 parts boracic acid, 12 parts pure borax, 20 parts starch, 1,000 parts distilled water; dip in this while it is hot; dry and iron.

Fire Kindlers.—To make very nice fire kindlers take resin any quantity and melt it, putting in for each pound being used 2 or 3 ounces of tallow and when all is hot stir in pine sawdust to make very thick; while yet hot spread it out about 1 inch thick upon boards which have fine sawdust sprinkled upon them to prevent it from sticking. When cold break up in lumps about an inch square; but if for sale take a thin board and press upon it while yet warm, to lay it off into inch squares. This makes it break regularly if you press the crease sufficiently deep. Grease the marked board to prevent it sticking.

Flies, To Drive From a Room.—Place a castor-oil plant in the room and the flies will leave.

Sticky Fly Paper.—Boiled linseed oil and resin; melt and add honey. Soak the paper in a strong solution of alum, then dry before applying the above. (See also "Pests.")

Ice, To Keep.—1. Small quantities of ice may be preserved in summer by making a bag large enough to hold the ice; then make another much larger bag and fill the space between with sawdust or feathers. 2. Cut a piece of flannel about 9 inches square and secure it by a ligature round the mouth of an ordinary tumbler, so as to leave a cup-shaped depression of flannel within the tumbler of about half its depth. In the flannel cup so constructed pieces of ice may be preserved many hours; all the longer if a flannel 4 or 5 inches square be used as a loose cover to the ice-cup; cheap flannel with comparatively open meshes is preferable, as water easily drains through it, and the ice is thus kept quite dry; when good flannel with close texture is employed a small hole must be made in the bottom of the flannel cut, otherwise it holds water and facilitates the melting of the ice.

Lamp Chimneys, To Prevent Cracking.—1. Place the chimney in a pot filled with cold water; add a little cooking salt, allow the mixture to boil well over a fire and cool slowly; chimneys become very durable by this process, which may be extended to crockery, stoneware, porcelain, etc.; the process is simply one of annealing, and the slower the process. especially the cooling portion of it, the more effective will be the work. 2. If the chimney glass of a lamp be cut with a diamond on the convex side it will never crack, as the incision affords room for expansion produced by the heat, and the glass, after it is cool, returns to its original shape, with only a scratch visible where the cut is made.

Lamp-Lighters.—Cut old postal cards lengthwise into strips ⅛ of an inch wide: they burn readily, do not give off sparks and leave scarcely a trace of ashes.

Lamps, Night, to Make.—1. Take a cork about 1 inch across, and cut a piece off the top about ⅛ inch thick; make a hole in the center; take a piece of tin the size of the little finger nail and make a small hole in the center sufficient to hold a common white cord; fill a common goblet ¾ full of water and pour over that about ⅛ inch sperm oil; place the tin on the cork and put a piece of cord 1 inch long through the holes, then set the cork afloat on the oil, and you have a good night lamp; kerosene or other low test oils should not be used. **2.** If sulphide of lime be enclosed in a bottle the figures on the face of a watch may be distinguished by its aid. To renew the luminosity of the mass place the bottle each day in the sun or in strong daylight, or burn a strip of magnesium wire close to the bottle; it will thus absorb light, which will again be available at night time. **3.** Take a stick of phosphorus and put it into a large dry vial, not corked, and it will afford a light sufficient to discern any object in the room when held near it; the vial should be kept in a cool place, where there is no current of air, and it will continue its luminous appearance for 12 months.

Matches, Care Of.—Parlor matches light the most readily, and are much more dangerous than the common matches. The general stock should be kept in a tin box. For each room where matches are used there should be a match safe of some kind; in the kitchen and bedroom, or wherever else matches are in frequent use. have the match safe fixed in one place, so that it can be found, if need be, in the dark.

Milk, Sour, To Sweeten.—Milk or cream may be sweetened after it has become slightly sour by a small portion of carbonate of magnesia; saleratus will also correct the acid, but slightly injures the flavor, unless very delicately managed.

Milk, To Prevent Souring.—1. Put 1 teaspoonful of scraped horseradish into each pan. and it will keep sweet for several days. **2.** Dissolve ½ thimbleful of California borax in hot water; put into the milk and it will keep perfectly sweet.

Milk, To Test the Richness Of.—Procure any long glass vessel—a cologne bottle or long phial. Take a narrow strip of paper. just the length from the neck to the bottom of the phial. and mark it off with 100 lines at equal distances. or into 50 lines. and count each as two, and paste upon the phial. so as to divide its length into 100 equal parts. Fill it to the highest mark with milk fresh from the cow. and allow it to stand in a perpendicular position 24 hours. The number of spaces occupied by the cream will give you its exact percentage in the milk without any guess work.

Rubber, To Restore Elasticity of.—Use a simple mixture composed of 1 part of aqua ammonia with 2 parts of water in which the articles should be immersed until they resume their former elasticity, smoothness, and softness, the time required varying from a few minutes to an hour.

Scissors, To Sharpen.—Take a fine file and sharpen each blade, being careful to keep the same angle as they had at first; file till the rough places are all taken out; put a little oil on the edges of the blades, and snap together; then wipe off.

Stoves, Cracks in, To Mend.—**1.** Good wood ashes are to be sifted through a fine sieve, to which are to be added the same quantity of clay, finely pulverized, together with a little salt; the mixture is to be moistened with water enough to make a paste, and the crack in the stove filled with it.   **2.** An excellent cement for iron stoves and furnaces is a paste of soluble glass and barytes, with or without some fine fireclay; or the soluble glass may be replaced by a solution of borax, and both these and barytes by a mixture of clay and powdered glass.

Taste of Wood, To Remove.—To prevent this scald the vessel well with boiling water, letting the water remain in it until cold; then dissolve some pearlash or soda in lukewarm water, adding a little lime to it; wash the inside of the vessel well with the solution; afterward scald it well with hot water, and rinse with cold water before using.

To Mend Tinware by the Heat of a Candle.—Take a phial about ⅔ full of muriatic acid and put into it little bits of sheet zinc as long as it dissolves them; then put in a crumb of sal ammoniac and fill up with water, and it is ready for use. Then, with the cork of the phial, wet the place to be mended with the preparation; then put a piece of zinc over the hole and hold a lighted candle or spirit lamp under the place, which melts the solder on the tin, and causes the zinc to adhere without further trouble. Wet the zinc also with the solution; or a little solder may be put on instead of the zinc or with the zinc.

To Mend Iron.—Mix finely some sifted lime with the white of an egg till a thin sort of paste is formed, then add some iron filings. Apply this to the fracture and the vessel will be found nearly as sound as ever.

Water, To Ascertain if Hard or Soft.—**1.** Dissolve ½ ounce of good white soap in 1 pint of rain water; let it cool and settle; mix about 1 ounce of this with 1 pint of the water to be tested and let stand a few minutes; if the water is soft, it will remain clear; if hard, it will turn opalescent. **2.** Procure a small quantity of soap dissolved in alcohol; let a few drops of it fall into a glass of water to be tried; if the water becomes milky, it is hard, but if little or no milkiness results, the water may be said to be soft.

Window Glass, To Prevent Frosting.—Apply a very thin coat of glycerine on both sides of the glass; this will prevent the formation of moisture.

ADDITIONAL RECIPES.

UNCLASSIFIED.

Burning Fluid.—Four quarts alcohol, 1 pint spirits of turpentine; mix well. It is the best in use.

Centennial Illuminating Oil.—Recipe for making 1 gallon: Take ⅞ gallon benzine or crude petroleum, add to it ½ ounce gum camphor, ½ ounce alcohol, ½ pint common salt. ½ ounce oil of sassafras; stir and mix it well for about 5 minutes; let it stand for 24 hours and it is ready for use. It is better to buy the benzine from Pittsburg, Pa., as the druggists usually charge 2 or 3 times the wholesale price.

I. X. L. Baking Powder.—Take 1 pound tartaric acid in crystals, 1½ pounds bicarbonate of soda, and 1½ pounds potato starch; each must be powdered separately, well dried by a slow heat, well mixed through a sieve; pack hard in tinfoil, tin, or paper glazed on the outside. The tartaric acid and bicarbonate of soda can, of course, be bought cheaper of wholesale druggists than you can make them, unless you are doing things on a large scale, but potato starch any one can make. It is only necessary to peel the potatoes, and to grate them up fine into vessels of water, to let them settle, pour off the water, and make the settlings into balls, and to dry them. With these directions anyone can make as good baking powder as is sold anywhere. If he wants to make it very cheap he can take cream of tartar and common washing (carbonate) soda instead of the articles named in the recipe, but this would be advisable only where customers insist on excessively low prices in preference to the quality of the goods.

Wash for Carpets.—Mix together 30 cents' worth of ground soap-tree bark (which can be purchased at any drug store), 5 cents' worth of ammonia, 1 cup vinegar, 1½ pails of water; boil this mixture one hour in a boiler, and use it on the carpet with a sponge.

Indestructible Lamp Wicks.—Steep common wicks in a concentrated aqueous solution of tungstate of soda, and then dry thoroughly in an oven.

Wax Stains on Cloth.—An old-fashioned way of removing wax stains from cloth is the following: Lay over the stains 2 thicknesses of blotting paper and apply for a moment the pressure of a moderately hot iron. The wax becoming melted will be absorbed by the two layers of paper, and the stains will be instantaneously and entirely removed.

Holes in Stockings.—To mend large holes in stockings or merino underwear, tack a piece of net over the rent and darn through it.

Fluid Extracts for Sarsaparilla Syrups.—Sarsaparilla

3 ounces, burdock 3 ounces. taraxacum 2 ounces, sassafras 1 ounce; put 1 teaspoonful of the mixture into 3 teaspoonsful of water, or in that proportion, and take 1 tablespoonful 3 times a day.

To Preserve Cut Flowers.—A bouquet of freshly cut flowers may be preserved alive for a long time by placing them in a glass or vase with fresh water. in which a little charcoal has been steeped, or a small piece of camphor dissolved. The vase should be set upon a plate or dish. and covered with a bell glass, around the edges of which. when it comes in contact with the plate, a little water should be poured to exclude the air.

To Preserve Flowers.—Take a jar sufficiently large to contain the flower to be preserved, and in the bottom place a lump of clay or some similar substance in which the flower must be stuck upright. Then pour in carefully fine dry sand till the flower is completely embedded in it. This must be done very slowly and cautiously so as not to disturb the leaves of the flower. Dried in this way. flowers preserve their form and much of their color for months, and are interesting and pretty for the winter decoration of rooms.

To Cleanse Bottles.—Make a lye by boiling equal quantities of soda and quicklime. When cold. put this in the bottles with some pebbles, and shake well. Set the bottles to drain thoroughly, then warm them, and blow inside with a pair of bellows to absorb all moisture.

To Clean Wine Decanters.—Use a little pearl ash or soda and some cinders and water; rinse them out with water.

To Clean China.—Use a little of Fuller's earth, and soda or pearl ash with water.

To Frost Window Panes.—Take epsom salts and dissolve in beer. Apply with a brush and you have the finest window frosting known.

To Keep Salt Dry.—To keep salt so it can be easily shaken from the cruet, mix 1 teaspoonful of corn starch with each cup of salt. This will prove effectual.

Preserving Wood.—There have been a number of processes patented for preserving wood. One of them, very generally used. consists in immersing the timber in a bath of corrosive sublimate. Another process consists in first filling the pores with a solution of chloride of calcium under pressure. and next forcing in a solution of sulphate of iron, by which an insoluble sulphate of lime is formed in the body of the wood. which is thus rendered nearly as hard as stone. Wood prepared in this way is now very largely used for railroad ties. Another process consists in impregnating the wood with a solution of chloride of zinc. Yet another way is to thoroughly impregnate the timber with oil of tar containing creosote and a crude solution of acetate of iron. The process consists in putting the wood in a cylindrical vessel, connected with a powerful air pump. The air is withdrawn, and the liquid subjected to pressure, so that as much of it as possible is forced into the pores of the wood. The processes above given not only season the timber so that it is not subject to dry rot, but also keep it from being injured by the weather, or being attacked by insects or worms.

Fireproof Wood.—Soak 27.5 parts by weight of sulphate of zinc, 11 of potash, 22 of alum and 11 of manganic oxide in luke-warm water in an iron boiler, and gradually add 11 parts by weight of 60 per cent sulphuric acid. The wood to be prepared is placed upon an iron grating in an apparatus of suitable size, the separate pieces being placed at least an inch apart. The liquid is then poured into the apparatus, and the wood allowed to remain completely covered for three hours, and is then air-dried.

To Preserve Wooden Posts.—The ends of the thoroughly dry posts which are to be put in the ground are placed in lime water 1.18 to 1.57 inches deep, and after taking out and drying, painted with diluted sulphuric acid. The posts thus treated become hard as stone and are far more durable than when carbonized or coated with tar.

To Prevent Warping of Wood and of wooden objects in damp air, saturate them with copaiba balsam. Articles already warped on one side can be straightened by saturating the other side with the balsam.

To Marble Books or Paper.—Marbling of books or paper is performed thus: Dissolve 4 ounces of gum arabic in 2 quarts of fair water, then provide several colors mixed with water in pots or shells, and with pencils peculiar to each color: sprinkle them by way of intermixture upon the gum water, which must be put into a trough or some broad vessel: then with a stick curl them or draw them out in streaks to as much variety as may be done. Having done this, hold your book or books close together and only dip the edges in, on the top of the water and colors, very lightly; which done, take them off and the plain impression of the colors in the mixture will be upon the leaves: doing as well the ends as the front of the book in like manner, and afterward glazing the colors.

To Make Paper into Parchment.—To produce this transformation take unsized paper and plunge it into a solution of 2 parts concentrated sulphuric acid combined with 1 part water; withdraw it immediately and wash it in clean water, and the change is complete. It is now fit for writing, for the acid supplies the want of size, and it becomes so strong that a strip 2 or 3 inches wide will bear from 60 to 80 pounds weight, while a like strip of parchment will bear only about 25 pounds.

How to Keep Eggs Fresh.—The great secret in keeping eggs consists in entirely excluding the air from the interior. The lining next to the shell is, when in its natural state, impervious to air, and the albumen is calculated to sustain it, but dampness and heat will cause decay, and if the egg is allowed to lie in one position, especially on one side, the yolk sinks through the albumen and settles upon the lining and, not possessing proper qualities for preserving the skin in a healthy condition. it dries. and air penetrates and begins the work of destruction. Where eggs are set upon their small ends, the yolk is much less liable to reach the lining of the shell. Where eggs are packed in barrel, keg, or bucket it is a good plan to turn the whole quantity onto a different side once in a while.

To Print a Picture from the Print Itself.—The page or picture is soaked in a solution, first of potassa and then of tartaric acid. This produces a perfect diffusion of crystals of bitartrate of potassa through the texture of the unprinted part of the paper. As this salt resists oil, the ink roller may now be passed over the surface, without transferring any part of its contents except to the printed part.

Premium Paint, Without Oil or Lead.—Slack stone lime with boiling water in a tub or barrel to keep in the steam; then pass 6 quarts through a fine sieve. Now to this quantity add 1 quart of coarse salt and 1 gallon of water; boil the mixture and skim it clear. To every 5 gallons of this skimmed mixture add 1 pound alum, ½ pound copperas, and by slow degrees ¾ pound potash and 4 quarts sifted ashes or fine sand; add any coloring desired. A more durable paint was never made.

To Prevent Mold.—A small quantity of carbolic acid added to paste, mucilage. or ink will prevent mold. An ounce of the acid to a gallon of whitewash will keep cellars and dairies from the disagreeable odor which often taints milk and meat kept in such places.

Waterproofing for Clothing.—Boiled oil 15 pounds, beeswax 1 pound, ground litharge 13 pounds; mix and apply with a brush to the article, previously stretching against a wall or on a table, well washing and drying each article before applying the composition.

How to Thaw Out a Water Pipe.—Water pipes usually freeze up when exposed, for inside the walls, where they cannot be reached, they are or should be packed to prevent freezing. To thaw out a frozen pipe bundle a newspaper into a torch, light it, and pass it along the pipe slowly. The ice will yield to this much quicker than to hot water or wrappings of hot cloths, as is the common practice.

Whitewash that Will Not Rub Off.—Mix up ½ pailful of lime and water, ready to put on the wall; then take ¼ pint of flour, mix it up with water, then pour on it the boiling water, a sufficient quantity to thicken it; then pour it while hot into the whitewash, stir all well together, and it is ready for use.

Imitation Frost Crystals.—A very pretty winter ornament for a parlor table, or to set on the showcase in the store, can be prepared as follows: Dissolve 456 grains of nitrate of lead in 6 fluid ounces of water. If the solution is turbid, filter through paper. Place the solution in a vessel on the table where it is intended to remain, and drop into it 200 grains of sal ammoniac in long fibrous crystals. Small crystals of chloride of lead form and ascend through the denser liquid, presenting the appearance of an ascending snow storm. When the lead is all precipitated the crystals of chloride of lead begin to descend as a genuine miniature snow storm, forming grotesque masses resembling a winter's landscape. If the vessel containing the crystals is not disturbed it often preserves its beauty for a week or two.

To Straighten Round Shoulders.—A stooping figure and a halting gait, accompanied by the unavoidable weakness of lungs incidental to a narrow chest, may be entirely cured by a very simple and easily-performed exercise of raising one's self upon the toes leisurely in a perpendicular position several times daily. To take this exercise properly one must take a perfectly upright position, with the heels together and the toes at an angle of forty-five degrees. Then drop the arms lifelessly by the sides, animating and raising the chest to its full capacity muscularity, the chin well drawn in, and the crown of the head feeling as if attached to a string suspended from the ceiling above. Slowly rise upon the balls of both feet to the greatest possible height, thereby exercising all the muscles of the legs and body; come again into standing position without swaying the body backward out of the perfect line. Repeat this same exercise, first on one foot, then on the other. It is wonderful what a straightening-out power this exercise has upon round shoulders and crooked backs, and one will be surprised to note how soon the lungs begin to show the effect of such expansive development.

Black Tracing Paper.—Rub smooth a little lampblack and mix with sweet oil. Paint over the paper, and dab it dry with a fine piece of linen. Put this under the pattern, and upon the material to which you wish the pattern transferred, and go over the lines with a hard point of wood or metal. If you wish it, the transferred lines may be fixed by using a pen with a kind of ink composed of a little stoneblue well mixed with water in a cup, with a small piece of sugar added to it.

To Make Cloth Waterproof.—There have been various devices for rendering cloth waterproof without the use of India rubber. The most successful of these, no doubt, is the Stenhouse patent. This consists of the application of paraffine combined with drying oil. Paraffine was first used alone, but it was found to harden and break off from the cloth after a time. When drying oil was added, however, even in a very small quantity, it was found that the two substances, by the absorption of oxygen, became converted into a tenacious substance very like resin. To apply this the paraffine is melted with drying oil, and then cast into blocks. The composition can then be applied to fabrics by rubbing them over with a block of it, either cold or gently warmed. Or the melted mixture may be applied with a brush and the cloth then passed through hot rollers in order to cover its entire substance perfectly. This application makes cloth very repellant to water, though still pervious to air.

Preservation of Ropes.—Dip the dry ropes into a bath containing 20 grains of sulphate of copper per quart of water, and after allowing them to lie in soak in this solution for four days, dry them. The ropes will thus have absorbed a certain quantity of sulphate of copper, which will preserve them alike from rot and from the attacks of animal parasites. The copper salt may be fixed in the fiber by a coating of tar or by soapy water. In tarring the rope it is said to be better to pass it through a bath of boiled tar, hot, drawing it through a thimble to press back the excess of tar, and suspending it afterward on a staging to dry and harden. According to another process the rope is soaked in a solution of 100 grains of soap per quart of water; the copper soap thus formed in the fiber of the rope preserves it from rot even better than the tar, which acts mechanically to imprison the sulphate of copper which is the real preservative.

Protecting Lead Water Pipes.—To protect lead water pipes from the action of water, which often affects them chemically, partially dissolving them, and injuring the pipes, as well as poisoning the water, fill the pipes with a warm and concentrated solution of sulphite of potassium or sodium; leave the solution in contact with the lead for about 15 minutes and then blow it out. This coats the inside of the pipes with sulphide of lead, which is absolutely insoluble, and cannot be acted upon by water at all.

Leg Ulcers.—Good results in the treatment of leg ulcers can be obtained by painting them with lead carbonate and linseed oil, in the following proportion; Pure white lead, ground in oil, 10 drams, raw linseed oil 4 drams, mix well and label. Paint the ulcer once or twice a day, after washing it with warm water. Dry well before painting. The best thing to apply the remedy with is a camel's-hair brush. Lead carbonate is a sedative, astringent and possesses disinfectant properties.

Court Plaster.—The preparation of court plaster is very simple; the basis of the first stratum is isinglass. Bruise a sufficient quantity of isinglass, and let it soak for 24 hours in a little warm water; expose it to heat over the fire, to dissipate the greater part of the water, and supply its place by proof spirits of wine, which will combine with the isinglass.

To Caseharden Iron.—If you desire to harden to considerable depth put the article into a crucible with cyanide of potash, cover over and heat altogether, then plunge into the water. This process will harden perfectly to the depth of two or three inches.

To Remove Rust from Iron or Steel.—For cleaning purposes, etc., kerosene oil or benzine are probably the best things known. When articles have become pitted by rust, however, these can, of course, only be removed by mechanical means.

such as scouring with fine powder, or flour of emery and oil, or with very fine emery paper. To prevent steel from rusting rub it with a mixture of lime and oil, or with mercurial ointment, either of which will be found valuable.

To Preserve Steel Articles from Rust.—Paint the articles over with white beeswax dissolved in benzole; the benzole rapidly evaporates, leaving the steel covered with a thin coating of the wax. As the solution is very volatile it should be kept in a bottle tightly corked.

To Melt Steel as Easily as Lead.—This apparent impossibility is easily performed by heating the bar of iron or steel red hot and then touching it with a roll of brimstone, when the metal will drop like water.

To Mend Ironware.—Sulphur 2 parts, fine black lead 1 part; put the sulphur in an iron pan over a fire until it melts; then add the lead; stir well; then pour out; when cool break into small pieces. A sufficient quantity of this compound being placed upon the crack of the ware to be mended, can be soldered by an iron.

To Prevent Iron from Rusting.—Warm it; then rub with white wax; put it again to the fire until the wax has pervaded the entire surface; or immerse tools or bright work in boiled linseed oil and allow it to dry upon them.

To Joint Lead Pipes.—Widen out the end of one pipe with a taper wood drift and scrape it clean inside; scrape the end of the other pipe outside a little tapered and insert it in the former; then solder it with common lead solder, as before described; or if required to be strong, rub a little tallow over and cover the joint with a ball of melted lead, holding a cloth (2 or 3 plies of greased bed tick) on the under side and smoothing over with it and the plumber's iron.

Silver Imitations.—Copper 1 pound, tin ¾ ounce; melt. This composition will roll and ring very near to silver. Brittania Metal: Copper 1 pound, tin 1 pound, regulus of antimony 2 pounds; melt together with or without a little bismuth. Genuine German Silver: Iron 2½ parts, nickel 31½ parts, zinc 25½ parts, copper 40½ parts; melt. Fine White German Silver: Iron 1 part, nickel 10 parts, zinc 10 parts, copper 20 parts; melt.

Artificial Gold.—This is a new metallic alloy which is now very extensively used in France as a substitute for gold. Pure copper 100 parts, zinc, or preferably tin, 17 parts, magnesia 6 parts, sal ammoniac 3-6 parts, quicklime ⅛ parts, tartar of commerce 9 parts; are mixed as follows: The copper is first melted and the magnesia, sal ammoniac, lime and tartar are then added separately and by degrees, in the form of a powder. The whole is now briskly stirred for about half an hour, so as to mix thoroughly; and then the zinc is added in small grains by throwing it on the surface and stirring until it is entirely fused; the crucible is then covered, and the fusion maintained for about 35 minutes. The surface is then skimmed, and the alloy is ready for casting. It has a fine grain, is malleable, and takes a splendid polish. It does not corrode readily, and, for many purposes, is an excellent substitute for gold. When tarnished its brilliancy can be restored by a little acidulated water. If tin be employed instead of zinc, the alloy will be more brilliant. It is very much used in France, and must ultimately attain equal popularity here.

Fictitious Gold.—Copper 16 parts, plantinum 7 parts, zinc 1 part; fused together. This alloy resembles gold of 16 carats fine or ⅔, and will resist the action of nitric acid, unless very concentrated and boiling.

DEPARTMENT V.

ALL TRADES.

THE CONFECTIONER AND BAKER.

The stages through which sugar passes in the process of candy-making are as follows: It is first boiled until it becomes a transparent syrup; then, by further boiling, it reaches a condition that, when "touched" between the thumb and forefinger, it draws out into a fine thread, which crystalizes and breaks: this is the "thread" stage. If boiled again, it will draw into a larger string, and, if blown, small bubbles or bladders will appear; this is called the "blown," or boiled "to the blow." Continued boiling produces the "feathered" stage, then the "caramel" and finally the "crackled," or true candy state. The fire must be gentle—not too fierce—and care must be taken to test frequently according to the kind of candy desired to make. Glucose is used in the manufacture of many candies.

Artificial Maple Syrup.—Dark C sugar (driest) 2 pounds, water ⅓ pint, butter 2 ounces, melted; flavor with maple flavor; boil to a ball, cream in the pan. Pour before it gets too stiff.

Almond Bars.—Same as peanut, only add the almond nuts in time to allow them to roast a little in the boiling sugar. One-fourth of a pint of New Orleans syrup added to the boiling sugar improves the flavor and color.

A Number One Chocolate Drop.—Molding cream, granulated sugar 20 pounds, water 3 quarts; boiled to a thread, set off, add 3 pounds of glucose dissolved; pour, let get cold. Cream, melt, add pinch of glucose to 1 pint simple syrup; 4 tablespoons of glycerine; stir; mold.

Butter Creams.—White sugar 1½ pounds, C sugar ½ pound, glucose ¾ pound, molasses ¼ pint, water 1¼ pints; boil to the hard snap, add 6 ounces of butter, set off until it melts; set on and let boil, to well mix the butter; pour out. Have 1 pound of hard cream dough thoroughly warmed, just so you can handle it. When the batch is cold enough on the stove to handle. place the warm cream lengthwise on the center of it and completely wrap the cream up in it. Place this on your table before your heater, spin out in long strips, have some one to mark them heavy or good. When cold, break where marked.

Boston Chips.—White sugar 3 pounds. cream of tartar ½ pipe, water 1¼ pints; boil with a lid over it to the hard snap; pour; pull this only half as much as any other candy, for too much pulling takes out all the gloss when done; flavor on the hook; wear your gloves, place it before your heater on the table, flatten out and spin out into thin ribbons, break off and curl them up in little piles. Strawberry chips can be made the same way, adding a pinch of cochineal paste.

Butter-Scotch.—C sugar 3 pounds, water 1¼ pints; cream of tartar 1 full pipe dissolved in ⸗ up of cider vinegar. molasses ½ pint, butter 8 ounces, (no flavor⸗ Add all except the vinegar, cream of tartar and butter. Boil to medium ball, then add the cream of tartar in the vinegar and butter; stir all the time carefully; boil to light snap.

Cheap Chocolates.—Quick work. Make a batch of the above number one. Exactly the same process. After the glucose is dissolved in the batch do not pour out, but add 5 pounds of the hard factory cream in pieces. Stir, flavor, melt. Set this kettle in a kettle of boiling water, have a boy to stir and watch it; do not allow it to get so thin as to simmer, only thin enough to run into your starch prints. This cream saves time and labor.

Common Twist Candy.—Boil 3 pounds of common sugar and 1 pint of water over a slow fire for half an hour without skimming. When boiled enough take it off, rub your hands over with butter; take that which is a little cooled and pull it as you would molasses candy, until it is white; then twist or braid it and cut it up in strips.

Cream Candy.—Take 1 pound of white sugar, 1 cupful of water, ½ teaspoonful of cream of tartar, 2 teaspoonfuls of vinegar, 2 teaspoonfuls of vanilla, butter the size of an egg; boil until it hardens when dropped into water. Pour upon a buttered platter and when nearly cold, pull.

Chocolate Caramels.—Grated chocolate 1 cupful, brown sugar 1 cupful, molasses 1 cupful, sweet milk ½ cupful: boil until it hardens when dropped in water. Then add a piece of butter the size of an egg, and one cupful of chopped English walnut meats; pour into a buttered pan, and when partly cold cut in squares.

Chocolate Coating.—Use sweet confectioner's or confectioner's plain (never use the ¼ and 1 pound grocery packages, as it contains too much sugar to melt good). Place a small piece of paraffine the size of a hickory nut and 1 small teaspoonful of lard in a rice cooker; melt; add ½ pound of chocolate; stir until dissolved; dip balls of cream in this chocolate, drop on wax paper to cool, and you have fine hand-made chocolate drops.

Cold Sugar Icing—For dipping cream drops. Confectioner's sugar with the white of eggs and a small amount of dissolved gum arabic in water; make this into a batter. If thick the drops will be rough; if thin, the drops will be smooth.

Cocoanut Cream Ice.—Two pounds granulated sugar, ¾ pint water, boil to a light crack; set off, add 4 ounces glucose (or the amount of cream of tartar you can hold on the point of a penknife) set back on the fire, just let come to a boil to dissolve the glucose; set off again, add immediately ¼ ounce shaved paraffine, 6 ounces cream dough cut up fine, 1 grated cocoanut· Stir all until it creams, pour out into a frame on brown paper dusted with flour, mark and cut with a knife when cold.

Crystalized Popcorn.—Put into an iron kettle 1 tablespoonful of butter, 3 tablespoonfuls of water and 1 teacupful of white sugar; boil until ready to candy, then throw in 3 quarts of nicely popped corn, stir briskly until the candy is evenly distributed over the corn. Care should be taken not to have too hot a fire, or the corn will be scorched while crystalizing. Nuts of any kind may be treated in the same way.

Candy Penny Popcorn Pieces.—Cook a batch of glucose to a light snap, flavor well pour thin. While hot, place your popcorn sheet hard down on the candy, mark deep, cut and wrap. I have put boys on this work in the shop at $5 a week pay, and knew them to clear for the proprietor from $5 to $20 daily for several months; one to pop corn, one to cook syrup, one to press and one to cut them; girls to wrap and box.

Date and Fig Creams.—Seed dates, cut a piece out of the end V shape, insert a white or pink cream ball, press it in, and stick a clove in the end, it looks like a pear. Cut figs in strips, place the seedy side around a piece of cream dough. The handmade cream can be made in various varieties of candies to suit your fancy.

Factory Cream Dough.—This recipe is worth $25 to any candy maker. When the cream is first done it appears flaky and coarse, but the next morning it is fine, and the longer it sets the better it is. When made up it never gets stale or hard. Never use flour to roll out cream when you can get the XXX lozenge sugar. Forty pounds granulated sugar, 5 quarts water; boil to a stiff ball; set off; add quickly 12 pounds glucose; do not stir; set on the fire, let it come to a boil until you see even the scum boiled in (do not allow the glucose to boil in the sugar). Pour out, wait only till you can lay the back of your hand on the top of the batch. Never let it get colder, it is better to cream while hot than cold like other goods. Cream it with 2 garden hoes or cream scrapers. Add while creaming ¼ pint scant measure of glycerine; no need of kneading it: scrape into your tub for use. If A1 sugar is used the cream is sticky.

French Creams.—Take 2 cupsful of granulated sugar, add to it ½ cupful milk; set upon the stove and bring slowly to a boil and boil for 5 minutes; take off the fire and set in a pan of cold water; stir rapidly until it creams; shape into balls with the hands and nuts on top of some of the creams, or it can be arranged in layers and figs or dates placed between; then cut into squares. Fine chocolate creams can be made of this mixture by dipping the balls into melted chocolate, leaving until cold upon buttered white paper.

French Creams No. 2.—Break the white of an egg into a glass and add an equal quantity of milk or water; then stir in enough XXXX confectioners' sugar to make sufficiently stiff to roll into shape; about 1½ pounds will be needed; use different flavorings to make a variety.

Fine Peppermint Lozenges.—Best powdered white sugar 7 pounds, pure starch 1 pound, oil of peppermint to flavor; mix with mucilage.

Fig Candy.—Take 1 pound sugar and 1 pint water; set over a slow fire; when done add a few drops of vinegar and a lump of butter, and pour into pans in which figs are laid.

Flavorings.—To any kind of oil take 8 times in bulk the amount of alcohol; stir; let set in a warm place a short time; can be used if needed immediately.

Home-Made Maple Sugar.—To 2 pounds of maple (bricks not cakes) add 1 pint water. ⅛ pipe cream of tartar (or 4 ounces glucose is best); boil slow to a smooth degree. cool, skim; white sugar can be used. To keep molasses from sugaring in the barrel when making the molasses, to every barrel add 20 ponnds of glucose; stir it in. To lighten the color and aid the flavor of rank, dark molasses, do the same as above. To allow molasses to cool slowly makes it dark; it should be stirred lively until cool. Also to improve sour, rank molasses, take the molasses, for instance, 10 gallons; take 5 pounds dry C sugar, 5 pounds of glucose, water 2 quarts; boil the sugar and glucose until thoroughly dissolved; add the molasses; boil 5 minutes. You can make fine syrup this way.

How to Ornament Cakes.—You need 4 cups of confectioners' finest sugar, whites of 2 eggs; beat the eggs just a little, add the sugar gradually; juice 1 lemon; beat this stiff until the sugar will bend when you hold the paddle up. Now take a sheet of thick writing paper, fold it into a funnel shape. hold it in your left hand; fill this with the icing prepared as above, about ⅗ full, fold in the top and place both thumbs on it, cut off a little of the small end of the funnel to allow the icing to come out when you press with your thumbs. Next with a knife cover your cake with icing sugar smoothly; if it sticks to the knife wet it a little. Let dry half hour; then with a lead pencil make leaves or designs. and with your paper funnel ice your pencil designs. ›Colored icing looks well.

Imitation Hand-Made Chocolate.—Take a suitable hand made; make your plaster paris prints; take a quantity of the above cream, melt in a bath; flavor and mold; dip.

Italian Cream Operas.—Melt 4 ounces of butter with 4 ounces plain chocolate; take a batch of the opera cream; when cooked add the above, stir it in the kettle until it creams, then pan and work it as you do the operas.

Jap Cocoanut.—One pound XXX confectioners' sugar dampened a little, 1½ pounds glucose; stir when cooked to a soft ball; add all the grated cocoanut it will stick together; boil; stir to the lightest crack.

Kisses.—Two cupsful powdered sugar, the whites of 3 eggs, 2 cupsful cocoanut, 2 teaspoonsful baking powder; mix all together; drop upon buttered paper and bake until slightly brown in a brisk oven.

Molasses Candy.—1. Take 4 cupsful sugar, 2 cupsful molasses, and ½ cupful vinegar; boil until it crisps in cold water, then stir in 1 tablespoonful baking soda; pour into well buttered dishes; leave until sufficiently cool; then pull. **2.** Boil molasses over a moderately hot fire, stirring constantly. When you think it is done, drop a little on a plate and if it is sufficiently boiled it will be hard. Add a small quantity of vinegar to make it brittle, and any flavoring ingredient you prefer. Pour in buttered tin pans. If nuts are to be added strew them in the pans before pouring out the candy.

Maple Caramels.—Use one-half maple sugar with C sugar. No flavor.

Molasses Pop-Corn Balls.—Always sift your corn after it is popped. For home use add butter and lemon flavor to your syrup. This is too expensive for retail and factory use, though some use lard sparingly. Boil molasses to a stiff ball, wet your tub, put in your corn; now with a dipper pour over your candy and stir with a paddle through the corn, wet your hands in cold water, make your balls and wrap in wax paper, twisting the ends close to the balls,

Molasses Taffy.—New Orleans molasses 1 pint, C sugar 1½ pounds, water ½ pint (no doctor); stir all the time to a good light snap; lemon flavor; work as above.

Nougat.—Almonds and other nuts for nougat should be blanched, drained, and skinned some time before they are chopped. The nougat is made by melting pounded sugar in a copper sugar boiler, put a dessertspoonful of lemon juice to each pound, then adding double the weight of sugar in almonds, either colored or white, filberts, pistachios, and a little sweet liquor. The almonds or nuts should be hot when put into the syrup. For lining molds small pieces of the nougat should be pressed in with a lemon till the mold is covered, when the nougat should be turned out.

Nut Taffy.—Use the cream candy recipe. Just before the

candy is done cooking stir in any kind of nut goodies; pour out, and when cool enough not to run, form it into a block; cut or break it with a hammer.

Opera Creams.—Two pounds white sugar, ¾ pint cows' cream; boil to a soft ball; set off; add 2 ounces glucose; set on; stir easy until it commence to boil, then pour out; let get ¾ cold and stir it until it turns into a cream; then work into 2 tablespoons vanilla; line a pan with wax paper, flatten the batch in it, and mark it in squares. Set aside 2 hours to harden.

Pine Tree Tar Cough Candy.—First have 1 tablespoonful oil of tar dissolved in 2 tablespoons of alcohol. Cook to a hard snap 20 pounds sugar (white), 3 quarts of water, 3 pounds glucose; pour out; scatter over it while cooling 20 drops tar, 2 tablespoons oil of capsicum. 3 tablespoons oil of wintergreen; work all well into the batch (do not pull this on the hook). Place before your heater on the table and spin it out in large round sticks. Have some one to keep them rolling until cold. Cut into sticks about 3½ inches long. Wrap them in printed labels if for sale.

Peppermint, Rose, or Hoarhound Candy.—These may be made as sour lemon drops. Flavor with essence of rose, or peppermint, or finely powdered hoarhound. Pour it out in a buttered paper placed in a square tin pan.

Raisin Candy.—Can be made in the same manner as fig creams, substituting stoned raisins for the figs Common molasses candy is very nice with any kind of nuts added.

Sour Lemon Drops.—Make a batch of barely squares. Just as soon as you pour it on the slab sprinkle over it ¾ ounces dry tartaric acid, 2 tablespoons lemon flavor; turn the cold edges in to the center of the batch, work it like bread dough; place this before a hot stove on your table and cut into little pieces with your scissors or run the batch through a drop machine. All the goods that you want to spin out or run through a machine or cut with the scissors should be kept warm by a sheet-iron stove, on a brick foundation, fitted in the table evenly, and the candy placed in front to keep warm. Should the candy slab, after it is greased, act sticky, not allowing the candy to come up freely, throw a dust of flour over the sticky place after it has been greased.

Stick Candy.—Stick candy is made precisely the same as the peppermint (which see), by keeping the batch round, and a second person to twist them and keep them rolling until cold. This can be done only by practice. The sticks are then chopped in the desired length by heavy shears.

Strawberry.—Same, only flavor with strawberry; color with liquid coloring lightly.

Sugar Candy.—Take 2 cupfuls A coffee sugar, ⅓ cupful of good vinegar, ⅔ cupful water; boil without stirring until it crisps in cold water. Turn out upon a buttered plat---- and pour the desired flavor over it. When sufficiently cool pull until white and light, pulling directly from you without twisting. Have the hands clean and dry; do not use butter on them. This rule is varied by using different flavorings, and makes excellent candy by pouring it over nuts or popcorn.

Popcorn, White or Red.—Sugar and glucose half and half, water to melt, and boil as above. Work the same. To make 600 bricks a day and pop this corn, put a coarse sieve in a box or barrel bottom, instead of the natural bottom. Sift your corn. Have your popper made with a swinging wire, hanging down from the ceiling over the furnace to save labor. Have a stout, thick, wide board for the floor of your press; make a stout frame the width that two bricks will measure in length, as long as 12 bricks are thick, and have your boards 6 or 8 inches wide. Put your frame together; now make a stout lid of 1 inch lumber to fit in your frame; have 4 cleats nailed crosswise to make it stout, and a 2x4 piece nailed lengthwise across the top of these (shorter than the lid is); now for a lever get a hard 2x4, 6 to 8 feet long; fasten the ends of this lever to the floor, giving it 6 inches of the rope to play in. Now you are ready; wet your flour board and dust it with the flour; do the lid and frame the same. To every 30 pounds melted scraps of candy use 2 pounds butter. (You can't cut the bricks without it). Cook to a hard ball. To ¾ tub of corn pour 3 small dippers of syrup; pour this when mixed in your frame on the flour board, put on the lid, with the lever press once the center, once each end, and once more the center; take out the lid, lift the frame, dump out on the table. When ⅔ cool, cut lengthwise with a sharp, thin knife, then cut your bricks off crosswise. Penny popcorn bricks are made the same way.

To Make a Candy House.—House for a show window. Take any design you fancy, of card board; cut out the windows; place this on your candy slab. Now with a lead pencil mark out your design, and as many of each piece as you need (it is a good idea to make an extra piece so if you break one you can go ahead). Now take off the icing sugar and fill your paper funnel as if for cake icing. and overline the pencil marks you made on the stone. When done you find you have a frame that will hold hot candy. Boil a batch of barley square goods and pour on some in a dipper; take this and pour in your icing sugar frame or patterns you made on the stone. when half cold, so as not to run; run a thin knife under them carefully. lift them and lay them in a different place on the stone; when you have molded all, cut off the icing sugar that sticks to the candy. Then put your candy house together, sides first, and take pieces of lemon stick candy, dip them in the hot candy, and stick in the bottom and top corners of your house; hold them a few seconds to cool, then finish likewise. When done, take your icing sugar and funnel paper and on the outside corners of the candy house put icing sugar and the windows finish the same. Candies, if desired, can be stuck on with the icing sugar, etc. The icing sugar should be stiff for a nice job, and will hide the corners. Candy pyramids can be made this way also.

To Make a Delicious Cocoanut Candy Cake.—Have your cake layers cold. Place in your rice steamer ½ grated cocoanut and a chunk of hand-made cream the size of your fist; stir until mixed and you can spread it; do not melt it more than necessary. This cake will not dry out if made with factory cream. I gave this recipe to two London cake bakers, and they said it beat any cake recipe they had ever received. Put your mind to work, and with a little practice you will get up candies of your own invention, from the knowledge you derive here in this book.

To Work Over Scraps of Candy.—To 30 pounds of scraps use 1 gallon of water; stir until it boils; set off, for it would never melt any more by boiling; continue stirring until all is dissolved. Set aside until cold; skim off the top. This can be worked into hoarhound or dark penny goods, popcorn bricks, etc.

To Cook Over Maple Sugar.—To 60 pounds broken up maple, add water (according to the hard or soft grain of the sugar) enough to dissolve; stir until melted. If the grain was soft, add 15 pounds granulated sugar, if the hard grain only add that amount of C sugar. Boil to 244 degrees by thermometer or good ball. Take out some in a porcelain sauce pan, grain until cloudy (to make quick work always have a small portion in the same sauce pan for the next stirring). Pour in molds greased, or put in tub of cold water.

To Shell Cocoanuts.—Take the nut in the left hand with the three eyes up; strike from the nut down with your hatchet; peel with a knife or spoke shave, cut them into 4 pieces, cover them with water, set on the furnace, and let come to a boil. If the nuts are sour, strain and add fresh cold water quickly so as the heat will not darken them, and repeat. If very sour scrape the insides out. Grate them, taking out one piece at a time, as the air does them no good.

Walnut Caramels.—Same as the first. (*See Chocolate Caramels*). When done, stir in sufficient nuts to suit. A better caramel can be made with white sugar, and milk instead of water. Still better, by using cream 1 quart, and when cream cannot be had, condensed milk dissolved in milk works fine. All caramels are made from the same recipe, the only difference being in the flavoring.

ICE CREAMS, ICES, ETC.

DIRECTIONS FOR FREEZING.

The essential points in freezing ice cream are to have the ice finely crushed, to use the right proportion of coarse rock salt, and to beat the mixture thoroughly during the freezing. Salt has a great attraction for water and causes the ice to melt, and ice, in changing from a solid to a liquid, absorbs heat. The mixture of melted ice and salt is many degrees colder than ice alone. The melting ice absorbs heat from the cream, or whatever may be placed in the freezer, and reduces the temperature to the freezing point. The finer the ice is crushed the quicker it melts, and the more the mixture is stirred, the sooner all parts come in contact with the cold surface of the can and become chilled. For this reason the ice should be crushed until fine and mushy, not merely broken into lumps; and also because large pieces with sharp edges will dent the can.

The melted ice and salt should surround the can, and not be drawn off as fast as melted. It is evident, therefore, that any freezer with an outlet for the water in the bottom, and with directions for drawing off the water as soon as the ice is melted, is constructed upon erroneous principles. The outlet should be just below the top of the can and should always be open, and then the water will run out before it can get inside the can. Do not draw it off during the process of freezing, unless the tub is so full that the ice clogs the outlet.

Use 1 part salt to 3 or 4 parts ice. Coarse fine salt will do the work, but not so satisfactorily as rock salt or Turk's Island salt. A mixture of snow and salt answers when ice cannot be obtained. The ice and salt may be mixed before putting them into the tub, but many prefer to put them in separately, in alternate layers. See that the can is clean, the bearings, gears and socket in the tub are well oiled, and that the can and gear frame are properly adjusted, before putting in the cream. Be sure that the bail of the tub hangs over the latch end, for if on the other side, the crank of the gear frame will interfere with it when lifting the tub. Then lift off the gear frame, being careful not to pull the beater shaft out of the socket. Turn in the cream, adjust the cover and gear frame, fasten the latch, and then pack in the ice and salt.

Put in a layer of ice 3 inches deep (pack it in solidly), then a measure or saucerful of salt, sprinkle it evenly on the ice, then 3 measures of ice and 1 of salt, etc., till the tub is full. When only a small quantity of cream is being frozen, it is sufficient for the ice to come a few inches above the cream in the can. Pack each layer in closely with a wooden paddle and turn the crank occasionally while packing. Turn slowly or occasionally for the first 10 minutes, then rapidly till you can turn no longer. Remove the beater, scrape off the cream from the sides and pack it down closely in the can. Put a cork in the opening of the cover, and lay the gear frame over, to keep the can down in the ice. Cover with a piece of old carpeting wet in the salt water. If the ice and salt have been well packed, and the cream is to be served within an hour and not molded, no more ice will be heeded. But if it is to be kept longer, draw off the water and add more ice and salt.

All ice creams are richer, and of better body, flavor. and texture, if allowed to remain in the ice and salt at least an hour to ripen.

NOTE.—The recipes for Ice Creams and Water Ices are not arranged alphabetically, but according to their degree of excellence and superiority.

Ice Cream (General Recipe).—Two quarts thick cream, pound A sugar, ¼ ounce French gelatine, yolks 3 eggs; add 1 quart of the cream and gelatine, set on the fire; stir; do not let boil; melt; set off, add the eggs and sugar stirred up together with a little of the cream, stirring all the time; set on, let get hot; set off, add the other quart of cream; stir, strain, freeze. Break your ice fine; use salt from 1 pint to 1 quart. Flavor after it is frozen.

Philadelphia Ice Cream.—One quart cream, 1 scant cup sugar; flavor to taste. This is a name generally applied in this country to all ice creams made with pure cream and no eggs. There are three ways of making this ice cream. First. Mix the sugar and flavoring with the cream, and when the sugar is dissolved strain it into the freezer. This is the quickest and easiest method; the cream increases in bulk considerably and is of a light snowy texture. 2d. Whip the cream until you have taken off a quart of the froth, mix the sugar and flavoring with the unwhipped cream, strain into the freezer, and when partly frozen add the whipped cream and freeze again until stiff. This gives a very light delicate texture to the cream. Third. Heat the cream in a double boiler until scalding hot, melt the sugar in it, and when cold add the flavoring. This is considered by many the best method, as the cream has a rich body and flavor, and a peculiarly smooth, velvety appearance. It also prevents the cream from turning sour. The cream may be whipped first, and the froth removed until you have a pint, then scald the remainder of the cream with sugar, and when cold add the whipped cream. Thin cream or single cream is rich enough for ice cream, but it should be all cream, not thick cream diluted with milk. When milk is used with thick cream, eggs or flour should be used to thicken the milk, or the milk should be well scalded with the cream.

Ice Cream with Gelatine.—One quart milk, 8 eggs, 1 saltspoon salt, 1 pint cream, 1½ cups sugar, ¼ box Nelson's gelatine, lemon, coffee, wine or any strong flavoring. Soak the gelatine in ½ cup of the measure of cold milk; boil the remainder of the milk and cream; beat the eggs till creamy, add the sugar and salt and beat again; add the hot milk, then put into the double boiler, stir constantly and cook till it thickens and coats the spoon; add the soaked gelatine, and more sugar if needed, and when dissolved strain it and set away to cool. When cold flavor highly with lemon, wine, or any flavoring strong enough to disguise the taste of the gelatine.

Vanilla Ice Cream.—1. The simplest way to make vanilla ice cream is to make either of the 5 kinds given as a foundation, and just before freezing flavor with 1 or 2 tablespoonsful of the extract of vanilla; the amount will depend upon the strength and purity of the extract. **2.** Make whichever foundation cream is preferred and use ¼ less than the sugar given in the recipe; just before freezing add from 1 to 2 tablespoonsful of vanilla sugar, or enough to give the flavor desired.

Vanilla Sugar.—Split 1 ounce Mexican vanilla beans, remove the fine seeds and soft part; put them in a mortar with ½ pound sugar and bruise them till the seeds are separated and thoroughly mixed with the flour; sift through a fine strainer, letting all the fine seeds go through with the sugar; cut the outer part of the bean into small pieces, bruise with another ½ lb. of sugar; sift and pound again until all is fine; the sugar that has the seeds may be kept for ice creams, as the presence of the seeds is desirable in genuine vanilla cream. The second portion may be used for flavoring custards, etc.

Caramel Ice Cream.—Put ⅓ cup of granulated sugar in a saucepan over the fire and stir till melted and dark brown; add ½ cup boiling water and simmer 10 minutes. Make either ice cream you prefer, using ½ the sugar given in the recipe; add enough of this caramel to give the desired flavor and color. Caramel may be added to a vanilla or coffee ice cream. Whipped cream may be served with it or stirred in when the caramel cream is partly frozen.

Lemon Ice Cream.—Make ice cream by the Philadelphia recipe. Pare the rind from the lemon, cut it in halves, remove the seeds and squeeze out the juice; if the rind and seeds are pressed with pulp much of their bitter flavor will be given to the juice; strain the juice (there should be about 2 tablespoonsful), and mix with an equal amount of water; freeze as usual; sweeten to taste, adding the flavor after freezing. A tablespoonful of extract may be used to a quart of cream if preferred.

Chocolate Ice Cream.—Make the foundation ice cream after either recipe, and whip 1 pint of cream to serve with it; heat 2 bars sweetened vanilla chocolate with 2 tablespoonsful water, or enough to melt it; when smooth add gradually a little of the hot cream or custard, and strain through a fine strainer or cloth into the remainder of the cream. If unsweetened chocolate is used, add 2 tablespoonsful of sugar to it while melting. Half of a level teaspoonful of Ceylon cinnamon may be mixed with the chocolate, or ½ inch of stick cinnamon may be boiled with the cream or milk; it gives a rich, spicy flavor; or you may have another variety by the addition of 1 tablespoonful of caramel.

Strawberry Ice Cream.—Sprinkle 2 cups of sugar over 2 quarts of strawberries; mash them and let them stand ½ hour or until the sugar is dissolved. Meanwhile prepare the ice and pack the freezer; turn the berries into a large square of cheese-cloth which has been placed over a bowl; gather up the edges of the cloth, twist them, and squeeze as long as any juice or pulp will come; then empty the pulp and seeds left in the cloth into a pan and pour on gradually about 1 pint of milk, mix it well with the pulp until the pulp is separated from the seeds; squeeze again until perfectly dry. There should be nothing left in the cloth save a ball of seeds. The pulp will thicken the milk, and it is much nicer than the juice alone. Add to this pulpy juice as much cream as you may have, from 1 cup to 3 pints, and sugar to make it very sweet. The cream should be scalded and cooled. Freeze as usual. This is delicious and a great improvement over that made by simply mashing the fruit, where the presence of the seeds is objectionable. Make other berry ice cream in the same manner.

Peach Ice Cream.—Pare 2 quarts of ripe white peaches, cut them fine and mash quickly with a wooden masher; then add 1 cup of sugar and a few of the peachstone meats, and keep it closely covered until the sugar is dissolved. Make the ice cream after either recipe, and when the cream is thoroughly chilled strain the peach pulp through coarse cheesecloth and stir it into the cream. Freeze as usual.

Banana Ice Cream.—Peel 6 ripe bananas, split and remove the seeds and dark portion in the center; rub the pulp through a puree strainer; add to it the juice of 1 lemon, a saltspoonful of salt, and sugar to make it quite sweet; add this pulp to either recipe for ice cream, and freeze as usual.

Almond Ice Cream.—Select the best paper-shell almonds; remove the shell and put them into boiling water for a minute, or until the skin can be rubbed off easily; then drain, put them in cold water and remove the brown skin; dry them on a towel. There should be ¼ pound of the selected nuts; pound them in a mortar with a few drops of rose water and ¼ cup each of sugar and cream, till like a fine paste. Make the Philadelphia ice cream with a scant cup of sugar and add to it when well chilled, a few drops of bitter almond extract, a teaspoonful of vanilla, and the nut paste; mix it thoroughly, freeze again, and when hard let it stand 2 hours to ripen. Nut ice creams require a long time to freeze and ripen, owing to their oily nature.

Pistachio Ice Cream.—Shell, blanch and pound 4 ounces of pistachio nuts, as directed for almonds in the preceding recipe. Make the Philadelphia ice cream, and scant the proportion of sugar. Flavor it with a delicate flavor of vanilla and almond and add the pistachio paste. Color it a pale green with spinach coloring, by mixing the spinach sugar with a little of the cream till smooth. Use enough to give the desired shade, then freeze as usual.

Mock Pistachio Ice Cream.—Make the almond ice cream as directed, and color it green with the spinach coloring. The flavor of the pistachio nuts is similar to the sweet almond, and as the real pistachio nuts are expensive, a very good imitation may be made in this way.

Harlequin Ice Cream.—This is a mixture of creams of different colors, served together. Sometimes they are molded together, either in uniform layers or irregularly, so that when turned out and served they have a streaked or mottled effect. Chocolate or pine-apple, strawberry, pistachio and vanilla make a pleasing variety.

Moss Ice Cream, Mousse.—This form of a "Frozen Dainty" has a frothy, moss-like texture, produced by freezing whipped cream without stirring it during the process of freezing. A great variety of delicate dishes may be made by varying the flavoring and molding the mousse alone, or in sherbet or ice cream of a contrasting shade and agreeable flavor. The following rules will illustrate the preparation of the cream and the manner of freezing: Sweeten and flavor a pint of cream. Use vanilla, lemon, caramel, melted chocolate, sherry wine, or maraschino. Place the bowl containing the cream in a pan of broken ice or snow, and have ready a granite or bright tin pan placed in another of broken ice. Put a sieve or puree strainer into the pan. Pack a plain mold or the freezer can, minus the beaters, in broken ice and salt, that it may become icy cold. Whip the cream with a syllabub churn, skim off the froth and put it into the strainer. If any liquid part drain through into the pan, put it back into the bowl and whip again; when all is whipped put it into the mold or can. Pack it in closely enough to fill all the spaces, but be careful not to break up the froth. Cover the mold and let it stand 3 or 4 hours. When a fluted or fancy mold is used the mousse will turn out better if the mold is first lined with ice cream or sherbet frozen just stiff enough to pack in smoothly.

SHERBETS AND WATER ICES.

These are made with the juice of fruit, water, and sugar. When fresh fruit cannot be obtained you may use syrups which have been made of fruit juices and sugar, and sealed in air-tight bottles; or canned fruits, mashed and sifted, using pulp as well as juice; or fruit jellies heated in water until melted. While such ices are acceptable in an emergency, they are never equal to those made from fresh fruit.

Lemon Ice.—Seven lemons, the juice only; juice 3 oranges; take 1 pint water, dissolve in ½ ounce French sheet gelatine; then add whites of 2 eggs. 1¼ pounds A sugar dissolved; add all together with 3 pints cold water; freeze as for ice cream. Keep machine running briskly until finished.

Lemon Sherbet with White of Egg.—Two quarts boiling water, 8 lemons, white of 1 egg, 1 quart sugar. Spread part of the sugar on a shallow plate or board, and after wiping the lemons with a clean damp cloth, roll them in the sugar to extract the oil. Then cut in halves, remove the seeds, and squeeze out the juice. Boil all the sugar and water until clear. Remove the scum as it rises. Add the lemon juice to the syrup, strain it, and pour it gradually into the beaten egg. Then freeze as usual.

Orange Sherbet.—Made in the same way, using oranges instead of lemons.

Pineapple Sherbet.—One pint fresh or 1 can grated pineapple, 1 pint sugar, 1 pint water, 1 tablespoonful gelatine, 1 lemon. Pare the pineapple, remove all the eyes, and pick off the tender part with a fork, rejecting all the hard core. If still too coarse chop a little. Add the sugar, water, lemon juice, and gelatine, which should be first soaked in cold water and then dissolved in boiling water. Freeze as usual.

Currant or Cherry Sherbet.—One pint fruit juice, 1 pint boiling water, 1 pound sugar. Mash the fruit and strain through a strong bag until all the juice is out; boil the sugar and water 5 minutes, remove the scum, and strain through fine cheesecloth. Cool and add the fruit juice. Freeze without stirring much, until mushy, or stir constantly and freeze until hard.

Strawberry or Blackberry Sherbet.—One quart of berries or enough to make 1 pint juice, 1 pint sugar, 1 lemon. Mash the berries, add the sugar, and after standing till the sugar is dissolved, add the water and lemon juice. Press through fine cheesecloth and freeze. Vary the sugar as the fruit requires. All of these fresh fruits are improved by the addition of the lemon.

Lemon Sherbet.—Four lemons, 1 pint sugar, 1 quart boiling water. Shave off the peel from 2 lemons in thin, waferlike parings, being careful to take none of the lighter colored rind below the oil-cells. Put the parings into a bowl, add the boiling water and let it stand 10 minutes closely covered. Cut the lemons in halves, remove the seeds, squeeze out the juice and add it with the sugar to the water. Add more sugar if needed. When cold strain it through a fine strainer into the can and freeze.

Lemon-Ginger Sherbet.—Cut 4 ounces candied ginger in fine pieces and steep it with the lemon, as directed above.

Lemon Sherbet, with Gelatine.—One tablespoonful gelatine, 3½ cups cold water, 6 lemons, ½ cup boiling water, 1 pint sugar. Soak the gelatine in ½ cup cold water 20 minutes. Put the sugar and the remaining cold water into a large lip bowl or pitcher. Pare the lemons, cut in halves, remove all the seeds, and press out the juice with a lemon-squeezer; add it to the syrup. Dissolve the scaked gelatine in the boiling water, add it to the other mixture. If liked sweeter, add more sugar. When the sugar is dissolved strain through a fine wire strainer or cheesecloth, turn into the freezer and freeze as directed. Sherbet made in this way has none of the volatile lemon oil. which to a delicate stomach often proves indigestible.

Fruit Cream.—One-half can apricots, 3 bananas, 3 oranges, 3 lemons. 3 cups sugar, 3 cups water. Put a puree strainer or sieve over a large granite pan or bowl. turn in the apricots and rub all but the skin through. Peel the bananas, remove the seeds and dark portions and sift the pulp. Pour the water in gradually to help the pulp go through the strainer   Squeeze the oranges and lemons and strain through into the fruit pulp. Add all the sugar, and when dissolved, freeze as usual. From 1 cup to 1 pint of cream may be mixed with the fruit just before freezing, but it is delicious without it, as the fruit pulp gives body to the frozen mixture. **2.** Prepare 1 pint of any ripe, firm fruit or canned fruit, drained, such as peaches, apricots, cherries, etc. Rub it through a puree strainer, and sweeten to taste; then stir in quickly 1 quart whipped cream. Freeze as usual.

Mixed Ices or Macedoines.—One cup currant and 1 cup raspberry juice: or 1 cup orange, 1 cup pineapple, and ½ cup of lemon; or 1 cup grape and 1 cup plum; or 1 cup strawberry 1 cup cherry, and 1 cup currant. Use as much water as fruit juice, and sugar to make the mixture quite sweet. Freeze as usual.

Frozen Fruits.—Ripe fruit sweetened and thoroughly chilled is an acceptable substitute for sherbets or ice cream, and in hot weather is very refreshing at the beginning of the morning meal. The prepared fruit is simply put in the freezer can minus the beaters: the can is surrounded with ice and salt. and left without stirring until the fruit is chilled. It usually takes about an hour.

BERRIES of all kinds should be hulled or stemmed, picked over. and sprinkled with fine sugar.

BANANAS should be peeled. sliced thinly. and sprinkled with sugar and lemon juice. A speck of salt and cinnamon mixed with the sugar is a great improvement.

ORANGE PULP prepared as directed in recipe for orange or lemon sherbet. may be used in place of the lemon juice with the bananas; or may be sweetened and chilled by itself.

PINEAPPLES should have the outer rind and eyes removed and the soft part cut in small cubes and sweetened to taste.

PEACHES and ripe yellow pears should be pared and cut in halves. the cores or stones removed, and sprinkled with sugar. A little lemon juice improves the pears.

WATERMELON AND CANTELOUPE. Take out the melon pulp in small. uniform pieces, and sprinkle slightly with salt and sugar.

TOMATOES.—Peel, cut in ½ inch slices and sprinkle with salt and sugar.

Frozen Beverages.—COFFEE. Prepare 2 quarts of strong clear coffee. and sweeten to taste. When cold put it in freezer and turn the crank until it is like soft mush.

TEA.—Prepare 1 quart of tea, sweeten to taste, and when cool add a little lemon juice. Freeze until mushy.

EGGNOGG.—Beat 2 eggs until light and creamy. add 2 tablespoonsful sugar and beat again; add 2 tablespoonsful of wine or brandy and 1 cup cream or milk. Put in the freezer and turn the crank until half frozen.

SYRUPS AND FLAVORS.

Artificial Honey.—Take 8 pounds of white sugar, add 2 Quarts water; boil 4 minutes, then add 1 pound bee's honey; strain while hot. Flavor with a drop of the oil of peppermint and a drop of the oil of rose.

Acid Fruit.—The juice of any acid fruit can be made into syrups by using 1 pound white sugar to 1 pint of juice, and adding some peel; boil 10 minutes, strain, and cork.

Ambrosia.—1. A mixture of equal parts of vanilla and strawberry syrup. **2.** Raspberry syrup 2 pints, vanilla syrup 2 pints, hock wine 3 ounces.

Apple.—Boil in clarified syrup an equal quantity of fruit cut in small squares, but not washed or broken. The syrup extracts the flavor and may be poured off after standing 24 hours; the apples can be used for other purposes.

Banana.—Oil of banana 2 drams, tartaric acid 1 dram, simple syrup 6 pints.

Blackberry.—Make a simple syrup of 1 pound of sugar to each pint of water; boil until thick, add as many pints of the expressed juice of ripe blackberries as there are pounds of sugar; put ½ grated nutmeg to each quart of syrup; boil 15 or 20 minutes; then add ½ gill fourth proof brandy for each quart of syrup; allow it to become cold, then bottle for use.

Candying, To Prevent.—The candying or crystalization of syrup, unless it be over saturated with sugar, may be prevented by the addition of a little citric or acetic acid (2 or 3 drams per gallon). Confectioners add a little cream of tartar to the sugar to prevent granulation.

Catawba Syrup.—Simple syrup 1 pint, catawba wine 1 pint. Note—All wine syrups are made in about the same proportions as this recipe.

Champagne Syrup or Flavor.—Rhine wine 2 pints, brandy 2 ounces, sherry wine 1 ounce, granulated sugar 3 pounds; dissolve the sugar without heat.

Cherry Syrup.—Take sour cherries (a convenient quantity), bruise them in a mortar, to break the stones; express the juice; set aside 3 days to ferment, and proceed according to directions given for strawberry syrup No. 1.

Chocolate.—Chocolate 8 ounces, syrup sufficient, water ½ pint, white of 1 egg: grate the chocolate and rub in a mortar with the egg; when mixed, add water gradually and triturate till a uniform mixture is obtained; add syrup to make 4 pints, and strain.

Cinnamon.—Oil of cinnamon 30 minims, carbonate of magnesia 60 grains, water 2 pints, granulated sugar 56 ounces; rub the oil first with the carbonate of magnesia, then with the water gradually added. filter through paper. (*See Filtration in Department* I.) In the filtrate dissolve the sugar without heat.

Clarifying.—Mix the white of eggs or a solution of gelatine with the mixture to be clarified.

Excelsior Syrup.—Simple syrup 1 pint, syrup of wild cherry bark 4 ounces, port wine 4 ounces.

Grape.—Brandy ½ pint, spirits of lemon ¼ ounce, tincture of red sanders 2 ounces, simple syrup 1 gallon.

Lemon.—Havana sugar 1 pound; boil in water down to 1 quart; drop in the white of 1 egg; strain it; add ¼ ounce tartaric acid; let stand 2 days; shake often; 12 drops essence of lemon will improve it.

Lemon Extract.—Oil of lemon 3 ounces; cut with 95 per cent proof alcohol; add 1 gallon 80 per cent proof alcohol, and filter through cotton or felt; put up in 2-ounce bottles.

Maple Syrup.—Dissolve 3½ pounds of maple sugar in 1 quart of water.

Mulberry.—Mulberries not quite ripe 6 pounds, sugar, powdered, 6 pounds; place in a kettle and boil, stirring until the boiling syrup marks 30 degress Baume; throw in a strainer and allow to strain thoroughly.

Nectar.—Vanilla syrup 5 pints, pineapple syrup 1 pint, strawberry, raspberry or lemon syrup 2 pints.

Orange Flower.—Orange flower water 1 pint, granulated sugar 28 ounces; dissolve without heat.

Orange.—Oil of orange 30 drops, tartaric acid 4 drams, simple syrup 1 gallon; rub the oil with the acid, then mix.

Raspberry.—1. Raspberry juice 1 pint, simple syrup 2 pints, solution of citric acid 2 drams. **2.** First make a syrup with 36 pounds of white sugar and 10 gallons of water, and put it into a plain barrel; dissolve ¼ pound of tartaric acid in 1 quart of cold water and add to the syrup; take ½ pound of orris root and pour over it ⅓ gallon of boiling water; let it infuse until cold, then filter and put it into the barrel, stirring it well.

Sarsaparilla.—Oils of wintergreen. anise and sassafras, of each 10 drops, fluid extract of sarsaparilla 2 ounces, simple syrup 5 pints. powdered extract of licorice ½ ounce.

Sherbet. — Mix equal parts of orange, pineapple and vanilla.

Sherry Cobbler.—Sherry wine 1 pint, simple syrup 1 pint, 1 lemon cut in thin slices; macerate 12 hours and strain.

Simple Syrup.—To make, use in proportions of 1 pound of white sugar to 1 pint of water.

Strawberry.---1. Use strawberries of good flavor to obtain syrup of fine flavor, mash the fruit in a suitable vessel and leave the pulp 12 or 24 hours at a temperature between 70 and 80 degrees; stir occasionally; press; set the juice aside for 1 night; add for every pound of juice 1 ounce Avoirdupois of cologne spirits or deodorized alcohol: mix: set aside for a night and filter; for 1 pound of filtered juice take 10 pounds of sugar, and heat to the boiling point. taking care to remove from the fire as soon as the mixture begins to boil; remove the scum: bottle in clean bottles. rinsed with cologne spirits; this syrup, as well as those made by the same process. is strong enough to be mixed with 2 or 3 times its weight of simple syrup for the soda fountain. **2.** Strawberry juice 1 pint, simple syrup 3 pints; solution of citric acid 2 drams.

Vanilla Cream.—1. Fluid extract of vanilla 1 ounce, simple syrup 3 pints, cream (or condensed milk) 1 pint. color with carmine. **2.** Cream syrup 1 pint, vanilla syrup 1 pint, oil of bitter almonds 4 drops.

NOTE.—An excellent cream syrup is made as follows: Fresh cream 1 pint, fresh milk 1 pint. powdered sugar 1 pound; mix by shaking and keep in a cool place. The addition of a few grains of bicarbonate of soda will retard souring.

Vanilla Syrup.—Fluid extract of vanilla 1 ounce, citric acid ½ ounce, simple syrup 1 gallon; rub the acid with some of the syrup; add the extract of vanilla and mix.

Wild Cherry.—Wild cherry bark (in coarse powder) 5 ounces; moisten the bark with water and let it stand 24 hours in a close vessel. then pack firmly in a percolator and pour water upon it until 1 pint of fluid is obtained: add sugar 28 ounces.

Wintergreen.—Oil of wintergreen 25 drops. simple syrup 5 pints, burnt sugar to color.

NOTE.—Essences are made with 1 ounce of any given oil added to 1 pint of alcohol. Peppermint is colored with tincture turmeric. cinnamon with tincture red saunders. wintergreen with tincture kino. Tinctures are made with 1 ounce of gum. root or bark. etc., dried, to each pint of proof spirits, and let it stand 1 week and filter.

BEVERAGES.

Medicinal Liquors and Drinks. Vinegars.

Aerated Lemonade.—Into each bottle put lemon syrup 1 to 1½ ounces, essence of lemon 3 drops, susqui-carbonate of soda ½ dram, water of sufficient quantity to nearly fill the bottle; have the cork fitted and ready at hand; then add of tartaric acid 1 dram; instantly close the bottle and wire down the cork; it should be kept inverted in a cool place and preferably immersed in a vessel of ice cold water before using.

Almond Milk.—Two ounces of sweet almonds, ½ ounce of bitter almonds, 2 ounces of loaf sugar, 1 tablespoonful of orange flower water, 1 pint of spring water. Blanch the almonds and pound them with the sugar and orange flower water, in a mortar, adding a few drops of water occasionally whilst pounding, to prevent too much oiliness. When the mixture looks creamy and smooth, pour it into a clean basin, add the cold spring water, and stir it with a silver or thin wooden spoon. Leave it for 2 hours, then strain and keep it either on ice or in a very cool place, as it is likely otherwise to turn sour. Almond milk is served with an equal amount of water.

Ambrosial or Nectar Cream Soda.—Two ounces tartaric acid, 2 ounces cream of tartar, 2½ pounds white sugar, 1 quart water, whites of 4 eggs well beaten, 2 tablespoonfuls wheat flour; put all in a tin dish and heat, but not to boiling point; add 2 drops fine oil of lemon or other flavoring if preferred, and that will complete the syrup; when ready to use, pour 3 tablespoonfuls of the syrup into a tumbler ⅔ full of water, add as much soda as can be held on a dime and drink immediately. A cool, refreshing summer drink.

Angostura Bitters.—Gentian 4 parts, calisaya bark, Canada snake root, Virginia snake root, licorice root, dandelion root, pimento root, angostura bark, each 10 parts, cardamon, rhubarb, galangal, each 4 parts, orange peel 16 parts, caraway seed, cinnamon, nutmeg, each 2 parts, cloves ½ part, coriander, catechu, wormwood, each 2 parts, mace 1 part, red sanders 12 parts, curcuma 8 parts, alcohol 65° 1450 parts, honey 480 parts; either maceration or percolation may be employed.

Aniseed Cordial.—Aniseed oil 2 ounces (or essential oil 1½ dram), sugar 3 pounds per gallon. **2.** Aniseed 4 ounces, coriander and sweet fennel seed (bruised), each 1 ounce, rectified spirits ½ gallon, water 3 quarts; macerate 5 or 6 days; draw over 7 pints and add lump sugar 2½ pounds. **3.** Oil of aniseed 15 drops, oil of cassia and caraway seeds each 6 drops; rub them with a little sugar, then dissolve in spirits, 3 quarts, by shaking together. Filter and dissolve in the liquor; sugar 1½ pounds.

Aperient Lemonade.—Sugar 1 ounce, lemon juice ¾ fluid

ounce, sulphate of soda 3 drams, water 8 fluid ounces; put them into a soda water bottle without shaking; have the cork ready fitted; add of sesqui-carbonate of soda ½ dram, and instantly cork the bottle; wire it down and keep in a cool place, the bottle inverted.

Apricot Wine.—Twelve pounds of ripe apricots, 6 ounces of loaf sugar to every quart of liquor. Wipe the apricots, cut them in pieces and let them boil in two gallons of water. After boiling up, let them simmer till the liquor is strongly impregnated with the flavor of the fruit. Strain through a hair sieve and put 6 ounces to every quart of liquor. Boil up again, skim very carefully, and as soon as no more scum appears. put it into an earthen pan. Bottle next day if it is quite clear and put one lump of sugar into each bottle. It should be a fine wine in 6 months.

Aromatic Bitters.—Macerate 1⅜ pounds ground dried orange apples, ⅛ pound ground orange peel, 1 ounce ground dried calamus root, 1 ounce ground dried pimpinella root, ½ ounce ground dried cut hops for 14 days with 5 gallons of spirits at 45°; press and add 1¼ pounds brown sugar syrup; filter.

Artificial Cider.—Sugar 1 pound, tartaric acid ½ ounce, good yeast 2 tablespoonfuls, water 1 gallon; agitate to effect solution, and allow to ferment 12 hours or more. **2.** Eighteen gallons of water, enough sulphuric acid to give the water an agreeable tartness. 25 pounds sugar, 2 ounces alum, 1½ ounces ginger, 2½ ounces cloves. 3 ounces bitter almonds; boil the last 4 ingredients in 1 gallon water for 2 hours; strain and add it to the remaining water. **3.** Put in a cask 5 gallons hot water. 15 pounds brown sugar, 1 gallon molasses, ½ gallon hops or brewer's yeast, good vinegar 6 quarts; stir well, add 25 gallons cold water and ferment.

Baked Milk.—Put the milk in a jar, covering the opening with white paper, and bake in a moderate oven until thick as cream. May be taken by the most delicate stomach.

Beet Vinegar.—One bushel sugar beets mixed with 9 bushels of apples makes a cider richer than that produced from apples alone. Sugar beet juice can be converted into vinegar the same as cider. It make a stronger article, equally as good, but of a different flavor.

Blackberry Cordial.—Wash and pick over the berries; mash with a wooden spoon in a preserving kettle; let them come to a boil; strain; to every pint of juice add ½ pint water, 1 pound loaf sugar. 1 ounce each of cloves, mace, and cinnamon. 1 grated nuneg, 1 ounce pounded green ginger; boil ½ hour; strain, and when cool add to each pint 1 gill of brandy. Keep in a cool dry place.

Blackberry Wine.—1. Gather when ripe on a dry day; put into a vessel with the head out and a tap fitted near the bottom: pour on boiling water; mash the berries with your hands, and let them stand covered till the pulp rises and forms a crust in 3 or 4 days; then draw off the liquid into another vessel, and to every gallon add 1 pound of sugar; mix well and put it into a cask to work for 1 week or 10 days, and throw off any remaining lees. When the working has ceased, bung the cask. After 6 or 12 months it may be bottled. **2.** Gather the berries when ripe: measure and bruise them; to every gallon add 1 quart of boiling water. Let the mixture stand 24 hours, stirring occasionally; strain off the liquor into a cask, to every gallon adding 2 pounds of sugar; cork tight and let it stand until October, and you will have wine for use without any further steaming or boiling.

Black Cherry Wine.—Twenty-four pounds of small black cherries, 2 pounds of sugar to each gallon of liquor; bruise the cherries but leave the stones whole, stir well, and let the mixture stand 24 hours, then strain through a sieve, add the sugar, mix again, and stand another 24 hours; pour away the clear liquor into a cask, and when the fermentation has ceased, bung it closely; bottle in 6 months' time. It will keep from 12 to 18 months.

Boker's Bitters.—Rasped quassia 1½ ounces, calamus 1½ ounces, powdered catechu 1½ ounces, cardamons 1½ ounces, dried orange peel 2 ounces: macerate 10 days in ½ gallon strong whisky: filter and add 2 gallons of water; color with mallow or melva flowers.

Bottle Soda Water, Without Machine.—In each gallon water, dissolve ¾ pound crushed sugar and 1 ounce super-carbonate of soda; then fill pint bottles with this water; drop into each bottle ½ dram pulverized citric acid; immediately cork and tie down; handle the bottles carefully and keep cool; more sugar may be added if desired.

Bromo and Cocoa.—Bromo and Cocoa can be made the same as chocolate. Equal parts of milk and water can be used in preparing these drinks, if pure milk is considered too rich, but they will be found lacking in flavor, as nothing brings out the rich flavor of these compounds like pure milk.

Barley Water.—Two ounces pearl barley, 2 quarts of boiling water, 1 pint of cold water. Wash the barley in cold water; put it into a saucepan with the above proportion of cold water, and when it has boiled for about a quarter of an hour, strain off the water, add the 2 quarts of fresh boiling water. Boil it until the liquid is reduced ½; strain it, and it will be ready for use. It may be flavored with lemon-peel, after being sweetened, or a small piece may be simmered with the barley. When the invalid may take it, a little lemon-juice gives this pleasant drink in illness a very nice flavor.

Cafe Noir.—This is usually handed round after dinner, and should be drunk well sweetened. The coffee should be made very strong and served in very small cups, but never mixed with milk or cream. Cafe Noir may be made of the essence of coffee, by pouring a dessertspoonful into each cup, and filling it up with boiling water. This is a very simple and expeditious manner of preparing coffee for a large party, but the essence for it must be made very good and kept well corked until required for use.

Champagne, Artificial.—Take 2 or 3 sliced lemons, 2 tablespoonfuls tartaric acid, 2 ounces race ginger, 3 pounds bright Demarara sugar; pour over them 5 gallons boiling water; when blood warm add ½ pint distillery yeast or 1 pint home brewed; let the whole stand in the sun for 1 day; in the evening bottle and wire the corks; it will be ready to drink in 2 or 3 days, and will sparkle and effervesce like genuine champagne, while to the palate and stomach it will prove agreeable and wholesome. **2.** Stoned raisins 7 pounds, loaf sugar 21 pounds, water 9 gallons, crystalized tartaric acid 1 ounce, cream of tartar ½ ounce, honey or sugar 1 pound, sweet yeast ½ pint; ferment, skimming frequently, and when the fermentation is nearly over, add of coarsely powdered orris root 1 dram, orange flower water ½ pint, lemon juice 1 pint; in 3 months fine it down with isinglass ½ ounce; in 1 month more, if not sparkling, fine it down, and in 2 weeks bottle it, observing to put a piece of double refined white sugar the size of a pea in each bottle; lastly, wire down the corks and cover with tin foil, after the manner of champagne.

Cherry Cordial.—Macerate 30 pounds red sour cherries, made into a pulp, with 4½ gallons 95º alcohol; press, and add syrup of 42 pounds and sugar 3½ gallons water, filter.

Ching-Ching.—A good orange, a few drops of essence of cloves, ditto peppermint, 3 or 4 lumps of sugar, a tumblerful of ice.

To Make Chocolate.—Allow ½ ounce of chocolate to each person; to every ounce allow ½ pint of water, ½ pint of milk. Make the milk hot; scrape the chocolate into it, and stir the mixture constantly and quickly until the chocolate is dissolved; bring it to the boiling point, stir it well, and serve directly with white sugar.

Cider, Canned.—Cider may be preserved for years by putting up in air-tight cans, after the manner of preserving fruit. The liquid should be first settled and drawn off from the dregs, but fermentation should not be permitted to commence before canning.

Cider Champagne.—Good cider, pale 1 hogshead, spirits 3 gallons, honey or sugar 20 pounds; mix and let them rest for 2 weeks; then fine with skimmed milk ½ gallon. This will be very pale; and a similar article, when bottled in champagne bottles and silvered and labeled, has often been sold to the ignorant for champagne. A raisin placed in each bottle increases the effervescence.

Cider, Cherry.—Thirty gallons apple cider made from bitter apples, which are the best for making cider; 8 quarts dried blackberries, 2 quarts dried blueberries, 1 quart elderberries, 75 pounds brown sugar. To make smaller quantities use less of the ingredients.

Cider Clearing.—To clear and improve cider take 4 pints of ground horseradish and nearly 1 pound thick gray filtering paper to the barrel; shake or stir until the paper has separated into shreds, and let it stand 24 hours, and then draw off with a siphon.

Cider, Preserving.—1. Fermentation may be largely prevented by filtration of the juice, when first expressed, by which much of the material on which fermentation works is removed. **2.** When the cider in the barrel is in a state of lively fermentation, add white sugar equal to ¼ or ¾ pound to each gallon of cider (according as the apples are sweet or sour); let the fermentation proceed until the liquid has the taste to suit, then add ¼ ounce sulphite (not sulphate) of lime to each gallon of cider; shake well and let it stand 3 days and bottle for use. The sulphite should first be disolved in 1 quart or so of cider before introducing it into the barrel of cider. **3.** Cider may be kept good in large quantities if 1 quart pure refined linseed or olive oil is poured in at the bung. This spreading over the top of the cider will prevent the air from coming in contact with it, and so keep it sweet. After the cider has been nearly all drawn this oil may be saved for another year, if desired, or used for other purposes.

Cider Vinegar.—When cider has done fermenting, fill into a keg, then take strips of straw paper and dip them into New Orleans molasses and put them into the keg of cider; set in a warm place near the stove, and in a few weeks the contents will have turned into sharp vinegar. The straw paper acts as mother.

Cider Without Apples.—To 1 gallon cold water add dark brown sugar 1 pound, tartaric acid ½ ounce, yeast 3 tablespoonfuls. Shake well together.

Sour Cider, To Sweeten.—If cider is long made or souring when you get it, about 1 quart hickory ashes (or a little more of other hardwood ashes) stirred into each barrel will sweeten and clarify it, but if it is not rectified it must be drawn off to get clean of the pomace, as with this in it it will soon sour. Oil or whisky barrels are best to put cider in, or ½ pint sweet oil to 1 barrel or 1 gallon whisky to 1 barrel, or both may be added with decidedly good effects. Isinglass 4 ounces to 1 barrel helps to clarify and settle cider that is not to be rectified.

Cocoa.—Allow 2 teaspoonfuls of some well prepared cocoa to 1 breakfast-cup; boiling milk and boiling water. Put the cocoa into a breakfast-cup, pour over it sufficient cold milk to make it into a smooth paste, then add equal quantities of boiling milk and boiling water, and stir all well together. Care must be taken not to allow the milk to get burnt, as it will entirely spoil the flavor of the preparation. The rock cocoa, or that bought in a solid piece should be scraped, and made in the same manner, taking care to rub down all the lumps before the boiling liquid is added. All cocoa is better boiled for a minute or two.

Coffee.—In preparing tea or coffee, it is of the first importance to begin right. See that the teakettle is clean, and the water pure. A teakettle that is filled with lime, or other sediment, is unfit for use, and water that has stood in the house over night, or for some hours, is impure. To begin then. rinse the teakettle thoroughly and fill with fresh water, put on the fire, and bring to a boil quickly. For coffee, procure of a good reliable dealer a mixture of ⅓ Mocha, to ⅔ Java, freshly roasted and ground. Allow a tablespoonful of ground coffee for every person to be served, and put in an extra spoon for every 5 or 6 persons. If an ordinary pot is used, mix the coffee with an egg, put it in the coffee pot and add to it about a cupful of cold water; set it on the stove and bring to a boil quickly. The moment it begins to boil, add boiling water (about 2 quarts to 5 spoonfuls of ground coffee) and set it on the back part of the stove where it will keep hot, but on no account allow it' to boil, as that destroys the aroma. The coffee will be ready to serve in 6 or 8 minutes after hot water has been added. If a drip coffee pot is used, the coffee must be ground very fine. Good directions usually accompany the different kinds of coffee pots in use. However, great care must be taken to keep the strainer, whether made of cloth or wire, clean and free from all obstruction. If made of wire, it should be washed and cleaned with a brush, at least once a day.

Coffee, Another Method of Making.—Allow ½ ounce, or 1 tablespoonful of coffee to each person; to every ounce allow ½ pint of water. Have a small iron ring made to fit the top of the coffee pot inside, and to this ring sew a small muslin bag (the muslin for the purpose must not be too thin). Fit the bag into the pot, pour some boiling water in it, and when the pot is well warmed, put the ground coffee into the bag; pour over as much boiling water as is required, close the lid. and when all the water has filtered through, remove the bag and send the coffee to the table. Making it in this manner prevents the necessity of pouring the coffee from 1 vessel to another, which cools and spoils it. The water should be poured on the coffee gradually, so that the infusion may be stronger, and the bag must be well made, that none of the grounds may escape through the seams, and so make the coffee thick and muddy.

Coffee, Essence of.—To every ¼ pound of ground coffee allow 1 small teaspoonful of powdered chicory, 3 small teacupfuls, or 1 pint of water. Let the coffee be freshly ground, and, if possible, freshly roasted: put it into a percolator, or filter, with the chicory, and pour slowly over it the above proportion of boiling water. When it has all filtered through, warm the coffee sufficiently to bring it to the simmering point, but do not allow it to boil; then filter it a second time, put it into a clean and dry bottle, cork it well, and it will remain good for several days. Two tablespoonfuls of this essence are quite sufficient for a breakfast-cupful of hot milk. This essence will be found particularly useful to those persons who have to rise extremely early; and having only the milk to make boiling, it is very easily and quickly prepared. ·When the essence is bottled, pour another 3 teacupfuls of boiling water slowly on the grounds, which, when filtered through, will be very weak coffee. The next time there is essence to be prepared, make this weak coffee boiling, and pour it on the ground coffee instead of plain water; by this means a better coffee will be obtained. Never throw away the grounds without having made use of them in this manner; and always cork the bottle well that contains this preparation, until the day that it is wanted for making the fresh essence. Prepared coffee essence can now be bought at a reasonable price, and of good quality. It needs to be mixed with boiling water or milk, to be filtered once, then brought to the boiling point, and allow 2 tablespoonfuls for a breakfastcupful of hot milk.

Coffee in a Saucepan.—Have an earthenware or fire-proof China pan, put in freshly, but not too finely ground coffee with water, a dessertspoonful to every ½ pint. Set it over the fire till it is just about to boil. Take it off, stir it well, put it on again, and again let it nearly boil. Repeat this twice, when a thick scum will have risen. Set it by the side of the fire, covered to settle, and serve with boiling milk.

Coffee, To Roast.—It being an acknowledge fact that French coffee is of decidedly superior quality, and as the roasting of the berry is of great importance to the flavor of the preparation, it will be useful and interesting to know how they manage these things in France. To obtain this flavor before roasting, they add to every 3 pounds of coffee a piece of butter the size of a nut, and a dessertspoonful of powdered sugar; it is then roasted in the usual manner. A tin in a slack oven, or a frying-pan over the fire will serve, with care. A rotating coffee roaster is of course better. The addition of the butter and sugar develops the flavor and aroma of the berry; but it must be borne in mind that the quality of the butter must be the very best.

Corn Coffee.—Roast an ear of dry corn until the tips of the kernels are black. Break the ear in pieces, put in a bowl; then pour over it a pint of boiling hot water. Drink cold.

Cottage Beer.—Good wheat bran 1 peck, water 10 gallons, hops 3 handfuls, molasses 2 quarts, yeast 2 tablespoonfuls; boil the bran and the hops in the water until both bran and hops sink to the bottom: then strain through a sieve, and when lukewarm put in the molasses and stir until assimilated; put in a cask and add the yeast when fermentation ceases; bung, and it is ready in 4 days. This is an excellent beer.

Cream of Tartar Drink.—Dissolve ½ an ounce of cream of tartar in ½ a pint of syrup of sugar and water, add 20 drops of essence of lemon, and keep it in a bottle to be diluted with water, or soda water, as required. It will keep a long time.

Curacoa Cordial.—Curacoa orange peel 2 pounds, ½ pound Ceylon cinnamon; soak in water; boil 5 minutes with juice of 32 oranges and 14 gallons plain white syrup; add 6 gallons alcohol (95°); strain; filter, color dark yellow with burnt sugar coloring.

Currant Water.—One pound of fine red currants, ½ pound of raspberries, 1 pound of crushed loaf sugar water. Pick the fruit, add ½ a pint of water, and crush with a wooden spoon, then put the pulp into a preserving pan with half the sugar. Stir till it is beginning to simmer, then filter through a hair sieve. Make the rest of the sugar into a syrup with 3 gills of water, pour it to the fruit syrup, add a pint and a half of water. Let it cool, then decant like wine for use.

Currant Wine.—**1.** To 10 quarts juice add 5 pounds sugar; pour through a cloth into a stone jar; after 4 or 5 days add 3 pounds more sugar; skim every day. When through fermenting pour in a clean wooden cask; let it remain to the end of March. When bottled let it remain in a dark, cool place; take care to lay the bottles down to prevent bursting. **2.** Take 4 quarts juice, 8 quarts water, 12 pounds granulated sugar; ferment in tubs and skim every day until it has done singing, then put it in a barrel; put the bung in loosely till it has stopped working, then drive it in tight and it will be ready to bottle in January.

Damson Wine.—One gallon of boiling water to every 8 pounds of bruised fruit, 2½ pounds of sugar to each gallon of juice. Well bruise the fruit and pour the boiling water on it; let it stand 48 hours. Then strain the mixture into a cask and put in the sugar. When fermentation ceases fill up the cask and bung closely. Bottle in 10 months' time. It will be fit for use in a year, but improves with keeping.

Economical Vinegar.—Take a quantity of maple, beech, or basswood chips and soak them in good vinegar 3 or 4 days; with these chips fill a barrel which has been pierced with a large number of holes all around the sides to admit fresh air among the chips. Cut another barrel in halves: place ½ below the barrel with the chips, the other ½ above; pierce the bottom of the top tub with a number of gimlet holes, and place in the holes several threads of twine to make the vinegar flow evenly over the chips. The liquid drains down slowly among the chips and out of a faucet near the bottom of the barrel into the lower tub. It then should be pumped or baled back, running through the top tub into the barrel again. Leach any of the following preparations through the shavings. One and one-half pounds sugar to each gallon water. ½ gallon water to 2 gallons cider. The water should be soft, and 2 quarts of yeast should be added to every barrel. This vinegar can be made in 3 days, and should be prepared in warm weather or in a room where a high temperature is kept up.

Effervescing Gooseberry Wine.—To every gallon of water allow 6 pounds of green gooseberries, 3 pounds of lump sugar. This wine should be prepared from unripe gooseberries, in order to avoid the flavor which the fruit would give to the wine when in a mature state. Its briskness depends more upon the time of bottling than upon the unripe state of the fruit, for effervescing wine can be made from fruit that is ripe as well as that which is unripe. The fruit should be selected when it has nearly attained its full growth, and consequently before it shows any tendency to ripen. Any bruised or decayed berries, and those that are very small should be rejected. The blossom and stalk ends should be removed, and the fruit well bruised in a tub or pan, in quantities as to ensure each berry being broken without crushing the seeds. Pour the water (which should be warm) on the fruit, squeeze and stir it with the hand until all the pulp is removed from the skin and seeds, and cover tne whole closely for 24 hours; after which strain it through a coarse bag, and press it with as much force as can be conveniently applied, to extract the whole of the juice and liquor the fruit may contain. To every 40 or 50 pounds of fruit 1 gallon more of hot water may be passed through the marc, or husks, in order to obtain any soluble matter that may remain, and be again pressed. The juice should be put into a tub or a pan of sufficient size to contain all of it, and the sugar added to it. Let it be well stirred until the sugar is dissolved, and place the pan in a warm situation; keep it closely covered and let it ferment for a day or two. It must then be drawn off into clean casks, placed a little on one side for the scum that rises to be thrown out, and the casks kept filled with the remaining "must," that should be reserved for that purpose. When the active fermentation has ceased, the casks should be plugged upright, again filled, if necessary, the bungs be put in loosely, and, after a few days when the fermentation is a little more languid (which may be known by the hissing noise ceasing), the bungs should be driven in tight and a spile-hole made to give vent if necessary. About November or December, on a clear fine day, the wine should be racked from its lees into clean casks, which may be rinsed with brandy. After a month it should be examined to see if it is sufficiently clear for bottling; if not, it must be fined with isinglass, which may be dissolved in some of the wine; 1 ounce will be sufficient for 9 gallons. In March or April, or when the gooseberry bushes begin to blossom, the wine must be bottled in ordered to insure its being effervescing.

Egg Wine.—One egg, 1 tablespoonful and ½ glass of cold water, 1 glass of sherry, sugar, and grated nutmeg to taste. Beat the egg, mixing with it a tablespoonful of cold water; make the wine and water hot, but do dot boil; pour it on the egg, stirring all the time. Add sufficient lump sugar to sweeten the mixture, and a little grated nutmeg: put all into a very clean saucepan, set it on a gentle fire, and stir the contents until they thicken, but do not allow them to boil. Serve in a glass with sippets of toasted bread or plain crisp biscuits. When the egg is not warmed, the mixture will be found easier of digestion, but it is not so pleasant a drink.

Fair Ground Lemonade.—Take 1 barrel of water; dissolve in 1 quart of warm water 25 cents' worth citric acid; dissolve $2 worth A sugar in 1 gallon water. Stir all together. A few cut up pieces of lemon may be added for appearance's sake.

Flaxseed Lemonade.—Steep 2 tablespoonfuls of flaxseed in 1 quart of hot water for 10 minutes. Stir in and add the juice of 3 lemons, a large cupful of sugar, and a wineglassful of wine. Drink either hot or cold. This is an excellent drink for persons suffering with colds or lung troubles.

German Bitters.—Chamomile 2 parts, sweet flag 6 parts, orris root 8 parts, coriander 3 parts, centuary 1 part, orange peel 3 parts, alcohol 588 parts, water 672 parts, sugar 24 parts.

Ginger Beer.—1. Lump sugar 1 pound, first-class unbleached Jamaica ginger (bruised) 1 ounce, cream of tartar ¾ ounce, or tartaric acid ½ ounce, 2 or 3 lemons (sliced). boiling water q. s. 2. Into each bottle put 1 drop concentrated essense of ginger, simple syrup ½ ounce, and fill with aerated water by means of bottling machine. Superior article for sale.

Ginger Lemonade.—Half cup of vinegar, 1 cup sugar, 2 teaspoonfuls ginger; stir well; put in a quart pitcher and fill with ice water; make sweet or sour by adding necessary ingredients.

Ginger Mead.—One gallon water, 1 pound loaf sugar ½ ounce race ginger, 1 lemon sliced without seeds, 1 teacupful yeast; let stand over night to ferment; then pour off without stirring; add to each bottle 1 raisin; cork tight.

Gooseberry Vinegar.—Two pecks of crystal gooseberries, 6 gallons of water, 12 pounds of beet sugar of the coarsest brown quality. Mash the gooseberries (which should be quite ripe) in a tub with a mallet; put to them the water nearly milk-warm; let this stand 24 hours, then strain it through a sieve, and put the sugar to it; mix it well and turn it. These proportions are for a 9 gallon cask, and if it be not quite full, more water must be added. Let the mixture be stirred from the bottom of the cask 2 or 3 times daily for 3 or 4 days to assist the melting of the sugar; then paste a piece of linen cloth over the bunghole and set the cask in a warm place, but not in the sun; any corner of a warm kitchen is the best situation for it. The following spring it should be drawn off into stone bottles, and the vinegar will be fit for use 12 months after it is made. This will be found a most excellent preparation, greatly superior to much that is sold under the name of the best white vinegar. Many years' experience has proved that pickle made with this vinegar will keep, when bought vinegar will not preserve the ingredients. The cost per gallon is merely nominal, especially to those who reside in the country and grow their own gooseberries; the coarse sugar is then the only ingredient to be purchased.

Grape Vinegar.—1. Vinegar from grapes may be made as follows: The wine is stirred into a cask which contains lees, and when mixed is squeezed through cloth sacks into an iron-bound vat, whence, after standing some hours, it is drawn off into casks for fermenting. These casks have only a small opening at the top and are kept at 77 to 86 degrees Fahrenheit. After 14 or more days the vinegar is drawn off cautiously into barrels which contain birchwood chips. This clarifies it, and after standing a few days it may be siphoned off into casks. The residue containing mother is employed to ferment all the subsequent liquor by simply pouring the latter into the cask used previously. **2.** Take full-grown green grapes before they turn sweet put them in a porcelain-lined kettle with water to cover them, and stew until tender; then pour into a hair sieve and let it stand to drain, pressing slightly, then sweeten slightly and heat the juice to the boiling point, and can in bottles or vials. This will spoil if not canned in a little longer time than common stewed fruit, but it will not produce mother nor breed vinegar weels. It can be used to acidify cabbage, and in the place of lemon or lime juice. The strained grapes can be returned to the kettle and sweetened, and with the addition of water, will prove sour enough for sauce.

Grape Wine, Home-Made.—1. One quart grape juice, 3 quarts water, 2½ pounds common brown sugar, keep in an open barrel 19 days, covered only with muslin to exclude insects, then put in a close cask, fasten and bung and set aside till spring, then rack off and bottle. **2.** Let the grapes gathered be rather ripe, with all decayed ones removed; mash; strain and measure. To each gallon juice add 1 pound white sugar; let stand for 2 or 3 days; skim, strain, and measure as before, and to each gallon add 1 pound of sugar; let stand again for 2 or 3 days and add 1 pound white sugar to each gallon; cork and put away. Do not add a drop of water to the juice if you want rich wine.

Hamburg Bitters.—Ageric 2 parts, cinnamon 5 parts, cassia 4 parts, grains of paradise ½ part, quassia 3 parts, cardemon 1 part, gentian 3 parts, orange peel 3 parts, alcohol 556 parts, water 684 parts, acetic ether 2 parts; mix by either maceration or percolation.

Home-Brewed Ale.—Take 8 bushels malt, hops 12 pounds, yeast 5 quarts. The malt being crushed or ground is mixed with 72 gallons water at 160 degrees, and covered 3 hours, when 40 gallons are drawn off, into which the hops are put to infuse: 60 gallons of water at 170 degrees are then added to the malt in the mash-tub and well mixed, and after standing 2 hours 60 gallons are drawn off. The wort from these 2 mashes is boiled with the hops for 2 hours, and after being cooled down to 660 degrees is strained through a flannel bag into a fermenting tub, where it is mixed with the yeast and left to work 24 to 30 hours. It is then run into barrels to cleanse, a few gallons being reserved for filling up the cask as the yeast works over.

Home-Made Soda.—Forty grains each carbonate soda and fine loaf sugar, 50 grains lemon or tartaric acid; mix these in 4 glasses water; stir and drink; if a sliced lemon be substituted for the acid, this drink will be improved.

Hop Beer.—1. Sugar 4 pounds, hops 6 ounces, 4 ounces ginger (bruised); boil the hops 3 hours with 5 quarts water; then strain; add 5 more quarts of water and the ginger; boil a little longer; again strain; add the sugar, and when luke warm add 1 pint yeast. After 24 hours it will be ready for bottling. **2.** Mix 14 pounds molasses and 11 gallons water well together and boil 2 hours with 6 ounces hops. When cool add 1 cupful yeast and stir well, 1 or 2 gallons at a time. Let it ferment 16 hours in a tub covered with a sack: then put it in a 9 gallon cask and keep it filled up. Bung in 2 days, and in 7 days it will be fit to drink.

Hop Bitters.—Orange peel 2 parts, sweet flag and pimpinella root, each 1 part, hops ½ part, alcohol and water, each 320 parts, sugar 30 parts; when completed, color with burnt sugar. (See also Medical Department.)

Iced Tea.—Make a pitcherful of tea 2 or 3 hours before wanted. It should be made stronger than if it were to be served hot, as the melting ice weakens it. About 10 or 15 minutes before serving, add to the tea a quantity of chopped ice. Put a lump of ice in each cup or glass, and serve.

Imperial Cream Nectar Soda.—Part **1.** Water 1 gallon, loaf sugar 6 pounds, tartaric acid 6 ounces, gum arabic 1 ounce. Part **2.** Flour 4 teaspoonfuls, white of 5 eggs; beat finely together; add ½ pint water. When the first part is blood warm put in the second; boil 3 minutes; to 3 tablespoonfuls of syrup to ⅔ glass of water add ½ teaspoonful carbonate of soda made fine; stir well and drink.

Jelly Water.—Put in a tumbler a tablespoonful of current jelly, and a tablespoonful of wine: mix them well together, then fill the glass with ice water. If the patient is feverish, leave out the wine.

Koumiss (sometimes called milk beer.)—Into 1 quart of new milk put 1 gill fresh buttermilk and 3 or 4 lumps white sugar; mix well and see that the sugar dissolves; put in a warm place to stand 10 hours, when it will be thick; pour from the vessel to another until it becomes smooth and uniform in consistency. Bottle and keep in warm place 24 hours; it may take 36 in winter. The bottles must be tightly corked and the corks tied down. Shake well 5 minutes before opening. It makes a very agreeable drink, which is especially recommended for persons who do not assimilate their food, and young children may drink it as freely as milk. Instead of buttermilk, some use a teaspoonful of yeast. The richer your milk, which should be unskimmed, the better will be your koumiss.

Lemonade for Invalids.—One-half a lemon, lump sugar to taste, 1 pint of boiling water. Pare off the rind of the lemon thinly; remove as much as possible of the white outside pith and all the pips; cut the lemon into slices. Put the slices of lemon, the peel and lump sugar into a jug; pour over the boiling water; cover it closely, and when it is cold, it will be fit to drink. It should either be strained or poured off from the sediment.

Lemon Beer.—**1.** To 20 gallons, boil 6 ounces of ginger root (bruised), ¼ pound cream of tartar for 20 or 30 minutes in 2 or 3 gallons of water; strain in 13 pounds of sugar in which is put ½ ounce oil of lemon and 6 good lemons squeezed, having warm water enough to make the whole 20 gallons, just so hot you can hold your hand in it. Put in 1½ pints yeast worked into paste with 5 or 6 ounces flour; let it work over night, then strain and bottle. **2.** Sugar 1 pound, boiling water 1 gallon, 1 sliced lemon, bruised ginger 1 ounce, yeast 1 teacupful; let it stand 12 or 20 hours, after which bottle.

Lemon Cordial.—Macerate fresh and dried lemon peel, each 2 ounces, and fresh orange peel 1 ounce in proof spirit 1 gallon for 1 week; strain with expression; add clear soft water q. s. to reduce it to desired strength; with lump sugar 3 pounds to the gallon. A little orange flower or rose water improves it.

Lemonade Powder.—Powdered citric or tartaric acid 12 grains, powdered white sugar ½ ounce, essence of lemon 1 drop (or a little of the yellow pulp of the lemon rubbed off on a piece of sugar;) mix for 1 glass. **2.** White sugar 4 pounds, of citric or tartaric acid 1½ ounces, essence of lemon ¼ ounce; mix well and preserve in a bottle for use. One to 2 dessertspoonfuls make a glass of lemonade; it is also put up in papers containing about 2½ drams each.

Lime-Juice Drink.—Fresh lime, ice water, loaf sugar, a little liqueur. Squeeze the juice from the limes, strain it, and add pounded sugar to taste, and a little flavoring of liqueur, if liked. Put a little of this mixture in a glass, and fill up with water. All the cups, such as champagne and claret cup, are improved by the introduction of slices of fresh fruit, such as apricots or pineapple.

Maple Beer.—To 4 gallons boiling water add 1 quart maple syrup and ½ ounce essence of spruce; add 1 pint yeast, and proceed as with ginger beer.

Mead.—Mix 1 quart boiling water with 2¼ pounds brown sugar, 2 ounces tartaric acid and ½ pint molasses; when cool add ½ ounce of any flavoring extract; 2 fingers of the syrup in a glass of ice water makes a refreshing summer drink; serve each glass with ¼ teaspoonful bicarbonate of soda.

Milk or Cream, Substitute for.—Allow 1 new-laid egg to every large breakfast-cupful of tea or coffee. Beat up the whole of the egg in a basin, put it into a teacup (or a portion of it, if the cup be small), and pour over it the tea or coffee very hot. These should be added very gradually and stirred all the time to prevent the egg from curdling. In point of nourishment, both these beverages are much improved by this addition.

Molasses Beer.—Hops 1 ounce, water 1 gallon; boil 10 minutes; strain; add molasses 1 pound, and when luke-warm, yeast 1 spoonful; ferment.

Mulled Buttermilk.—The well beaten yolk of an egg added to boiling buttermilk and allowed to boil up; or add to the boiling buttermilk a little thickening of flour and cold buttermilk.

Nourishing Lemonade.—One and ½ pint of boiling water, the juice of 4 lemons, the rinds of 2, ½ pint of sherry. 4 eggs, 6 ounces of loaf sugar. Pare off the lemon-rind thinly, put it into a jar with the sugar, and pour over the boiling water. Let it cool, then strain it; add the wine, lemon-juice, and eggs, previously well beaten, and also strained, and the beverage will be ready for use. If thought desirable, the quantity of sherry and water could be lessened, and milk substituted for them. To obtain the flavor of the lemon-rind properly, a few lumps of the sugar should be rubbed over it, until some of the yellow is absorbed.

Orangeade.—**1.** Juice of 4 oranges, thin peel of 1 orange, lump sugar 4 ounces, boiling water 3 pints. **2.** Juice and peel of 1 large orange, citric acid 15 grains, sugar 3 ounces, boiling water 1 quart.

Orangeade Powders.—Powdered sugar 14½ ounces, powdered orange peel 12 granes, oil of orange peel 60 drops, essence of cedrat 12 drops, bicarbonate of soda 3½ ounces; mix and put 145 grains in each blue paper. In white paper put 32 grains tartaric acid or 30 grains citric acid, or the alkaline and acid powders may be put in separate bottles with a measure holding the proper proportions of each. The orange peel may be omitted. To use, mix the powders in water.

Orange Wine.—Oranges, 32 pounds of lump sugar, water. Break up the sugar into small pieces and put it into a dry, sweet 9 gallon cask, place in a cellar or other storehouse where it is intended to be kept. Have ready, close to the cask 2 large pans or wooden keelers, into one of which put the peel of the oranges, pared quite thin, and into the other the pulp after the juice has been squeezed from it. Strain the juice through a piece of double muslin, and put it into the cask with the sugar; then pour about 1½ gallon of cold spring water on both the peels and pulp; let it stand for 24 hours, and then strain it into the cask; add more water to the peels and pulp when this is done, and repeat the same process every day for a week. It should take about a week to fill up the cask. Be careful to apportion the quantity as nearly as possible to the 7 days, and to stir the contents of the cask each day. On the third day after the cask is full—that is, the tenth day after the commencement of making—the cask may be securely bunged down. This is a very easy and simple method, and the wine made according to it will be pronounced to be most excellent. There is no troublesome boiling, and all fermentation takes place in the cask. When the above directions are attended to, the wine cannot fail to be good. It should be bottled in 8 or 9 months, and it will be fit for use in 12 months after the time of making. Ginger wine may be made in precisely the same manner, only with the 9 gallon cask for ginger wine, 2 pounds of the best whole ginger, bruised, must be put with the sugar. It will be found convenient to tie the ginger loosely in a muslin bag.

Ottawa Beer.—Take 1 ounce each of sassafras, allspice, yellow dock, and wintergreen, ½ ounce each wild cherry bark and coriander, ½ ounce hops, 3 quarts molasses; pour sufficient boiling water on the ingredients, and let stand 24 hours; filter, and add ½ pint yeast. Ready for use in 24 hours.

Peach Cordial.—Make a rich syrup of 1 quart peach juice and 1 pound white sugar; when cold, add ½ pint best brandy; for a drink, dilute with water.

Peppermint Cordial.—1. Pour 1 quart boiling water on ½ pound of loaf sugar; stir till sugar dissolves; add 24 drops oil of peppermint; bottle while warm. **2.** Good whisky and water, of each 10 gallons, white sugar 10 pounds, oil of peppermint 1 ounce in 1 pint alcohol, 1 pound flour well worked in the fluid, ½ pound burnt sugar to give color; mix, and let stand 1 week before using.

Peruvian Bitters.—Peruvian bark and orange peel of each 8 parts, cinnamon, cloves, nutmeg and cayenne, of each ¼ part, alcohol and water, of each 492 parts; mix by maceration or percolation.

Pineapple Water.—One large, ripe pineapple, 1 pint of boiling syrup, juice of 1 lemon. Peel the pine, slice and mash it well in a basin, then pour on the syrup and lemon juice; stir well and cover. Let it stand 2 hours, then filter through a fine silk sieve and add a quart of spring water.

Pomegranate Drink.—Four pomegranates, ½ pound of pounded loaf sugar, 1 pint of water, the juice of 2 limes. Put the red pips of the fruit into a basin with the sugar, bruise all together, pour over the water, then the lime-juice and strain several times through muslin.

Pop.—Cream of tartar 3 ounces, ginger 1 ounce, white sugar 24 ounces, lemon juice 1 ounce, boiling water 1½ gallons; when cool strain and ferment with 1 ounce yeast; bottle.

Portable Lemonade.—Tartaric acid 1 ounce, white sugar 2 pounds, essence of lemon ¼ ounce; powder and keep dry for use. One dessertspoonful will make a glass of lemonade.

Raisin Wine.—Ten pounds of raisins, 1 pound of sugar. The raisins must be sound and large. Pick them very clean and chop finely. Pour a gallon of hot water on them and press the liquor through a bag. Let it stand 12 hours, then put in the sugar and leave it to ferment. When this is over, cask it, bung it and leave it for 3 months; then draw it off into another cask, quite filling it. Bung very closely and bottle in 10 months' time. It will be fit to drink in a year.

Raspberry Shrub.—Place red raspberries in a stone jar, cover them with good cider vinegar and let stand over night, in the morning strain, and to each pint of juice, add 1 pint of sugar; boil 5 minutes, skim and let cool; then bottle and cork tightly.

Raspberry Vinegar.—To every 3 pints of the best vinegar allow 4½ pints of freshly gathered raspberries; to each pint of liquor allow 1 pound of pounded loaf sugar, 1 wineglassful brandy; let the raspberries be freshly gathered; pick them from the stalks and put 1½ pints of them into a stone jar, pour 3 pints of the best vinegar over them and let them remain for 24 hours; then strain the liquor over another 1½ pints of fresh raspberries. Let them remain another 24 hours, and the following day repeat the process for the third time; then drain off the liquor without pressing, and pass it through a jelly bag (previously wet with plain vinegar), into a stone jar. Add to every pint of the liquor 1 pound of pounded loaf sugar; stir them together, and when the sugar is dissolved, cover the jar; set it upon the fire in a sauce pan of boiling water and let it boil for an hour, removing the scum as fast as it rises; add to each pint a glass of brandy; bottle it and seal the corks. This is an excellent drink in cases of fever and colds; it should be diluted with cold water according to the requirements of the patient. To be boiled 1 hour.

Raspberry Wine.—Gather the raspberries when ripe; bruise them; strain through a bag into jars; boil the juice and to every gallon put 1½ pounds lump sugar; now add whites of eggs and let the whole boil for 15 minutes, skimming as the froth rises; when cold and settled decant into a cask, adding yeast to make it ferment. When this has taken place, add 1 pint white wine or ½ pint proof spirits to each gallon, and hang in the cask a bag containing 1 ounce bruised mace. In 3 months, if kept in a cool place, it will be excellent.

Red Currant Wine with Raspberries.—Ten gallons of red currant juice, 1 pint of raspberry juice, 20 gallons of water, 18 pounds of finely sifted loaf sugar. Put the ingredients together and let them stand until the sugar is dissolved, then put the liquor into a cask, and bung lightly, for the air to aid in the fermentation. Let it cease fermenting, then bung tightly. Bottle in a year's time, using sound corks and sealing them. It will be in excellent condition in three months.

Rhubarb Sherbet.—Boil in 3 pints water 6 or 8 green stalks rhubarb and 4 ounces raisins or figs; when the water has boiled ½ hour, strain and mix it with 1 teaspoonful rosewater, and orange or lemon syrup to taste. Drink it cold.

Root Beer.—1. Take 3 gallons molasses and 10 gallons water at 160° Fahr.; let this stand 2 hours, then pour into a barrel and add powdered sassafras and wintergreen bark each ½ pound, bruised sassafras root ½ pound, yeast 1 pint, water to fill the barrel; ferment 12 hours and bottle. 2. For 10 gallons beer take 3 pounds common burdock root or 1 ounce essence sassafras, ½ pound good hops, 1 pint corn, roasted brown; boil in 6 gallons pure water till the strength is obtained; strain while hot into a keg; add cold water to make 10 gallons; when nearly cold add molasses or syrup until palatable; add also as much fresh yeast as will raise a batch of 8 loaves of bread. Place in the keg in a cool place, and in 48 hours it will be first-rate beer. 3. For each gallon water take hops, burdock, yellow dock, sarsaparilla dandelion, and spikenard root (all bruised) of each ⅓ ounce:

boil 20 minutes; strain while hot; add 8 or 10 drops of oil of spruce and sassafras mixed in equal proportions. When cool enough put 2 or 3 tablespoonfuls of yeast; molasses ⅜ pint or white sugar, ½ pound gives the right sweetness.

Royal Cordial.—Take a stone bottle and put into it 2 quarts best brandy, add 2 drams angelic seed, 1 ounce coriander seeds, 1 teaspoonful each fennel and aniseeds, previously bruised in a mortar; squeeze into the mixture the juice of 2 fresh lemons, putting in the rinds cut small; add 1 pound loaf sugar, and agitating the jug from time to time. let the whole infuse 5 days; after this, pass it through filtering paper and bottle it, corking tightly; 2 tablespoonfuls to a small wineglass of water is the dose.

Sacramental Wine.—Bruise the grapes and let them stand over night, then press out the juice in a vessel of water on the stove; when the water reaches the boiling point cork tightly and seal with wax. Box and set away in a cool place. Bottled in this way the juice of the grape remains as when pressed out for years. When a bottle is opened it must be used soon, as fermentation begins in a few hours.

Sarsaparilla Beer.—Sarsaparilla (sliced) 1 pound. guaiacum bark (bruised small) ¼ pound. guaiacum wood (rasped) and licorice root (sliced), of each 4 ounces, aniseed (bruised) 1½ ounces, mezereon root bark 1 ounce, cloves (cut small) ¼ ounce, moist sugar 3½ pounds, hot water (not boiling) 9 quarts; mix in a clean stone jar, and keep in a moderately warm room, shaking 2 or 3 times daily until fermentation sets in, then let it stand 1 week, when it will be fit for use.

Sarsaparilla Mead.—One pound Spanish sarsaparilla; boil 5 hours, so as to strain off 2 gallons; add 16 pounds sugar and 10 ounces tartaric acid; ½ wineglass of syrup to ½ pint tumbler of water, and ⅛ teaspoonful soda powder is a fair proportion for a drink.

Sassafras Mead.—Three and ½ pounds nice brown sugar; 1½ pints goods molasses, 3 quarts boiling water, ¼ quart tartaric acid; when cool strain into a jug and mix with this ½ ounce essence of sassafras. Put in bottles, cork tightly and keep in a cool place. For a drink put 2 spoonfuls of this syrup into ⅗ glass ice water, and then add ⅓ teaspoonful soda

Sherbet.—Eight ounces carbonate of soda, 6 ounces tartaric acid, 2 pounds powdered loaf sugar, 3 drams essence of lemon; mix thoroughly; keep corked and dry; stir in 2 teaspoonfuls to 1 pint cold water, and drink.

Slippery Elm Bark Tea.—Break the bark into bits, pour boiling water over it. cover. and let it infuse until cold. Sweeten ice, and take for summer disorders, or add lemon juice and drink for a bad cold.

Small Beer.—Take 1 quart New Orleans molasses, 1 ounce essence of spruce, 1 ounce of essence of wintergreen, ½ ounce essence of sassafras; fill a pail with hot water; mix well; let stand 10 or 12 hours; bottle, and in 3 hours it is fit for use.

Soda Powders.—1. Tartaric acid 1 ounce, bicarbonate soda 1 ounce, 54 grains, or bicarbonate of potassa 1 ounce, 2 drams, 40 grains; reduce the acid and either bicarbonate separately to fine powder; divide each of these into 16 powders and preserve the acid and alkaline powders in separate papers of different colors. **2.** Citric acid 9 drams, bicarbonate of soda 11 drams, or bicarbonate of potassa 13 drams. Proceed as last, dividing each into 18 parts. **3.** Tartaric acid (in crystals) 10 drams, bicarbonate of soda 11 drams, or bicarbonate of potassa 13 drams. Reduce them to power, and divide into 18 parts.

Spruce Beer.—1. Essence of spruce ½ pint, pimento and ginger (bruised), of each 5 ounces, hops ½ pound, water 3 gallons; boil the whole for 10 minutes; then add moist sugar 12 pounds; warm-water 11 gallons; mix well, and when only luke-warm add of yeast 1 pint. After the liquor has fermented 24 hours, bottle. **2.** Cold water 10 gallons, boiling water 11 gallons: mix in a barrel; add molasses 30 pounds, or brown sugar 24 pounds, oil of spruce 1 ounce; add 1 pint yeast; ferment; bottle in 2 or 3 days. If you wish white spruice beer use lump sugar. For ginger flavor use 17 ounces ginger root (bruised) and a few hops; boil 30 minutes in 3 gallons water; strain and mix well; let it stand 2 hours and bottle, using yeast. Birch beer can be made by using oil of birch instead of spruce. **3.** Boil 1 handful of hops and 2 handsful of chips of sassafras root in 10 gallons of water; strain and turn on while hot 1 gallon molasses, 2 spoonfuls essence of spruce, 2 spoonfuls of ginger, and 1 spoonful pounded allspice; put into a cask, and when cold enough add 1 pint good yeast; stir well; stop it close. When clear, bottle and cork.

Stomach Bitters (Equal to Hostetter's, which see in "Medical Preparations)."—Take of European gentian root 1½ ounces, orange peel 2½ ounces, cinnamon ¼ ounce, aniseed and coriander seed of each ½ ounce, cardamon seed ⅛ ounce, ungronnd peruvian bark 1½ ounce, gum kino ¼ ounce: bruise: put into best alcohol 1 pint: let stand 1 week; pour off the clear tincture; boil the dregs a few minutes in 1 quart water; strain, and press out the strength: then dissolve 1 pound loaf sugar in the hot liquid, adding 3 quarts cold water, and mix with the spirit tincture first poured off.

Stoughton Bitters.—Orange peel 12 parts, gentian 16 parts, Virginia snake root 3 parts, American saffron and red sanders, of each 1 part, alcohol 104 parts, water 56 parts; mix by percolation or maceration.

Straight Lemonade.—1. Take 2 lemons, divide them, and put each ½ into a lemon squeezer; when all the juice is extracted put the remainder of the lemons into a pitcher and pour boiling water on them; after they have stood a little, squeeze all the goodness from them; add the juice to some loaf sugar to sweeten pleasantly; then pour on enough cold water to make the desired strength. Ice must be added. **2.** Citric acid 1 to 1½ drams, essence lemon 10 drops, sugar 2 ounces, cold water 1 pint; agitate together until dissolved.

Strawberry Cordial.—One quart strawberries, fully ripe, 1 lemon, 1 orange, 3 pints water, 1 pound sifted sugar; mash the strawberries through a sieve; add juice of lemon and orange and the water, and work together; let stand 2 hours; put the sugar into a bowl and strain the juice over it, stirring till sugar is dissolved; stand on ice before serving; a delicious drink.

Strawberry Sherbet.—Crush 1 quart ripe berries; add juice of 1 lemon, 2 tablespoonfuls orange flower water, and 3 pints water; let them stand several hours; then strain over ¾ pound sugar; set in ice an hour before using. (For delicious summer drinks, see Syrups.)

Strawberry Water.—One pound fine strawberries, ½ pound of loaf sugar, juice of 1 lemon. Crush the sugar finely, and sift over the strawberries, which should be red and ripe. Add ½ a pint of cold water, filter through a sieve, add a quart of spring water, and the strained juice of a lemon.

Strawberry Wine.—**1.** To 1 quart of strawberry juice add 1 quart water and 1 pound sugar; stir well and let it ferment in an open jar. When it has entirely stopped fermenting draw off in bottles and cork. **2.** Take 3½ gallons cold water, 3 gallons cider and 3 gallons strawberries; let them ferment and add to them 8 pounds sugar, 1½ ounces red tartar in fine powder, the juice and rind of 1 lemon, 1 quart brandy. This will make 9 gallons of wine. The fruit should be picked when there has been two or three days clear weather, and it should be bottled when the atmosphere is clear. The bottles must be sound and clean, and the corks new and made to fill the necks of the bottles so as to render them air tight. All wine should be kept in a cool cellar, the bottles laid on their side.

Tea, Perfect Method of Making.—There is very little art in making good tea. If the water is boiling and there is no sparing of the fragrant leaf, the beverage will almost invariably be good. The teapot must be kept dry. Delicately flavored tea is better made in an earthen than a metal pot. The old-fashioned plan of allowing a teaspoonful to each person, and one over, is still practiced. Warm the teapot with boiling water; let it remain for 2 or 3 minutes for the vessel to become thoroughly hot, then pour it away. Put in the tea, pour in from ⅓ to ¾ of a pint of freshly boiling water, close the lid and let it stand for the tea to draw from 5 to 10 minutes: then fill up the pot with water. The tea will be quite spoiled unless made with water that is actually boiling, as the leaves will not open, and the flavor not be extracted from them; the beverage will consequently be colorless and tasteless—in fact, nothing but tepid water. Neither will it be good if the water has simmered for hours. When there is a very large party to make tea for, it is a good plan to have 2 teapots instead of putting a large quantity of tea into 1 pot; the tea, besides, will go farther. When the infusion has been once completed, the addition of fresh tea adds very little to the strength; so, when more is required, have the pot emptied of the old leaves, scalded, and fresh tea made in the usual manner. Economists say that a few grains of carbonate of soda added before the boiling water is poured on the tea, assist to draw out the goodness. If the water is very hard, perhaps it is a good plan, as the soda softens it; but care must be taken to use this ingredient sparingly, as it is liable to give tea a soapy taste if added in too large a quantity. For mixed tea the usual proportion is 4 spoonfuls of black to 1 of green; more of the latter when the flavor is very much liked; but strong green tea disagrees with some persons and should never be partaken of by them.

NOTE.—The tea-float is a very useful addition to the teapot. The tea is placed in the float, and the float in the teapot. Boiling water is added as in ordinary tea-making. The float rises to the surface and thus retains the tea at the hottest part of the water instead of its sinking to the bottom, which is the coldest part. By this application of natural laws and the chemistry of tea-making, all the strength of the tea is withdrawn and the infusion is far stronger than when prepared in the usual way. A smaller quantity of tea is therefore required when the tea-float is used.

Toast Water.—Toast a slice of bread very brown, break it into pieces, and pour over it a cupful of boiling water. When cold it makes a nourishing drink.

Welsh Nectar,—One pound of raisins, 3 lemons, 2 pounds of loaf sugar. 2 gallons of boiling water. Cut the peel of the lemon very thin, pour upon it the boiling water, and, when cool, add the strained juice of the lemons, the sugar, and the raisins, stoned and chopped very fine. Let it stand 4 or 5 days, stirring it every day, then strain it through a jelly bag and bottle it for present use.

Whey.—To a pint of warm new milk add a teaspoonful of prepared rennet. Let it stand, and then strain it through a piece of muslin. This can sometimes be taken when milk cannot. It is a useful drink in feverish complaints. White wine whey is made by pouring a wineglassful of sherry into a breakfast cupful of boiling milk, and then straining through muslin. Treacle posset is made of boiling milk, with 1 or 2 tablespoonfuls of treacle, in the same way. Alum whey and tamarind whey are also occasionally made.

White Wine Vinegar.—Mash up 20 pounds raisins; add 10 gallons of water; let it stand in a warm place 1 month and you will have pure white wine vinegar. The raisins may be used a second time.

Wild Cherry Bitters.—Wild cherry bark 4 parts, partridge-berry (Michella reptans) 1 part, juniper-berries ½ part, prickley ash ¼ part; exhaust with water 40 parts; after filtering add sugar 8 parts, alcohol 6 parts.

VARIOUS RECIPES FOR THE SICK-NURSE.

Sago, Cream, and Extract of Beef.—Two ounces of sago, ¼ pint of water, ½ pint of cream, yolks of 4 eggs, 1 quart of beef tea. Wash 2 ounces of sago until the water poured from it is clear. Then stew the sago in half a pint of water until it is quite tender and very thick; mix with it half a pint of good cream and the yolks of 4 eggs, and mingle the whole with 1 quart of beef tea, which should be boiling. Useful in cases of lingering convalescence after acute disease.

Tapioca and Cod Liver.—Quarter pound of tapioca, 2 quarts of water, ½ pint of milk, 1 pound of fresh cod liver, salt, pepper. Boil a quarter of a pound of tapioca till tender in 2 quarts of water, drain it, add half a pint of milk, salt and pepper to season, add 1 pound of fresh cod liver cut in pieces. Simmer very slowly for half an hour till the liver is quite cooked. Press on it with a spoon to get as much oil into the tapioca as possible. After taking away the liver, mix the tapioca. If too thick, add a little more milk. Tapioca thus cooked is nourishing and easily digested.

Burdete's Restorative Jelly.—Three ounces of isinglass, 2 ounces of gum arabic, 2 ounces of sugar candy, a bottle of sherry. Put them in a jar, cover it closely, and let it stand all night; then set it in a saucepan of water, and let it simmer till it is dissolved.

Invalid's Jelly.—Twelve shanks of mutton, 3 quarts of water, a bunch of sweet herbs, pepper and salt to taste, 3 blades of mace, 1 onion, 1 pound of lean beef, a crust of bread toasted brown. Soak the shanks in plenty of water for some hours, and scrub them well; put them, with the beef and other ingredients, into a saucepan with the water, and let them simmer very gently for 5 hours. Strain the broth, and, when cold, take off all the fat. It may be eaten either warmed-up or cold as a jelly.

Meat Juice.—Scrape the meat very fine with a knife, and take away all fat and fibre. The finer it is scraped the better. Put it in a glass with its own weight of cold or lukewarm water, and let it stand twenty minutes. Then strain it. Children sometimes take it mixed with sugar. The appearance can be disguised with Liebig's extract.

Beef-Tea Custard.—In those cases where some variation from beef-tea is desired, the following may be found useful: Take a gill of beef-tea, the yolks of 2 eggs, the white of 1, and a pinch of salt. Mix all thoroughly together, butter an earthenware cup very thoroughly, pour in the mixture, tie buttered paper over, and steam it for twenty minutes. Turn it out, and serve hot or cold, or put a few pieces into a cup of broth. The water should not bubble after the custard is in.

Beef Jelly.—Cut 3 pounds of lean shin of beef into small pieces, and put it in a jar with seasoning, and just enough water to cover it. Lemon-peel, celery, or spice may be added to flavor. Tie it closely down with brown paper, and set it in a *cool* oven, where it should remain for 4 or 5 hours. Then strain off the liquor into very small moulds or cups, out of which it should turn in a jelly. If steak is used, it is necessary to add a little gelatine or isinglass. To be served cold. It can sometimes be retained on the stomach when ordinary hot beef-tea is at once rejected, but, if made for such a patient, should be without flavoring.

Bread-and-Water Poultice.—(*Abernethey's Plan.*)—First scald out a basin; then, having put in some boiling water, throw in coarsely-crumbled bread, and cover it with a plate. When the bread has soaked up as much water as it will imbibe, drain off the remaining water, and there will be left a light pulp. Spread this a third of an inch thick on folded linen, and apply it when of the temperature of a warm bath. To preserve it moist, occasionally drop warm water on it.

Linseed-Meal Poultice.—A linseed poultice being always needed hot, care should be taken that it is made so. Put the meal into the oven to heat for a quarter of an hour, and scald out the basin in which it is to be mixed with boiling water. Next pour in as much boiling water as is needed according to the size of the poultice required; then, stirring with a knife all the time, shake in the hot meal till the poultice is sufficiently thick. In some cases it is better to put the poultice upon the skin, when, to prevent its sticking, it may be slightly oiled. A paper cut rather larger than the poultice will then serve for spreading it on. When it is preferred that it should not touch the skin, an old thin handkerchief answers well for a wrapper, the surplus being turned over at the back of the poultice. In either case it should be covered with cotton-wool and oil-silk to retain the heat as long as possible.

Poultice for Chilblains.—Bake a common white turnip and scrape out the pulp; mix it with a tablespoonful of salad-oil, one of mustard, and one of grated horseradish. In this way form a poultice, and apply it to the chilblains on a piece of linen ag.

GLUES AND CEMENTS.

GLUES.

Botanical.—1. Used for mounting ferns and botanical specimens: Gum arabic 5 parts, white sugar 3 parts, starch 2 parts; add very little water; boil, stirring until thick and white. 2. For mosses: Clarified glue, dissolved in water to the thickness of molasses; add a thickening of flour and water while the glue is boiling until about as thick as clear starch; apply to the moss or lichen, and to the surface to which it is to be attached.

Drapers' Glue, For Joining Purposes.—Glue, cut in small pieces, 3 parts, water 8 parts; let stand for several hours; then add hydrochloric acid ¾ part and sulphate zinc 1 part; expose the whole to a temperature of 178 to 192 degrees Fahrenheit during a period of 10 or 12 hours; will not gelatinize; needs only to settle; an excellent glue.

Fireproof Glue.—Take the best glue; pour on water to cover; soak over night; melt over a gentle heat, and add fine Paris white, or white lead; mix well, and add a little acetic acid, carbolic acid or any ethereal oil to prevent putrefaction; adapted for flexible objects like leather; will not withstand boiling water.

Fire and Waterproof Glue.—Mix a handful of quick-lime with 4 ounces of linseed oil; thoroughly lixiviate the mixture; boil it to a good thickness, and spread it on tin plates in the shade; it will become very hard, but can be dissolved over a fire, like common glue, and is then fit for use.

Glue for Damp Places.—Take the best and strongest glue enough to make a pint when melted. Soak this until soft. Pour off the water as in ordinary glue making and add a little water if the glue is likely to be too thick. When melted, add 3 tablespoonfuls of boiled linseed oil. Stir frequently and keep up the heat until the oil disappears, which may take the whole day and perhaps more. If necessary add water to make up for that lost by evaporation. When no more oil is seen, a tablespoonful of whiting is added and thoroughly incorporated with the glue.

Labeling on Metal or Glass.—Good yellow glue, broken into small pieces; soak a few hours in cold water; pour off the water; place the glue in a wide-mouthed bottle; add sufficient glacial acetic acid to cover the glue; facilitate solution by placing the bottle in warm water; will stick anything; a little chloride of calcium added to glue will prevent cracking, and cause it to adhere to anything, metal, glass, etc.

Liquid Glue.—**1.** To 1 ounce of borax in 1 pint of boiling water, add 2 ounces of shellac, and boil until the shellac is dissolved. **2.** Dissolve 1 pound best glue in 1½ pints of water, add 1 pint of vinegar; ready for use at any time without warming.

Liquid Glues.—Dissolve 33 parts best (Buffalo) glue on the steam bath in a porcelain vessel, in 36 parts of water. Then add gradually, stirring constantly, 3 parts of aqua fortis, or as much as is sufficient to prevent the glue from hardening when cool. Or, dissolve 1 part of powdered alum in 120 parts of water, add 120 parts of glue, 10 parts of acetic acid and 40 parts of alcohol, and digest.

Leather Cement.—**1.** Take gutta percha, cut in chloroform to right consistency for use. Equal to Cook's best, for putting patches on leather, cloth shoes or boots. **2.** Rubber 1 ounce, pack tightly as possible in a bottle and cover it with bisulphate of carbon. When the rubber is dissolved you will have the best cement in the world. There is a fortune in this to an energetic man, as it sells at 25 cents a dram and costs but little to make it. This is the cement used by shoemakers to put invisible patches on shoes.

Mineral Glue for Geologists and Mineralogists.—Take 2 ounces clear gum arabic, 1½ ounces of fine starch, and ½ ounce white sugar; pulverize the gum arabic, and dissolve it in as much water as the laundress would use for the quantity of starch indicated; dissolve the starch and sugar in the gum solution; then cook the mixture in a vessel suspended in boiling water until the starch becomes clear. The cement should be as thick as tar and kept so. It can be kept from spoiling by dropping in a lump of gum camphor or a little oil of cloves or sassafras. This cement is very strong indeed, and will stick perfectly to glazed surfaces, and is good to repair broken rocks, minerals, or fossils. The addition of a small amount of sulphate of aluminum will increase the effectiveness of the paste, besides helping to prevent decomposition.

Marine Glue.1—. This is probably the strongest cement known. When well made and properly applied it will unite wood, metal, glass, leather, etc., with a strength that is remarkable. Dissolve 3 parts shellac and 1 part india rubber in separate vessels in ether free from alcohol, applying a gentle heat; when dissolved mix the 2 solutions. Use rectified sulphuric ether and unvulcanized rubber. It is well to cut the rubber into small pieces before pouring the ether on; stir while melting. This glue resists water, hot or cold, and most acids. If thinned with ether and appied as a varnish to leather along the seams it renders it water-tight. **2.** Finely divided india rubber 1 part, dissolved in crude naphtha 40 parts. The solution is complete in 10 or 12 days if repeatedly agitated. To it is then added gum lac 2 parts by weight to 1 of solution. Then place over a fire and thin until perfectly liquid and even. Cool on a stone slab and break into pieces for use. To use, heat to 212° Fahrenheit and coat the edges to be joined with a thin coating, pressing firmly together. It is valuable in foundries, caulking ships, joining blocks of marble and granite, uniting wood to iron, etc. Can be made as hard as desired by increasing the lac. **3.** Dissolve 4 parts india rubber in 34 parts coal tar naphtha—aiding the solution with heat and agitation; add to it 64 parts powdered shellac, which must be heated in the mixture till the whole is dissolved. While the mixture is hot it is poured upon metal plates in sheets like leather. When required for use, it is heated in a pot till soft, and then applied with a brush to the surfaces to be joined. Two pieces of wood joined with this glue can scarcely be sundered.

Metal.—(See Labeling.)

Mouth or Lip Glue.—(See Portable Glue).—Take isinglass and parchment, each 1 ounce, sugar candy and gum tragacanth each 2 drams; add to them 1 ounce water, and boil the whole together till the mixture appears (when cold) of the consistency of glue; then pour it into any form you please. If this glue be wet with the tongue and rubbed on the edges of the paper, silk or leather that are to be cemented they will, on being laid together, pressed tightly, and suffered to dry, be as firmly united as other parts of the subtance. It is fine to seal letters.

Portable Glue.—Useful for repairing book-bindings, leather goods, bank bills, parchments, etc. To use, hold over steam a moment or wet with the tongue and rub on the surfaces to be cemented. It is of great strength. Prepare as follows: White shell glue 2 pounds: boil and strain until clear; then boil 8 ounces of Cooper's isinglass to a creamy consistency; mix the 2 substances while hot in a clean double glue pot; add 1 pound good brown sugar to the mass, and boil, stirring until thick: pour off into shallow pans when nearly cold; cut in pieces for the desk or the pocket. This is a valuable recipe. Try it.

Parchment Glue.—Parchment shavings 1 pound. water 6 quarts; boil until dissolved; then strain and evaporate to the proper consistency. Use a water bath if wanted light colored.

Prepared Liquid Glue.—Take of best white glue 16 ounces, white lead, dry, 4 ounces, rain water 2 pints, alcohol 4 ounces; with constant stirring dissolve the glue and lead in the water by means of a water bath; add the alcohol and continue the heat for a few minutes. Lastly pour into bottles while it is still hot.

Rubber Glue.—Bottle india rubber dissolved in highly rectified spirits of turpentine.

Spalding's Liquid Glue.—One pound fine isinglass and 1 pint rain water; boil and prepare an ordinary glue, then add slowly stirring continually, 2 ounces nitric acid; bottle, and it is fit for use. It will permanently adhere to wood, leather, paper, and everything else.

To Fasten Rubber to Wood or Metal.—As rubber plates and rings are nowadays used almost exclusively for making connections between steam and other pipes and apparatus, much annoyance is often experienced by the impossibility or imperfection of an air-tight connection. This is obviated entirely by employing a cement which fastens alike well to the rubber and to the metal or wood. Such cement is prepared by a solution of shellac in ammonia. This is best made by soaking pulverized gum shellac in 10 times its weight of strong ammonia, when a slimy mass is obtained, which in 3 or 4 weeks will become liquid without the use of hot water. This softens the rubber and becomes, after volatilization of the ammonia, hard and impermeable to gases and fluids.

To Fasten Paper to Tin.—Take good, clear, pale yellow glue, break it into rather small pieces, and let it soak a few hours in cold water: pour off the supernatant water, place the glue thus softened in a wide-mouthed bottle; add sufficient glacial acid to cover the glue, and facilitate the solution by standing the bottle in warm water. This acetic will stick almost anything.

Waterproof Glue.—Soak glue in water until it is soft, but still retains its form: then put it into raw linseed oil and apply a gentle heat until it is dissolved by the oil. Use like ordinary glue. It soon dries and water has no effect upon it

---

CEMENTS.

BUILDING.

Concrete, Gravel.—To 8 barrows slaked lime, well deluged with water, add 15 barrows sand, do not use river or beach sand, as this absorbs dampness; mix to a creamy consistency and add 60 barrows coarse gravel; work well. You can throw stones of any shape into this mixture, from 9 to 10 inches in diameter, and it will soon grow as hard as rock.

External, For the Outside of Buildings.--1. Powdered quicklime 1 part, powdered baked clay 2 parts; mix; then add 1 part freshly baked and powdered gypsum to 2 parts powdered baked clay; after mixing, add them to the former powder and incorporate the two; mixed with water and apply like mortar. **2.** Sand 1 part, ashes 2 parts, clay 2 parts; mix with linseed oil; hard and durable, and resists the weather almost like marble.

Fireproof.--Used for walls and to mend broken pieces of stone, steps, etc. Fine river sand 20 parts, litharge 2 parts, quicklime 1 part, linseed oil sufficient to form a thin paste.

Floor Cements.--Take $\frac{2}{3}$ lime and $\frac{1}{3}$ coal ashes well sifted with a small quantity of loamy clay; mix the whole together; temper with water, making it into a heap; let it lie a week or 10 days, and temper it again; heap it up for 3 or 4 days, repeating the tempering until it becomes smooth and gluey; the floor being leveled, apply with a trowel 2½ to 3 inches thick: the hotter the atmosphere the better.

Mortar, To Make.—Reduce quicklime and sand to a paste with water; the lime pure, free from carbonic acid, and in fine powder; the sand free from clay (partly fine sand and partly gravel); the water pure and, if previously saturated with lime, the better. The proportions are 3 parts fine and 4 parts coarse sand, 1 part quicklime, recently slaked, and as little water as possible. The addition of burnt bones, hair, etc., improves mortar by giving it tenacity, but should not exceed ¼ of the lime employed. Black mortar is made by mixing with lampblack.

Portland Cement.—Gray chalk mixed with ¼ its weight of clay in a pug-mill supplied with warm water, and run off into a settling pond, where the superfluous water is removed. The sediment is dried on a floor provided with flues, then burnt in a kiln and ground between millstones.

Roofing Cement.—Melt together in an iron pot 2 parts by weight of common pitch and 1 part gutta-percha. This is easily applied. To repair gutters, roofs, etc., clean out of the cracks all earthy matter, warm the edges with a plumber's soldering iron, then pour the cement upon the cracks hot; finish by going over the cement with a moderately hot iron, so as to make a smooth joint.

Wall Finish.—(For coating walls of rooms.) A coat of oxide of zinc mixed with size is first applied, and over that a coat of chloride of zinc prepared as the first. The oxide and chloride form a combination and make a cement as smooth as glass. Claimed to be superior to plaster of paris. **2.** Slack 1 peck of lime. and while hot and thick like cream, add 1 pint linseed oil ¼ pound dissolved glue; let it stand ½ day before using. For interior walls this is superior to lime and water.

Water-Proof and Fire-Proof Cement for Roofs of Houses.—Slack stone lime in a large tub or barrel with boiling water, covering the tub or barrel to keep in the steam. When thus slacked pass 6 quarts through a fine sieve. It will then be in a state of fine flour. To this add 1 quart rock salt and 1 gallon of water; boil the mixture and skim it clean. To every 5 gallons of this skimmed mixture add 1 pound of alum and ½ pound copperas; by slow degrees add ¾ pound potash and 4 quarts fine sand or wood ashes sifted. Both of the above will admit of any coloring you please. It looks better than paint and is as durable as slate.

MISCELLANEOUS BUILDERS' CEMENTS.

Cement for Terraces, Floors, Roofs, Reservoirs, etc. —In certain localities where a limestone impregnated with bitumen occurs, it is dried, ground, sifted, and then mixed with about its own weight of melted pitch, either mineral, vegetable, or that of cold tar. When this mixture is getting semifluid, it may be moulded into large slabs or tiles in wooden frames lined with sheet iron, previously smeared over with common lime mortar, in order to prevent adhesion to the moulds, which, being in moveable pieces, are easily dismounted so as to turn out the cake of artificial bituminous stone. This cement is manufactured upon a great scale in many places, and used for making Italian terraces, covering the floors of balconies, flat roofs, water reservoirs, water conduits, &c. When laid down, the joints must be well run together with hot irons. The floor of the terrace should be previously covered with a layer of Paris plaster or common mortar, nearly an inch thick, with a regular slope of one inch to the yard. Such bituminous cement weighs 144 pounds the cubic foot; or a foot of square surface, one inch thick, weighs 12 pounds. Sometimes a second layer of these slabs or tiles is applied over the first, with the precaution of making the seams or joints of the upper correspond with the middle of the under ones. Occasionally a bottom bed, of coarse cloth or gray paper, is applied. The larger the slabs are made, as far as they can be conveniently transported and laid down, so much the better.

Mastic Cement for Covering the Fronts of Houses.—Fifty parts, by measure, of clean dry sand, fifty of limestone (not burned) reduced to grains like sand, or marble dust, and 10 parts of red lead, mixed with as much boiled linseed oil, as will make it slightly moist. The brick, to receive it, should be covered with three coats of boiled oil, laid on with a brush, and suffered to dry, before the mastic is put on. It is laid on with a trowel like plaster, but it is not so moist. It becomes hard as stone in a few months. Care must be exercised not to use too much oil.

Cement for Outside Brick Walls.—Cement for the outside of brick walls, to imitate stone, is made of clean sand 90 parts, litharge parts, plaster of Paris 5 parts, moistened with boiled linseed oil. The bricks should receive two or three coats of oil before the cement is applied.

Cement for Coating the Fronts of Buildings.—The cement of dihl for coating the fronts of buildings consists of linseed oil, rendered dry by boiling with litharge, and mixed with porcelain clay in fine powder, to give it the consistence of stiff mortar. Pipe-clay would answer equally well if well dried, and any color might be given with ground bricks, or pottery. A little oil of turpentine to thin this cement aids its cohesion upon stone, brick or wood. It has been applied to sheets of wire cloth, and in this state laid upon terraces, in order to make them water tight; but it is a little less expensive than lead.

Cement for Steps and Brick Walls.—A cement which gradually indurates to a stony consistence, may be made by mixing twenty parts of clean river sand, two of litharge, and one of quicklime, into a thin putty with linseed oil. The quicklime may be replaced with litharge. When this cement is applied to mend broken pieces of stone, as steps of stairs, it acquires after some time a stony hardness. A similar composition has been applied to coat over brick walls, under the name of mastic.

A Hard Cement for Seams.—An excellent cement for seams in the roofs of houses, or for any other exposed places, is made with white lead, dry white sand, and as much oil as will make it into the consistency of putty. This cement gets as hard as stone in a few weeks. It is a good cement for filling up cracks in exposed parts of brick buildings; and for pointing up the base of chimneys, where they project through the roofs of shingled houses.

Another Good Cement.—Dissolve 1 pound of alum in boiling water, and while it is boiling add 5 pounds of brown soap, cut into small pieces; boil the mixture about 15 minutes. It then becomes sticky like shoemaker's wax. Now mix it with whiting to a proper consistency for filling up seams, &c. It becomes partially hard after a few months, and strongly adheres to wood. The wood should be perfectly dry. To make it adhere it must be well pressed down. When dry it is impervious to water, and is slightly elastic.

Cement for Tile-Roofs.—The best cement for closing up seams in tile-roofs is composed of equal parts of whiting and dry sand and 25 per cent. of litharge, made into the consistency of putty with linseed oil. It is not liable to crack when cold, nor melt, like coal-tar and asphalt, with the heat of the sun.

Coarse Stuff.—Coarse stuff, or lime and hair, as it is sometimes called, is prepared in the same way as common mortar, with the addition of hair procured from the tanner, which must be well mixed with the mortar by means of a three-pronged rake, until the hair is equally distributed throughout the composition. The mortar should be first formed, and when the lime and sand have been thoroughly mixed, the hair should be added by degrees, and the whole so thoroughly united, that the hair shall appear to be equally distributed throughout.

Parker's Cement.—This cement, which is perhaps the best of all others for stucco, as it is not subject to crack or flake off, is now very commonly used, and is formed by burning argillaceous clay in the same manner that lime is made. It is then reduced to powder. The cement, as used by the plasterer, is sometimes employed alone, and sometimes it is mixed with sharp sand; and it has then the appearance, and almost the strength of stone. As it is impervious to water, it is very proper for lining tanks and cisterns.

Hamelein's Cement.—This cement consists of earthy and other substances insoluble in water, or nearly so; and these may be either those which are in their natural state, or have been manufactured, such as earthenware and china; those being always preferred which are least soluble in water, and have the least color. When these are pulverized, some oxide of lead is added, such as litharge, gray oxide, or minium, reduced to a fine powder; and to the compound is added a quantity of pulverized glass or flint stones, the whole being thoroughly mixed and made into a proper consistence with some vegetable oil, as that of linseed. This makes a durable stucco or plaster, that is impervious to wet, and has the appearance of stone. The proportion of the several ingredients is as follows: To every 560 pounds of earth, or earths, such as pit sand, river sand, rock sand, pulverized earthenware or porcelain, add 40 pounds of litharge, 2 pounds of pulverized glass or flint, 1 pound of minium and 2 pounds of gray oxide of lead. Mix the whole together and sift it through sieves of different degrees of fineness, according to the purposes to which the cement is to be applied. The following is the method of using it: To every 30 pounds of the cement in powder, add about 1 quart of oil, either linseed, walnut, or some other vegetable oil, and mix it in the same manner

as any other mortar, pressing it gently together either by tread-
ing on it, or with the trowel; it has then the appearance of
moistened sand. Care must also be taken that no more is mixed
at one time than is required for use, as it soon hardens into a
solid mass. Before the cement is applied, the face of the wall to
be plastered should be brushed over with oil, particularly if it
be applied to brick, or any other substance that quickly imbibes
the oil; if to wood, lead, or any other substance of a similar
nature, less oil may be used.

Plaster in Imitation of Marble, Scagliola.—This
species of work is exquisitely beautiful when done with taste and
judgment, and is so like marble to the touch, as well as appearance, that it is scarcely possible to distinguish the one from the
other. We shall endeavor to explain its composition, and the
manner in which it is applied; but so much depends upon the
workman's execution, that it is impossible for anyone to succeed
in an attempt to work with it without some practical experience. Procure some of the purest gypsum, and calcine it until
the large masses have lost the brilliant, sparkling appearance by
which they are characterized, and the whole mass appears uniformly opaque. This calcined gypsum is reduced to powder, and
passed through a very fine sieve, and mixed up, as it is wanted
for use, with glue, isinglass, or some other material of the same
kind. This solution is colored with the tint required for the
scagliola, but when a marble of various colors is to be imitated,
the several colored compositions required by the artist must be
placed in separate vessels, and they are then mingled together in
nearly the manner that the painter mixes his color on the pallet.
Having the wall or column papered with rough plaster, it is
covered with the composition, and the colors intended to imitate
the marble, of whatever kind it may be, are applied when the
floating is going on. It now only remains to polish the work,
which, as soon as the composition is hard enough, is done by
rubbing it with pumic-stone, the work being kept wet with
water applied by a sponge. It is then polished with Tripoli and
charcoal, with a piece of fine linen, and finished with a piece of
felt, dipped in a mixture of oil and Tripoli, and afterwards with
pure oil.

Maltha, or Greek Mastic.—This is made by mixing lime
and sand in the manner of mortar, and making it into a proper
consistency with milk or size, instead of water.

Fine Stuff.—This is made by slacking lime with a small portion of water, after which so much water is added as to give it
the consistence of cream. It is then allowed to settle for some
time, and the superfluous water is poured off, and the sediment
is suffered to remain till evaporation reduces it to a proper
thickness for use. For some kinds of work, it is necessary to add
a small portion of hair.

Stucco for Inside of Walls.—This stucco consists of fine
stuff already described, and a portion of fine washed sand, in the

proportion of 1 of sand to 3 of fine stuff. Those parts of interior walls are finished with this stucco which are intended to be painted. In using this material, great care must be taken that the surface is perfectly level. and to secure this it must be well worked with a floating tool or wooden trowel. This is done by sprinkling a little water occasionally on the stucco, and rubbing it in a circular direction with the float. till the surface has attained a high gloss. The durability of the work very much depends upon the care with which this process is done; for if it be not thoroughly worked, it is apt to crack.

Higgins' Stucco,—To 15 pounds of the best stone lime, add 14 pounds of bone ashes, finely powdered, and about 95 pounds of clean, washed sand, quite dry, either coarse or fine, according to the nature of the work in hand. These ingredients must be intimately mixed, and kept from the air till wanted. When required for use, it must be mixed up into a proper consistence for working with lime water, and used as speedily as possible.

Gauge Stuff.—This is chiefly used for moldings and cornices which are run or formed with a wooden mold. It consists of about 1-5 of plaster of paris. mixed gradually with 4-5 of fine stuff. When the work is required to set very expeditiously, the proportion of plaster of paris is increased. It is often necessary that the plaster to be used should have the property of setting immediately it is laid on, and in all such cases gauge stuff is used, and consequently it is extensively employed for cementing ornaments to walls or ceilings, as well as for casting the ornaments themselves.

Composition.—This is frequently used, instead of plaster of paris, for the ornamental parts of buildings, as it is more durable, and becomes in time as hard as stone itself. It is of great use in the execution of the decorative parts of architecture, and also in the finishings of picture frames, being a cheaper method than carving by nearly 80 per cent. It is made as follows: Two pounds of the best whitening, 1 pound of glue, and ⅛ pound of linseed oil are heated together, the composition being constantly stirred until the different substances are thoroughly incorporated. Let the compound cool, and then lay it on a stone covered with powdered whitening. and heat it well until it becomes of a tough and firm consistence. It may then be put by for use, covered with wet cloths to keep it fresh. When wanted for use, it must be cut into pieces, adapted to the size of the mold, into which it is forced by a screw press. The ornament, or cornice, is fixed to the frame or wall with glue or with white lead.

Foundations of Buildings.—The nature and condition of the soil upon which houses are to be built should receive far more attention than is usually bestowed upon such subjects. A soil which is spongy and damp. or contains much loose organic matter, is generally unhealthy; whereas a dry, porous soil affords a healthy site for buildings. Wherever we find a soil deficient in gravel or sand. or where gravel and sand-beds are underlaid with clay, there should be a thorough sub-soil drainage, because the clay retains the water, and a house built in such a spot would otherwise always be damp and unhealthy. When the sub-soil is swampy, which is the case with many portions of various cities that have been filled in with what is called made earth, fever is liable to prevail in houses built in such localities, owing to the decay of organic matter underneath, and its ascension in the form of gas through the soil. When good drainage cannot be effected in such situations, and it is found necessary to build houses on them, they should all have solid floors of concrete, laid from the outside of the foundations and covering the whole area over which the structure is erected. These floors tend to prevent dampness in houses, consequently they are more comfortable and healthy than they otherwise would be. Such floors also tend to prevent the cracking of the walls, owing to the solidity and firmness imparted to their foundations.

Concrete Floors.—The lower floors of all the cellars of houses should be composed of a bed of concrete about 3 inches thick. This would tend to render them dry, and more healthy, and at the same time prevent rats from burrowing under the walls on the outside, and coming up under the floor—the method pursued by these vermin where houses are erected on a sandy soil. This concrete should be made of washed gravel and hydraulic cement. Common mortar mixed with pounded brick and washed gravel, makes a cement for floors nearly as good as that formed with hydraulic cement. Such floors become very hard, and are much cheaper than those of brick or flagstone.

Fireproof Composition to Resist Fire for Five Hours.—Dissolve, in cold water, as much pearlash as it is capable of holding in solution, and wash or daub with it all the boards, wainscoting, timber, etc. Then diluting the same liquid with a little water, add to it such a portion of fine yellow clay as will make the mixture the same consistence as common paint; stir in a small quantity of paperhanger's flour paste to combine both the other substances. Give 3 coats of this mixture. When dry, apply the following mixture: Put into a pot equal quantities of finely pulverized iron filings, brick dust and ashes; pour over them size or glue water; set the whole near a fire, and when warm stir them well together. With this liquid composition, or size, give the wood 1 coat, and on its getting dry, give it a second coat. It resists fire for 5 hours, and prevents the wood from ever bursting into flames. It resists the ravages of fire, so as only to be reduced to coal or embers, without spreading the conflagration by additional flames; by which 5 clear hours are gained in removing valuable effects to a place of safety, as well as rescuing the lives of all the family from danger! Furniture, chairs, tables, etc., particularly staircases, may be so protected. Twenty pounds of finely sifted yellow clay, 1½ pounds of flour for making the paste, and 1 pound of pearlash, are sufficient to prepare a square rood of deal-boards.

CEMENTS FOR OTHER PURPOSES.

NOTE.—(*See also Glues*).

Acid Proof.—Resin 6 pounds; dried red ochre, 1 pound; calcined plaster of Paris, ½ pound; linseed oil, ¼ pound. Incorporate by stirring together when melted. Used for cementing troughs for holding acids. Will stand boiling sulphuric acid.

Alabaster.—Used to join or mend alabaster, marble and other stone of similar character, and to fill up cracks, supply chips out of corners, etc. Apply hot, the surfaces having been previously warmed. **1.** Yellow resin, 2 parts; melt and stir in plaster of paris, 1 part. **2.** Yellow resin, beeswax and plaster of paris, equal parts. **3.** Resin, 8 parts; wax, 1 part; melt and stir in plaster of paris, 4 parts.

Aquarium Cement.—Used for the marine as well as the fresh water aquaria, as it resists the action of salt water. 1 gill of litharge: 1 gill plaster of paris: 1 gill dry white sand; ⅓ gill finely powdered resin. Sift, and keep corked tight until required for use, when it is made into a putty by mixing in boiling linseed oil with a little drying fluid combined. Never use it after it has been mixed with the oil over 15 hours. The tank can be used immediately, but it is better to give it 3 or 4 hours to dry.

Bucklands.—Used for all the purposes of mucilage and as a cement for labels. It does not become brittle or crack. White sugar, 1 ounce: starch, 3 ounces: gum Arabic, 4 ounces; all to be separately reduced to a fine powder and mixed together in a dry mortar, then little by little add cold water until of the thickness of melted glue, then put in a wide mouth bottle and cork close.

Chinese.—For mending china, glass and fancy ornaments. Dissolve shellac in enough rectified spirits to make a liquid the consistency of molasses. This will join wood so strongly that it will resist the flexion of a bow. The fluid is thinly smeared over each face to be united.

Coppersmiths.—Used to secure the edges and rivets of copper boilers, to mend leaks from joints, etc. Bullock's blood, thickened with finely powdered quicklime. It must be used as quick as mixed, as it soon becomes hard. Is extremely durable and cheap.

Druggists.—Used for cementing stoppers. Litharge, finely powdered, and concentrated glycerine, painted around the cork or stopper. Quickly dries and becomes hard, but may be easily scraped off when necessary to open the bottle.

Diamond Cement.—Used to unite bits of glass, polished steel, and for cementing precious stones on jewelry. **1.** Dissolve 5 or 6 bits of gum mastic, each the size of a large pea in as much rectified alcohol as will render it liquid; and in another vessel dissolve as much isinglass, previously softened in water (although none of the water must be used), in French brandy or good rum, as will make a 2-ounce vial of strong glue, adding 2 small bits of gum galbanum or ammoniacum, which must be dissolved. Mix the whole with sufficient heat and fill vial, which must be closely stopped. When used, set the vial in boiling water. **2.** Isinglass, 6 ounces; gum mastic and olibanum, each, 2 ounces; pure water, 9 ounces; rectified spirits of wine, 12 ounces; dissolve the isinglass in the water, then stir in the mastic, previously dissolved in the spirits of wine, and lastly, stir in the olibanum in the state of a fine powder.

Earthenware.—1. A good cement is made by dissolving gum shellac in alcohol, apply the solution, bind the parts together and let dry. **2.** White of egg, thickened with powdered quicklime.

Elastic.—(*See Glues, Cements for Uniting Leather, etc.*)

Entomologists.—Used to rejoin the dislocated parts of insects, etc. To a solution of gum-ammoniac in proof spirits, add best isinglass, and unite with gentle heat. Valuable.

French.--Used by naturalists in mounting specimens; by artificial flower makers, and by confectioners, to stick wafers, ornaments, etc., on cakes. Mix thick mucilage of gum Arabic with powdered starch. A little lemon juice is sometimes added.

Glass Cements.—1. Pulverized glass, 10 parts; powdered fluor spar, 20 parts; soluble silicate of soda, 60 parts. Both glass and fluor spar must be in the finest powder. The mixture must be made by quick stirring, and when incorporated, must be used at once. **2.** Used for mending valuable articles in glass. A strong solution of gelatine, to which is added for every 5 parts gelatine, 1 part solution acid chromate of lime. The mixture becomes insoluble in water under the action of light, in consequence of the partial reduction of the chromic acid; with a fresh preparation of the solution, cover the surfaces to be united as evenly as possible; press them together and tie them. Expose the glass to the sun a few hours. Boiling water has no effect on the oxydized cement, and the fracture can scarcely be recognized.

Glycerine.—(*See Druggists' Cement*).

Iron.—(See "To mend Iron" in *Household Miscellany*). 5 parts fire clay and 1 part fine iron filings, mixed into a paste with linseed oil. When hard it resists heat, but is not good for mending cracks in stoves, as it will crack under the red heat.

Ivory Cement.—Dissolve 1 part of isinglass and 2 parts of white glue in 30 parts of water; strain, and evaporate to 6 parts; add 1-30 part of gum mastic dissolved in ½ part of alcohol, and 1 part of white zinc; when required for use, warm and shake it; used also for mother of pearl.

Japanese.—This elegant cement is made by mixing rice flour intimately with cold water, and then gently boiling. It is used by the Japanese in the manufacture of all their works in paper and laquer, and from it many handsome articles can be made·

when dry, the articles made from it are susceptible of a high polish and are durable.

Jeweler's.—(*See Diamond Cement.*) **1.** Dissolve 5 or 6 pieces gum mastic the size of a pea in just as much methylated spirits as will make it liquid; soften isinglass by steeping in water; having dried it, dissolve in as much good brandy as will make a 2-ounce vial of strong glue, to which add 2 small pieces of gum ammoniacum; mix the two and keep closely corked. Set the vial in boiling water before using.

Lamp Cement.—This is used for cementing the tops on kerosene lamps. One part caustic soda 5 parts water; mix with ½ the weight of plaster of paris.

Leather Cements.—(*See Glues.*)

Leather to Rubber.—Used for uniting sheet rubber or gutta percha to leather, soles of shoes, etc. Gutta percha 50 pounds, Venice turpentine 40 pounds, shellac 4 pounds, caoutchouc 1 pound, liquid storax 5 pounds. The Venice turpentine should first be heated; then the gutta percha and shellac added; when dissolved add the others; stir well and do not burn.

Leather to Metal.—Fifty-six pounds good glue; melt and add 3½ pounds gum ammoniac; stir well till reduced to an even mass; remove from the fire and pour in gradually 3½ pounds nitric acid, and incorporate with the rest. This has been proven the best among metal binders, as it is not susceptible to the action of oil.

Metal to Fibrous Material.—A preparation made of good glue dissolved in hot vinegar with ⅓ its volume of white pine pitch, also hot, is said will give sure results with any metal.

Metal to Glass.—Take 1 pound shellac dissolved in 1 pint of strong methylated spirits, to which is added 1-5 part of solution of India rubber in carbon bisulphide.

Microscopic.—Used for mounting opaque objects for the microscope. Put into a bottle 2 parts isinglass and 1 part gum arabic; cover with proof spirits; cork the bottle loosely and place in water and boil till a solution is effected; strain for use.

Opticians.—**1.** Shellac softened with rectified spirits or wood naphtha. For fine work. **2.** Beeswax 1 ounce, resin 15 ounces; melt and add whiting (previously made red hot and still warm) 4 ounces.

Rubber Cement.—(*See Glues.*) Used for uniting leather or rubber that has not been vulcanized. Sixteen parts gutta percha, 4 parts India rubber. 2 parts common caulker's pitch, 1 part linseed oil; melt together; use hot.

Safety Envelope.—To be used in two portions, neither of which is of any value without the other, makes it an impossibility to open letters or separate paper when each is moistened and applied to the other. **1.** This is composed of a preparation of chromium, and is made by dissolving crystalized chromic acid in water, the proportions being 2-5 grams of acid to 15 grams of water; 15 grams of ammonia are added to this, then 10 drops sulphuric acid: finally 30 grains sulphate of ammonia and 4 grams white paper. **2.** Dissolve 1 part acetic acid, 7 parts of water; dissolve in this a quantity of isinglass. Apply No. 1 to the envelope and No. 2 to the place where it unites with the paper.

Universal Cement.—Used for cementing wood, iron, leather, glass, paper and almost all kinds of household articles Best isinglass, ½ ounce. Rub it between the hands until it breaks into a powder. Put in a bottle and put as much acetic acid to it as will wet the mass through. Stand the bottle in some boiling water and the paste will dissolve and be ready for use. It will be solid when cold, but can be easily warmed to a state of liquidity. Leave the cork out when warming, as there is danger of bursting the bottle.

Cements of various kinds should be kept for occasional use. Flour paste answers very well for slight purposes; if required stronger than usual, boil a little glue or put some powdered resin in it. White of egg, or a solution of glue and a strong gum water are good cements. A paste made of linseed meal dries very hard and adheres firmly. A soft cement is made of yellow wax, melted with its weight of turpentine, and a little Venetian red to give it color. This when cool is as hard as soap, and is very useful to stop up cracks, and is better to cover the corks of bottles than sealing wax or hard cement. The best cement for broken china or glass is that sold under the name of Diamond Cement. It is colorless and resists moisture. This is made by soaking isinglass in water until it is soft, and then dissolving it in proof spirits; add to this a little gum ammoniac or galbanum or mastic, both dissolved in as little alcohol as possible. When the cement is to be used, it must be gently liquified by placing the vial containing it in boiling water. The vial must be well closed with a good cork, not by a glass stopper, as they become forced. It is applied to the broken edges by a camel's hair pencil. When objects are not to be exposed to the moisture, the white of an egg alone mixed with finely powdered quicklime, will answer very well. Shellac dissolved in water is better. A very strong cement for all earthenware is made by boiling slices of skim-milk cheese and water into a paste, then grinding the quicklime in a marble mortar, or on a slab with a mallet.

ADDITIONAL UNCLASSIFIED CEMENTS.

Armenian or Diamond Cement.—This article, so much esteemed for uniting pieces of broken glass, for repairing precious stones, and for cementing them to watch cases and other ornaments, is made by soaking isinglass in water until it becomes quite soft, and then mixing it with spirit in which a little gum mastic and ammoniacum have been dissolved. The jewelers of Turkey, who are mostly Armenians, have a singular method of ornamenting watch cases, etc., with diamonds and other precious stones, by simply glueing or cementing them on. The stone is set in silver or gold, and the lower part of the metal made flat, or to correspond with the part to which it is to be fixed; it is then warmed gently, and has the glue applied, which is so very strong that the parts so cemented never separate; this glue, which will strongly unite bits of glass, and even polished steel, and may be applied to a variety of useful purposes, is thus made in Turkey: Dissolve 5 or 6 bits of gum mastic, each the size of a large pea, in as much spirits of wine as will suffice to render it liquid; and in another vessel, dissolve as much isinglass, previously a little softened in water (though none of the water must be used), in French brandy or good rum, as will make a 2-ounce vial of very strong glue, adding 2 small bits of gum albanum, or ammoniacum, which must be rubbed or ground till they are dissolved. Then mix the whole with a sufficient heat. Keep the glue in a vial closely stopped, and when it is to be used, set the vial in boiling water. Some persons have sold a composition under the name of Armenian cement, in England; but this composition is badly made; it is much too thin, and the quantity of mastic is much too small. The following are good proportions: isinglass, soaked in water and dissolved in spirit, 2 ounces (thick); dissolve in this 10 grains of very pale gum ammoniac (in tears), by rubbing them together; then add 6 large tears of gum mastic, dissolved in the least possible quantity of rectified spirit. Isinglass, dissolved in proof spirit, as above, 3 ounces; bottoms of mastic varnish (thick but clear) 1¼ ounces; mix well. When carefully made, this cement resists moisture, and dries colorless. As usually met with, it is not only of very bad quality, but sold at exorbitant prices.

Cements For Mending Earthen and Glass Ware.—1. Heat the article to be mended, a little above boiling water heat, then apply a thin coating of gum shellac, on both surfaces of the broken vessel, and when cold it will be as strong as it was originally. **2.** Dissolve gum shellac in alcohol, apply the solution, and bind the parts firmly together until the cement is perfectly dry.

Cement for Stoneware.—Another cement in which an analogous substance, the curd or caseum of milk is employed, is made by boiling slices of skim-milk cheese into a gluey consistence in a great quantity of water, and then incorporating it with quicklime on a slab with a muller, or in a marble mortar. When this compound is applied warm to broken edges of stoneware, it unites them very firmly after it is cold.

Iron-Rust Cement.—The iron-rust cement is made from 50 to 100 parts of iron borings, pounded and sifted, mixed with 1 part of sal ammoniac, and when it is to be applied moistened with as much water as will give it a pasty consistency. Formerly flowers of sulphur were used, and much more sal ammoniac in making this cement, but with decided disadvantage, as the union is effected by oxidizement, consequent expansion and solidification of the iron powder, and any heterogeneous matter obstructs the effect. The best proportion of sal ammoniac is, I believe, 1 per cent of the iron borings. Another composition of the same kind is made by mixing 4 parts of fine borings or filings of iron, 2 parts of potter's clay and 1 of pounded potsherds, and making them into a paste with salt and water. When this cement is allowed to concrete slowly on iron joints it becomes very hard.

Architectural Ornaments in Relief.—For making architectural ornaments in relief, a molding composition is formed of chalk, glue and paper paste. Even statues have been made with it, the paper aiding the cohesion of the same.

Electrical and Chemical Apparatus Cement.—Electrical and chemical apparatus cement consists of 5 pounds of resin, 1 of beeswax, 1 of red ochre, and 2 tablespoonfuls of paris plaster, all melted together. A cheaper one for cementing voltaic plates into wooden troughs is made with 6 pounds of resin, 1 of red ochre, ½ of plaster of paris and ¼ pound of linseed oil. The ochre and the plaster of paris should be calcined beforehand, and added to the other ingredients in their melted state. The thinner the stratum of cement that is interposed, the stronger, generally speaking, is the junction.

Cement for Iron Tubes, Boilers, Etc.—Finely powdered iron 66 parts, sal ammoniac 1 part, water a sufficient quantity to form into paste.

Cement for Ivory, Mother of Pearl, Etc.—Dissolve 1 part of isinglass and 2 of white glue in 30 of water, strain and evaporate to 6 parts. Add 1·30 part of gum mastic, dissolved in ½ part of alcohol, and 1 part of white zinc. When required for use, warm and shake up.

Cement for Holes in Castings.—The best cement for this purpose is made by mixing 1 part of sulphur in powder, 2 parts of sal ammoniac and 80 parts of clean powdered iron turnings, sufficient water must be added to make it into a thick paste, which should be pressed into the holes or seams which are to be filled up. The ingredients composing this cement should be kept separate, and not mixed until required for use. It is to be applied cold, and the castings should not be used for 2 or 3 days afterwards.

Cement for Coppersmiths and Engineers.—Boiled linseed oil and red lead mixed together into a putty are often used by coppersmiths and engineers, to secure joints. The washers of leather or cloth are smeared with this mixture in a pasty state.

A Cheap Cement.—Melted brimstone, either alone, or mixed with resin and brick dust, forms a tolerably good and very cheap cement.

Plumber's Cement.—Plumber's cement consists of black

resin 1 part, brick dust 2 parts, well incorporated by a melting heat.

Cement for Bottle Corks.—The bituminous or black cement for bottle corks consists of pitch hardened by the addition of resin and brick dust.

China Cement.—Take the curd of milk, dried and powdered. 10 ounces; quicklime 1 ounce, camphor 2 drams. Mix, and keep in closely stopped bottles. When used, a portion is to be mixed with a little water into a paste, to be applied quickly.

Cement for Leather.—A mixture of India rubber and shellac varnish makes a very adhesive leather cement. A strong solution of common isinglass, with a little diluted alcohol added to it, makes an excellent cement for leather.

Marble Cement.—Take plaster of paris, and soak it in a saturated solution of alum, then bake the two in an oven, the same as gypsum is baked to make it plaster of paris; after which they are ground to powder. It is then used as wanted, being mixed up with water like plaster and applied. It sets into a very hard composition capable of taking a very high polish. It may be mixed with various coloring minerals to produce a cement of any color capable of imitating marble.

A Good Cement.—Shellac dissolved in alcohol, or in a solution of borax, forms a pretty good cement.

Cement for Marble Workers and Coppersmiths.—White of egg alone, or mixed with finely sifted quicklime, will answer for uniting objects which are not exposed to moisture. The latter combination is very strong, and is much employed for joining pieces of spar and marble ornaments. A similar composition is used by coppersmiths to secure the edges and rivets of boilers; only bullock's blood is the albuminous matter used instead of white of egg.

Transparent Cement for Glass.—Dissolve 1 part of India rubber in 64 of chloroform, then add gum mastic in powder 16 to 24 parts, and digest for two days with frequent shaking. Apply with a camel's hair brush.

Cement to Mend Iron Pots and Pans.—Take 2 parts of sulphur, and 1 part, by weight, of fine black lead; put the sulphur in an old iron pan, holding it over the fire until it begins to melt, then add the lead: stir well until all is mixed and melted; then pour out on an iron plate, or smooth stone. When cool, break into small pieces. A sufficient quantity of this compound being placed upon the crack of the iron pot to be mended, can be soldered by a hot iron in the same way a tinsmith solders his sheets. If there is a small hole in the pot, drive a copper rivet in it and then solder over it with this cement.

Cement to Render Cisterns and Casks Water-Tight.—An excellent cement for resisting moisture is made by incorporating thoroughly, 8 parts of melted glue, of the consistence used by carpenters, with 4 parts of linseed oil, boiled into varnish with litharge. This cement hardens in about 48 hours, and renders the joints of wooden cisterns and casks air and water tight. A compound of glue with ¼ its weight of venice turpentine, made as above, serves to cement glass, metal and wood, to one another. Fresh-made cheese curd, and old skim-milk cheese, boiled in water to a slimy consistence, dissolved in a solution of bicarbonate of potash, are said to form a good cement for glass and porcelain. The gluten of wheat, well prepared, is also a good cement. White of eggs, with flour and water well mixed, and smeared over linen cloth, forms a ready lute for steam joints in small apparatus.

Cement for Repairing Fractured Bodies of All Kinds.—White lead ground upon a slab with linseed oil varnish, and kept out of contact of air, affords a cement capable of repairing fractured bodies of all kinds. It requires a few weeks to harden. When stone or iron are to be cemented together, a compound of equal parts of sulphur with pitch answers very well.

Cements for Cracks in Wood.—Make a paste of slacked lime 1 part, rye-meal 2 parts, with a sufficient quantity of linseed oil. Or, dissolve 1 part of glue in 16 parts of water, and when almost cool stir in sawdust and prepared chalk a sufficient quantity. Or, oil-varnish thickened with a mixture of equal parts of white lead, red lead, litharge, and chalk.

Cement for Joining Metals and Wood.—Melt resin and stir in calcined plaster until reduced to a paste, to which add boiled oil a sufficient quantity, to bring it to the consistence of honey: apply warm. Or, melt resin 180 parts, and stir in burnt umber 30, calcined plaster 15, and boiled oil 8 parts.

Gasfitters' Cement.—Mix together, resin 4½ parts, wax 1 part, and Venetian red 3 parts.

Impervious Cement for Apparatus, Corks, etc.—Zinc-white rubbed up with copal varnish to fill up the indentures; when dry, to be covered with the same mass, somewhat thinner, and lastly with copal varnish alone.

Cement for Fastening Brass to Glass Vessels.—Melt resin 150 parts, wax 30, and add burnt ochre 30, and calcined plaster 2 parts   Apply warm.

Cement for Fastening Blades, Files, etc.—Shellac 2 parts, prepared chalk 1, powdered and mixed. The opening for the blade is filled with this powder, the lower end of the iron heated and pressed in.

Hydraulic Cement Paint.—If hydraulic cement be mixed with oil, it forms a first-rate anti-combustible and excellent waterproof paint for roofs of buildings, outhouses, walls, etc.

Valuable Cement.—Two parts, by weight, of common pitch, and 1 part gutta percha, melted together in an iron vessel, makes a cement that holds together, with wonderful tenacity, wood, stone, ivory, leather, porcelain, silk, woollen, or cotton. It is well adapted to aquariums.

Plumbers' Cement.—Black resin, 1 part; brick dust, 2 parts; well incorporated by a melting heat. Boiled linseed oil and red lead mixed together into a putty are often used by coppersmiths and engineers to secure joints; the washers of leather or cloth are smeared with this mixture in a pasty state.

Cement for Rubber or Leather.—Dissolve 1 ounce of gutta percha in ½ pound chloroform. Clean the parts to be cemented, cover each with the solution and let them dry 20 or 30 minutes, warm each part in the flame of the candle, and press very firmly together till dry.

Tin Box Cement.—To fix labels to tin boxes either of the following will answer: **1.** Soften good glue in water, then boil it in strong vinegar, and thicken the liquid while boiling with fine wheat flour, so that a paste results. **2.** Starch paste, with which a little Venice turpentine has been incorporated while warm.

Roofing Cement.—Mix ordinary red oxide of iron and boiled linseed oil so as to form a paint, add to every quart 1 gill of Japan dryer and then add equal parts of Roman water lime and Venetian red until the mixture is as thick as desired for the work to be done. This cement will be found very useful for flashings or for repairing leaky roofs, as it dries quickly and can be applied by means of a small brush to leaks on a standing seam roof where it would be impossible to solder. It is also useful for repairing cracked seams where the tin has become too rusty to be soldered.

Jeweler's Turkish Cement.—Put into a bottle 2 ounces of isinglass and 1 ounce of the best gum Arabic; cover them with proof spirits, cork loosely, and place the bottle in a vessel of water, and boil it till a thorough solution is effected; then strain for use; best cement known.

Cement for Mending Valuable Glassware.—Mix 5 parts of gelatine with 1 part of a solution of acid chromate of lime. Cover the broken edges with the cement, press the parts together and expose to sunlight. The light hardens the cement, which will then withstand boiling water.

Best Cement for Aquaria.—It is the same as that used in constructing the tanks of the Zoological Gardens, London. One part, by measure, say a gill of litharge; 1 gill of plaster of paris; 1 gill of dry, white sand; ¼ of a gill of finely powdered resin. Sift, and keep corked tight until required for use, when it is to be made into a putty by mixing in boiled oil (linseed) with a little patent drier added. Never use it after it has been mixed (that is, with the oil) over 15 hours. This cement can be used for marine as well as fresh-water aquaria, as it resists the action of salt water. The tank can be used immediately, but it is best to give it 3 or 4 hours to dry.

Coppersmith's Cement, etc.—Bullock's blood thickened with finely-powdered lime. Use as soon as mixed, as it rapidly gets hard.

Liquid Cement.—Cut gum shellac into 70 per cent alcohol, put it in vials, and it is ready for use. Apply it to the edge of the broken dish with a feather, and hold it in a spirit lamp as long as the cement will simmer, then join together evenly, and when cold the dish will break in another place first, and is as strong as new.

Crystal Cement.—Dissolve 1 pound of white glue in 1½ pints of hot water, then cut 1 ounce gum shellac in 1½ pints alcohol, and mix with the glue, then stir in 2 ounces of dry white lead, and add 1 ounce of turpentine. This makes the best cement of anything that has been discovered. It will stand heat, and articles will break in another place sooner than where put together. This is a fortune to an enterprising man.

Cement for Leather.—1. Virgin India rubber dissolved in bisulphide of carbon. Add bisulphide until of proper consistency to apply. After applying hold a moderately warm iron over the patch. 2. Take gutta percha, cut in chloroform to right consistency for use. Equal to Cook's best, for putting patches on leather, cloth shoes or boots. Well worth $100.

Egyptian Cement.—For mending china, glass or wooden-ware. Take 1 pound of the best white glue, ½ pound dry white lead 1 quart soft water, ½ pint alcohol. Put the three first articles in a dish, and that dish in a pot of boiling water. Let it boil until dissolved, then add the alcohol, and boil again until mixed. A little camphor should be added, to preserve it and disguise its composition. Put in small bottles.

Cement for Seams in Roofs.—Take equal quantities of white lead and white sand, and as much oil as will make it into the consistence of putty. It will in a few weeks become as hard as stone.

Cement for Rubber Boots.—A good cement for rubber boots is made by dissolving crude rubber in bisulphuret of carbon, making the solution rather thin. Put the cement upon the patch and the boot, heat both and put them together.

Powerful Cement for Broken Marble.—Take gum arabic, 1 pound; make into a thick mucilage; add to it powdered plaster of paris, 1½ pounds; sifted quicklime, 5 ounces; mix well; heat the marble, and apply the mixture.

———————

MUCILAGES.

Commercial Mucilage.—The best quality of mucilage in the market is made by dissolving clear glue in equal volumes of water and strong vinegar, and adding ¼ of an equal volume of alcohol, and a small quantity of a solution of alum in water. Some of the cheaper preparations offered for sale are merely boiled starch or flour, mixed with nitric acid to prevent their gelatinizing.

Cream Mucilage.—Take the curd of skim milk, carefully freed from cream or oil, wash thoroughly and dissolve to saturation in a cold concentrated solution of borax. This mucilage keeps; is creamy in appearance, and surpasses gum arabic for adhesiveness.

Dextrine.—Dissolve sufficient yellow dextrine in hot water to bring it to the consistency of honey. This forms a strong paste, used on the back of labels, envelopes, postage stamps, etc. The following is said to be the formula for the mucilage used on United States postage stamps: Dextrine 2 ounces, acetic acid 1 ounce, water 5 ounces, alcohol 1 ounce; add the alcohol to the other ingredients when the dextrine is dissolved.

Elastic Mucilage.—Dissolve 1 part of salicylic acid in 20 parts of alcohol, add 3 parts of soft soap and 3 parts of glycerine; shake thoroughly and add the mixture to a mucilage prepared from 93 parts of gum arabic and the requisite amount of water (about 180 parts). This mucilage keeps well, and, when it dries, remains elastic without tendency to cracking.

Gum Arabic.—This is the principal material from which mucilage is made. Put 3 ounces gum arabic into ½ pint of cold water, and stir frequently until dissolved.

Gum Tragacanth.—Powdered tragacanth 1 dram, glycerine 6 drams, water q. s. to make in all 10 ounces; rub the tragacanth in a mortar with the glycerine, then add the water; makes an excellent mucilage. Equal parts of gum tragacanth and gum arabic dissolved in sufficient water makes a better mucilage than either alone.

Labeling.—To adhere paper to wood, tin, or metal make a mucilage of gum arabic, to which add a solution of sulphate of aluminum (1 part of aluminum to 10 parts water); 10 grains of aluminum are sufficient for 250 grains of mucilage. This preparation will not become moldy.

Liquid Mucilage.—Fine clean glue 1 pound, gum arabic 10 ounces, water 1 quart; melt by heat in glue kettle or water bath. When entirely melted, add slowly 10 ounces strong nitric acid; set off to cool. Then bottle, adding a couple of cloves to each bottle.

Mucilage for Labels.—Dextrine 2 ounces, glycerine 1 dram, alcohol 1 ounce, water 6 ounces.

Peach-Tree Gum.—Take the gum found on peach trees, put into a bottle and add equal parts of alcohol and water, until of the proper consistence. This is good, and easily obtained where there are peach trees.

To Preserve Mucilage.—The use of salicylic acid, corrosive sublimate, boracic acid, cloves. or any essential oil will prevent mucilage or paste from becoming sour, ropy, and unfit for use.

PASTES.

An Excellent Paste for Envelopes.—Mix in equal quantities gum arabic (substitute dextrine) and water in a vial, place it near a stove or on a furnace register, and stir or shake it well until it dissolves; add a little alcohol to prevent its souring.

A Perpetual Paste is a paste that may be made by dissolving an ounce of alum in a quart of warm water; when cold add as much flour as will make.it the consistency of cream. then stir into ½ teaspoonful of powdered resin and 2 or 3 cloves; boil it to a consistency of mush, stirring all the time. It will keep for 12 months, and when dry may be softened with warm water.

A Paste for Scrap Books.—Take ½ teaspoonful of starch, same of flour; pour on a little boiling water; let it stand a minute, add more water, stir and cook it until it is thick enough to starch a shirt bosom. It spreads smooth, sticks well. and will not mold or discolor paper. Starch alone will make a very good paste.

A Strong Paste.—A paste that will neither decay nor become moldy. Mix good clean flour with cold water into a thick paste well blended together, then add boiling water, stirring well up until it is of the consistency that can be easily and smoothly spread with a brush; add to this a spoonful or two of brown sugar, a little corrosive sublimate and about ½ dozen drops of oil of lavender, and you will have a paste that will hold with wonderful tenacity.

A Brilliant Paste.—A brilliant and adhesive paste, adapted to fancy articles, may be made by dissolving caseine precipitated from milk by acetic acid and washed with pure water in a saturated solution of borax.

A Sugar Paste.—In order to prevent the gum from cracking, to 10 parts by weight of gum arabic and 3 parts of sugar, add water until the desired consistency is obtained. If a very strong paste is required, add a quantity of flour equal in weight to the gum, without boiling the mixture. The paste improves in strength when it begins to ferment.

Acid-Proof Paste.—A paste formed by mixing powdered glass with a concentrated solution of silicate of soda makes an excellent acid-proof cement.

Bookbinder's.—Place ½ gill of flour in a saucepan and as much cold water as will cover it; break all the lumps while in a state of dough; then pour on 2 quarts cold water and 1 ounce powdered alum; set on the fire and stir constantly, while boiling, until thick.

Corn Starch.—Corn starch makes a good paste for scrapbooks. Dissolve a small quantity in cold water, then cook thoroughly; do not get it too thick. When cold it should be thin enough to apply with a brush. It is not so liable to mold and stain the paper as paste made from other flours or starches.

Flour Paste That Will Not Sour.—Mix good flour with cold water to a paste, then add boiling water, stirring up well until of a consistence capable of being spread with a brush; add a little brown sugar, a little corrosive sublimate, and 6 drops oil of lavender. Keep 2 days before using.

Perpetual Paste.—Used for leather, paper, or card board. Let 4 parts by weight of glue soften in 15 parts cold water for 15 hours; then heat until clear; add to this 65 parts boiling water without stirring. In another vessel mix 30 parts starch paste with 20 parts cold water, stirring well. Into this pour the boiling solution; stir thoroughly; keep at boiling heat; when cool add 10 drops carbolic acid. Preserve in closed bottles and it will keep for years.

Photographic.—Used for mounting photographs. Mix thoroughly 630 grains finest Bermuda arrow root with 375 grains cold water; then add 10½ ounces of water and 60 grains of gelatine; boil, with stirring, 5 minutes, or until clear; when cold, stir in 375 grains of alcohol and 5 or 6 drops of carbolic acid; keep in well-closed vessels, and before using, work up a portion with a brush in a dish. (*See also Perpetual Paste.*)

Paste That Will Not Sour.—Dissolve ½ ounce of alum in a pint of boiling water, add an equal weight of flour. made smooth in a little cold water, and a few drops of oil of cloves, and let the whole come to a boil; put it into glass or ointment jars. It will keep for months.

Paper and Leather Paste.—Cover 4 parts, by weight, of glue, with 15 parts of cold water, and allow it to soak for several hours, then warm moderately till the solution is perfectly clear. and dilute with 60 parts of boiling water, intimately stirred in. Next prepare a solution of 30 parts of starch and 200 parts of cold water, so as to form a thin homogeneous liquid, free from lumps. and pour the boiling glue solution into it with thorough stirring, and at the same time keep the mass boiling.

Paste to Fasten Cloth to Wood.—Take a plump pound of wheat flour, 1 tablespoonful of powdered resin, 1 tablespoonful of finely powdered alum, and rub the mixture in a suitable vessel, with water. to a uniform, smooth paste; transfer this to a small kettle over a fire, and stir until the paste is perfectly homogeneous without lumps. As soon as the mass has become so stiff that the stirrer remains upright in it, transfer it to another vessel and cover it up so that no skin may form on its surface. This paste is applied in a very thin layer to the surface of the table; the cloth, or leather, is then laid and pressed upon it, and smoothed with a roller. The ends are cut off after drying. If leather is to be fastened on. this must first be moistened with water. The paste is then applied. and the leather rubbed smooth with a cloth.

Starch Paste.—Mix starch and cold water, carefully working the lumps out of the starch, and a mass is formed not too thick; pour into this boiling water slowly, stirring rapidly, until the mass becomes transparent, showing the formation of paste; a little alum preserves it.

SEALING WAX.

Black Sealing Wax.—1. Purchase the best black resin 3 pounds, beeswax ½ pound and finely powdered ivory black 1 pound; melt the whole together over a slow fire, and make it into sticks. **2.** Shellac 3 pounds, venice turpentine 19 ounces, finest cinnabar 2 pounds: mix. **3.** Rectified spirits of wine 8 ounces, camphor 1 ounce, shellac 2½ pounds, black resin 1½ pounds, lampblack 4 ounces.

Bottle Wax, Black.—Black resin 6½ pounds, beeswax ½ pound, finely powdered ivory black 1½ pounds; melt together. **Red.**—As the last, but substitute venetian red or red lead for the ivory black.

Brown.—Shellac 7½ ounces. venice turpentine 4 ounces; color with 1 ounce brown ocher and ⅓ ounce cinnabar: mix thoroughly by a gentle heat and mold as required.

Gold.—Bleached shellac 3 pounds, venice turpentine 1 pound, dutch leaf, ground fine, 1 pound; prepare as others.

Green.—Shellac 2 parts, yellow resin 1 part, verdigris 1 part; powder and mix by heating slowly; blue can be made by using ultramarine blue for coloring.

Marbled.—Mix 2 or 3 different kinds just as they begin to grow solid.

Red Sealing Wax.—1. The red sealing wax is made thus: Take of venice turpentine 2 pounds, camphor 4 ounces, vermilion 1¼ pounds, rectified spirits of wine 16 ounces. Dissolve the camphor first in the spirits of wine. in a suitable vessel, over a slow fire, taking care that no flame touches the evaporating spirit; then add the shellac, and when that has become of a uniform smoothness, by a moderate application of heat, add the turpentine, and lastly the vermilion, which should be passed through a hair-sieve over the melted mass, in order that it may not get into clots. When the whole is well incorporated, it is ready to be formed into sticks of whatever size may be desired. It may be added, that it is usual to weigh out the soft wax into balls, and roll them on a mahogany table into the lengths desired, and then to flatten them by pressure. They are polished by being held over charcoal fire in a chaffing dish, then drawn over a piece of mutton suet, or tallow candle, and rubbed with a piece of soft leather. **2.** Purchase 4 pounds shellac, 1½ pounds venice turpentine, 3 pounds finest cinnabar and 4 ounces venetian; mix the whole well together, and melt over a very slow fire. Pour it on a thick, smooth glass, or any other flat, smooth surface, and make it into 3, 6 or 10 sticks.

Red, For Cans.--Melt together yellow wax 1 ounce, American vermilion 3 ounces, gum shellac 5 ounces, resin 16 ounces; run into molds.

White.--Mix 3 parts resin, 1 part caustic soda and 5 parts water; this is then to be mixed with ½ its weight of plaster of paris. The compound sets in ¾ hour, adheres strongly, is not permeable like plaster alone and is affected but slightly by warm water.

Yellow.--Pale shellac 4 ounces, resin 1¼ ounces, venice turpentine ¾ ounce, sulphuret of arsenic to color; mix well by heat.

PERTAINING TO METALS.

SOLDERS, ALLOYS, ETC.

A Good Solder.—Take 1 pound of pure banca tin, and melt it, then add ½ pound clean lead, and when it is melted, stir the mixture gently with a stick or poker, and pour it out into solder strips.

Coppersmith's Solder.—Tin 2 parts, lead 1 part. When the copper is thick, heat it by a naked fire; if thin, use a tinned copper tool. Use muriate or chloride of zinc, or resin, as a flux. The same solder will do for iron, cast iron, or steel; if thick, heat by a naked fire, or immerse in the solder.

Soldering.—The solder for joints requires to be of some metal more fusible than that of the substances to be joined. For copper, usual solder 6 to 8 parts brass to 1 of zinc; 1 of tin sometimes added. A still stronger solder, 3 parts brass, 1 of zinc. To prepare this solder: Melt the brass in a crucible, when melted add in the zinc, and cover over for 2 or 3 minutes till the combination is effected, then pour it out, over a bundle of twigs, into a vessel of water, or into a mould composed of a number of little channels, so that the solder may be in long strips convenient for use. Brass filings alone will answer very well. To braze with this solder: Scrape the surfaces perfectly clean, and secure the flange or joint carefully; cover the surfaces to be brazed with borax powder moistened; apply the solder, and melt it in with the flame of a clear coke fire from a smith's hearth; particular care being taken not to burn the copper.

Soldering Fluid.—Take 2 ounces of muriatic acid; add zinc till bubbles cease to rise; add ½ teaspoonful of sal ammoniac and 2 ounces of water. Damp the part you wish to solder, and with a piece of hot iron or soldering iron solder the part.

Solders, To Prepare.—For lead, the solder is 1 part tin, 1 to 2 of lead. Tin; 1 to 2 parts tin to 1 of lead. Zinc: 1 part tin to 1 to 2 of lead. Pewter: 1 part tin to 1 of lead, and 1 to 2 parts of bismuth. Steel Joints: 19 parts of silver. 1 copper. 2 brass; melt together. Hard Solder: 2 parts of copper, 1 zinc; melt together. **1.** Gold: 7 parts of silver, 1 copper, with borax: **2.** 2 parts of gold, 1 silver, 1 copper. **3.** 3 parts of gold, 3 silver, 1 copper, ½ zinc. Silver: 2 parts of silver, 1 brass, with borax; or 4 silver 3 brass, 1-16 zinc, with borax. Brass: 3 parts of copper, 1 zinc, with borax. Platina: Gold. with borax. Iron; The best solder for iron is good tough brass, with a little borax. Copper: 6 parts of brass, 1 zinc, 1 tin; melt together. mix well, and pour out to cool. The surfaces to be joined are made perfectly clean and smooth, and then covered with sal ammoniac or resin, or both; the solder is then applied, being melted in and smoothed over by the soldering iron.

Fusible Metal.—**1.** Bismuth 8 parts; lead 5 parts; tin **3** parts; melt together. Melts below 212o Fahrenheit. **2.** Bismuth 2 parts; lead 5 parts; tin 3 parts. Melts in boiling water. **3.** Lead 3 parts; tin 2 parts; bismuth 5 parts; mix. Melts at 197o Fahrenheit. Remarks: The above are used to make toy-spoons, to surprise children by their melting in hot liquors; and to form pencils for writing on asses' skin, or paper prepared by rubbing burnt hartshorn into it.

Metallic Cement.—M. Greshiem states that an alloy of copper and mercury, prepared as follows, is capable of attaching itself firmly to the surfaces of metal, glass, and porcelain. From 20 to 30 parts of finely divided copper, obtained by the reduction of oxide of copper with hydrogen, or by precipitation from solution of its sulphate with zinc, are made into a paste with oil of vitriol and 70 parts of mercury added, the whole being well triturated. When the amalgamation is complete, the acid is removed by washing with boiling water, and the compound allowed to cool. In 10 or 12 hours, it becomes sufficiently hard to receive a brilliant polish, and to scratch the surface of tin or gold. By heat it assumes the consistence of wax; and, as it does not contract on cooling, M. Greshiem recommends its use by dentists for stopping teeth.

Artificial Gold.—This is a new metallic alloy which is now very extensively used in France as a substitute for gold. Pure copper 100 parts, zinc, or preferably tin 17 parts, magnesia 6 parts, sal ammoniac 3-6 parts, quicklime 1-8 parts, tartar of commerce, 9 parts, are mixed as follows: The copper is first melted, then the magnesia, sal ammoniac, lime, and tartar, are then added, separately and by degrees, in the form of powder; the whole is now briskly stirred for about half an hour, so as to mix thoroughly; and then the zinc is added in small grains by throwing it on the surface and stirring till it is entirely fused;

the crucible is then covered and the fusion maintained for about 35 minutes. The surface is then skimmed and the alloy is ready for casting. It has a fine grain, is malleable and takes a splendid polish. It does not corrode readily, and for many purposes is an excellent substitute for gold. When tarnished, its brilliancy can be restored by a little acidulated water. If tin be employed instead of zinc, the alloy will be more brilliant. It is very much used in France, and must ultimately attain equal popularity here.

● **Ormolu.**—The ormolu of the brassfounder, popularly known as an imitation of red gold, is extensively used by the French workmen in metals. It is generally found in combination with grate and stove work. It is composed of a greater portion of copper and less zinc than ordinary brass, is cleaned readily by means of acid, and is burnished with facility. To give this material the rich appearance, it is not unfrequently brightened up after "dipping" (that is cleaning in acid) by means of a scratch brush (a brush made of fine brass wire), the action of which helps to produce a very brilliant gold-like surface. It is protected from tarnish by the application of lacquer.

Blanched Copper.—Fuse 8 ounces of copper and ½ ounce of neutral arsenical salt, with a flux made of calcined borax, charcoal dust and powdered glass.

Browning Gun Barrels.—The tincture of iodine diluted with ½ its bulk water, is a superior liquid for browning gun barrels.

Silvering Powder for Coating Copper.—Nitrate of silver 30 grains, common salt 30 grains, cream of tartar 3½ drams; mix, moisten with water, and apply.

● **Alloy for Journal Boxes.**—The best alloy for journal boxes is composed of copper, 24 pounds; tin, 24 pounds; and antimony, 8 pounds. Melt the copper first, then add the tin, and lastly the antimony. It should be first run into ingots, then melted and cast in the form required for the boxes.

Alloy for Bells of Clocks.—The bells of the pendules, or ornamental clocks, made in Paris, are composed of copper 72.00 tin 26.56, iron 1.44, in 100 parts.

An Alloy for Tools.—An alloy of 1000 parts of copper and 14 of tin is said to furnish tools, which hardened and sharpened in the manner of the ancients, afford an edge nearly equal to that of steel.

● **Alloy for Cymbals and Gongs.**—An alloy for cymbals and gongs is made of 100 parts of copper with about 25 of tin. To give this compound the sonorous property in the highest degree, the piece should be ignited after it is cast, and then plunged immediately into cold water.

Solder for Steel Joints.—Silver 19 pennyweights, copper 1 pennyweight, brass 2 pennyweights. Melt under a coat of charcoal dust.

Soft Gold Solder.--Is composed of 4 parts gold, 1 of silver, and 1 of copper. It can be made softer by adding brass, but the solder becomes liable to oxidize.

Files.--Allow dull files to lay in diluted sulphuric acid until they are bit deep enough.

To Prevent Rusting.--Boiled linseed oil will keep polished tools from rusting if it is allowed to dry on them. Common sperm oil will prevent them from rusting for a short period. A coat of copal varnish is frequently applied to polished tools exposed to the weather.

Anti-Attrition, and Axle-Grease.--One part of fine black lead, ground perfectly smooth, with 4 parts of lard.

To Galvanize.--Take a solution of nitro-muriate of gold (gold dissolved in a mixture of aquafortis and muriatic acid) and add to a gill of it a pint of ether or alcohol, then immerse your copper chain in it for about 15 minutes, when it will be coated with a film of gold. The copper must be perfectly clean and free from oxide, grease, or dirt, or it will not take on the gold.

RARE AND VALUABLE COMPOSITIONS.

Recipes for the use of machinists, iron and brass founders, tinmen, coppersmiths, turners, dentists, finishers of brass, brittannia, and German silver, and for other useful and important purposes in the practical arts.

The larger number of the following recipes are the result of inquiries and experiments by a practical operative. Most of those which relate to the mixing of metals and to the finishing of manufactured articles have been thoroughly tested by him and will be found to produce the results desired and expected. The others have been collected from eminent scientific works.

Yellow Brass for Turning.—(Common article.) Copper 20 pounds, zinc 10 pounds, lead 1 to 5 ounces. Put in the lead last before pouring off.

Red Brass for Turning.—Copper 24 pounds, zinc 5 pounds, lead 8 ounces. Put in the lead last before pouring off.

Red Brass, Free, for Turning.—Copper 160 pounds, zinc 50 pounds, lead 10 pounds, antimony 44 ounces.

Another Brass for Turning.—Copper 32 pounds, zinc 10 pounds, lead 1 pound.

Best Red Brass for Fine Castings.—Copper 24 pounds, zinc 5 pounds, bismuth 1 ounce. Put in the bismuth last before pouring off.

Bronze Metal.—1. Copper 7 pounds, zinc 3 pounds, tin 2 pounds. **2.** Copper 1 pound, zinc 12 pounds, tin 8 pounds.

Bell Metal for Large Bells.—Copper 100 pounds, tin from 20 to 25 pounds.

Bell Metal for Small Bells.—Copper 3 pounds, tin 1 pound.

Cock Metal.—Copper 20 pounds, lead 8 pounds, litharge 1 ounce, antimony 3 ounces.

Hardening for Britannia.—To be mixed separately from the other ingredients. Copper 12 pounds, tin 1 pound.

Good Britannia Metal.—Tin 150 pounds, copper 3 pounds, antimony 10 pounds.

Britannia Metal.—Second quality. Tin 140 pounds, copper 3 pounds, antimony 9 pounds.

Britannia Metal for Casting.—Tin 210 pounds, copper 4 pounds, antimony 12 pounds.

Britannia Metal for Spinning.—Tin 100 pounds, Britannia hardening 4 pounds, antimony 4 pounds.

Britannia Metal for Registers.—Tin 100 pounds, hardening 8 pounds antimony 8 pounds.

Best Britannia for Spouts.—Tin 140 pounds, copper 3 pounds. antimony 6 pounds.

Best Britannia for Spoons.—Tin 100 pounds, hardening 5 pounds, antimony 10 pounds.

Best Britannia for Handles.—Tin 140 pounds, copper 2 pounds, antimony 5 pounds.

Best Britannia for Lamps, Pillars, and Spouts.—Tin 300 pounds copper 4 pounds, antimony 15 pounds.

Casting.—Tin 100 pounds, hardening 5 pounds, antimony 5 pounds.

Lining Metal for Boxes of Railroad Cars.—Mix tin 24 pounds, copper 4 pounds, antimony 8 pounds, for a hardening; then add tin 72 pounds.

Fine Silver-Colored Metal.—Tin 100 pounds, antimony 8 pounds, copper 4 pounds, bismuth 1 pound.

German Silver, First Quality, for Casting.—Copper 50 pounds, zinc 25 pounds, nickel 25 pounds.

German Silver, Second Quality, for Casting.—Copper 50 pounds, zinc 20 pounds, nickel (best pulverized) 10 pounds.

German Silver for Rolling.—Copper 60 pounds, zinc 20 pounds, nickel 25 pounds.

German Silver for Bells and Other Castings.—Copper 60 pounds, zinc 20 pounds, nickel 20 pounds, lead 3 pounds, iron (that of tin plate being best) 2 pounds.

Imitation of Silver.—Tin 3 ounces. copper 4 pounds.

Pinchbeck.—Copper 5 pounds, zinc 1 pound.

Tombac.—Copper 16 pounds, tin 1 pound, zinc 1 pound.

Red Tombac.—Copper 10 pounds, zinc 1 pound.

Hard White Metal.—Sheet brass 32 ounces, lead 2 ounces, tin 2 ounces, zinc 1 ounce.

Metal for Taking Impressions.—Lead 3 pounds, tin 2 pounds, bismuth 5 pounds.

Spanish Tutania.—Iron or steel 8 ounces, antimony 16 ounces, niter 3 ounces. Melt and harden 8 ounces tin with 1 ounce of the above compound.

Another Tutania.—Antimony 4 ounces, arsenic 1 ounce, tin 2 pounds.

Gun Metal.—Bristol brass 112 pounds, zinc 14 pounds, tin 7 pounds.

Rivet Metal.—Copper 32 ounces, tin 2 ounces, zinc 1 ounce.

Rivet Metal for Hose.—Tin 64 pounds, copper 1 pound.

Fusible Alloy which Melts in Boiling Water.—Bismuth 8 ounces, tin 3 ounces, lead 5 ounces.

Solder for Gold.—Gold 6 pennyweights, silver 1 pennyweight, copper 2 pennyweights.

Solder for Silver.—(For use of jewelers.) Fine silver 19 pennyweights. copper 1 pennyweight, sheet brass 10 pennyweights.

White Solder for Silver.—Silver 1 ounce, tin 1 ounce.

White Solder for Raised Britannia Ware.—Tin 100 pounds, copper 3 ounces; to make it free add lead 3 ounces.

Best Soft Solder for Cast Britannia Ware.—Tin 8 pounds, lead 5 pounds.

Yellow Solder for Brass or Copper.—Copper 1 pound, zinc 1 pound.

Yellow Solder for Brass or Copper.—Stronger than the last.—Copper 32 pounds, zinc 29 pounds, tin 1 pound.

Solder for Copper.—Copper 10 pounds, zinc 9 pounds.

Black Solder.—1. Copper 2 pounds, zinc 3 pounds, tin 2 ounces. **2.** Sheet brass 20 pounds, tin 6 pounds, zinc 1 pound.

Soft Solder.—Tin 15 pounds, lead 15 pounds,

Silver Solder for Plated Metals.—Fine silver 1 ounce, brass 10 pennyweights.

Yellow Dipping Metal.—Copper 32 pounds, zinc 2 pounds, soft solder 2¼ ounces.

Quick Bright Dipping Acid for Brass Which Has Been Ormoloud.—Sulphuric acid 1 gallon, nitric acid 1 gallon.

Dipping Acid.—Sulphuric acid 12 pounds. nitric acid 1 pint, niter 4 pounds, soot 2 handsful, brimstone 2 ounces. Pulverize the brimstone and soak in water 1 hour; add the nitric acid last.

Good Dipping Acid for Cast Brass.—Sulphuric acid 1 quart, niter 1 quart, water 1 quart. A little muriatic acid may be added or omitted.

Dipping Acid.—Sulphuric acid 4 gallons, nitric acid 2 gallons, saturated solution of sulphate of iron (copperas) 1 pint, solution of sulphate of copper 1 quart.

Ormolu Dipping Acid for Sheet Brass.—Sulphuric acid 2 gallons, nitric acid 1 pint, muriatic acid 1 pint, water 1 pint, niter 12 pounds. Put in the muriatic acid last, a little at a time, and stir with a stick.

Ormolu Dipping Acid for Sheet or Cast Brass.—Sulphuric acid 1 gallon, sal ammoniac 1 ounce, sulphur (in flour) 1 ounce, blue vitriol 1 ounce, saturated solution of zinc in nitric acid, mixed with an equal quantity of sulphuric acid, 1 gallon.

To Prepare Brass Work for Ormolu Dipping.—If the work is oily boil it in lye; and if it is finished work, filed or turned, dip it in old acid, and then it is ready to be ormeloed: but if it is unfinished and free from oil, pickle it in strong sulphuric acid, dip in pure nitric acid, and then in the old acid, after which it will be ready for ormeloing.

To Repair Old Nitric Acid Ormolu Dips.—If the work after dipping appears coarse and spotted, add vitriol till it answers the purpose. If the work after dipping appears too smooth add muriatic acid and niter till it gives the right appearance. The other ormolu dips should be repaired according to the recipes, putting in the proper ingredients to strengthen them. They should not be allowed to settle, but should be stirred often while using.

Tinning Acid for Brass or Zinc.—Muriatic acid 1 quart, zinc 6 ounces. To a solution of this add water 1 quart, sal ammoniac 2 ounces.

Vinegar Bronze for Brass.—Vinegar 10 gallons, blue vitriol 3 pounds, muriatic acid 3 pounds, corrosive sublimate 4 grains, sal ammonia 2 pounds, alum 8 ounces.

Directions for Making Lacquer.—Mix the ingredients and let the vessel containing them stand in the sun or in a place slightly warmed 3 or 4 days, shaking it frequently till the gum is dissolved, after which let it settle from 24 to 48 hours, when the clear liquor may be poured off for use. Pulverized glass is sometimes used in making lacquer, to carry down the impurities.

Lacquer for Dipped Brass.—Alcohol, proof specific gravity not less than 95-100th, 2 gallons, seed lac 1 pound, gum copal 1 ounce, English saffron 1 ounce, annotto 1 ounce.

Lacquer for Bronzed Brass.—To 1 pint of the above lacquer add gamboge 1 ounce; and after mixing it add an equal quantity of the first lacquer.

Deep Gold-Colored Lacquer.—Best alcohol 40 ounces, Spanish annotto 8 grains, tumeric 2 drams, shellac ½ ounce, red sanders 12 grains; when dissolved, add spirits of turpentine 30 drops.

Gold-Colored Lacquer for Brass Not Dipped.—Alcohol 4 gallons, tumeric 3 pounds, gamboge 3 ounces, gum sanderach 7 pounds, shellac 1½ pounds, turpentine varnish 1 pint.

Gold-Colored Lacquer for Dipped Brass.—Alcohol 36 ounces, seed lac 6 ounces, amber 2 ounces, gum gutta 2 ounces, red sandalwood 24 grains, dragon's blood 60 grains, oriental saffron 36 grains, pulverized glass 4 ounces.

Good Lacquer for Brass.—Seed lac 6 ounces, amber or copal 2 ounces, best alcohol 4 gallons, pulverized glass 4 ounces, dragon's blood 40 grains, extract of red sandalwood obtained by water 30 grains.

Lacquer for Dipped Brass.—Alcohol 12 gallons, seed lac 9 pounds, turmeric 1 pound to a gallon of the above mixture; Spanish saffron 4 ounces. The saffron is to be added for bronze work.

Good Lacquer.—Alcohol 8 ounces, gamboge 1 ounce, shellac 3 ounces, annotto 1 ounce, solution of 3 ounces of seed lac in 1 pint of alcohol; when dissolved add ½ ounce venice turpentine. ¼ ounce dragon's blood, will make it dark; keep in a warm place 4 or 5 days.

Pale Lacquer for Tin Plate.—Best alcohol 8 ounces, tumeric 4 drams, hay saffron 2 scruples, dragon's blood 4 scruples, rec sanders 1 scruple, shellac 1 ounce, gum sanderach 2 drams, gum mastic 2 drams, Canada balsam 2 drams; when dissolved add spirits of turpentine 30 drops.

Red Lacquer for Brass.—Alcohol 8 gallons, dragon's blood 4 pounds, Spanish annotto 12 pounds, gum sanderach 13 pounds, turpentine 1 gallon.

Pale Lacquer for Brass.—Alcohol 2 gallons, cape aloes, cut small, 3 ounces, pale shellac 1 pound, gamboge 1 ounce.

Best Lacquer for Brass.—Alcohol 4 gallons, shellac 2 pounds, amber gum 1 pound, copal 20 ounces, seed lac 3 pounds, saffron to color, pulverized glass 8 ounces.

Color for Lacquer.—Alcohol 1 quart, annotto 4 ounces.

Lacquer for Philosophical Instruments.—Alcohol 80 ounces, gum gutta 3 ounces, gum sandarach 8 ounces, gum elemi 8 ounces, dragon's blood 4 ounces, seed lac 4 ounces, terra merita 3 ounces, saffron 8 grains, pulverized glass 12 ounces.

Brown Bronze Dip.—Iron scales 1 pound, arsenic 1 ounce, muriatic acid 1 pound, zinc (solid) 1 ounce. Let the zinc be kept in only while it is in use.

Green Bronze Dip.—Wine vinegar 2 quarts, verditer green 2 ounces, sal ammoniac 1 ounce, salt 2 ounces, alum ⅛ ounce, French berries 8 ounces; boil the ingredients together.

Aquafortis Bronze Dip.—Nitric acid 8 ounces, muriatic acid 1 quart, sal ammoniac 2 ounces, alum 1 ounce, salt 2 ounces, water 2 gallons. Add the salt after boiling the other ingredients, and use it hot.

Plumber's Solder.—Lead 2 parts, tin 1.

Tinman's Solder.—Lead 1 part, tin 1.

Pewterer's Solder.—Tin 2 parts, lead 1.

Common Pewter.—Tin 4 parts lead 1.

Best Pewter.—Tin 100 parts, antimony 17.

A Metal That Expands in Cooling.—Lead 9 parts, antimony 2, bismuth 1. The metal is very useful in filling small defects in iron castings, etc.

Queen's Metal.—Tin 9 parts, antimony 1, bismuth 1, lead 1 part.

Mock Platinum.—Brass 8 parts, zinc 5.

Composition Used to Weld Cast Steel.—Borax 10 parts: sal ammoniac 1; grind or pound them roughly together, then fuse them in a metal pot over a clear fire, taking care to continue the heat until all spume has disappeared from the surface. When the liquid appears clear, the composition is ready to be poured out to cool and concrete; afterwards being ground to a fine powder, it is ready for use. To use this composition the steel to be welded is raised to a heat which may be expressed by "bright yellow," it is then dipped among the welding powder, and again placed in the fire until it attains the same degree of heat as before, it is then ready to be placed under the hammer.

Cast Iron Cement.—Clean borings or turnings of cast iron 16 parts, sal ammoniac 2, flour of sulphur 1; mix them well together in a mortar and keep them dry. When required for use, take of the mixture 1 part, clean borings 20; mix thoroughly, and add a sufficient quantity of water. A little grindstone dust added improves the cement.

Booth's Patent Grease for Railway Axles.—Water 1 gallon, clean tallow 3 pounds, palm oil 6 pounds, common soda ½ pound; or tallow 8 pounds, palm oil 10. The mixture is to be heated to about 210° Fahrenheit and well stirred until it cools down to about 70°, when it is ready for use.

Cement for Steampipe Joints, with Faced Flanges.—Mixed white lead 2 parts, red lead 1; or otherwise mix them to a consistence of thin putty, apply interposed layers with 1 or 2 thicknesses of canvas or gauze wire, as the necessity of the case may be.

Olive Bronze Dip for Brass.—Nitric acid 3 ounces, muriatic acid 2 ounces; add titanium or palladium; when the metal is dissolved add 2 gallons pure soft water to each pint of the solution.

Brown Bronze Paint for Copper Vessels.—Tincture of steel 4 ounces, spirits of niter 4 ounces, essence of dendi 4 ounces, blue vitriol 1 ounce, water ½ pint. Mix in a bottle. Apply it with a fine brush, the vessel being full of boiling water. Varnish after the application of the bronze.

Bronze for All Kinds of Metal.—Muriate of ammonia (sal ammoniac) 4 drams, oxalic acid 1 dram, vinegar 1 pint; dissolve the oxalic acid first; let the work be clean. Put on the bronze with a brush, repeating the operation as many times as may be be necessary.

Bronze Paint for Iron or Brass.—Chrome green, 2 pounds, ivory black 1 ounce, chrome yellow 1 ounce, good japan 1 gill; grind all together and mix with linseed oil.

To Bronze Gun Barrels.—Dilute nitric acid with water and rub the gun barrels with it; lay them by for a few days, then rub them with oil and polish them with beeswax.

For Tinning Brass.—Water 2 pails full, cream of tartar ¼ pound, salt ½ pint. Shaved or Grained Tin—Boil the work in the mixture, keeping it in motion during the time of boiling.

Silvering by Heat.—Dissolve 1 ounce of silver in nitric acid; add a small quantity of salt; then wash it and add sal ammoniac, or 6 ounces of salt and white vitriol; also ¼ ounce of corrosive sublimate; rub them together till they form a paste: rub the piece which is to be silvered with the paste, heat it till the silver runs, after which dip it in a weak vitriol pickle to clean it.

Mixture for Silvering.—Dissolve 2 ounces of silver with 3 grains of corrosive sublimate; add tartaric acid 4 pounds, salt 8 quarts.

Separate Silver from Copper.—Mix sulphuric acid 1 part, nitric acid 1 part, water 1 part; boil the metal in the mixture till it is dissolved, and throw in a little salt to cause the silver to subside.

Solvent for Gold.—Mix equal quantities of nitric and muriatic acids.

Varnish for Smooth Molding Patterns.—Alcohol 1 gallon, shellac 1 pound, lamp or ivory black sufficient to color it.

Fine Black Varnish for Coaches.—Melt in an iron pot, amber 32 ounces, resin 6 ounces, asphaltum 6 ounces, drying linseed oil 1 pint; when partly cooled add oil of turpentine, wormed, 1 pint.

Chinese White Copper.—Copper 40.4 parts, nickel 31.6 parts, zinc 25.4 parts, iron 2.6 parts.

Bath Metal.—Brass 32 parts, zinc 9.

Speculum Metal.—Copper 6 parts, tin 2, arsenic 1; or, copper 7 parts, zinc 3, tin 4.

Blanched Copper.—Copper 8, and arsenic ½ parts.

Britannia Metal.—Brass 4, and tin 4 parts; when fused, add bismuth 4, and antimony 4 parts. This composition is added at discretion to melted tin.

Soft Cement for Steam-boilers, Steampipes, Etc.—Red or white lead, in oil, 4 parts; iron borings 2 or 3 parts.

Hard Cement.—Iron borings and salt water, and a small quantity of sal ammoniac with fresh water.

Staining Wood and Ivory.—YELLOW.—Diluted nitric acid will produce it on wood.

RED.—An infusion of Brazil wood in stale urine, in the proportion of a pound to a gallon for wood; to be laid on when boiling hot, and should be laid over with alum water before it dries; or a solution of dragon's blood in spirits of wine, may be used.

BLACK.—Strong solution of nitric acid for wood or ivory.

MAHOGANY.—Brazil, madder and logwood, dissolved in water and put on hot.

BLUE.—Ivory may be stained thus: Soak it in a solution of verdigris in nitric acid, which will turn it green; then dip it into a solution of pearlash boiling hot.

PURPLE.—Soak ivory in a solution of sal ammoniac in 4 times its weight of nitrous acid.

Silver Plating Fluid.—Dissolve 1 ounce of nitrate of silver in crystal in 12 ounces of soft water; then dissolve in the water 2 ounces cyanuret of potash; shake the whole together and let it stand until it becomes clear. Have ready some ½ ounce vials and fill half full of Paris white or fine whiting; and then fill up the bottles with the liquor, and it is ready for use. The whiting does not increase the coating power; it only helps to clean the articles, and save the silver fluid, by half filling the bottles.

● **To Loosen Rusted Screws.**—One of the simplest and readiest ways of loosening a rusted screw is to apply heat to the head of the screw. A small bar or rod of iron, flat at the end, if reddened in the fire and applied for 2 or 3 minutes to the head of the rusty screw will, as soon as it heats the screw, render its withdrawal as easy by the screw-driver as if the screw had been only recently inserted. As there is a kitchen poker in every house, that instrument, if heated at its extremity and applied for a few minutes to the head of the screw or screws, will do the work of loosening; an ordinary screw-driver will do the rest without causing the least damage, trouble, or vexation of spirit.

LEATHER.

CARE OF AND POLISHES FOR.

Boot and Shoe Blacking.—Ivory black 1 pound, molasses 2 ounces. olive oil 4 ounces, oil of vitriol 4 ounces, alcohol 8 ounces, rye flour 1 pound; mix them together in a kettle.

Boots. To make leather boots waterproof saturate them with castor oil. To stop squeaking, drive a peg into the middle of the sole.

Boot Cleaning.—Three good brushes and good blacking must be provided; one of the brushes hard, to brush off the mud; the other soft. to lay on the blacking; the third of a medium hardness, for polishing. The blacking should be kept corked or covered except when in use. When boots come in very muddy wash off the mud, and wipe them dry with a sponge: then leave them to dry gradually on their sides, taking care they are not placed near the fire.

Brilliant French Varnish for Leather.—Spirit of wine ¾ pint, vinegar 5 pints, gum senegal in powder ½ pound, loaf sugar 6 ounces, powdered galls 2 ounces. green copperas 4 ounces; dissolve the gum and sugar in the water; strain, and put on a slow fire, but don't boil; now put in the galls, copperas, and the alcohol; stir well for five minutes; set off: and when nearly cool strain through flannel, and bottle for use. It is applied with a pencil brush. Most superior.

Cleaning Patent Leather Boots.—They require to be wiped with a wet sponge, and afterwards with a soft dry cloth, and occasionally with a soft cloth and sweet oil, blacking and polishing the edges of the sole in the usual way, but so as not to cover the patent polish with blacking. A little milk may also be used with very good effect for patent leather boots.

Cheap Tanning Without Bark or Mineral Astringents.—The astringent liquor is composed of water 17 gallons, aleppo galls ½ pound, Bengal catechu 1½ ounces, and 5 pounds of tormentil or septfoil root. Powder the ingredients. and boil in the water 1 hour; when cool, put in the skins (which must be prepared by being plunged into a preparation of bran and water for 2 days previously); handle them frequently during the first 3 days, let them alone the next 3 days, then handle 3 or 4 times in 1 day; let them lie undisturbed for 25 days more, when the process will be complete.

Enameled Leather Shoes, Polish for.—One pint pure sweet cream. ½ pint linseed oil; make warm separately; then mix together. Having cleaned the shoes. rub them over with a sponge dipped in the mixture, then rub with a soft dry cloth until a luster is produced.

French Polish or Dressing for Leather.—Mix 2 pints best vinegar with 1 pint soft water; stir into it ¼ pounds glue, broken up, ⅛ pound logwood chips, ¼ ounce finely powdered indigo, ¼ ounce best soft soap, and ¼ isinglass; put the mixture over the fire, and let it boil ten minutes or more; then strain, bottle, and cork. When cold it is fit for use. Apply with a sponge.

French Polish.—Boil in a quart of liquid, consisting of 2 parts of vinegar and 1 part of water, ¼ pound of glue and the same quantity of logwood chips, with about the sixth part of an ounce of the following ingredients: Soft soap, isinglass, and finely-powdered indigo. When boiled ¼ of an hour it should be strained off, and when cold be fit for use. It should be applied with a piece of soft rag or sponge, the shoes being quite dry and free from dirt.

Harness.—1. Molasses ½ pound, lampblack 1 ounce, yeast 1 spoonful; sugar, olive oil, gum tragacanth and isinglass each 1 ounce, and a cow's gall, mix with 2 pints stale beer, and let stand upon the fire 1 hour. **2.** Four ounces best glue, 1½ pints best vinegar, 2 ounces gum arabic, ½ pint black ink, 2 drams isinglass. Dissolve the gum in the ink, and melt the isinglass in another vessel with as much water as will cover it. Steep the glue in the vinegar until soft. Dissolve it by the aid of heat, stirring to prevent burning. Add the ink to the gum and heat generally. Lastly, mix in the solution of isinglass and remove from the fire. When used, a small portion must be heated until fluid, then applied with a sponge and permitted to dry. Dried in the sun, or by the fire, it will have a better polish.

Liquid Blacking for Boots and Shoes.—1. Four ounces molasses, ½ ounce lampblack, 1 teaspoonful yeast, 1 teaspoonful oil of turpentine; mix well; apply with a sponge. **2.** Soft water, 4 gallons, logwood extract, 6 ounces. Dissolve by gentle heat. Soft water 1 gallon, borax 6 ounces, shellac 1½ ounces, boil until solution is effected. Potassium bichromate ¾ ounces, water ½ pint; dissolve all together. Add to this before boiling 3 ounces spirits of water or ammonia. **3.** Three ounces ivory black, 2 ounces molasses, ½ ounce sweet oil; mix to a paste; add gently ½ ounce of vitriol, then add ½ pint vinegar and 1¾ pints water or sour beer. The oil of vitriol may be mixed with sweet oil. **4.** One dram isinglass, ½ dram indigo, ½ ounce soft soap, 2 ounces glue, small handful logwood raspings. Boil all slowly together in 1 pint vinegar until reduced one half. Clean the shoes of all dirt and blacking with a wet sponge. Dry the shoes and apply polish with a sponge.

Oil Paste for Blacking Boots and Shoes.—Two ounces oil of vitriol, 4 ounces tanner's oil, mix and let stand 48 hours, then add 5 ounces molasses and 1 pound ivory black; stir well and then put up for sale. This has been the fortune of Mason, of Philadelphia.

Patent Blacking.—One gallon alcohol, 1 ounce sulphur

acid. 1½ pounds gum shellac; let stand 48 hours, then add ¼ pound ivory black. Let stand 24 hours, then carefully pour off the top; this is ready for use, and is waterproof. This recipe costs $50, and is for the polish of all leather. It sells in 4 ounce bottles at $1 per bottle.

Paste Blacking for Boots and Shoes.—1. Four ounces oil of vitriol, 10 ounces tanner's oil, 2 pounds ivory black, 10 ounces molasses. Mix the vitriol and oil together, and let stand 24 hours; then add the ivory black and molasses and mix into a thick paste; will not injure the leather. **2.** Mix 3 pounds lampblack, ½ pound bone black, and 5 pounds molasses and glycerine in equal parts; melt 2½ ounces gutta percha in an iron saucepan; add 10 ounces olive oil and 1 ounce stearine or tallow; stirring; add to this the first mixture, and stir thoroughly; dissolve 5 ounces gum senegal in 1½ pints water, and 1 ounce each oils of rosemary and lavender. Stir well into the double mixture. For use, dilute the blacking with 3 or 4 parts water.

Patent Leather, To Restore Enamel.—When the enamel has chipped off, clean the parts well with fullers earth and water, and then apply the following varnish: 2 ounces pure Prussian blue, 1 ounce vegetable black, with a little copal or amber varnish. Melt at a heat of 160o Fahrenheit, but be sure that the pigments are carefully ground in the drying oils. Don't add the varnish till the third and last coat. Polish with a piece of pumice stone.

Stains on Leather.—A piece of cloth dipped in spirits of wine and rubbed on soiled leather will remove every spot on it.

Varnish for Leather.—Spirits of wine (alcohol) ¾ pint, vinegar 5 pints, senegal gum in powder ½ pound, loaf sugar 6 ounces, powdered galls 2 ounces, green copperas, 4 ounces; dissolve the gum and sugar in the water, strain and put on a slow fire, but don't boil. Now put in the galls, copperas, and alcohol; stir well 5 minutes; set off; when nearly cool strain through a flannel and bottle for use. Apply with a brush.

To Tan Raw Hide.--When taken from the animal spread it flesh side up; then put 2 parts of saltpeter and alum combined, make it fine, sprinkle it evenly over the surface, roll it up, let it alone a few days till dissolved; then take off what flesh remains and nail the skin to the side of a barn in the sun; stretch tight, to make it soft like harness leather, put neat's foot oil on it, fasten it up in the sun again; then rub out all the oil you can with a wedge-shaped stick, and it is tanned with the hair on.

Waterproof for Leather.--Take linseed oil 1 pint, yellow wax and white turpentine each 2 ounces, burgundy pitch 2 ounces; melt and color with lampblack.

Waterproof Blacking for Boots and Shoes.—Take an old pair india rubber shoes, cut them up, and pull off the cloth lining, put the rubber in about 1 pint neat's foot oil, and set on the stove until the rubber is melted, stirring once in a while, and don't let it boil or burn. It will take about 2 days to melt. As soon as melted stir in about ⅓ pound beef or mutton tallow and ¼ pound beeswax: if it is not black enough add lampblack; wash the boots clean and when nearly dry apply the waterproof. If the weather is cold work near the stove, rubbing it in well with the hands.

Waterproof Blacking for Harness.—Melt in a glazed saucepan 2 ounces black resin; add 3 ounces beeswax; when melted take from the fire. add ½ ounce fine lampblack and ¼ dram prussian blue in fine powder; stir them so as to be perfectly mixed: then add spirits of turpentine to form thin paste. When cool apply with a linen rag evenly, and polish with a brush.

HINTS FOR TRAPPERS AND HUNTERS.

Angler's Secret.—**1.** Mix the juice of lovage or smellage with any kind of bait. **2.** Mullen seed pulverized and mixed with dough and sprinkled on the surface of still water intoxicates the fish, and makes them turn up on the top of the water

Hunters' and Trappers' Secret.—Take equal parts of oil of rhodium, anise oil, sweet oil, and honey. and mix well. Put a few drops on any kind of bait. For musk rats use sweet apples or vegetables for bait. For mink use a chicken's head or a piece of fresh meat.

Skinning Animals.—As soon as possible after an animal is dead and dry. attend to skinning. For fur alone, small animals should be skinned by beginning at one of the hind feet. slitting the skin down to the anus; cutting around this and thence up to the other foot. To strip the skin from the tail pull the skin back from 2 or 3 of the first joints: tie them firmly with a strong cord. and attach it to a strong hook in the wall; then introduce a cleft stick between the vertebræ and the skin: then force the stick to the extremity and the tail bones will come out of the skin. Peel the skin off by drawing it wrong side out over the body; leave the fur side in. Larger animals are skinned by cutting from the front of the lower jaw to the anus, and peeling (without slitting) the legs if possible: but if inconvenient slit in a straight line on the inside of the leg from one foot to the other. making a double cross: chop off the feet. and remove the hide as before. In removing the skin from the otter and other wide-tailed animals. rip the skin along the under side of the tail, and open it out, stretched flat on a board.

Stretching and Drying.—In drying skins it is important that they should be stretched tight, like a drum-head. There are 3 modes of stretching: The Board Stretcher is of light wood. and of various sizes. For a small one prepare a board 2 feet, 3 inches long, 3½ inches wide at one end, and 2⅛ inches at the other, and ⅜ inches thick; bevel it from centre to sides all most to an edge; round and bevel the small end 1 inch up on the sides; saw this board through the middle, and make a wedge of same length and thickness, 1 inch wide at the large end. ¾ inches at the other, and drive it between 2 pieces. This is suitable for a mink or marten. Two larger sizes, with similar proportions are required for the larger animals. The largest size, suitable for the full-grown otter or wolf, should be 5½ feet long, 7 inches wide at the large end when fully spread by the wedge, and 6 inches at the small end. For the fox, raccoon, fisher and some other animals, the board should be 3 feet 7 inches long, 4½ inches wide at widest part, 3⅝ inches at narrowest, and the wedge about the same width as given for a mink. These stretchers require that the skin of the animal should not be ripped through the belly, but stripped off whole. The skin should be drawn over the 2 pieces, stretched and tacked, the wedge driven in and all made solid by a tack in the end of the tail; hang up to dry. For musk-rat and other small animals, take a thin board, 20 inches long, 6 inches wide at one end, tapering to 5½ inches at 6 inches from the small end, beveled and rounded as before; stretch the skin on tight and tack. The Bow Stretcher: Take a strip of any elastic wood, such as hickory, birch, elm, etc., bend it into the shape of an ox bow, and shove it into the skin, which is drawn tight and fastened by splitting down a sliver in the bow, and drawing the skin of the lip into it. For curing in this manner a musk-rat skin, for instance, the feet are cut off; the skin is ripped with a knife from the centre of the under jaw down the middle of the belly, a little beyond the holes left by the forelegs; the skin is next cut loose around the lips, ears and eyes, and finally stripped backwards off the body. The Hoop Stretcher: The skins of large animals are best dried by spreading them at full size, in a hoop. Cut a stick of hickory, or other flexible wood, long enough to entirely surround the skin when bent, or splice together 2 small ones; place this in the skin, and lop and tie the ends. The skin of the legs must not be ripped in this method. This is the proper method of stretching the skin of the deer. When it is dry, it may be taken from the hoop, and is ready for packing and transportation. Skins stretched by these methods should not be dried in the sun, nor by the fire, but in a cool place, and sheltered from rain. No salt or other preservative is used upon skins intended for the market.

Stuffing and Mounting Birds.—1. Before skinning, measure girth and length. From these data an artificial body is constructed as follows: On a piece of straight wire, a bunch of excelsior is secured by repeated winding with thread. This bundle is molded to resemble the bird's body; it is attached to the end of the wire, the long protruding portion of which serves as a foundation for the neck; the extremity of the wire is clipped to a point, and forced diagonally upward through the skull, on top of which it is clinched flat. Cotton batting is wound about the wire between the skull and body, sufficient to fill the skin of the neck.

Paint the inside of the skin with arsenical soap; then draw the skin back to envelop the false body; a needle and thread are thrust through the nostrils to make a loop for convenience in handling; the finest pair of forceps is employed to pull the eyelid skin into place; arrange the feathers, and pull up the cotton in the orbits. More cotton is pushed down the throat until filled; 2 pieces of wire are then sharpened at one extremity; taking the wire in one hand and guiding it with the other, shove it into the leg from the ball of the foot up alongside the thigh bone, the skin being turned back; cotton is then wound about both wire and bone to fill the thigh out, and the same process repeated for the other side, the ends of the wire below protruding to support the bird on the perch; the upper ends are pushed clean through the artificial body from below, and clinched on the upper side: this secures the legs, which are afterward bent in natural position; the bird can now be set up. For small birds, the cut in the breast need not be sewn up; a chicken or larger fowl will require a few stitches. If the tail feathers are to be spread, a wire is thrust across the body and through each feather; the wings are then gathered closely into the body, and 2 wires, one from each side are pushed in diagonally from up, own and through the skin of the second joint. The wings are thus held, and the wires, as well as that through the tail, are left protruding. A touch of glue within the eyelids prepared for the eyes, which may be purchased from taxidermists; for smaller birds, black beads will answer. If plain glass beads can be readily obtained, by the aid of a little paint they can be made to imitate the eyes of a chicken. After the eyes are inserted, a needle is used to pull the lids around them and into place; then, with a fine pair of forceps, adjust the feathers, smoothing them with a large camel's-hair brush. Thread must then be wound over the body loosely, beginning at the head, and continuing until all the feathers are bound. The bird is left to dry for a day or two, when the thread is removed, the ends of the wire cut off close to the body, and the work is complete. In ducks, hens, etc., the neck is so long and narrow that the skin cannot be drawn over the head with these birds; therefore, skin the neck and cut it off; make a cut through the skin from the angle of the jaw to the bottom of the piece of neck attached to head, and remove the neck, brain, tongue, etc., through the opening. **2.** A simple manner of stuffing a bird is as follows: The entrails are removed, taking care not to injure the feathers; then the brain taken out through the mouth, taking care not to tear the membranes of the bill; then fill the inside of the skull and the body with a mixture of pepper, salt and alum. Put the bird in a cool place for a short time, then dry before a fire. Then take out the pepper, etc., and fill the bird with some soft substance, and arrange as you wish it to remain. The wings and tail can be kept in position with the wire.

Stuffing and Mounting Small Animals.—Select a piece of wire of such thickness that 4 pieces, introduced into the legs, will support the animal. A thinner piece, 2 feet long, is next taken and bent ⅛ its length into an oval shape smaller than the hand, the two ends united together, leaving one end shorter than the other; then the wire must be cut the same length as the tail, independent of the oval. Wrap the wire in flax, constantly increasing toward the oval; rub the whole with paste to preserve the shape. With a small brush put a little of the preparation into the tail, and coat the towed wire with the same, and put it into the skin of the tail; place the oval end within the body; this serves to fix the tail to the iron backbone. Take 5 pieces of iron wire, the diameter of a straw; 1 a foot longer than the body of the animal and 4 others the length of the legs they are to support; the point must be sharp at one extremity in a triangular form. Form a ring at the unpointed end of the long wire, large enough to pass the little finger through, bending the wire back on itself 1½ turns with round pinchers; form a similar ring on the same wire, by one turn, in the part that will come between the animal's shoulders. The rest of the wire must be straight and pointed triangularly. Having annointed the skin with preservatives, fill the hollows of the head with chopped flax; insert one end of the long piece of wire into the middle of the skull, and restore the head to its place: stuff the skin of the neck with the same, preserving dimensions. The second ring of the wire must correspond with the pelvis. Next take one of the foot wires and pass it behind the bone of the front leg, placing the point which comes out at the sole under the highest ball of the foot; then draw the bones of the leg up within the skin, and tie the wire to the bone of the arm and forearm with pack thread; anoint the parts, and twist them with chopped flax. To fix the forelegs pass their wires through the little ring of the middle or back wire and twist the ends together with pincers. For an animal the size of a fox the pieces left to twist should be 5 or 6 inches in length. Bind the wires on the under side against the back wire and fasten with pack thread; replace the two legs and bend them according to the attitude intended. The skin of the shoulders and belly are next stuffed, putting sufficient flax under the back wire. Sew the anterior part of the opening, preserving the appearance of the scapulae, and that thickness which appears at the junction of the shoulder and bones of the fore foot. The wires for the hind legs should be longer than for the fore legs, and be inserted into the paw loosely fastened to the thigh and leg bone, and the flax applied. If the whole is bound round with thread it will prevent slipping up when the leg is placed within the skin. Pass the extremities of the wires of the hind legs through the second ring of the back wire, which ring should be at the pelvis; bend the ends and twist them in opposite directions around the ring. To give strength pass a piece of pack thread several times around these three wires and tie it. Replace the body with chopped flax, laying it under the wires, preserving the general appearance of the animal; then with a triangle pointed needle and strong silk, sew up the incision down the belly; pass the needle from the inner surface, dividing the hairs to prevent their being drawn in with the edge of the skin.

When the skin is sewed up turn the subject in all directions, and press into correct shape, restoring the appearance of the muscles. Next take a board and drill 4 holes the same size as the foot wires at a distance to suit the position of the feet; insert the wires of the feet through the holes, and with pincers draw them down close to the board, so that the soles remain firm; bend the wires on the under side of the board and clinch with short nails or brads. The specimen being erect, give proper position to the head, imitating the muscles by stuffing in cotton at the orifices. Put in the eyes while the eyelids are fresh. Place cotton inside the lips, and secure by pins; distend the nostrils with cotton closely pressed, and the flesh saturated with the preservative. If the ears are to be erect, pass a connecting thread through the base of each, tightening it until sufficiently near to each other. If the ears are large, pasteboard of the same form may be placed within and fastened around the edges with small pins. Anoint the ears, nose, lips and paws with a brush dipped in spirits of turpentine, and afterwards wipe the hair with cotton. Repeat this 7 or 8 times at intervals of some days. When quite dry the wire which passes from beyond the head may be cut.

Stuffing, Preparation for.—Camphor 1 ounce, corrosive sublimate 1 ounce, alum ½ ounce, sulphur 1 ounce; all powdered and mixed. **2.** Tanner's bark, dried and powdered, 2 ounces, burnt alum 1 ounce, snuff 1 ounce; mix, and add arsenic ¼ ounce, sulphur 1 dram, camphor ¼ ounce. **3.** Arsenic 4 ounces, tanner's bark 8 ounces; mix and reduce to powder. Sift fine; add camphor (reduced to powder with spirits of wine) 2 ounces, musk 30 grains. Keep in a closed jar. **4.** (Arsenical soap.) Camphor 5 drams, arsenic 4 ounces, white soap 4 ounces, carbonate of potash 12 ounces, air-slacked lime 4 ounces; make a stiff paste with a little water.

Tanning With the Hair On.—First scrape off all the fat with a blunt knife to avoid cutting the hide. This should be done on a log having a couple of legs on one end, like a trestle, the other end resting on the ground. After the fat is cleaned off take the brains of the animal, or of any other recently killed, and work them into the hide; this renders it pliable. Take 1 spoonful of alum, 2 of saltpeter; pulverize and mix; sprinkle on the flesh side. If the hair side is greasy a little weak lye will take it out. Yellow ochre mixed with the brains gives a fine color to the under side. The whites of several eggs or the soaking of the skin ½ day in oil or lard is said to produce the same effect as brains. This process is good for deerskins, sheepskins and all small furs.

Tanning Without the Hair.—Flesh it with a dull knife, and grain by scraping with a sharp instrument; then soak in pure water several days, and afterward in lime-water until the hair pulls out easily; remove the hair by scraping backward and replace the skin in fresh weak lime-water. Altogether the skin should be in lime-water 2 or 3 weeks, changing the water every 4 or 5 days. Take out, scrape, trim, rinse in clean water, and put in a mixture of wheat bran and water; after 2 weeks transfer to a mixture of alum, salt, and water; stir well, and replace for a day or two in the bran mixture; remove to a dry room; stretch for a while, and then soak in warm water. While soaking prepare a paste in the following proportions, increasing or decreasing quantity as necessary; Salt ½ pound, alum 1 pound 3 ounces, wheat flour 3 pounds, yolks of 16 eggs; mix with water, dissolving first the alum, then the salt. This is to be used in the next step, a little of the paste to a great deal of water. Take the skin and place it in a tub containing this preparation beaten to a froth; tramp and work well; then remove; stretch dry, and lastly run over with a warm flat iron. This process, though slow, makes a splendid leather, and is good for all small animals—dogs, sheep, calf, etc.

THE PAINTER AND DECORATOR.

PAINTS.

In this department will be found recipes and formulas for paints, polishes, stains, bronzes, japans, lacquers, varnishes, and waterproofing materials for cloth, etc.

To Mix.—Before the colors can be applied they must be mixed with linseed oil or spirits of turpentine or certain proportions of each. For inside work, walls, etc., flat colors are used principally, which are simply the paints mixed with turpentine alone, which dries almost immediately, and must be applied carefully. The base (usually white lead) for ordinary work must first be mixed with the oil; then the tint color added until the proper tint has been accomplished; then add the dryer, either turpentine or japan. A small quantity of the mixed color should be reserved for a guide, in case it is desired to make up an extra quantity of the color. The paint should be strained before use, and be of the consistency to spread easily, care being exercised not to get either too thick or too thin. The following tables will give the proportions by weight in mixing paints, also the colors needed to produce certain desired tints:

TABLE I.

100 parts white lead require	12 parts oil
100 parts zinc white require	14 parts oil
100 parts chrome green require	15 parts oil
100 parts chrome yellow require	19 parts oil
100 parts vermilion require	25 parts oil
100 parts light red require	31 parts oil
100 parts madder lake require	62 parts oil
100 parts yellow ochre require	66 parts oil
100 parts light ochre require	72 parts oil

100 parts Berlin blue require.......................112 parts oil
100 parts ivory black require........................112 parts oil
100 parts cobalt ....125 parts oil
100 parts florentine brown ....150 parts oil
100 parts burnt terra sienna require................181 parts oil
100 parts raw terra sienna require........ ....140 parts oil

TABLE II—TO MIX PAINTS FOR TINTS.

Red and black make............ ....Brown
Lake and white make ....Rose
White and brown make ....Chestnut
White, blue, and lake make ....Purple
Blue and lead color make..................................Pearl
White and carmine make......................................Pink
Indigo and lampblack make ....Silver gray
White and lampblack make............................Lead color
Black and venetian red make....... ....Chocolate
White and green make............................Bright green
Purple and white make ....French white
Light green and black make............. ....Dark green
White and green make..... ....Pea green
White and emerald green make.. ....Brilliant green
Red and yellow make............. ....Orange
White and yellow make...........................Straw color
White, blue, and black make............. ....Pearl gray
White, lake, and vermilion make ....Flesh color
Umber, white, and venetian red make......................Drab
White, yellow, and venetian red make.....................Cream
Red, blue, black, and red make ....Olive
Yellow, white, and a little venetian red make ....Buff

Combinations of green and white or black make the various
tints of green

TINTING.

Lead Color is to be made with blue-black and lampblack,
heightened with indigo or Prussian blue.

Lilac is made with the same tints, and purple lake or Indian
red.

Flesh Color is made with lakes, carmine, and a little blue,
with some yellow.

Buff Color is made with a little chrome yellow, yellow ochre,
and white.

Carnations, of carmine or scarlet lake, and the best and
clearest dry white. Perhaps the damar varnish, used so as to
dry without gloss, would be the best vehicle for such delicate
colors, in which carmines and lakes are used.

Orange.—Vermillion and chrome yellow, and cheaper orange
mineral and Indian red.

Bronze Green.—Chrome green, subdued with burnt umber.

Olive.—Umber and fine yellow ochre or stone ochre. ·Where the ochre predominates mixed with white, a fine Portland stone color is obtained.

Freestone Color.—Made with purple, brown, yellow ochre, and a little blue-black and white.

Chocolate Color.—Spanish brown or venetian red and black.

MIXING PAINTS.

A Beautiful White Paint.—For inside work, which ceases to smell and dries in a few hours. Add 1 pound of frankincense to 2 quarts of spirits of turpentine; dissolve it over a clear fire, strain it and bottle for use; then add 1 pint of this mixture to 4 pints of bleached linseed oil, shake them well together, grind white lead in spirits of turpentine and strain it; then add sufficient of the lead to make it proper for painting; if too thick in using, thin with turpentine, it being suitable for the best internal work on account of its superiority and expense.

For a Pure White Paint.—Nut oil is the best; if linseed oil is used, add ⅓ of turpentine.

To Mix Common White Paint.—Mix or grind white lead in linseed oil to the consistency of paste, add turpentine in the proportion of 1 quart to a gallon of oil; but these proportions must be varied according to circumstances. Remember to strain your color for the better sort of work. If the work is exposed to the sun, use more turpentine for the ground color to prevent its blistering.

For Knotting.—Mix white or red lead powder in strong glue size and apply it warm.

Common Flesh Color.—Stain your white lead with red lead, and mix with oil and turps.

Fine Flesh Color.—It is composed of white lead, lake and vermilion.

A Beautiful Color for Carriages, Etc.—Mix carmine lake with black japan.

Cream Color.—This is a mixture of chrome yellow, the best English venetian red, white lead, and red lead in oil.

Pearl Gray.—White lead with equal portions of Prussian blue and lampblack, mixed with oil and turps.

Fawn Color.—Grind some burnt and raw terra sienna very fine. Two or 3 pounds of this is sufficient to stain white lead for a large building. This color is of a superior shade, and very excellent for inside work.

Blue.—Grind Prussian blue in turps; other blue very fine in linseed oil, and mix it with white paint to the tint required

Buff.—This is a mixture of French yellow chrome yellow and white lead, tinged with a little venetian red, oil and turps.

Straw.—A mixture of chrome yellow and white lead, oil and turps.

Drab.—**1.** Raw and burnt umber and white lead, with a little venetian red, linseed oil, and turps. **2.** Burnt umber and white lead, with a little venetian red, oil and turps as before.

Steel.—Mix white lead, Prussian blue, fine lake and verdigris in such proportions as to produce the required color.

Purple.—White lead, Prussian blue and vermilion or lake with oil and turps.

Violet.—Is composed of vermilion mixed with blue-black and a little white.

French Gray.—White lead and Prussian blue, tinged with vermilion; and for the last coat substitute carmine for the vermilion; mix with oil and turps.

Silver.—Use white lead, indigo, and a small portion of blue-black, as the shade may require.

Gold.—Mix Naples yellow or patent yellow with a small quantity of orange chrome and a little Spanish white.

Dark Chestnut.—Mix red ochre and black; use yellow ochre when you require to lighten the color, in oil.

Salmon.—White lead, tinged with the best English venetian red, oil and turps.

Peach Blossom.—White lead, tinged with orpiment; mixed with oil and turps.

Drab.—**1.** White lead with a little Prussian blue and French yellow, linseed oil and turps. **2.** White lead with a little French yellow and lampblack, linseed oil and turps. **3.** White lead with a little chrome green and blue-black.

Lead.—This is a mixture of lampblack and white lead, with a little litharge.

Chocolate.—Mix lampblack and venetian red with a little red lead or litharge to harden the color and give a drying quality. The colors must be ground and mixed with boiled oil and a little turps.

Dark Red for Common Purposes.—Mix English venetian red in boiled oil with a little red lead and litharge, to give a drying quality.

Orange.—Mix red lead and French yellow with linseed oil and turps, or use deep chrome yellow.

Bright Yellow for Floors, Etc.—White lead and linseed oil mixed with some French yellow, and a little chrome yellow to brighten it; some red lead, burnt white vitriol, and litharge added to it to give it a very drying quality. This color mixed with equal parts of boiled oil and turpentine and used very thin

Dark Yellow.--Mix French yellow in boiled oil, adding to it a little red lead and litharge, to give the paint a drying quality.

Light Yellow.—1. This is a mixture of French yellow, chrome yellow, and white lead, with oil and turps. **2.** French yellow, white lead, and red lead. **3.** Grind raw terra sienna in turps and linseed oil; mix with white lead. If the color is required of a warmer cast, add a little burnt terra sienna ground in turps.

Olive Green.—A suitable, cheap and handsome color for outside work, such as doors, carts, wagons, etc. **1.** Grind separately Prussian blue and French yellow in boiled oil, then mix to the tint required with a little burnt white vitriol to act as a drier. **2.** Black and blue mixed with yellow, in such quantities as to obtain the colors or shades required. For distemper use indigo and yellow pink mixed with whiting or white lead powder. **3.** This is a mixture of Prussian blue, French yellow, a small portion of Turkey umber, and a little burnt vitriol; ground the same way. **4.** (In Oil.) Mix Prussian blue and chrome yellow; grind the same. **5.** (Another shade.) A mixture of Prussian blue and French yellow, with a small quantity of white lead and Turkey umber and burnt white vitriol; grind the same.

Light Green.—White mixed with verdigris. A variety of shades may be obtained by using blue and yellow with white lead.

Grass Green.—1. Yellow mixed with verdigris. **2.** Mix 1 pound of verdigris with 2 pounds of white lead. Walnut oil is the best for this purpose.

Invisible Green for Outside Work.--Mix lampblack and French yellow with burnt white vitriol. These colors mix in boiled oil. Burnt vitriol is the best drier for greens, as it is powerful and colorless, and consequently will not injure the color.

To Paint a Bronze.—Grind good black with chrome yellow and boiled oil; apply with a brush, and when nearly dry use the bronze powder at certain parts and the edges also; the effect will be a brassy hue.

A Good Imitation of Gold.—Mix white lead, chrome yellow, and burnt sienna, until the proper shade is obtained.

Tar Paint for Fences, Roofs, Etc.—Common tar mixed with whiting, venetian red or French yellow, according to the color required. This should be warmed in a large iron kettle in the open air, and applied with a large painting brush. It is an excellent preservative of the wood, and looks well for rough work.

Paint Dryers.—LITHARGE. This is a useful dryer, and may be used in all kinds of paints, except greens and very delicate colors. WHITE VITRIOL OR COPPERAS. This turns into water, especially when used in black paints; and is almost useless for any color till the water of crystallization is evaporated, and then it becomes a powerful dryer, and may be used for every delicate color, as it is perfectly transparent; but when used in its raw state in white paint has the effect of turning it yellow. SUGAR OF LEAD. This is a very useful and transparent dryer; not so powerful as white vitriol, but it may be used with it to advantage.

Milk Paint for Indoor Work.—The quantity for 100 square feet: One quart skimmed milk, 3 ounces of lime, 3 ounces of linseed or poppy oil, 1½ pounds of Spanish white or whiting; put the lime into a clean bucket, add sufficient of the milk to slake the lime, add the oil a few drops at a time, stirring the mixture with a flat stick till the whole of the oil is incorporated in the mass; then add the remainder of the milk, and afterward the Spanish white or whiting, finely powdered and sifted gently over the mixture by degrees. Curded milk will do for the purpose, but it must not be sour. One coat of this will do for ceilings and staircases in general; 2 coats or more for new wood. Where color is required you may use powdered umber, ochres, chromes, greens, blues, pinks, etc., ground in milk. For particular work strain the color through a hair sieve.

Lime Whitewash.—Lime whitewash is made from lime well slaked. Dissolve 2½ pounds of alum in boiling water and add it to every pailful of whitewash. Lime whitewash should be used very thin, and when it is sufficiently bound on the wall by means of alum, two thin coats will cover the work better. Most whitewashers apply their wash too thick, and do not mix a proportionate quantity of alum to bind it, consequently the operation of the brush rubs off the first coat in various parts and leaves an uneven surface, and the original smooth surface of the wall is entirely destroyed.

Italian Marble.—This looks bold and is well adapted for columns, etc., and is easy to imitate. The ground a light buff. For the graining colors prepare a rich, warm buff, made in the following manner: Mix stiff in boiled oil, white lead, and good stone ochre, and tinge with vermilion, then grind some burnt terra sienna very fine in boiled oil, and put it into another pot; mix some pure white stiff in oil, and keep this separate. Thin these colors with turpentine, have ready a brush for the buff and another for the terra sienna. Proceed to work as follows: Take the brush intended for the buff moderately full of color and dab it on freely and carefully in different patches, some of them larger than others, and varying them as much as possible. When these are laid on take the other brush and fill in with the terra sienna the spaces between; as soon as this is done, take a dry duster or softener and blend the edges together, making it appear as soft as possible. Proceed in this manner till the whole is finished, then take a hair pencil and draw a few thin white veins over the work, varying them as much as is necessary; take another pencil for the terra sienna, and run a few thin lines intermixing with the whole; varnish when dry.

To Imitate Granite.—For the ground color, stain your white lead to a light lead color, with lampblack and a little rose-pink. Throw on black spots with a graniting machine, and fill up with the white a little before the ground is dry.

A Cheap Oak Varnish.—Two quarts of boiled oil, 1½ pounds of litharge. ¾ pound gum shellac. All boiled together and stirred up till dissolved, then take off the fire and add 2 quarts of turps. When settled, strain into a bottle and cork for use.

Common Oil Varnish.—Take 1 gallon of quick-drying oil, 2 pounds of resin, and 1 quart of turpentine: put the resin with the drying oil into a varnish kettle, and let it dissolve in a gentle heat; take it from the fire and gradually pour in the spirits of turpentine. If too thick add more of the turpentine.

Transparent Varnish for Pictures.—Take the white of 4 eggs and 2 ounces of loaf sugar; beat them up in lime water to the proper consistency of varnishing.

For Varnishing on Wood, Unpainted.—Quarter of a pint of wood naphtha, ¼ pint spirits of wine, 4 ounces of benzoin, 4 ounces of orange shellac, added all together. If not thick enough with those ingredients for your purpose, add more of the gums benzoin and shellac.

Waterproof Varnish, for Linen or Calico.—One pint of turpentine, 1½ pints of linseed oil, 7 ounces of litharge, 1 ounce of sugar of lead. Strain it, apply with a brush, and dry in the sun or in a warm place.

Instructions.—Oil of turpentine deadens the color of paints; varnishes, copal, etc., brighten the color.

TABLE III.

1 gallon priming color will cover ....50 square yards.
1 gallon white zinc will cover.......... ....50 square yards.
1 gallon white lead will cover...... ....44 square yards.
1 gallon lead color will cover....................50 square yards.
1 gallon black paint will cover...................50 square yards.
1 gallon stone color will cover...................44 square yards.
1 gallon yellow paint will cover..................44 square yards.
1 gallon blue color will cover..... ....45 square yards.
1 gallon green paint will cover............. .....45 square yards.
1 gallon bright emerald green will cover.... ....25 square yards.
1 gallon bronze green will cover. ....45 square yards.

Anti-Corrosive Paint.—Take equal parts, by weight, of whiting and white lead, with half the quantity fine sand, gravel or road-dust, and sufficient coloring matter. This mixture is made in water, and can be used as a water color; but it is more durable to dry it in cakes after mixing, and then use it as an oil paint by grinding in linseed oil. The preparation of oil for this purpose is 12 parts, by weight, of linseed oil, 1 part boiled linseed oil, and 3 parts sulphate of lime, mixed; 1 gallon of this oil to 7 pounds powder.

Artificial Asphaltum.—Coal tar, by gentle evaporation, assumes the appearance of mineral pitch, and at last, by a combination of the process, attains the consistence of asphaltum. This artificial asphalum is found to answer nearly all the purposes of the natural production in the coarse black varnishes, such as are used for coach-tops, various japanned wares, and other common articles which require protection from rust. The artificial asphaltum has a feature so nearly resembling the natural, that it is difficult to distinguish them by external inspection; the artificial is blacker than the real asphaltum. The most certain method of detecting the difference between them, is by the smell. Artificial asphaltum must be rejected for etching ground, as it contains ammonia, which will be affected by nitric acid. It appears, also, that genuine Syrian asphaltum is the proper substance for etching ground; or Burgundy pitch, for such purpose, is scarcely less important.

Brunswick Black.—Take of asphaltum 2 pounds, oil of turpentine 2 pints, boiled linseed oil, ½ pound. Melt first the asphaltum, to which add the linseed oil, and afterwards the oil of turpentine. This varnish is used for grates, and other common purposes; it is best applied warm, or even hot.

Black Japan Varnish.—Take of asphaltum 3 ounces, boiled linseed oil, 4 pints, burnt amber (in powder), 4 ounces. Oil of turpentine, a sufficient quantity to make the varnish of a proper consistence. Melt first the asphaltum, to which add the linseed oil gradually, it being first made hot; then add the burnt amber, and lastly the oil of turpentine. A useful varnish for leather.

Blue.—Blue black, ½ cwt.; whiting, 1 cwt.; wood-dust, 2 cwt.; blue, ½ cwt., lime water, 12 gallons; factitious linseed oil to grind.

Brown.—Venetian red or Spanish brown 1 hundredweight, road dust 3 hundredweight, common soot 28 pounds, lime water 15 gallons, factitious linseed oil to grind.

Cream.—First coat: White lead, in oil, 66.66 parts, French yellow 3.33 parts, Japan varnish 1.33 parts, raw oil 28 parts, spirits of turpentine 2.25 parts. Second coat: White lead, in oil, 70 parts, French yellow 3.33 parts, Japan varnish 1.33 parts, raw oil 24.5 parts, spirits of turpentine 2.25 parts. One square yard of new brick work requires for first coat 75 pounds; second coat, 3 pounds.

Drab.—1. White lead with a little Prussian blue and French yellow, linseed oil and turps. 2. White lead with a little Prussian blue and lampblack, linseed oil and turps.

Flexible.—Cut soap into slices, and to every ¾ pound add 2 quarts boiling water, and while hot mix with 62 pounds oil paint; excellent for canvas.

Fireproof Paint.—Take a sufficient quantity of water for use; add as much potash as can be dissolved therein. When the water will dissolve no more potash, stir into the solution first, a quantity of flour paste of consistency of painter's size; second, a sufficiency of pure clay to render it of the consistency of cream. Apply with a painter's brush. The above will admit of any coloring you please

Green.—Lime water 6 gallons, whiting and road dust, of each 1 hundredweight, blue black 30 pounds, yellow ochre 28 pounds, wet blue, previously ground in prepared residue oil, 20 pounds; grind together. For use, thin with equal parts prepared residue oil and linseed oil. **2.** A yellow ocher and wet blue, of each 1 hundredweight, road dust 1½ hundredweight, blue black 10 pounds, lime water 6 gallons, prepared fish oil 4 gallons, prepared residue and linseed oils, of each 7½ gallons. **3** (Pea). Take 1 pound genuine mineral green, 1 pound precipitate of copper, 1½ pounds blue verditer, 3 pounds white lead, 3 ounces sugar of lead and 3 ounces burnt white vitriol; mix these in linseed oil; grind fine; it will produce a bright mineral pea green paint; preserve a blue tint and keep any length of time in any climate, by putting water over it; to use for house or ship painting, take 1 pound of green paint with some pale boiled oil; mix together: this will produce a strong pea green paint. The tint may be altered by adding a proportionate quantity of white lead to the green, ground in linseed oil, and thinned with spirits of turpentine for use. It may also be used for venetian window blinds, by adding white lead and mixing the color with boiled oil. For all the aforesaid preparations it will retain a blue tint.

How to Kill Grease Spots Before Painting.—Wash over smoky or greasy parts with saltpeter, or very thin lime whitewash. If soap-suds are used, they must be washed off thoroughly, as they prevent the paint from drying hard.

Lead Color.—Whiting 1 hundredweight, blue black 7 pounds, white lead, ground in oil 28 pounds, road dust 56 pounds, lime water 5 gallons, prepared residue oil 2½ gallons.

Metallic Paint.—Break common resin into dust or small pieces' and then dissolve in benzoline or turpentine until the solution acquires the consistency of syrup; or equal parts of each of the above spirits, or hydrocarbon that will dry and combine with drying oils can be used instead of benzoline or turpentine. When the solution is complete, it is gradually added to oxide of zinc, which has previously been made into paste with boiled linseed oil, until the whole mixture acquires the consistency of paint suitable for use; a white paint is thus produced of a durable and glossy character. Other pigments, such as sulphate of barytes, oxide of iron, Brunswick green or red lead can be added to make any desired color of paint. One great advantage of its use, it is said, is its effectual resistance to heat and moisture. It never blisters or cracks, even under the hottest sun or in the most inclement weather.

Outside Work, Durable Paint for.—**1.** Take some charcoal and pulverize it fine; add sufficient litharge as a drier and levigate with linseed oil; a good black paint is produced, to which, if yellow ochre is added, an excellent green will ensue, which is preferable to the bright green used by painters for garden work, and does not fade in the sun. **2.** For weather-worn weather-boarding take ½ common whiting and ½ white lead; throw in small portions red lead and chrome yellow to overcome the blackness of the wood, or add umber for a drab color. Fresh paint is always best. Where persons wish to do their own painting it is sometimes best to buy the paint dry. Take a board with a smooth surface, find a muller 3 inches in diameter at one end and conveniently shaped to hold with both hands, and you can mix up the paint readily. Use flaxseed oil; a little turpentine will make the paint flow freely from the brush. Small portions of venetian red and lampblack will do for dark colors.

Paint for Rough Woodwork.—Six pounds melted pitch, 1 pound linseed oil, and 1 pound yellow ochre,

Phosphorescent.—1. Heat strontium theo-sulphate 15 minutes over a Bunsen lamp, and then 5 minutes over a blast lamp. **2.** Heat equal parts of strontium carbonate and lac sulphuris gently 5 minutes, then strongly 25 minutes over a Bunsen lamp, then over a blast lamp 5 minutes. **3.** Precipitate strong aqueous solution of strontium chloride by means of sulphuric acid; dry in a current of hydrogen; then over a Bunsen lamp for 10 minutes and 20 minutes over a blast lamp. Mix any of the above with pure melted paraffine for use as a paint, and expose for a time to sunlight. The two former yield a greenish phosphorescence in the dark, the latter a bluish light. **4.** Take oyster shells and clean them with warm water; put them into the fire ½ hour; then take them out; when cold powder into a crucible in alternate layers with flowers of sulphur: put on the lid and cement with sand made into a stiff paste with beer; when dry put into the fire and bake 1 hour; wait until cold before opening the lid. The product ought to be white. Separate all gray parts. Make a sifter in the following manner; Take a jam pot; put a piece of fine muslin loosely across it; tie round with string; put the powder into the top and rake about with a bit of stick until only the coarse remains. Open the pot and you will find a very fine powder. Mix into a thin paint with gum water. Two thin applications are better than one thick one.

Reddish Brown.—1. (Dark.) For a common purpose. Mix venetian red in boiled oil, with a little red lead and litharge to give a drying quality. **2.** (Lighter.) Mix equal parts venetian red and red lead in boiled oil and turps. **3.** (Imitation Vermilion.) Grind together in oil, red lead and rose pink. **4.** (Deep Red.) Mix in oil, vermilion with a dust of ventian red or red lead.

Superior Paint for Brick Houses.—To lime whitewash add, for a fastener, sulphate of zinc, and shade with any color you choose, as yellow ochre, venetian red, etc. It outlasts oil paint.

Steel.—Mix ceruse, Prussian blue, fine lac and vermilion with oil and turps.

Stone.—Lime water 4 gallons, whiting 1 hundredweight, white lead ground in oil 28 pounds, road-dust 56 pounds, prepared fish, linseed, and residue oils, of each 3 gallons.

Straw.— A mixture of chrome yellow, white lead, oil, and turps.

To Harden Wood.—One often desires to impart the hardness of oak to shutters, doors, etc., made of soft wood. This is often done by giving them a first coating of common gray paint, and then sifting some very fine sand over it. When a dry coat of paint is laid on, after which the surface becomes so hard that it will resist the action of the sun and rain for many years without undergoing the slightest alteration.

The Art of Painting on Glass.—The only difference between ordinary painting and painting on glass is, that in the latter all transparent colors are used instead of opaque ones and the color is ground up with turpentine and varnish instead of oil. In painting upon glass it is necessary to place the picture between the artist and the light to enable him to see the effect, the light having the property of casting a yellowish tinge upon all colors so exposed. To persons having a knowledge of coloring, this art is easily learned, and affords a handsome remuneration. **2.** One ounce of clear resin; melt it in an iron vessel; when all is melted, let it cool a little, but not harden; then add oil of turpentine sufficient to keep it in a liquid state. When cold, use it with ground colors in oil.

To Imitate Ground Glass.—**1.** Two ounces of spirits of salts, 2 ounces of oil of vitriol, 1 ounce of sulphate of copper, 1 ounce of gum arabic, mixed together, and dabbed on with a brush. **2.** Dab your squares regularly over with putty; when dry, go over them again, the imitation will be executed. **3.** Mix Epsom salts with porter, and apply it with a brush.

To Paint in Imitation of Ground Glass.—Grind and mix white lead in ¾ of boiled oil, and ¼ of spirits of turpentine; and to give the mixture a very drying quality, add sufficient quantities of burnt white vitriol and sugar of lead. The color must be made exceedingly thin, and put on the panes of glass with a large painting-brush in as even a manner as possible. When a number of the panes are thus painted, take a dry duster, quite new, dab the ends of the bristles on the glass in quick succession, till you give it an uniform appearance; repeat this operation till the work appears very soft, and it will then appear like ground glass. When the windows require fresh painting, get the old coat off first by using strong pearl-ash water.

White.—1. The white destined for varnish or oil, requires a metallic oxide, which gives a body to the color. Take ceruse; reduced to powder; grind it with oil of pinks, and ¼ ounce sulphate of zinc for each pound oil. Apply the second coat without the sulphate of zinc, and let dry; cover the whole with a stratum of sandarac varnish. This color is durable and brilliant. Boiled linseed oil may be employed instead of oil of pinks, but the color will injure the purity of white. 2. Pure white oxide of lead, ground with a little essence, added to oil of pinks, and mixed with gallipot varnish. The color may be mixed with essence diluted with oil, and without varnish. which is reserved for the two last coatings. If for a lively white, heighten with a little Prussian blue or indigo, or prepared black; the latter gives it a gray coat. Pure white lead is reserved for valuable articles. If a durable white is required, grind with a little essence, and mix it with sandarac varnish.

Yellow, for Floors.—White lead and linseed oil, mixed with some French yellow and a little chrome yellow to brighten it, and some red lead, burnt white vitriol and litharge added, to give it a drying quality. Mix with equal parts boiled oil and turpentine, and use thin. (*See Glue Paint for Kitchen Floors, Cleaning and Repairing—Household Recipes.*)

COMPOUND COLORS.

These are formed by mixing two only, and will be the best and the richest.

Size.—The best size for distemper colors is made from the clippings of the skin of animals, which must be submitted to strong boiling. Take the quantity necessary, put it into an iron kettle, and fill it with water; let it stand 24 hours, till the pieces are thoroughly soaked. Let the size boil 5 hours, occasionally taking off the scum. When it is sufficiently boiled, take it from the fire, and strain it through a coarse cloth. If the size is to be kept for a length of time, dissolve 2 or 3 pounds of alum in boiling water, and add to every pailful. The size must then be boiled again till it becomes very strong; it must be strained a second time, put into a cool place, and it will keep good several months.

Brilliant Peach Blossom.—Orange lead (orpiment) and whiting, when properly mixed, composes a beautiful and unfading color; it is much used by paper-stainers. Dissolve whiting in water; then grind very fine in water a small quantity of orange lead, and mix with the whiting; add sufficient size to the mixture, and strain it through a sieve, and put into a cool place till fit for use. This color must be worked in a jelly, as the orange lead is heavy, and would otherwise separate from the other parts and sink to the bottom in a pure state.

Salmon Color.—An excellent salmon color can be made by dissolving whiting in water, and tinging it with the best English venetian red, finely ground in water. A little venetian red mixed with lime whitewash, and a proportionate quantity of alum, will answer very well for common purposes. It is important, when English red is required, that you obtain it genuin as a spurious article is frequently sold for it, which, when used, spoils the intended effect when applied to fine with.

Pink.—Dissolve in water, separately, whiting and rose pink, mix them to the texture required; strain the color through a sieve, and bind with size.

Lilac.—Take a small quantity of indigo finely ground in water and mix it with whiting till it produces a dark gray, then add to the mixture some rose pink: well mix and strain to the color and a beautiful lilac will be the result.

Light Gray.—A small quantity of lampblack mixed with whiting composes a gray; more or less black, of course, regulates the shade. With whiting, therefore, mixed with black in varying proportions, a wide range of shades may be obtained, from the darkest to the lightest gray.

French Gray.—Whiting predominates in this color; it is treated as other grays, but with this difference, that it admits of lake instead of black. Take the quantity, therefore, of whiting necessary and soak it in water, then add the Prussian blue and lake, which have been finely ground in water; the quantity of each of those colors should, of course, be proportioned to the warmth of color required. This is a handsome and delicate color for walls. Either of the preceding grays will answer for the first coat, as the French gray will cover upon it very well. Rose pink may be substituted, but it does not make so brilliant a color, neither is it so durable.

Orange Color for Walls and Stables.—Use 2 pounds of green copperas dissolved in hot water, just sufficient to dissolve it; mix it well with 8 gallons of fresh lime-wash. Stir it well while using. **2.** This is a mixture of whiting, French yellow, or Dutch pink and orange lead. These ingredients may be proportioned according to taste. This color cannot be worked except in a size-jelly, as the orange lead is a color which has great body.

Buff.—A good buff may be produced by dissolving separately whiting and French yellow in water; a little English venetian red must be added to give the yellow a warm cast; mix with size and strain as before directed.

An Excellent Green for Walls.—**1.** Take 2 pounds of mineral green and 6 pounds of good green verditer; mix them together and grind in water; mix with size, and work the color when it has formed a jelly. This green has a good body and is very durable. **2.** Mix a solution of common salt and blue vitriol in water; by putting copper plates therein, a green precipitate will be gradually formed, which may be mixed with whiting and then spread on a board to dry. **3.** (Good and Cheap.) Take 8 pounds Roman vitriol and 2 pounds of whiting, boil them in a brass or copper kettle in 3 gallons of water 1 hour, stirring the mixture the whole time till thoroughly dissolved. Pour it into an earthen pan, and let it stand several days. Decant the water, and mix the sediment with size; apply it to the walls with a whitewash brush. The shade may be altered or improved by adding a little Dutch pink or chrome yellow. When required for use it must be dissolved in water, mixed with size, etc. This color must not come in contact with iron, as the Roman vitriol powerfully attacks it, and thereby spoils the color.

Blue in Distemper.—A good blue is made by dissolving whiting in water, and mixing indigo with it.

Blue Verditer.—The best blue in use for distemper color on walls. Dissolve some pieces of copper in aqua-fortis, and when dissolved, produce a precipitation of it by adding quicklime, in such doses that it will be entirely absorbed by the acid. In order that the precipitate may be pure copper without any mixture, when the liquor has been decanted, wash the precipitate, and spread it out on a piece of linen cloth to drain. If a portion of this precipitate, which is green, be placed on a grinding-stone, and a little quicklime in powder be added, the green color will be changed into a beautiful blue. The proportion of lime added is from 7 to 10 parts in 100. As the whole matter has already acquired the consistency of paste, dissication soon takes place.

Straw Color in Size.—Dissolve the necessary quantity of whiting in water, then grind in water some chrome yellow or Dutch pink; mix to the shade required, and add some strong size; strain the color through a hair sieve, and set it in a cool place till fit for use.

Drab in Size.—(An excellent drab.) Dissolve in water, whiting, and grind some burnt umber very fine in water; mix it to the shade required. Strain the color as usual and mix with size. Raw umber will make a drab of a different shade. **2.** Dissolve separately some whiting and French yellow in water. Take a proportionate quantity of each and mix them together till a bright yellow is produced. Grind a little lampblack very fine in vinegar, and with it sufficiently stain the color to form a drab; another shade may be obtained by adding a little venetian red. Thus, by diversifying the proportions of the above-mentioned pigments, a great variety of shades may be produced.

Milk Paint for Out-Door Work.—The quantity for 100 square feet: One quart of skimmed milk, 3 ounces of lime, 2 ounces of linseed or poppy oil, 1½ pounds of Spanish white or whiting. Put the lime into a clean bucket, add sufficient of the milk to slake the lime, add the oil a few drops at a time, stirring the mixture with a flat stick till the whole of the oil is incorporated in the mass; then add the remainder of the milk and afterward the Spanish white or whiting, finely powdered and sifted gently over the mixture by degrees. Curded milk will do for the purpose, but it must not be sour. One coat of this will do for ceilings and staircases in general, 2 coats or more for new wood. Where color is required you may use powdered umber, ochres, chromes, greens, blues, pinks, etc., ground in milk. For particular work strain through a hair sieve.

For Outdoor Work.—Eight ounces of lime newly slacked,

by dipping it in water, and allowing it to break down in the open air. Now take 2 ounces of Burgundy pitch, and dissolve by a gentle heat in 6 ounces of poppy or linseed oil; then add to the hot lime 2 quarts of skimmed milk while in a hot state. Add the mixture of pitch and oil a little at a time, stirring all the while. Lastly, add 3 pounds of powdered whiting.

To Whiten Ceilings or Walls.—Take the best whiting and break down in water, then boil some parchment-cuttings three hours, and strain off the liquor after the whole is mixed together. London size will be a good substitute for the above; if the double size, use nearly half water; if the single, use none. You must test the size, as some is much stronger than others. You may add a small piece of blue black to the whiting, and before using this wash you may stir in a little turpentine.

Distemper Color for Walls.—If distemper is to be applied to a wall or ceiling which is covered with plaster, some whiting is put into water, where it may be easily broken and diluted if allowed time to soak; it must be completely saturated, and when it has settled, the clear water must be poured off. To correct the too great whiteness and to prevent a yellow cast, grind separately in some water a little indigo or ivory black, and mix with it; then add to the mixture some strong size which has been previously warmed, well stirring the whole till properly mixed. The whole of the distemper must be strained while warm, in order to remove all impurities and thoroughly mix the color. When this is done the distemper may be put into a cool place till it is formed into a weak trembling jelly, which is the only proper state in which to apply it to the walls. All size distemper colors which are applied to walls, and which are mixed with whiting, should at all times be worked cold, and of a weak, trembling jelly, otherwise it will be impossible to make good work, and great care should be taken not to have too much body in the color, for it will certainly crack and fall off in scales, as it is not the strength of the size that causes the work to crack, but the body of color. There is a great advantage in having a sufficient quantity of size in the first coat of distemper, as it binds hard, and stops the suction of the wall, in consequence of which the next coat, if properly prepared, will not move the first strata, but it will work perfectly free, and when dry, the work will have a uniform and solid appearance. If these instructions are fully attended to the amateur cannot fail in his endeavors to execute his work in the best manner. This method of whitewashing and coloring walls is far superior to lime, as it works much smoother and when properly mixed and worked upon a new wall it will not crack and fall off in scales; it also covers better, and after being repeatedly applied for a number of years the walls need no scraping, as the color easily washes off with a whitewashing brush, after they have been well soaked with water.

Lime Whitewash.—This is made from lime well slaked. Dissolve 2½ pounds of alum in boiling water, and add it to every pailful of whitewash. Lime whitewash should be used very thin and when it is sufficiently bound on the wall by means of alum, two thin coats will cover the work better; this may be used for the first coat, thinned with water. Most whitewashers apply their wash too thick, and do not mix a proportionate quantity of alum to bind it, consequently the operation of the brush rubs off the first coat in various parts and leaves an uneven surface, and the original smooth surface of the wall is entirely destroyed.

To Make Paste for Paper-Hanging.—Mix 4 pounds of flour well with cold water, as thick as you can, then boil 2 gallons of water and add a little alum, then take a little of the hot water and mix with that you have stirred with the cold water, stirring the while till you have added the whole, then strain for use; thin with cold water; size your walls with thin glue size.

Color to Imitate Cherry Tree.—Grind raw and burnt terradasienna with whiting, then to 1 gallon of water add ½ pound of glue; let the water be warm to dissolve the glue. When the color is applied, it will do with or without varnish.

Transparent Color for Painting.—The best are made from vegetable or animal substances; minerals do not work so well with water, and are apt to fade.

Directions for Inside Painting,-- The first thing is to have the room free from dust; the next essential thing is to kill the knots of the wood. When the work is knotted, proceed to prime it, which must be made to dry exceedingly hard, in order to stop the unction of the wood, otherwise the second coat will, by the operation of the brush, rub off the priming in different parts of the work, and there will be no uniformity in the finishing coat, but it will leave some parts dead and others of a shining surface. The middle coat may be of size color applied warm. Use but little color in your size or it will scale. To prepare knotting grind some lead powder in water, and mix in with strong glue size; put it into an iron vessel, and when used it must be applied to the knots with a brush quite warm. To make priming, mix or grind red and white lead with linseed oil; then, for the dryers, take a little litharge and burnt white vitriol or patent dryers, which must be ground on a slab very fine in turpentine. Mix them altogether and thin with boiled oil. The burnt vitriol and litharge act, as it were, in opposition to each other, and render the paint exceedingly drying; and the turpentine, with the boiled oil, prevents the color from running down the quicks of the work. When the priming is dry, fill up the nail-holes and crevices with putty. Rub the surface of the work smooth with glass-paper and dust it well.

The Second Coat for White.--If this coat is intended as a finish too much oil must not be added or the work will turn yellow. Mix the white lead in raw linseed oil, with equal parts of oil and turps and a little litharge; but it does not require so much as in the priming, as it will dry in a little time if the first coat is hard. The white may be heightened with a little lamp-black or Prussian blue.

The Third Coat.—If this coat is intended to have but little gloss the white lead must be mixed in linseed oil, but not too stiff, and thinned with spirits of turpentine, adding to it a little litharge and burnt white vitriol, and also a very small portion of lampblack. For white; If a dead white is required for the finishing coat the white lead must be ground as stiff as possible in linseed oil, and made quite thin with spirits of turpentine, which requires no dryers. A small portion of lampblack may be added to heighten the white, and ground exceedingly fine and strained.

Painting in Dead Colors for Inside Work.—If the work is to be painted in a superior manner new wood requires 3 coats of oil color and a flat, as the flat is not intended to give body to the work, but is a thin wash, merely to beautify and give a smooth, solid, and uniform appearance: and to apply this last coat, which is generally about the third day after the last coat of oil paint, as the flatting will then appear soft. If the last coat of paint remains to get hard the flatting will appear harsh and streaky. The proper method of flatting a door is to begin and finish the panels, taking care to cut them in clean; proceed with the styles, working the color quick, in order to keep it from setting before the door is finished; and if the flatting should set on any part of the work it must be rubbed up with fresh color as you proceed to finish, otherwise it will not have an uniform appearance.

To Flat a French Gray on Hard-Finished Walls.—In painting a new wall the oil should be put on quite warm, in order to make the paint adhere; without this precaution the paint would be apt to rise and fall off in scales. The first coat to be applied to the wall is of good boiled oil; when this is dry and hard, a thin coat of weak size may be put on tinged with red lead, in order to stop the suction of the wall, and bring the work to an uniform appearance. When this second coat is dry the wall must be painted with a thin coat of light lead color, mixed in boiled oil, to which a little spirits of turpentine and litharge must be added to harden it. When this coat is dry, rub it smooth with sandpaper, procure some of the best English ground lead, and mix it with equal parts of raw linseed oil and spirits of turpentine; then, to form the French gray, stain the white paint with Prussian blue and tinge it with vermilion to give it a warm appearance; some burnt white vitriol must also be added to give it a drying quality. Strain the color through a coarse cloth or a sieve made of fine wire. When it has stood 3 or 4 days the work will be in good order for flatting; but before this is put on the work should be lightly rubbed with sandpaper and dusted.

To Make and Apply the Flatting.—Mix the best English ground white lead with spirits of turpentine to the thickness of treacle, put in Prussian blue, finely ground, in equal parts of oil and turpentine. To make a superb gray, lake must be substituted for vermilion. Great care must be taken to match the shade of the last coat, by comparing the flatting with the remains of the last color which may have been left in the paint pot. It should be observed that the flatting must be made about one-third lighter, as the ground color will not be so apt to show through, and it will, therefore, give the work a more solid appearance. When the flatting is brought to the proper shade, strain it, and thin it to the proper consistency for use. Good soft-spreading brushes must be used, otherwise it will be impossible to make good work. If the wall be from 8 to 10 feet high, it will require two men to flat it. Fix a scaffold from one end of the wall to the other, a proper depth from the ceiling, in order to reach with care the top of the work. Let the color be properly thinned and stirred from the bottom, and be careful to have everything provided, as you cannot leave off work until one flank is finished. The bottom of the wall must be commenced first, painting not more than 12 or 18 inches wide at one time. Move the brush in a perpendicular direction, and when you have painted as high as you can conveniently reach, carefully cross the work with a light hand, in order to give the color a uniform extension. When this is done, finish the work by laying it off very lightly, beginning at the bottom and striking the brush up about a foot, then from the top lightly draw the brush to the bottom. When this is done, the man on the plank must begin where the other left off, and finish the top. In the meantime the man on the floor must begin another width, and so proceed until one side of the wall is finished. The same precaution will be highly necessary in flatting every other color.

Harmony of Colors.—Red looks well with blacks, whites, or yellows. Blues harmonize with whites and yellows. Greens with whites, black, or yellow. Gold with blacks or browns. White appears well with any color. Purple, pink, and white, etc.

To Prepare the Ground for the Oak Rollers.—Stain your white lead with raw terradasienna and red lead or with chrome yellow and venetian red; thin it with oil and turps, and strain it for use. When the groundwork is dry, grind in beer, vandyke brown, whiting, and a little burnt terradasienna for the graining color, or you may use raw terradasienna with a little whiting, umbers, etc.

Oil for Graining Oak.—Grind vandyke brown in turps; add as much gold size as will set it, and as much soft soap as will make it stand the comb. Should it set too quickly, add a little boiled oil. Put a teaspoonful of gold size ½ pint turps, and as much soap as will lay on a 25-cent piece; then take a little soda mixed with water and take out the veins.

Spirit Graining for Oak.—Take 2 pounds of whiting, ¼ pound of gold size, thinned down with spirits of turpentine; then tinge your whiting with vandyke brown and raw terradasienna ground fine, strike out your lights with a fitch dipped in turpentine, tinged with a little color to show the track, and every few strokes wipe off the color to show the lights. If your lights do not appear clear, add a little more turpentine. Turpentine varnish is a good substitute for the above-mentioned. This kind of graining must be brushed over with beer, with a clean brush. before varnishing. Strong beer must be used for glazing up top graining or shading.

Another Cream.—Mix raw terradasienna, red and white lead, to the tint required for the ground; when this is applied and dry and made smooth with fine glass-paper, the graining color may be applied, for which take 4 ounces of sugar of lead, 4 ounces of raw terradasienna, whiting, and vandyke brown, and grind them quite stiff in boiled linseed oil; take 8 ounces of beeswax and melt it in an iron ladle or earthen pipkin, and when fluid take it a distance from the fire, and pour in gradually spirits of turpentine, to the consistency of thick treacle; put a small quantity of this (grainer's cream) into the graining color in order to keep it from flowing together. If the composition should set too quick before it can be conveniently worked. add a small portion of boiled oil; or, should it flow too freely, add some of the cream. This style of oak requires working with combs of various sizes. Observe that for the purpose of graining moldings it will be necessary to prepare small combs in a variety of forms.

APPLICATION.—Spread the graining color over the surface of the work with a large paint brush, about half worn; take a coarse comb and pass over it in a straight direction. pressing moderately hard; after which, take a finer comb and pass over it several times in a wavy direction; then with an ivory comb, with the two outside teeth broken off, pass over the center of the work with a very tremulous motion of the hand, in order to produce the finest grain, which is in the center of the tree. To produce flowers or veins, use a piece of thin wash-leather, wrapped tight round the thumb, and wipe them out with the thumb-nail, or twist the leather to a point and hold it between the thumb and finger. By taking these methods the thickest or finest veins may be struck out successfully. When the whole of your work is dry, dip the flat hog's hair graining brush into a small quantity of burnt umber, ground up in ale very thin. and pass over it in a straight direction. This will leave the fine transparent grain so natural to this wood. When dry, varnish.

Another Oak.—This ground color is prepared with white lead and chrome yellow, heightened with a little venetian red. When your ground is dry. take burnt umber and grind it up in equal parts of boiled oil and turpentine; when this is done, take an equal proportion of copperas (white vitriol), previously baked in an oven or stove, till the moisture is evaporated. which will take place in a few minutes. This operation must be performed in a glazed earthen bowl, as it will adhere so firmly to any rough vessel that it would be difficult to separate them. When the copperas is burnt, it must be ground in raw linseed oil, and mixed with the above ingredients: then take one-sixth in bulk of castile soap. melted over the fire in a little boiled oil; mix this also with the other ingredients; thin the whole down with boiled oil and turpentine to the proper consistency for graining. If the grain should run together too freely, use a greater proportion of spirits of turpentine: or should it set too quick, add more boiled oil. Proceed to finish exactly as in the last.

To Imitate Oak in Distemper.—To prepare the ground for this, make a very light yellow with stone ochre and white lead. The graining colors used for this specimen are equal quantities of raw umber and stone yellow, ground very fine in ale. This should be kept in a well-corked bottle, in order to keep the dust and other impurities from it: and when required for use, it should be diluted with ale to a proper consistency for graining. When your ground is dry, take a large tool well filled with this color, rub it over the panel in an even manner, have ready a sponge, a bowl of water, and a straight-edge. Place the straight-edge against the work, and, with the sponge moistened with water, draw out the light shades in a perpendicular manner, then wipe with a brush the panel, striking the work with the end of the brush in quick succession till you get to the bottom, when, if done according to these directions, it will leave the natural grain of the wood. When this operation is finished, immediately take a piece of wash-leather, moistened, and wipe out the veins; and when this is dry, put in some dark veins of the same color; allow this to dry also, then, with a flat hog's hair brush, dipped into burnt umber thinly diluted with ale, pass over the panel in a perpendicular direction; and as soon as one panel is finished, take a wet rag or sponge and carefully wipe off all the color which may have gone beyond the panel. When all your panels are finished, commence on the middle upright styles varying the grain according to taste. but always in a downward direction. When all the middle styles are thus far completed, lay the straight-edge over the work finished, and pass the tool with a little of the graining color from top to bottom of the door; this will make a neat job, both at the end of the styles and panels. When dry, take the flat graining brush and dip it in the thin glaze of umber, and pass over the work, not too straight and formal, but in a spirited manner, occasionally giving a free turn to the brush, which will give a pleasing variety and make the imitation look quite natural. When dry, varnish. All distemper graining requires two good coats of varnish; beer it over before you varnish it a second time.

Another Method.—This method of imitating oak in distemper is so excellent, that should it be exposed continually to the hot rays of the sun; it will never fade. Make a rich ground color with stone ochre, burnt terradasienna, chrome yellow and white lead. For your graining color dissolve some gum arabic in hot water, and mix it with raw terradasienna, whiting and vandyke, ground in beer. When the ground is dry, spread the surface very even, then take a dry duster and draw it down upon the work, pressing moderately hard; comb the color while wet, and allow it to get perfectly dry, then with a camel-hair pencil, dipped in clear water, put in your veins. Allow the work to remain a few seconds till the water has dissolved the gum arabic, and then beat the veins out with a dry duster or cloth, in a downward direction. After this, use the flat brush, and pass over the work with a thin glaze of Turkey umber, ground in ale. Should the veins not beat out sufficiently clear, add a little more gum to the color, but care must be taken not to put too much, as the work would be likely to crack. When dry, varnish.

To Imitate Old Oak.—To make an exceedingly rich color for the imitation of old oak. The ground is a composition of stone ochre or orange chrome and burnt terradasienna. The graining color is burnt umber or vandyke brown, to darken it a little. Observe that the above colors must be used whether the imitation is in oil or distemper. When dry, varnish.

To Grain Oak in Distemper.—The ground either light or dark. When the ground is dry and made quite smooth, then with a fitch form your veins with a little ochre, ground in turpentine varnish. When the distemper color for the combining is applied after the veins are formed on the plain ground, then whip and comb in with your color mixed with beer. When dry, varnish: which varnish will bring the lights out which were first struck out. When dry, wet the whole with a little beer, glaze up and varnish.

To Imitate Old Oak in Oil.—Grind vandyke and whiting in turpentine, add a bit of common soap to make it stand the comb, and thin it with boiled oil.

Pollard Oak in Distemper, with a Roller or Hand-work.—Form large dark patches with vandyke brown on the ground; then with a softener draw from patch to patch, then take a short cut hair pencil or a small piece of sponge tied to the end of a stick, and by turning it round between the thumb and finger, form your curls or knots on the patches; to render it more showy, put in some patches of lake and burnt terradasienna and form knots in the same way as above: then top grain, which grain must cross all the other grains. As soon as dry, which will be in a few minutes, give it a coat of equal parts of gold size and turps, to be used as a varnish, as it dries quickly where expedition is required. When dry, glaze over with vandyke brown or ivory-black, ground in beer, then with a soft piece of rag or sponge take out your shades, soften, varnish and finish your work.

To Imitate Pollard Oak.—The ground color is prepared with a mixture of chrome yellow, vermilion and white lead, to a rich, light buff. The graining colors are vandyke brown and small portions of raw and burnt terradasienna and lake, ground in ale and beer. Fill a large tool with color, spread even the surface to be grained, and soften with a badger-hair brush. Take a moistened sponge between the thumb and finger, and dapple round and round in kind of knobs, then soften very lightly: then draw a softener from one set of knobs to the other while wet, to form a multiplicity of grains, and finish the knots with a hair pencil, in some places in thicker clusters than others. When dry put the top grain on in a variety of directions, and varnish with turps and gold size; then glaze up with vandyke and strong ale. To finish varnish with copal.

Pollard Oak in Oil.—The ground is a rich buff, prepared the same as the pollard oak in distemper. The graining colors are: Equal portions of burnt Turkey umber or vandyke, raw terradasienna and burnt copperas, ground separately in boiled oil or turps very stiff; then mix them together, and thin the whole with spirits of turpentine; then with a large sash tool rub a very light coat on the panel, and, while wet, take the flat graining brush, containing a very thin row of hairs, dip it into the color and in a spirited manner dapple in various directions, then dip the brush into the burnt umber, which has been made quite thin with spirits of turpentine, and throw on some very fine spirits. When the colors are set, take the same flat brush, dip it into a thin glaze of burnt umber, and put the grain on in a curly direction. Care must be taken to have a sufficient quantity of oil in the colors to bind them, and to finish but a small part of the surface at once, in order to keep it moist, the work will then blend itself.

A Good Ground for Mahogany.—One pound of the best English venetian red, 2 ounces of chrome yellow, ground together in equal portions of linseed oil and turpentine. If a light ground is required, use the same quantities of red lead and chrome yellow; a little vermilion will increase the richness of the color. Use for the graining color equal quantities of vandyke brown and burnt terradasienna, ground in ale or beer, well ground on a clean stone; a small piece of lake may be added for the light grain. The feather is formed with a graining-roller in a few seconds, ready for softening.

To Imitate Mottled Mahogany.—The ground is prepared with the best English venetian red, red lead, and a small portion of white lead. The graining colors required are burnt terradasienna ground in ale, with a small portion of vandyke brown, sufficient to take away the fiery appearance of the terradasienna. Cover the surface to be grained, soften with the badger's hair brush, and while wet take a mottling-roller and go over the lights a second time, in order to give a variety of shade; then blend the whole of the work with the badger softener. Put the top grain on with the same color; when dry, varnish.

Another Method.—This ground is prepared with vermilion and a very small portion of white lead and chrome yellow. The graining color is vandyke brown and a little crimson lake, ground up in ale. After the ground is dry and smooth spread a thick coat on the surface to be grained, and soften with the badger-hair brush; take out the lights on each side, and use a roller with the imitation carved on leather wetted with water; it is expeditious in forming a feather or mottling. Blend the whole together with the badger-hair brush till the work appears very soft. Top grain, and the effect will be beautiful. When dry, varnish.

To Imitate New Mahogany.—This is an excellent method of preparing for the imitation of new mahogany. The ground color must be prepared with equal quantities of chrome yellow and red lead, with a little burnt terradasienna. The graining color is prepared with equal portions of raw and burnt terradasienna, finely ground in ale or beer. After the ground is dry, spread a thick coat on the panel, then work with a mottler and softener. When dry, put on the top grain with the burnt terradasienna. Varnish when dry.

Another Method.—This ground is prepared with stone ochre, red lead, and a small quantity of burnt terradasienna. The graining color is a mixture of vandyke brown and dragon's blood; for the top grain a greater proportion of vandyke brown must be used. Varnish as before.

To Imitate Rosewood with Rollers.—Brush on the graining color as even as you can; then pass the graining rollers over to form the hearts. knots, etc. Previous to doing this let the rollers be wetted with water and rolled on a cloth. When the work is dry brush it over with a thin coat of gold size and turps; when this is dry top grain again with rollers and varnish it over. For the ground color mix the best English venetian red with linseed oil and turps, to which add a little patent dryer. Vermilion will form a superior ground, but is more expensive.

Another Method.—Mix vermilion and a small quantity of white lead for the ground. Take rose pink, tinged with a little lampblack or vandyke brown, and grind very fine in oil, then take a flat graining brush, with the hairs cut away at unequal distances, and put on the grain as if wending round a knot. When nearly dry take a graining comb that is used for oak and draw down the grain. This will give it the appearance of nature. When dry, varnish.

Another Method.—The ground is a bright red, prepared exactly the same. For the graining colors, grind separately some burnt terradasienna and ivory black, very fine in ale; mix them together and with the tool well cover the surface of the work, then wipe it with the softener, to form the small speckled grain. When dry take a small flat graining brush, well filled with ivory black, and put on the top grain in a knotty form; after this, cut the top grain asunder by putting in the heavy hearts with rollers. When the first coat of varnish is dry grind a small quantity of lake in ale, and with a camel-hair pencil touch round the knots and other parts of the work. When dry, finish with a coat of clear varnish.

✦**Another Method.**—This ground color is prepared with vermilion and small quantities of white lead and crimson lake. When the ground is dry and made very smooth, take vandyke brown, ground in oil, with a small tool spread the color over the surface in different directions, forming kind of knots. Before the work is dry take a piece of leather and, with great freedom, strike out the light veins; having previously prepared the darkest tint of vandyke brown or gum asphaltum, immediately take the flat graining brush, with a few hairs in it, draw the grain over the work and soften. When varnished the imitation will be excellent.

Another Method, in Size.—Mix venetian red, white lead powder, vermilion, and common size, the consistency of which when cold must be of a weak, trembling jelly. With this composition paint the work twice over. When the ground is dry take some lampblack finely ground in beer, and beat the white of an egg into it; take the flat graining brush dipped in the black and put on the grain. When dry stain the first coat of varnish with rose pink, finely ground in turpentine, and finish the work by giving it a coat of clear varnish.

To Imitate Bird's Eye Maple.—The ground is a light buff prepared with white lead, chrome yellow, and a little vermilion or English venetian red to take off the rawness of the yellow The graining color is equal parts of raw umber and terradasienna, ground in ale to the proper consistency. Spread the surface of the work with this color and, having some of the same prepared a little thicker, immediately take a sash-tool or sponge and put on the dark shades and soften with the badger hair brush; before the color is dry, put on the eyes by dabbing the dotting machine on the work. When dry, put on the grain with the camel's-hair pencil in the prominent parts to imitate the small hearts of the wood. When dry, varnish.

Another Method.—The ground for this prepare in oil, with white lead, turps, and stained with chrome or stone ochre, and a little red. The graining colors are 3 parts of raw umber and 1 of raw terradasienna ground fine in ale. Make part of this color quite thin, and rub a transparent coat over the work, and while wet take the flat hog's-hair graining brush and dip it into some thicker color, draw the veins very much curled, and rather inclining downward; then take a feather or goose-quill and pass over the work in the same direction as the flat brush was used, occasionally giving a sharp turn and, if necessary, pass over the work again; this will split them into a variety of forms. While wet soften the whole together and put in the eyes by dabbing the points of the fingers or rollers, etc., on the work, occasionally using the hair pencil. When the whole of the work is dry, top grain with a thin glaze of raw umber finely ground in ale. When dry, varnish.

To Imitate Curled Maple.—Prepare a light yellow for the ground by mixing chrome yellow and white lead, tinged with venetian red. The graining color is a mixture of equal portions of raw terradasienna and vandyke ground in ale. Spread the surface to be grained in an even manner, then with a piece of cork rub across the work to and fro to form the grains which run across the wood; soften, and when dry, lightly top grain with the same color. When dry, varnish.

Another Maple.— The ground is prepared precisely the

same. The graining colors are equal quantities of raw and burnt terradasienna ground in water and diluted with ale. Fill a tool with the color, and spread the surface even: then take a long piece of stout buff leather, cut to a straight edge, and by holding it each end, press the edge hard against the work, draw the leather down and it will leave the lights and shades, or use a patent roller to take out the lights, which is very expeditions in its operation; when softened, top grain and varnish when dry.

Another Method.—Put on the color with the tool; then with a sponge mottle and soften; then put in small eyes with your roller or fingers on the mottle; then put on the fine top grain with a fine pencil, forming the heart of the wood, and shade underneath with a bit of buff leather.

Curled Maple in Oil for Outside Work.—Prepare a rich ground by mixing chrome yellow, white lead, and burnt terradasienna. For the graining color grind equal parts of raw terradasienna and umber with a little burnt copperas in turpentine, and mix with it a small quantity of grainer's cream. Thin the color with boiled oil, then fill a tool and spread the surface even and rub out the lights with the sharp edge of a piece of buff leather, which must now and then be wiped to keep it clean; soften the edges of the work very lightly, and when dry, put on the top grain with burnt umber and raw terradasienna, ground in ale, with the white of an egg beat into it. When dry, varnish.

Satinwood.—This ground is prepared with white lead, stone ocher, and small quantities of chrome yellow and burnt terradasienna. The graining-color is $\frac{1}{3}$ of raw terradasienna and whiting, ground in pale ale very thin; then spread the color over the surface to be grained. While wet, soften, and have ready a wet roller or mottling-brush, in order to take out the lights; blend the whole with the badger hair-brush. When the work is dry, take the flat-brush, and, with the same color, put on the top grain; when dry, varnish.

Another Method.—Prepare the ground for this the same. The graining-colors are equal quantities of raw terradasienna and raw umber, with a little burnt terradasienna, and a very small portion of whiting, ground in ale or beer. Spread the color even over the surface of the work, and soften, then take the roller which has the feather carved on it. Soften, and when dry top grain with the same color. Varnish as before.

Another Method.—The ground make with white lead, chrome yellow, and a little vermilion, till a very light cream color is produced. Well cleanse the work from dust and grease, take a little of the best stone yellow, and a very small portion of burnt terradasienna and whiting, ground in pale ale, and cover with a thin coat the surface to be grained. Take a piece of wetted sponge and dab it on various parts of the work, and a roller, in order to take out the lights. As soon as you have produced as much dapple as required, soften the whole of the work. When dry. put on the top grain with a thin glaze of the same color, thinned with beer; when dry, varnish.

To Imitate Yew Tree.—The ground is a reddish buff. For the graining-color. grind in ale equal portions of vandyke brown and burnt terradasienna, with a small quantity of raw terradasienna. When the ground is dry, spread the surface even with the color, and soften; then with a piece of cork with a sharp edge, rub the work cross and cross. in order to form the fine grain as in curled maple. and soften the same way of the grain. When dry. dip the tip of your fingers in the graining-color to form the eyes or knots, and put in the small touches with the camel-hair pencil. When dry, put on the top grain, and when this is dry, varnish.

To Imitate Hair-Wood.—For the ground-color, take white lead and thin it with turpentine, and slightly stain it with equal quantities of Prussian blue and lampblack. For the graining-color, grind in ale a mixture of Prussian blue and raw terradasienna; when the ground is dry, spread a transparent coat of the graining-color on the surface of the work, and soften; then with the cork, mottle by rubbing it to and fro across the work to form the fine, long grain or mottle. When this is done. soften and top grain in a wavy but perpendicular direction; varnish when dry.

Hair-Wood for Chairs.—Paint the chair a light gray, by adding a little Prussian blue with white lead, ground very stiff in boiled linseed oil. and thinned down with turps to the consistency required. When this is dry, take some of the ground-color, made considerably thinner with turpentine. and with a common paint-brush put a very light coat on a small part of the work at once. as the grain must be laid on before the last coat sets, otherwise the colors will not blend together; having provided some thicker color, made darker by adding more Prussian blue, take a feather, or short gilder's-tip. dip it into the color, and put on the fine. long vein cross ways, similar to the grain of curled maple. When the work is thus far finished, take a small flat graining-brush, and put on the top grain with the same color; when the whole of the work is ornamented and quite dry, it may be completed with two coats of colorless copal varnish. If a green color is desired, substitute mineral green for Prussian blue, both for the ground and graining-colors.

To Imitate Oriental Verd-antique Marble.—Mix the ground black in oil-paint, and made quite smooth. For the graining-color, take white lead in oil, and made quite fluid in spirits of turpentine. This, laid on with a common sash-tool, in broad, transparent veins, so thin in places that the white is scarcely perceptible, and in other places nearly opaque. While the white is wet. take a piece of wash-leather, and dab it on in different parts of the work. leaving it in the form of shells or other fossil remains. While the color is still wet, take a square piece of cork, and notching it in two or three places, turn it round on the work between the thumb and finger. This will leave the circles more natural than pencil; when this is done, cut away part of a feather at unequal distances, pass this once over the white to take out irregular veins on the black ground, and by suddenly checking the hand, make it take an angular direction. When the work is sufficiently veined, let it remain till it gets dry before more can be done to it; when dry, it must be glazed over in distemper colors, in some places with raw terradasienna, in others, Prussian blue; and some parts must be left black and white. When the work is dry, take a feather and dip it into whiting ground fine in milk, and with it draw the fine veins over the work; a few fine lines with a camel-hair pencil may also be made to curl over the light parts with Prussian blue. When dry, it will be ready for the last glaze, which make of raw terradasienna and a small portion of Prussian blue, mixed together in equal parts of boiled oil and turpentine. This will give the whole of the work the appearance of a beautiful green; when dry, varnish. Observe that verdantique, Egyptian, and serpentine, are the three principal marble greens, and most varied in their colors; but those with all other greens may be produced in a similar manner to the verdantique; but it will be advisable for the learner to procure some specimens of the different kinds of green marbles before he attempts to imitate what he has never seen.

To Imitate Black and Gold Marble.—This description of marble is now in great use. The ground is a deep, jet black, or a dead color in gold size, drop black and turps; second coat, black japan, commence veining; mix white and yellow ochre with a small quantity of vermilion to give a gold tinge; dip the pencil in this color, and dab on the ground with great freedom some large patches, from which small threads must be drawn in various directions. In the deepest parts of the black a white vein is sometimes seen running with a great number of small threads attached to it: but care must be taken that these threads are connected with, and run in some degree in the same direction with the thicker veins. If durability is not an object, and the work is required in a short time, it may be executed very quick in distemper colors, and when varnished it will look well.

Dove Marble.—The ground is a lead color If the work is new, it will be necessary to give it two very thin coats of ground color. which must be made to dry hard, taking care to rub it smooth with fine glass paper after each coat, and not to rub the color off the sharp edges of the wood; it must now remain till quite hard. For the graining take some of the lead color, such as is used for the ground, and make it quite thin with turpentine and rub a light coat over a small part of the work, with some dryers in to give a drying quality, and make it thin with spirits of turpentine; then take a small granitating machine, with a whitish color, to form the small specks or other fossil remains; proceed in the same way till the whole surface is covered, taking the precaution to paint but a small part of the ground at once, that the colors may have sufficient time to blend together while wet.

otherwise the work will appear harsh. When these colors are set, take some of the thin ground color, and, with a fitch or small sash tool, put in the faint, broad veins; then take a camel-hair pencil and put in a multiplicity of very fine veins over the whole surface of the work, crossing each other in every direction. When this is done, make the color a few shades lighter by adding white lead, and with a feather dipped in the color, pass over the broad veins in the same direction, forming streams or threads. When this is done, take some thin white, and, with a camel-hair pencil, go partly over the same vein with short, thick touches; then with a fine stripping pencil, and with the same color, pass over the work, forming very fine lines, crossing each other in an angular direction. When the work is hard, rub it smooth with very fine glass paper, and finish by putting on a coat of colorless varnish. Observe that the first layer of veins must be exceedingly faint, so much so that they are scarcely perceptible, as the lighter shades are put on, the former veins will appear sunk from the surface of the work to the depth of several inches, which will give an admirable effect for chimney pieces, table tops, wash stands, etc., where the work is exposed to close inspection.

Another Method.—The ground is a light lead color, and perfectly dry, take a small paint-brush and scumble on irregular broad veins of white and black. Soften with a dry duster, and when sufficiently blended, the color must form light and dark shades, and not a decided black or white. This style of graining is well calculated for large columns, halls, and all outside work, as it has a strikingly bold and heavy appearance. A few veins may be added with advantage.

Another Method.—The ground the same as the last. The graining-colors are lampblack and a little Prussian blue, ground together very stiff in turps and a little white vitriol, to act as a dryer, and thinned with boiled oil. Mix small portions of these colors together with white lead, making the mixture a very little lighter than the ground color, and with a fitch put on the broad veins; then fill a camel-hair pencil and go over the same veins again with a lighter color; when this is done, go partly over the same vein again with white, slightly tinged with blue-black, made very thin with turpentine; a few white veins may be made to run over the surface of the work in various directions, being careful not to make them too prominent.

White-Veined Marble.—This ground is a pure white. For the graining color white lead ground stiff in raw oil and made very thin with turpentine: then with a paint brush rub a light coat on a small part of the surface; then with a fitch scumble over the work with broad, faint veins of white, heightened with a little Prussian blue and lampblack, and with a camel hair pencil go over the work in various directions, forming the fine angular lines, then with a little darker color go over the broad veins rater sparingly; when this is done make the color still darker, and with a fine pencil or feather go over the same veins, forming very small threads intersecting each other and running to a center, and then suddenly striking out again in all directions. A good effect may be given by passing a few fine dark veins across different parts of the work in an opposite direction to the veins already laid on. When the work is dry use colorless varnish.

Sienna Marble.—The ground is stone yellow or raw sienna. When the ground is dry, mix some stone yellow with white lead, have ready some white paint, and with these two colors, used separately, put in some broad transparent shades of white and yellow, and while wet, blend them them together with a soft duster. Take some venetian red a little Prussian blue mixed with it, and with a hair pencil put in some broad veins in the same direction as the shades run, then for the darker veins take a mixture of venetian red, lake, and Prussian blue and with a feather draw them over the first layer of veins in fine threads running to a center, and then striking out again fine transparent veins in different directions. When this is done mix Prussian blue and lake together, and with a fine pencil put in the darkest and finest veins over those previously laid on. Put in a few dark touches of burnt terradasienna between the fine veins, which are formed into small masses. If the first shades are not sufficiently varied a thin and separate glaze of burnt and raw terradasienna may be applied in different parts of the work. All the above graining colors should be ground in spirits of turpentine and gold size sufficient to bind them.

Italian Marble.—This looks bold, and is well adapted for columns, etc., and is easy to imitate. The ground is a light buff. For the graining colors prepare a rich, warm buff made in the following manner: Mix stiff in boiled oil, white lead, and good stone ochre, and tinge with vermilion; then grind some burnt terradasienna very fine in boiled oil and put it in another pot; mix some pure white stiff in oil, and keep this separate. Thin these colors with turpentine; have ready a brush for the buff and another for the terradasienna ·Proceed to work as follows: Take the brush intended for the buff moderately full of the color and dab it on freely and carefully in patches, some of them larger than others, and varying them as much as possible. When these are laid on take the other brush and fill in with the terradasienna the spaces between; as soon as this is done take a dry duster or softener and blend the ends together, making it appear as soft as possible. Proceed in this manner till the whole is finished; then take a hair pencil and draw a few thin white veins over the work, varying them as much as necessary; take another pencil for the terradasienna, and run a few lines intermixing the whole. Varnish when dry.

Red Marble.—For the ground put on a white tinged with lake or vermilion; then apply deep rich reds in patches, filling up the intermediate spaces with brown and white mixed in oil; then blend them together; if in quick drying colors use about ½ turps and gold size. When dry, varnish, and while the varnish is wet put in a multitude of fine white threads. crossing the whole work in all directions, as the wet varnish brings the pencil to a fine point.

Jasper Marble.—Put on a white ground lightly tinged with blue, then put on patches of rich reds or rose pink, leaving spaces of the white ground; then partly cover those spaces with various browns to form fossils, in places running veins; then put in a few spots of white in the center of some of the red patches, and leaving in places masses nearly all white. When dry, use the clearest varnish.

Blue and Gold Marble.—For the ground put on a light blue; then take blue, with a small piece of white lead and some dark common blue, and dab on the ground in patches, leaving portions of the ground to shine between; then blend the edges together with a duster or softener; afterwards draw on some white veins in every direction, leaving large open spaces to be filled up with a pale yellow or gold paint; finish with some fine white running threads, a coat of varnish last.

Imitation of Marbles in Distemper; White-Veined Marble.—This kind of marble has a splendid appearance on the walls of staircases, halls, bars of taverns, coffee-rooms, etc., and can be executed with great expedition. If the walls are broken and scaly they must be well scraped and dusted, and two thin coats of lime whitewash applied. The second coat must be whiting mixed in milk, and at the same time have a little indigo, lampblack, and venetian red ground separately in milk, which is sufficiently glutinous to bind the colors; have them all ready for use by putting each color into a separate bowl. A few long striping hair pencils will be necessary, with long handles to them, in order to give more spirit and freedom to the work. When all the colors and tools are procured commence by dividing the work into squares about 20x14 inches, to represent the blocks of marble; this may be done by a long straight-edge and a black lead pencil: the lines must be stout, in order to be seen through the last coat of whitewash. When the work is thus divided commence at the top of the wall by putting on a very thin coat of whitewash, working downward, taking the precaution to wet not more than one or two squares, as the whole of the work commenced upon must be blended with the dry duster and finisher before it gets dry. Immediately have ready in the bowl some whitewash slightly tinged with lampblack and venetian red, and with a large brush put in the broad faint vein, and blend it together with the brush used for the whitewash; then with a feather or the flat graining brush, containing a very thin row of hairs, draw the narrow veins in the same direction with the broad vein; then take a large hair pencil and put in some thick touches between the veins just laid on; immediately take some blue tinged with venetian red, and made quite thin with milk, and with a fine camel's hair pencil put in a multiplicity of very fine veins to represent, as it were, small streams of water running to a center, and suddenly striking out in various directions, but always inclining the same way the broad vein runs. When this is done take a fine hair pencil and put in a few fine white veins over the darkest shades. Have all the colors and tools in readiness before commencing work of this description. as it requires to be done with expedition. If the edges of the work should get too dry they must be damped with milk, and so proceed till the wall is finished. The next thing to be done is to draw the fine black lines with lampblack finely ground in size. in order to represent the small blocks, which is easily executed with a pencil, such as is generally used for drawing the joints of brickwork, and with a beveled straight-edge. It should be observed that the vein in each block should be made to run in a different direction, in order to distinguish one from another, and give the work a more natural appearance.

Italian Marble.—This kind of marble may be worked on walls. If a new wall. give it a coat of size worked in a jelly, in order to stop the suction of the wall. Mix a sufficient quantity of Indian red with strong beer, and put into an earthen bowl; mix in beer whiting add French yellow, and tinge with English venetian red till you produce a good buff. This you may know by drying it on a piece of paper and drying it by the fire, as it dries much lighter than it is while wet; then mix whiting with milk, as the beer would be apt to discolor it. or you may mix with size and apply it warm. These colors must be mixed to the consistency of cream. Having the colors and brushes in readiness proceed in the same manner as with oil colors. only instead of putting so many patches on the wall at once, you should dab on only 8 or 10, and those very quick and freely; then fill up the spaces with the red and blend the edges directly before the color sets, as it will be impossible to do anything with it after it dries. Proceed in the same manner till the whole of the wall is finished; put in the veins with distemper colors, as directed in oil colors.

Verd-Antique.—This is an easy and also a very excellent method of imitating this species of marble, and will be found very useful to the cabinet maker, as it is well adapted for the tops of tables, sideboards, wash-stands, etc. It may be produced with good effect by any person. although he may not be accustomed to the art of painting. If the work is new it may have one coat of dark lead color in oil paint, and when dry it should be made smooth with fine glass-paper. Grind separately some white lead powder and lampblack very fine in water and mixed with size. The black must be put on the work with a large sash tool, leaving various narrow spaces in different parts of the work. When this is dry the white lead must then be poured in thin streams on the black, and the table or wash-stand to be marbled is moved in various directions. taking the precaution to let the white fill up the small spaces which are left by the black. The floating must be repeated till the whole veins are sufficiently varied, and the small threads may be drawn from the wet masses of white over the dark parts by means of a feather. When the whole of the work is dry the shells or fossil figures are dabbed carelessly on with a camel-hair pencil. When these colors are dry have ready some raw terradasienna and Prussian blue, which has been finely ground in ale, and, with these colors used separately, put a thin glaze of each color on various parts of the work; allow this to dry also; then apply the green glaze, which is composed of raw terradasienna and Prussian blue, ground in spirits of turpentine, and mixed with copal varnish. When the work is varnished and polished it will look well.

Another Method.—The ground is black in oil paints, which well prepare and lay perfectly smooth on the surface of the work to be painted. It is necessary to give the work two thin coats, especially on mantel-pieces, fluted columns, etc., in order that the sharp edges of the wood may be completely covered; and further observe that in imitation of all fancy woods and marbles particular care should be taken in laying on the ground colors that the marks of the brush may not be visible; it will be better in all cases to give the surface to be grained two thin coats of ground color. Take lampblack and put it into an iron kettle, place it over the fire till it gets red-hot, then take it from the fire and extinguish it on the slab. It must be stiffly ground in boiled oil and thinned for use with spirits of turpentine; it will be necessary to add some burnt white vitriol and a small quantity of litharge. When the ground is dry commence graining by laying on white lead powder finely ground in water, and mixed with a small quantity of size, in order to bind and prevent its absorbing the varnish. The work must be entirely covered with white, but must be laid on in large streaks with a sash tool, having previously prepared some lampblack finely ground in size, with another sash tool fill up the spaces which are left by the white thereby covering the whole surface of the work; then with the badger-hair brush soften the whole of the work together while it is still wet, in order to make the veins run imperceptibly into each other. The whole of the work should be covered this way at once; then take a large hair pencil and dip it into the white, and on the darkest parts of the work dab the white carelessly, in spots of various sizes and forms, in order to represent the shells, etc. Take another pencil, dip it into the black and go over the lightest parts of the work in the same manner. The flat graining brush, containing a very thin row of hairs, may then be dipped into the white and drawn over the black, in order to form the small irregular veins. A dark blue vein may be made to run across the work: this should be put on in a wavy zigzag direction. When the work is perfectly dry in order to give it the green shade, it must have a thin glaze of Prussian blue and raw terradasienna, the latter predominating. The colors may be ground in spirits of turpentine and mixed in copal varnish. When this is dry the work may be finished by giving it another coat of varnish.

Marble to Resemble Jasper.—The ground is mixed the same as for mahogany, with venetian red, red lead, and a little chrome yellow, ground and thinned with equal parts of oil and turpentine; to increase the brilliancy of the color substitute vermilion or lake for the venetian red; then throw on spots of white paint with a graining machine while the ground is wet; blend them in with a softener or duster, and apply a little more white in the same manner. Blue, brown or yellow, may be thrown in the same way, and blended altogether. When nearly dry, take a hair pencil and form the large and small veins and threads; this latter part may be omitted or not, according to the taste of the workman. The above may be executed on a white ground and distemper colors applied with sash tools and pencils, then varnished.

To Polish Woods and Marbles.—Two and one-half ounces of spirits of wine, 1 dram of gum elemi, ½ ounce of orange shellac; pound the gums, and mix with the other ingredients.

To Imitate Porphry Marble.—The ground is purple, brown, and rose pink. The graining colors for this specimen are vermilion and white lead, ground separately in turpentine and a little gold size added to each color to bind them; but, as they cannot be ground sufficiently thin for use, more turpentine must be added to each color before it is applied. When the ground is quite dry, fill a large brush with vermilion, discharge nearly all the color by scraping the brush on the edge of a palette knife, then holding a rod of iron in the left hand, strike the handle of the brush against it, letting the small red spots fall on the work till the surface is covered, or, what is much preferable to it, a patent graniting machine, which will do the spotting much cleaner for all spotting purposes. Make the color a lighter shade by adding an equal quantity of white lead, and use it as before. Then with the clear, thin white, throw on the color the last time in very fine spots, and when dry, put in a few white veins across the work. When it gets quite hard give it two coats of varnish. This kind of marble may be successfully imitated in distemper, which is preferable for inside work. The process is precisely the same as in oil; and as a substitute for gold size and turpentine, take the white of a few eggs and beat up in ale. By this method the work is executed with greater expedition, as it may be varnished at once. It is necessary, in the imitation of this marble, to procure some sheets of paper to place at the extent of the surface to be grained, in order to receive the superfluous spots.

Another Method.—This ground is red, and prepared with venetian red, heightened with a little vermilion and white. For the graining color add a little more white to the ground color, and sprinkle the first layer on in the same manner as the last. When this coat is dry, the sprinkling may be repeated very sparingly, and in some parts more than others, with a mixture of venetian red and vermilion. Sprinkle the last time with white in very fine spots. You may put an opaque white vein across the work running among the spots, from which transparent threads must be drawn in various directions; but this can not be done till the whole of the work is quite dry and hard, when it may be performed with a sable pencil, and the threads drawn out with a feather. The work may then be varnished, and if due care be taken in sprinkling, the imitation will be excellent. Observe that in the application of each color a different circular brush will be required.

To Imitate Granite.—For the ground color stain your white lead to a light lead color with lampblack and a little rose pink. Throw on black spots, with a graniting machine, a pale red, and fill up with white a little before the ground is dry.

Another Method.—A black ground; when half dry, throw in vermilion, a deep yellow and white spots.

Another Method.—Oak, mahogany and green grounds, look well with the same spots as used on other grounds.

To Imitate Black and Gold Marble for Table Tops, Side-Boards. Etc.—The finest specimens of this marble are produced by spreading a leaf or two of gold in any part of the work where the gold veins are intended to run, and silver leaf where the white vein is to be displayed. The black ground may then be painted rather thickly over the whole surface, covering the gold and silver leaves: and after the color has been on a short time take a round-pointed bodkin and draw the color in small reticulate veins from off the gold and silver leaf; the metal will then show in fine lines. The larger masses may then be wiped off with leather. When the block is dry the yellow and white veins may be painted as before directed and drawn over the gold and silver leaf, which will, by this means, show through them: and when the work is properly varnished and polished it will give the appearance of nature. The colors may be ground in milk or strong beer, with the addition of a little size in the black.

To Imitate Tortoise Shell.—This beautiful color can be made in the following manner: Take of clear linseed oil 24 ounces. of Venice turpentine or shellac 1½ ounces, copal of an amber color 6 ounces, essence of turpentine 6 ounces. The copal is to be placed in a matrass and exposed to a moderate heat until it is liquefied; the linseed oil is then to be added in a boiling condition; then the Venice turpentine or shellac, liquefied also; finally, in small portions, the spirits of turpentine. To be applied in the ordinary way.

Varnish for Applying on Glass.—Take a quantity of gum tragacanth and dissolve it for 30 hours in the white of eggs, which should be well beat up: it is then gently to be rubbed on the glass with an ordinary brush.

Waterproof Polish.—This valuable article is made by putting ¼ ounce of gum sandarac, ¼ ounce of gum anime, and 2 ounces of gum benjamin into a pint of spirits of wine in a bottle tightly stopped. The bottle is to be placed either in a sand bath or in hot water till the gums are dissolved; the mixture must then be strained off; then shake it up with ¼ gill of the best clear poppy oil, and set aside till needed.

To Heighten the Color of Gold or Brass.—If you wish

to operate on yellow gold dissolve in water 1 ounce of alum, 6 ounces saltpeter, 2 ounces of copperas, 1 ounce of white vitriol. If for red gold take 4 ounces melted yellow wax, 2½ ounces of red ochre in fine powder, 1½ of calcined verdigris, ½ ounce of calcined borax. Dissolve in water; apply with a soft cloth and rub for a few minutes and the surface will be very bright.

To Dissolve Gold.—Take any given quantity platina or gold, dissolve it in nitro-muriatic acid, until no further effervescence will take place when heat is applied. The solution of gold thus formed, must be evaporated to dryness by a gentle heat; by this means it will be freed from any excess of acid, which is quite requisite; then re-dissolve the dry mass in as little water as possible; next take an instrument, which is used by chemists for dropping liquid, known by the name of separating-funnel, having a pear-shaped body, tapering to a fine sharp point, and a neck capable of being stopped with the finger or a cork, which may contain a liquid ounce or more; this must be filled about one-fourth full with the liquid, and the other three parts must be with the best sulphuric ether. If this is properly managed, the liquids will not mix. Then place the tube in a horizontal position, and gently turn it round with the finger and thumb. The ether will very soon be impregnated with the gold or platina, which may be known by its changing its color; replace it in a perpendicular position, and let it stand at rest for 24 hours, having first stopped up the upper orifice with a cork. The liquid will then be divided into two parts—the darkest coloring being underneath. To separate them, take out the cork and let the dark liquid flow out; when it has disappeared, stop the tube immediately with the cork, and what remains in the tube is fit for use, and may be called gilding liquid. It should be put up in a bottle and corked tightly. The muriate of gold or platina, formed by digesting these metals in nitro-muriatic acid, must be entirely free from any excess of acid; for otherwise it will act too forcibly on the steel, and cause the coating of gold to peel off. Pure gold must be employed. The ether must not be shaken with the muriate of gold, as advised in works of chemistry, for it will be sure then to contain acid; but if the two liquids be brought continually into contact by the motion described, the affinity between ether and gold is so strong as to overcome the obstacle of gravity, and it will hold the gold in solution. By gentle evaporation this etherial solution may be concentrated.

Gold Paint.—Take 1 pound of spirits of wine, ¼ pound of pure gum-lac, wash it till the water is no more red; when dry, grind it fine, and add it to the spirits of wine in a glazed earthen vessel of a size which will not be more than 3 parts filled by the ingredients. Place this vessel in another which contains the water, after the manner of a glue pot, over a fire without flame, keep it boiling till the gum is dissolved, and be careful that no lighted candle or flame come near it. Stir it while boiling with a piece of white wood. You may add a little tumeric root or not at your own discretion. In case of its taking fire by accident, have a cloth ready in water to extinguish the flame. When dissolved, strain it through a strong linen cloth, bottle, and well cork it. To use this, paint over the wood 3 times with a soft brush; let each coat well dry before applying the other. If the work be silvered over first, it will resemble fine gold.

POLISHING.

See also "*Cleaning and Repairing*," *Department 1V.*

Dining-Table.—One pint linseed oil; 2 ounces black resin; 2 ounces spirits of nitre; 4 ounces distilled vinegar; 1 ounce spirits salts, and 2 ounces butter of antimony. The tables are to be washed on alternate days; first day with boiling water; second day with the polishing liquid; third day with cold vinegar. The tables assume a lustrous appearance; hot dishes placed upon them without a mat will have no effect upon them, and any liquid spilt will, if wiped dry, leave no mark.

French Polish.—Shellac 3 parts, gum mastic, 1 part; gum sandarac 1 part; spirits wine 40 parts. The mastic and sandarac must first be dissolved in spirits of wine, and then the shellac. To do this put them into a bottle loosely corked, and place it in a vessel of water. heated to a little below 173° Fahrenheit, until solution is effected; the clear solution may be poured off into another bottle for use.

Ivory or Bone.—These admit of being turned very smooth, or, when filed, may afterwards be scraped. so as to present a good surface. Rub first with fine sand paper, and then with a piece of wet linen cloth dipped in powdered pumice stone; this will give a fine surface. and the polish may be produced by fine whiting, applied by a piece of cloth wetted in soapsuds. Care must be taken in this, and in every instance where articles of different fineness are successively used, that previous to applying a finer. every particle of the coarser material be removed, and that the rags be clean and free from grit.

White.—To make this splendid polish, grind dry zinc white with white varnish, which affords a glossy finish, to be laid on after the second coat. A more perfect surface may be obtained by covering the second coat with several other coats of hard drying paint, mixed with turpentine. japan and litharge; then rubbing with pumice stone, followed by a coat of polish white, and finished with a flow coat of white varnish. containing a little zinc white. Although this requires more time and trouble, the result will compensate. When the last coat is to be glossy, the previous coat must be flat or dead, and a flat coat for finishing should be preceded by a somewhat glossy coat.

Woods.—1. The wood is first well smoothed with fine sandpaper, then covered with a thin coating of size from transparent glue, or thin shellac. to prevent the varnish from sinking into the wood. When dry, pour some varnish into a saucer;

take a fine camel's hair brush, and commence to varnish at one corner, gradually spreading over the whole surface. Take care that there is not too much varnish on the brush, otherwise an even surface cannot be obtained. The first coating must be allowed to dry, which will take 2 or 3 hours; then sand-paper the surface smooth. This done, with great care spread the next coat of varnish, always using sand-paper when the surface does not turn out smooth. The whole, when dry, may be rubbed well with a piece of warm woolen till bright and smooth. **2.** To French polish, make the wood smooth; then pour some prepared polish into a saucer, and some linseed oil into another; take some pieces of woolen rag, and roll them up into a ball, covering them with a piece of linen drawn tightly over; the rags inside should first be saturated with the polish, and the whole should be taken in the fingers of the right hand in such a way that the linen may be drawn tightly over, and may present to the wood a smooth, rounded surface. Polish with free, circular strokes, and gradually traverse the whole surface; apply now and then a drop of polish and a drop of oil to the surface of the rubber. When the grain of the wood disappears, allow it to stand 1 hour, or until hard, and then sand-paper the whole; repeat the polishing until smooth. If dull patches appear, they may be removed by a few drops of spirits wine or a new rubber. **3.** Dissolve, by heat, so much beeswax in spirits turpentine, that when cold it shall be thick as honey. This may be applied to furniture or to work running in the lathe, by means of a piece of clean cloth, and as much as possible should then be rubbed off by means of a clean flannel. Beeswax alone is often used; upon furniture it must be melted by means of a warm flat-iron; but it may be applied to work in the lathe, by holding the wax against it until a portion of it adheres; a piece of woolen cloth should then be held upon it, and the lathe turned quickly, so as to melt the wax; the superfluous portion may be removed by a small piece of wood, when a light touch with a clean part of the cloth will give it a gloss. A good polish may be given to mahogany by rubbing it with linseed oil, and then holding against it a cloth dipped in fine brick dust. **4.** (Dark.) Seed lac 1 ounce, gum guaiacum, dragon's blood, and gum mastic, of each 2 drams. Put in a bottle with 1 pint spirits wine; cork close; expose to a moderate heat till dissolved; strain into a bottle for use, with ¼ gill linseed oil; shake together. **5.** Take a piece of smooth pumice stone and water and pass repeatedly over the work till the rising of the grain is cut down; then take powdered tripoli and boiled linseed oil, and polish bright.

STAINING.

Black.—1. Boil ½ pound chip logwood in 2 quarts of water; add 1 ounce pearlash, and apply it hot to the work with a brush; then take ½ pound logwood, boil it as before in 2 quarts of wa ter and add ½ ounce verdigris and ½ ounce copperas; stain, put in ½ pound rusty steel filings; with this go over the work a second time. **2.** (Ebony imitation.) Mix up a strong stain of copperas and logwood; to this add powdered nut-gall; stain with this solution; dry and rub down well; oil and use French polish, made tolerably dark with indigo, or finely powdered stone blue.

Black Walnut.—1. One-quarter pound asphaltum, ½ pound common beeswax, and 1 gallon of turpentine. If the mixture is found too thin, add more beeswax: if too light in color. add more asphaltum; a very little will make a great difference in the shade: varnishing is not necessary. A good stain for pine. **2.** Take 1 gallon very thin sized shellac, and add 1 pound dry burnt umber, 1 pound dry burnt sienna, ¼ pound lampblack; put these into a jug, and shake frequently till mixed; apply 1 coat with a brush; when dry sand-paper with fine paper, and apply 1 coat of shellac varnish. A good imitation of solid walnut. It may be used on pine and white wood.

Blue.—1. Into a clean glass bottle put 1 pound oil vitriol and 4 ounces best indigo, pounded in a mortar; take care to set the bottle in a basin or earthen glazed pan, as it will ferment; put the veneers into a copper or stone trough; fill it with rather more than ⅓ water. and add as much of the vitriol and indigo as will make a fine blue; let the veneers remain until the dye has struck through. The color will be improved if the solution of indigo in vitriol be kept a few weeks before using. The color strikes better if the veneers are boiled in plain water remaining a few hours thereafter to dry previous to immersing in the dye.

Brown.—Boil ½ pound vandyke brown and 2 ounces carbonate of soda in 12 ounces water, and add ½ ounce bichromate of potassa; or use a weak aqueous solution of permanganate of potassa in water.

Floor Stains.—The cheapest stain of any color is made with aniline colors dissolved in hot water. Some of these will fade, but yellow, red and brown, especially when covered with a coat of linseed oil will last a long time. Any shade can be obtained by mixing. See "Glue Paint for Kitchen Floors," *Department IV., Cleaning and Repairing.*

Light Reddish.—Boil ⅓ pint madder and ¼ pound fustic to 1 gallon of water; brush the work when boiling hot until properly stained.

Mahogany.—1. Break 2 ounces dragon's blood in small pieces and put in 1 quart alcohol; let the bottle stand in a warm place and shake it frequently; use when dissolved. An excellent imitation of mahogany for soft woods. **2.** (On maple.) Dragon's blood ½ ounce, alkanet ¼ ounce, aloes 1 dram, alcohol 16 ounces.

Oak.—Wash the wood carefully in a solution of 1 pound of copperas dissolved in 1 gallon strong lye water; when the wood is dry after saturation, oil it and it will look fresh for a year or two. When it becomes dim with age, restain and oil. The hands must be protected while applying the stain or they will become blistered.

Red, Cherry.—Rain water 3 quarts, annotto 4 ounces; boil in a copper kettle until the annotto is dissolved; then put in a piece of potash the size of a walnut; keep it on the fire ½ hour longer; then bottle for use.

SOME ADDITIONAL PROCESSES FOR STAINING WOOD.

A Red Stain.—Take of pearlash 1 ounce, Brazil wood, in chips, 1 pound, water 1 gallon. Let them stand together 2 or 3 days, during which time the mixture should be frequently stirred; then boil it for 2 or 3 hours, and while boiling hot, brush over the wood intended to be stained 2 or 3 times, or oftener, till the proper tint is obtained. While wet, brush it over with a solution of alum in water, made in the proportion of 2 ounces of alum to a quart of water.

A Light Red, Approaching to Pink.—Add to a gallon of the above infusion 2 additional ounces of pearlash. The wood in this case should be often brushed over with the solution of alum. By increasing the quantity of pearlash, the red may be rendered still paler; but when more pearlash is added, a proportionate quantity of the solution of alum will also be required.

A Very Dark Red Stain.—Take of salt of tartar 1 ounce, logwood, in chips, ½ pound, water 2 quarts. Boil the logwood chips in the water till it becomes of a very dark red color; then add the salt of tartar, and boil for 2 more hours. The decoction must be applied to the wood boiling hot.

The Old Method of Coloring Wood Red.—Dissolve 1 ounce of dragon's blood in 1 pint of rectified spirits of wine; brush the wood over with this varnish till it appears of the required color.

A Yellow Stain.—Take of turmeric root, in powder, 1 ounce, rectified spirits of wine 1 pint. Digest for 4 days, shaking occasionally the mixture, when it may be strained off for use. Let it be applied to the wood by brushing it over 3 or 4 times, taking care that the first stain is dry before the second is applied. If the color be required of a reddish cast, a little dragon's blood may be added to the mixture.

Another Yellow Stain.—Take of alum ½ ounce, French berries 1 pound, soft water 1 gallon. Boil them together for 2 hours, and while boiling brush over the wood with the decoction till it becomes of the required color. After the stain has been some hours applied, so that the wood is become quite dry, brush it over with a weak solution of alum water.

Blue Stains.—Wood may be stained blue by either a solution of copper or of indigo. Copper will produce a bright color, and is more generally practicable.

A Blue Stain with Copper.—Dissolve copper-filings or slips in aquafortis, adding the filings or slips to the acid till all effervescence ceases; to the solution add of starch, finely powdered, the weight of one-fifth of the weight of the copper dissolved. Make now a solution of pearl-ash in water; put as much of this solution to the solution of copper as will cause the copper to precipitate in a fine green powder. On the first addition of the pearl-ash solution, the liquid will appear of a dark muddy green; but by adding more of the pearl-ash solution, it will soon become clear, and the precipitate assumes a fine green color. The clear part must be poured off, and the precipitate washed in 3 or 4 quantities of clear water, till the water becomes tasteless. Let the precipitate be dried for use; which is, in fact, a "verditer." After the wood intended to be stained has been brushed over in a similar way, as described for other colors, till it is stained a dark green, make a solution consisting of 2 ounces of pearl-ash in a pint of water, and brush it over the wood boiling-hot, when it will appear of a fine deep blue color.

A Green Stain.—This may be made with the same precipitate of any tint, by merely melting the solution of pearl-ash, and brushing the mixture over the wood once or more, according to the required tint.

A Blue Stain with Indigo.—Dissolve indigo in sulphuric acid, or a liquid blue may be thus prepared: Put 3 ounces of indigo, in powder, to 1 pound of sulphuric acid. When the indigo is dissolved, which it will be in about 24 hours, provided the mixture has been occasionally stirred, add to the solution 1 pint of boiling water. This solution must be applied to the wood boiling-hot. Dissolve by boiling 3 ounces of cream of tartar in a quart of water; with this solution, used copiously, brush over the wood before the moisture of the indigo is quite absorbed.

A Purple Stain.—Take of Brazil-wood, in chips, 4 ounces, logwood chips, 1 pound, water, 1 gallon. Boil these together for 2 or 3 hours. The decoction must be applied boiling-hot. When dry, brush it over with a solution containing ¼ ounce pearl-ash to ½ gallon water. This solution must be carefully used, as it gradually changes its color from a brown-red, which it originally is, to a dark blue purple, and therefore its effects must be carefully noted to make the desired color.

A Black Stain.—Brush the wood several times with the hot decoction of logwood described in the last article, omitting the Brazil-wood; next prepare an infusion thus; Take of powdered galls, 4 ounces, water 2 quarts. Place them in a gentle heat for 3 or 4 days; brush the wood over with this infusion 3 or 4 times, and then pass over the wood again with a solution composed of 2 ounces of sulphate of iron, and a quart of water.

A Very Fine Black can be produced by brushing the wood several times with a solution of copper in aqua-fortis, and afterward with the decoction of logwood, which must be repeated till the desired color is obtained, and then the greenness of the copper wholly overcome.

A Common Black Stain is produced by immersing a pound of iron nails into ½ gallon of vinegar, with a small quantity of verdigris. This is the common black stain for chairs; it is also useful to mix with colors that require grain, rosewood, tulip, etc.

Mahogany Stains.—These stains are very useful, and if well prepared and applied to suitable wood, resemble red mahogany.

A Light-Red Brown Mahogany.—Take of fustic chips 4 ounces, madder root, in powder, ½ pound, water 1 gallon. Boil together for 2 or more hours. This decoction must be applied to the wood boiling hot, till the proper color is obtained. If the grain of the wood be not sufficiently varied, a varnish brush, dipped in the black stain and passed lightly over the wood while wet, will greatly improve it, and give it the appearance of dark Honduras mahogany.

A Fine Mahogany Stain is produced by mixing the tincture of dragon's blood and turmeric root in spirits of wine. By diminishing or increasing the proportion of each of the ingredients, the brown stain may be varied to a more red or yellow cast at pleasure.

Spanish Mahogany Stain.—Take of madder root, in powder, ½ pound, fustic chips 1 ounce, logwood chips 2 ounces, water 1 gallon. Boil for 2 or 3 hours. Apply the decoction boiling hot. When the wood has been brushed over several times, and is become dry, let it be slightly brushed over with a solution of ¼ of an ounce of pearlash in 1 quart of water. Any stain of intermediate colors may be made by varying the proportion of the ingredients.

Fancy Woods.—The preceding stains may, by judicious management, be combined in various ways, so as to represent many variegated woods. Rosewood in particular may thus be imitated.

Rosewood Stains.—The articles chiefly stained to imitate rosewood are chairs, which are commonly for such purposes made of beech. They are usually dipped in a large copper containing the boiling red stain, then taken out and dried before they are dipped again. When the red stain is acquired, a flat varnish brush, having its hairs separated, is dipped in the black stain, and drawn over the chairs which are stained red. The application of some polish to such woods as have just been given, is necessary to render them pleasing to the eye.

ᵔTo Make Sweet-Oil Turps Without Smell.—Half gallon of gray stone lime, slack it properly in 5½ gallons water to destroy its property, then put into a can, shaking it 3 or 4 times a day. leaving the cork out. Let it properly settle. then pour off the water from the lime, which will be oily, then add raw linseed oil 5½ pints, shaking it 3 or 4 times; after this add ¼ pint clarified vitriol to each gallon. It is then fit for use.

To Varnish Prints.—Dissolve 1 ounce of the best isinglass in a pint of water by boiling it over the fire; strain it through fine muslin and keep it for use. Try this size on a piece of paper moderately warm; if it glistens it is too thick, add more water. If it soaks into the paper it is too thin. Add or diminish the isinglass till it merely dulls the surface. Give the print 2 or 3 coats. letting it dry between each; bear lightly on your brush, which should be a flat tin camel's hair, then with best mastic varnish give it 2 or 3 coats.

To Polish on Paint.—Two and a half ounces of spirit of wine. 1 dram of oil of almonds, 1 dram of gum elemi, ½ ounce of orange shellac pounded fine and put altogether in a bottle to dissolve. When dissolved rub it on with soft woolen or cotton wadding.

Rosewood.—Alcohol 1 gallon, camwood 2 ounces; set in a warm place 24 hours, then add extract of logwood 3 ounces and aquafortis 1 ounce; when dissolved it is ready. This is a fine imitation of rosewood. Give 1 or 2 coats, as desired.

Satinwood.—Alcohol 2 pints, powdered gamboge 3 ounces, ground tumeric 6 ounces; steep to obtain full strength, strain through muslin; apply 2 coats with a fine sponge; sandpaper when dry and varnish or French polish.

Stains for Soft Woods.—Ebony: Make a strong decoction of logwood by boiling. Apply 3 or 4 times according to shade desired; then apply solution of acetate of iron. This is made by putting iron filings into strong vinegar. Mahogany, Rosewood. or Cherry: Mix venetian red with white or brown, according to color desired. with turpentine. Walnut; Burnt umber and turpentine. Apply any stain. according to color desired; continued applications making the color darker.

VARNISHES AND JAPANS.

Including lacquers for metals, etc. Care should be exercised in the application of varnishes, etc., as they dry quickly, and if not evenly applied present a rough unfinished appearance.

Amber Varnish, Pale.—Amber, pale and transparent, 6 pounds, fuse: add hot clarified linseed oil 2 gallons; boil till it strings strongly; cool a little and add oil turpentine 4 gallons. Soon becomes hard and is the most durable of oil varnishes, but requires time before fit for polishing.

Anti-Rust Varnish for Iron or Steel.—Resin 120 parts, sandarac 180 parts, gum lac 60 parts, essence of turpentine 120 parts, rectified alcohol 180 parts. Pound the first 3 ingredients, digest them by regular heat until melted; add the turpentine gradually. After solution has taken place, add the alcohol and filter through fine cloth. Keep in well-stoppered bottles.

Asphalt Varnish.—Boil coal tar until it shows a disposition to harden on cooling; this can be ascertained by rubbing a small quantity on a piece of metal; then add 20 per cent of lump asphalt, stirring it with the boiling tar until the lumps are melted; then let it cool. A very bright varnish for sheet metals, cheap and durable.

Basket Varnish.—Take sealing wax of the color desired; to every 2 ounces add 1 ounce alcohol; pound the wax fine, sift; put into a vial with the alcohol; shake occasionally; let it stand near the fire for 48 hours; then apply with a brush to the baskets. Let them dry: apply a second time.

Bleached Oil for Colorless Varnish.—Cover the bottom of a 4-gallon vessel with white lead to the depth of about 6 inches, nearly fill it with raw linseed oil; be careful that the vessel is covered with glass; this is necessary, not only to keep the dust and other impurities from it, but that it may admit the light and hot rays of the sun. It must remain exposed to the sun till it gets fat and colorless, and it will be fit for use. French yellow is an excellent substitute for white lead. and is used by many varnish-makers in preference, as it speedily draws the coloring matter out of the oil and soon renders it suitable for the varnish.

Black Japan.—1. Asphaltum 1 pound, balsam of capivi 1 pound, oil of turpentine q. s. The asphaltum is melted over a fire and the balsam, previously heated, is mixed in with it. The mixture is then removed from the fire and the turpentine stirred in. **2.** Moisten good lampblack with oil of turpentine and grind it very fine; then add sufficient copal varnish, and rub well together.

Black Rosewood Japan.—The work must be grounded black, after which mix some red lead and apply with a stiff flat brush, imitating the streaks in the wood. Then take a small quantity of lake ground fine, and mix with brown spirit varnish, observing to have no more color than will tinge the varnish; if too red, add a little umber, ground fine, and pass over the whole of the work intended to imitate black rosewood. If well done, when it is varnished and polished, it will scarcely be known from rosewood. Vandyke brown may be used instead of umber, it being more transparent.

Black Varnish.—1 (For Iron). Mix with a small quantity of oil of turpentine. drop by drop. oil of vitriol, until it forms a syrupy precipitate. which no longer increases in bulk. The mass is then poured over with water. stirred well, the water removed, and repeated as often as it shows a trace of acid on litmus paper: the remaining precipitate is then strained dry, and when required for use a portion of it is applied on the iron (stove. etc.)

and the stove heated and the powder burned; if too thick a layer it must be thinned and spread out with more turpentine, so as to give a uniform coating to the metallic surface: the residue left after burning is then rubbed in with a rag dipped in linseed oil until the proper polish is acquired. **3.** (For coal buckets.) Asphaltum 1 pound, lampblack ¼ pound. resin ½ pound, spirits of turpentine 1 quart; dissolve the asphaltum and resin in the turpentine, then rub up the lampblack with linseed oil to a paste and mix with the others. Apply with a brush.

Bookbinder's Varnish.—Shellac 8 parts, gum benzoin **3** parts. gum mastic 2 parts; bruise and digest in alcohol 48 parts, oil of lavender ½ part. Or digest shellac 4 parts, gum mastic 2 parts. gum dammer and white turpentine, of each 1 part, with alcohol (95 per cent) 28 parts.

Brass. Lacquer For.—I. Turmeric 1 ounce, saffron and annotto each ¼ ounce, rectified spirits 1 pint: digest at a gentle heat for several days; strain through coarse linen; bottle and add 3 ounces coarsely pulverized seed lac; place in a moderate heat and shake occasionally till dissolved. **2.** Alcohol 12 gallons. seed lac 9 pounds, turmeric 1 pound to 1 gallon of the above mixture, Spanish saffron 4 ounces; the saffron is to be added for bronze work. **3.** (Gold colored.) Alcohol 36 ounces. seed lac 6 ounces. amber 2 ounces, gum gutta 2 ounces, red sandalwood 24 grains. dragon's blood 60 grains, oriental saffron 36 grains, pulverized glass 4 ounces. **4.** (Red.) Alcohol 8 gallons, dragon's blood 4 pounds, Spanish annatto 12 pounds, gum sandarac 13 pounds, turpentine 1 gallon.

Brown Lacquer for Copper Bronze.—Two and one-half ounces shellac, 2 quarts wine spirits. 2 ounces gum sandarac, ¼ ounce gum elimi; mix and keep warm until a solution is effected, then strain and color with dragon's blood and aniline brown to suit.

Brushes, Varnish, Care Of.—Suspend them by the handles in a tightly covered can, keeping the points ⅓ inch from the bottom and apart from each other. The can should be filled with slowly drying varnish up to 1-16 inch above the bristles, and the can kept in a close cupboard. As wiping a brush on a sharp edge will ruin it, the top of the can should have a wire soldered along the edge of the tin, turned over. Finishing brushes should not be cleansed in turpentine. When taken from the can prepare them for use by working them out in varnish, and before replacing, clean the handles and binding with turpentine.

Cabinet Varnish.—Fuse 7 pounds of fine African gum copal; when it runs freely, pour into it ½ gallon clarified linseed oil; when clear remove from the fire, and mix 3 gallons spirits of turpentine with it and strain. If properly boiled, it will dry in 10 minutes; if boiled too much, it will not mix with the turpentine. Used by Japanner's, cabinet and coach makers.

Carriage Japan.—Forty gallons of raw linseed oil, 40

pounds litharge, 20 pounds red lead, 10 pounds black oxide manganese, 2 pounds white gum shellac; set the oil over the fire and bring to the boiling point; add by degrees litharge and red lead alternately and slowly; add the gum, and when melted put in the manganese, and keep the whole in rapid motion from the time the oil is at 200 Fahr. until the making is finished: when cool enough to bear the finger in it a moment, add from 20 to 30 gallons spirits of turpentine.

Carriage Varnish.—1. Eight pounds of second sorted African copal, 2½ gallons clarified oil; boil till very stringy; ¼ pound dried copperas, ¼ pound litharge, 5½ gallons strained turpentine, 8 pounds second sorted gum anime, 2½ gallons clarified oil, ¼ pound dried sugar of lead, ¼ pound litharge, 5½ gallons turpentine; mix with the first while hot. This varnish will dry hard if well boiled in four hours in summer, and six in winter. It is used for wheels, springs and carriage parts of coaches, chaises, etc.; it is used by house painters and decorators, because of its drying quality and strong gloss. **2.** Eight pounds of second sorted gum anime, 2¾ gallons fine clarified oil, 5¼ gallons turpentine, ¼ pound litharge, ¼ pound dried sugar of lead, ¼ pound dried copperas; boiled and mixed as before. When three runs are poured into the boiling pot, the driers put in, and well boiled, this varnish will dry hard in four hours in winter, and in two in summer. Used for varnishing dark carriage work or black japan, and by house painters for dark work.

Colorless Varnish.—1. Dissolve 1½ ounces shellac in 1 pint rectified spirits of wine; boil for a few minutes in 5 ounces wellburnt and recently heated animal charcoal; filter a small portion, and if not colorless add more charcoal. When all color is removed, press the liquor through a piece of silk and filter through blotting paper. This varnish should be used in a temperature at least 60° Fahr., perfectly free from dust. It dries in a few minutes, and is not liable afterward to chill or bloom. It is particularly applicable to drawings and prints that have been sized, and may be advantageously used upon oil paintings that are thoroughly hard and dry, as it brings out the colors with the purest effect. This quality prevents it from obscuring gilding and renders it valuable for all kinds of leather, as it does not yield to the warmth of the hand, and resists damp. Its useful applications are numerous; indeed to all the purposes of the best hard-spirit varnishes. **2.** A common lac varnish may be made by digesting 4 ounces clear grained lac in 1 pint spirits of wine in a wide-mouthed bottle, keeping in a warm place for 2 or 3 days, and occasionally shaking it. When dissolved, strain through flannel into another bottle for use.

Copal Varnish.—1. Gum copal 8 pounds, linseed oil 2 gallons, sugar of lead ½ pound, turpentine 3½ gallons; boil until stringy. **2.** Gum copal 8 pounds, oil 2½ gals., sulphate of iron ¼ pounds, turpentine 5½ gallons. Good for house and sign painting. In making the above melt the gum in a small quantity of boiling oil and pour gradually into the kettle containing the other on while boiling. When done and cool enough not to ignite the turpentine, add it. **3.** Fuse 8 parts fine African copal and add 2 gallons clarified oil; boil slowly 4 or 5 hours until stringy; then mix with 3½ gallons turpentine. **4.** (Transparent green.) A transparent green varnish is made by taking a small quantity of Chinese blue with about twice the amount finely powdered chromate of potash; stir these in copal varnish thinned with turpentine; thoroughly grind the mixture, intimately incorporating the ingredients, otherwise it will not be transparent. A preponderance of chromate of potash gives a yellowish shade and a deficiency increases the amount of blue. Thus colored it produces a striking effect in japanned goods, paper hangings, etc., and can be made very cheaply.

● Flexible Varnish.—This is used for balloons, gas bags, etc. **1.** India rubber cut small 1½ ounces, chloroform, mashed ether, or bisulphuret of carbon 1 pint; digest in the cold until solution is complete. Dries as soon as laid on. Pure gutta percha may be substituted for india rubber. **2.** India rubber 1 ounce, drying oil 1 quart; dissolve by heat: very tough; dries in 48 hours. **3.** Linseed oil 1 gallon, dried white copperas and sugar of lead, of each 3 ounces, litharge 8 ounces; boil with constant agitation until it strings; then cool slowly and decant the clear portion; if too thick thin with quick-drying linseed oil.

Furniture Varnish.—**1.** Shellac 1½ pounds. naphtha 1 gallon; dissolve. and it is ready without filtering. **2.** Shellac 12 ounces, copal 3 ounces; dissolve in 1 gallon naphtha. **3.** Shellac 1½ pounds, seed lac and sandarac, of each 4 ounces, mastic 2 ounces, rectified spirit 1 gallon; dissolve. **4.** Shellac 2 pounds, benzoin 4 ounces, spirit 1 gallon. **5.** Shellac 10 ounces, seed lac, sandarac, and copal varnish, of each 6 ounces, benzoin 3 ounces, naphtha 1 gallon. To darken use benzoin and dragon's blood; turmeric and other coloring matters are also added; to make it lighter use bleached lac, though some add oxalic acid to the ingredients. It is insoluble in spirit or naphtha. For ordinary purposes the first form is best, while its appearance is equal to any other.

● Glass Varnish.—Fuse together 15 parts powdered quartz or of fine sand, 10 parts of potash, and 1 of charcoal; pulverize the mass and expose it for some days to the air; treat the whole with cold water, which removes the foreign salts. etc.; boil the residue in 5 parts water until it dissolves. It is permanent in the air and not dissolved by cold water. Used to protect wood, etc., from fire.

Glass Varnish.—**1.** Wax 1 ounce, mastic ½ ounce, asphaltum ¼ ounce, turpentine ½ dram. **2.** Mastic 15 parts, turpentine 7 parts, oil of spike 4 parts.

Gold Varnish.—**1.** Turmeric 1 dram. gamboge 1 dram, oil of turpentine 2 pints, shellac 5 ounces, sandarac 5 ounces, dragon's blood 7 drams, thin mastic varnish 8 ounces; digest with agitation 14 days in a warm place; then set aside to fine, and pour off clear. **2.** Dutch leaf 1 part. gamboge 4 parts, gum dragon **4** parts, proof spirit 18 parts. Macerate 12 hours and then grind.

Grates, Varnish For.—Melt 4 pounds common asphaltum, add 2 pints linseed oil and 1 gallon oil turpentine. If too thick add more turpentine.

Grecian Varnish.—Three ounces balsam fir, 2 ounces alcohol, 1 ounce spirits turpentine. Mix together.

India Rubber Varnish.—**1.** Two ounces India rubber finely divided; place in a vial and digest in a sand bath with ¼ pound camphene and ½ ounce naphtha. When dissolved add 1 ounce copal varnish, which renders it more durable. **2.** Digest in a wide-mouthed glass bottle 2 ounces india rubber in shavings with 1 pound oil turpentine during 2 days without shaking; then stir with a wooden spatula. Add another pound oil of turpentine and digest with agitation until dissolved. Mix 1¼ pounds of this solution with 2 pounds white copal oil varnish and 1½ boiled linseed oil. Shake and digest in a sand bath until united in good varnish. **3.** Four ounces india rubber in shavings; dissolve in a covered jar by means of a sand bath in 2 pounds crude benzole, and then mix with 4 pounds hot linseed oil varnish and ½ pound oil turpentine. Dries well.

Linseed Oil Varnish.—Pour 25 pounds pure linseed oil in an enameled iron pot which holds about 40 pounds weight; then place in a moderately strong charcoal fire and heat the oil ¼ hour to boiling point; in the meantime rub 4 ounces pure oxide of manganese in linseed oil; put this mass into a small vessel provided with a spout and pour in drops into the boiling linseed oil, while being gently stirred with a wooden spatula. During effervesence of the oil the dropping in of the manganese must stop. As soon as the oil has settled the dropping in is continued to the last. The vessel is washed out with linseed oil. which is poured into the boiling oil. The varnish is now boiled slowly 1 hour, but if stronger varnish is desired boil ½ hour or 1 hour longer. When removed from the fire cover with a clean plate and let rest 24 hours; then carefully pour off into clean vessels: the sediment and other residue are used for the preparation of ordinary ground colors. The varnish when poured into glass bottles can then be bleached by exposure to the sun and moon. Moonlight bleaches quicker than sunlight. The bleached is used only for the finest white oil and lac colors, and for dissolving fine copal lacs, as well as a drying medium for fine oil colors.

Mahogany Varnish.—Gum anime 8 pounds clarified oil 3 gallons, litharge and powdered dry sugar of lead, of each ½ pound. Proceed as for body varnishes and thin with oil turpentine 5 gallons or a sufficient quantity.

Mastic Varnish.—**1.** Pale and bleached gum mastic 5 pounds, glass (pounded small, washed and dried) 3 pounds. finest newly rectified oil of turpentine (lukewarm) 2 gallons; put them into a 4-gallon tin bottle or can, bung down, and keep rolling it backwards and forwards smartly on a counter or other smooth place 4 hours: when the gum is dissolved, the varnish may be decanted, strained through muslin into another bottle and allowed to settle; if the solution is still incomplete the agitation must be continued longer or gentle warmth applied. Very fine. **2.** Mastic 4 pounds, oil turpentine 2 gallons; dissolve by heat. Used for pictures, etc.; when good it is tough, brilliant, and colorless; it improves by age and should never be used before 12 months old. Should it get chilled add 1 pound well-washed silicious sand, made moderately hot, to each gallon; agitate 5 minutes and let it settle.

Shellac Varnish.—One part gum shellac dissolved in 3 or 4 parts of alcohol, 92 per cent; mix with 1 part water; filtered, pressed, and the solution distilled until the alcohol is evaporated. The gum precipitated from this solution is dried on a water bath and dissolved in double its weight of alcohol of 96 to 98 per cent.

Stove Varnish.—Melt ½ pound asphaltum and add to it ¼ pint linseed oil and 1 pint turpentine; this will be enough for 4 grates. If too thick as it gets to the bottom, add more turpentine. It is for black stoves, which must be washed clean of dirt and black lead, and when dry apply the varnish with a brush.

Tar Varnish.—1. (For Iron.) Place a convenient quantity coal tar in small retorts, and heat until the oil commences to distil over; then let the retort cool somewhat; when they are opened and a proportionate quantity of heavy oil of tar added and the mixture well stirred; then pour the mixture out and the operation is complete. Made in this way it is preferable to tar and dries in from 24 to 48 hours. By incorporating naphtha of the lowest quality (to do which the mass must be warm) with the material made with light oil instead of heavy oil, a varnish may be obtained which will dry in 1 hour or less. **2.** Tar 2 gallons, tallow 1 pound; melt, then add ground ochre 7 pounds, spirits of turpentine 6 pounds; mix well. By regulating the quantity of ochre a very excellent chocolate paint for rough outdoor work will be produced.

Tin, Japan For.—Draw letters on paper to suit the piece of tin, having first cleaned it with diluted alcohol and a piece of cotton. Take whiting and rub it over the back of the paper upon which your design is made, and lay it upon the japanned tin; next place a weight upon the four corners of the paper; then, with a pointed piece of hard wood, trace the design. bearing upon the paper with the point hard enough to cause the whiting on the other side of the paper to adhere to the tin. After going over the whole you will have transferred the design in fine outline to the tin. Size with oil size, and when dry enough for gilding lay on the gold leaf and dab it down; brush off the loose gold with a flat camel's hair brush.

Tin, Lacquer For.—Put 3 ounces seed lac. 2 drams dragon's blood, 1 ounce turmeric powder, into 1 pint well rectified spirits; let the whole remain 14 days, and agitate once a day; when comhined, strain through muslin. It is bruised over tinware intended to imitate brass.

Turpentine Varnish.—Put 1 pint turpentine into a bottle, with ½ pound white resin in powder; dissolve in a gentle heat by placing the bottle in an iron pot surrounded by dry sand, over a moderate fire.

Transparent Japan.—1. Oil of turpentine 4 ounces, oil of lavender 3 ounces, camphor ½ dram, copal 1 ounce; dissolve. Used to japan tin, but quick copal varnish is mostly used instead. **2.** Copal varnish 35 parts, camphor 1 part, boiled oil 2 parts; mix.

Violin Varnish.—1. Rectified spirits of wine ½ gallon; add 6 ounces gum sandarac, 3 ounces gum mastic, and ½ pint turpentine varnish; put the above in a tin can by the stove, frequently shaking till dissolved; strain and keep for use. If you find it harder than you wish, thin with turpentine varnish. **2.** Heat together at a low temperature 2 quarts alcohol, ½ pint turpentine varnish and 1 pound clean gum mastic. When the latter is dissolved, strain through cloth. **3.** Coarsely powdered copal and glass of each 4 ounces, alcohol 64 per cent (1 pint), camphor ½ ounce. Heat the mixture with frequent stirring in a waterbath until the solution is complete. When cold decant the clear portion.

Wax Varnish.—1. Take of pure white wax 1 pound, melt with gentle heat; add of warm rectified spirits (specific gravity 83) 1 pint; mix and pour the liquid out upon a cold slab; grind to a smooth paste, adding more spirits as required. Put the paste into a marble mortar, make an emulsion with 3½ pints of water, gradually added, and strain through muslin. Used as a varnish for paintings. When dry a hot iron is passed over it. so as to fuse it and render it transparent; when cold it is polished with a clean linen cloth. The most protective of all varnishes. **2.** Wax 5 ounces, oil of turpentine 1 quart; dissolve. Used for furniture.

White Varnish.—1. Gum sandarac 3 ounces, mastic in drops 1 ounce, gum elemi ½ ounce, oil of spike lavender, ½ ounce; put into a 1 pint vial and fill up with best spirits of wine; let it stand in a rather warm place till the gums are dissolved, then pour off into a clean vial, and it is ready. **2.** (Imitation ivory.) Take ½ ounce isinglass, boiled gently in ½ pint of water till dissolved; then strain and add flake white powder till it becomes as white as cream. Give the box or carved wood three or four coats, letting each dry before the other is put on; then smooth with a damp rag. It has the appearance of ivory. If, when mixed it looks too white, a few grains of carmine will give it a pink look, or use chrome yellow. Either of these colors improve it.

GENERAL HINTS ON JAPANNING AND VARNISHING.

Japanning is the art of covering bodies by grounds of opaque colors in varnish, which may be afterward decorated by printing or gilding, or left in a plain state. It is also to be looked upon in another sense, as that of ornamenting coaches, snuff boxes, screens, etc. All surfaces to be japanned must be perfectly clean, and leather should be stretched on frames. Paper should be stiff for japanning. The French prime all their japanned articles, the English do not. This priming is generally of common size. Those articles that are primed thus, never endure as well as those that receive the japan coating on the first operation, and thus it is that those articles of japan work that are primed with size when they are used for some time, crack, and the coats of japan fly off in flakes. A solution of strong isinglass size and honey, or sugar candy, makes a good japan varnish to cover water colors on gold grounds. A pure white priming for japanning, for the cheap method, is made with parchment size, and one-third of isinglass, laid on very thin and smooth. It is the better for three coats, and when the last coat is dry, it is prepared to receive the coating painting or figures. Previous to the last coat, however, the work should be smoothly polished. When wood or leather is to be japanned, and no priming used, the best plan is to lay on 2 or 3 coats of varnish made of seed-lac and resin, 2 ounces each, dissolved in alcohol and strained through a cloth. This varnish should be put on in a warm place, and the work to be varnished should, if possible, be warm also, and all dampness should be avoided, to prevent the varnish from being chilled. When the work is prepared with the above composition and dry, it is fit for the proper japan to be laid on. If the ground is not to be white the best varnish now to be used is made of shellac, as it is the best vehicle for all kind of colors. This is made in the proportions of the best shellac, 5 ounces, made into powder, steeped in a quart of alcohol, and kept at a gentle heat 2 or 3 days and shaken frequently, after which the solution must be filtered through a flannel bag, and kept in a well corked bottle for use. This varnish for hard japanning on copper or tin will stand forever, unless fire or hammer be used to burn or beetle it off. The color to be used with shellac varnish may be of any pigments whatever to give the desired shade, as this varnish will mix with any color.

White Japan Grounds.—To form a hard, perfect white ground is no easy matter, as the substances which are generally used to make the japan hard, have a tendency, by a number of coats, to look or become dull in brightness. One white ground is made by the following composition: White flake or lead washed over and ground up with a sixth of its weight of starch, then dried and mixed with the finest gum, ground up in parts of 1 ounce gum to ½ ounce of rectified turpentine mixed and ground thoroughly together. This is to be finely laid on the article to be japanned, dried and then varnished with 5 or 6 coats of the following: Two ounces of the whitest seed lac to 3 ounces of gum anima reduced to a fine powder and dissolved in a quart of alcohol. This lac must be carefully picked. For a softer varnish than this, a little turpentine should be added, and less of the gum. A very good varnish and not brittle, may be made by dissolving gum anima in nut oil, boiling it gently as the gum is added, and giving the oil as much gum as it will take up. The ground of white varnish may of itself be made of this varnish, by giving 2 or 3 coats of it, but when used it should be diluted with pure turpentine. Although this varnish is not brittle, it is liable to be indented with strokes, and 't will not bear to be polished, but if well laid on it will not need polishing afterward; it also takes some time to dry. Heat applied to all oils, however, darkens their color, and oil varnishes for white grow very yellow if not exposed to a full clear light.

Gum Copal.—Copal varnish is one of the very finest varnishes for japanning purposes. It can be dissolved by linseed oil, rendered dry by adding some quicklime at a heat somewhat less than will boil or decompose the oil by it. This solution, with the addition of a little turpentine, forms a very transparent varnish, which, when properly applied and slowly dried is very hard and durable. This varnish is applied to snuff boxes, tea boards and other utensils. It also preserves paintings and renders their surfaces capable of reflecting light more uniformly. If powdered copal be mixed in a mortar with camphor, it softens and becomes a coherent mass, and if camphor be added to alcohol it becomes an excellent solvent of copal by adding the copal well ground, and employing a tolerable degree of heat having the vessel well corked which must have a long neck for the allowance of expansion, and the vessel must only be about ¼ filled with the mixture. Copal can also be incorporated with turpentine, with 1 part of powdered copal to 12 parts of pure turpentine, subjected to the heat of a sand bath for several days in a long necked mattras, shaking it frequently. Copal is a good varnish for metals, such as tin; the varnish must be dried in an oven, each coat, and it can be colored with some substances, but alcohol varnish will mix with any coloring matter. In white japans or varnishes, we have already shown that fine chalk or white lead was used as a basis, and the varnishes coated over it. To japan or varnish white leather, so that it may be elastic, is altogether different work from varnishing or japanning wood or metal, or papier mache. For white leather, oil is the principal ingredient, as it is well known that chalk is extensively used to give white leather its pure color, or speaking more philosophically, its fair colorless whiteness. White leather having already the basis of white varnish, it should get a light coat of the pure varnish before mentioned, and dried well in the oven, or a coat of the oil copal will answer very well. This being well dried, boiled nut oil nicely coated and successively dried, will make a most beautiful white varnish for leather, not liable to crack. This quality takes a long time to dry, and of course is more expensive. Coarse varnish may be made of boiled linseed oil, into which is added gradually the acetate of lead as a drier. This addition must be done very cautiously as the oil will be apt to foam over. A better and more safe drying mixture than the mere acetate of lead, is to dissolve the acetate of lead in a small quantity of water; neutralize the acid with the addition of pipe clay, evaporate the sediment to perfect dryness, and feed the oil when gently boiling gradually with it. These varnishes or japans, as far as described, have only reference to white grounds. There is some nice work to be observed, and there is much in applying the varnishes at the right time, knowing by the eye the proper moment when the mixture is perfect, or when to add any ingredient. These things require practice.

Black Grounds.—Black grounds for japans may be made by mixing ivory black with shellac varnish; or for coarse work, lampblack and the top coating of common seedlac varnish. A common black japan may be made by painting a piece of work with drying oil (oil mixed with lead), and putting the work into a stove, not too hot, but of such a degree, gradually raising the heat and keeping it up for a long time, so as not to burn the oil and make it blister. This process makes very fair japan and requires no polishing.

Black Japan.—Naples asphaltum 50 pounds, dark gum-anime 8 pounds, fuse, add linseed oil 12 gallons, boil, add dark gum amber 10 pounds, previously fused and boiled with linseed oil 2 gallons, add the driers, and proceed as last. Used for wood or metals.

Brunswick Black.—1. Foreign asphaltum, 45 pounds, drying oil, 6 gallons, litharge 6 pounds, boil as last, and thin with 25 gallons of oil of turpentine. Used for ironwork, etc. **2.** Black pitch and gas tar asphaltum, of each 25 pounds, boil gently for 5 hours, then add linseed oil 8 gallons, litharge and red lead, of each 10 pounds, boil as before, and thin with oil of turpentine 20 gallons. Inferior to the last, but cheaper.

Blue Japan Grounds. — Blue japan grounds may be formed of bright Prussian blue. The color may be mixed with shellac varnish, and brought to a polishing state by 5 or 6 coats of varnish of seedlac. The varnish, however, is apt to give a greenish tinge to the blue, as the varnish has a yellowish tinge, and blue and yellow form a green. Whenever a light blue is desired, the purest varnish must always be used.

Scarlet Japan.—Ground vermilion may be used for this, but being so glaring it is not beautiful unless covered over with rose-pink, or lake, which have a good effect when thus used. For a very bright crimson ground, safflower or Indian lake should be used, always dissolved in the alcohol of which the varnish is made. In place of this lake, carmine may be used, as it is more common. The top coat of varnish must always be of the white seedlac, which has been before described, and as many coats given as will be thought proper; it is easy to judge of this.

Yellow Grounds.—If turmeric be dissolved in the spirit of wine and strained through a cloth, and then mixed with pure seedlac varnish, it makes a good yellow japan. Saffron will answer for the same purpose in the same way, but the brightest yellow ground is made by a primary coat of pure chrome yellow, and coated successively with the varnish. Dutch pink is used for a kind of cheap yellow japan ground. If a little dragon's blood be added to the varnish for yellow japan, a most beautiful and rich salmon-colored varnish is the result, and by these two mixtures all the shades of flesh-colored japans are produced.

Green Japan Grounds.—A good green may be made by mixing Prussian blue along with the cromate of lead, or with turmeric, or orpiment (sulphuret of arsenic), or ocher, only the two should be ground together and dissolved in alcohol and applied as a ground, then coated with 4 or 5 coats of shellac varnish, in the manner already described. A very bright green is made by laying on a ground of Dutch metal, or leaf of gold, and then coating it over with distilled verdigris dissolved in alcohol, then the varnishes on the top. This is a splendid green, brilliant and glowing.

Orange-Colored Grounds.—Orange grounds may be made of yellow mixed with vermilion or carmine, just as a bright or rather inferior color is wanted. The yellow should always be in quantity to make a good full color, and the red added in proportion to the depth of the shade. If there is not a good full body of yellow the color will look watery, or bare, as it is technically termed.

Purple Japan Grounds.—This is made by a mixture of lake and Prussian blue, or carmine, or, for an inferior color, vermilion, and treated as the foregoing. When the ground is laid on and perfectly dried, a fine coat of boiled nut oil then laid on perfectly dried, is a good method to have a japan not liable to crack. But a better plan is to use this oil in the varnish given, the first coat, after the ground is laid on, and which should contain considerable of pure turpentine. In every case where oil is used for any purpose for varnish, it is all the better if turpentine is mixed with it. Turpentine enables oils to mix with either alcohol or water. Alkalies have this property also.

Black Japan.—**1.** Asphaltum 3 ounces, boiled oil 4 quarts, burnt umber 8 ounces. Mix by heat and when cooling thin with turpentine. **2.** Amber 12 ounces, asphaltum 2 ounces. fuse by heat, add boiled oil ½ pint, resin 2 ounces: when cooling add 16 ounces oil of turpentine. Both are used to varnish metals.

Japan Black for Leather.—**1.** Burnt umber 4 ounces, true asphaltum 2 ounces, boiled oil 2 quarts. Dissolve the asphaltum by heat in a little of the oil, add the burnt umber ground in oil and the remainder of the oil; mix, cool, and thin with turpentine. **2.** (Flexible.) Shellac 1 part, wood naphtha 4 parts; dissolve and color with lampblack. Inflexible.

Transparent Japan.—Oil of turpentine 4 ounces, oil of lavender 3 ounces, camphor ½ dram. copal 1 ounce; dissolve. Used to japan tin, but quick copal varnish is mostly used instead.

Japanner's Copal Varnish.—Pale African copal 7 pounds, fuse, add clarified linseed oil ⅛ gallon, boil for 5 minutes, remove it into the open air, add boiling oil of turpentine 3 gallons, mix well, strain it into the cistern, and cover it up immediately. Used to varnish furniture, and by japanners, coach-makers, etc. Dries in 15 minutes and may be polished as soon as hard.

Tortoise Shell Japan.—This varnish is prepared by taking of good linseed oil 1 gallon and of umber ½ pound, and boiling them together until the oil becomes very brown and thick, when they are strained through a cloth and boiled again until the composition is about the consistence of pitch, when it is fit for use. Having prepared this varnish clean well the copper or iron plate or vessel that is to be varnished (japanned), and then lay vermilion mixed with shellac varnish or drying oil. diluted with turpentine. very thinly on the places intended to imitate the clean parts of the tortoise shell. When the vermilion is dry brush over the whole with the above umber varnish diluted to a due consistence with turpentine. and when it is set and firm it must be put into a stove and undergo a strong heat for a long time, even 2 weeks will not hurt it. This is the ground for those beautiful snuff boxes and tea boards which are so much admired. and those grounds can be decorated with all kinds of paintings that fancy may suggest, and the work is all the better to be finished in an annealing oven.

Painting Japan Work.—The colors to be painted are tempered generally in oil. which should have at least ¼ of its weight of gum sandarac or gum mastic dissolved in it, and it should be well diluted with turpentine that the colors may be laid on thin and evenly. ❯In some instances it does well to put on water colors or grounds of gold, which a skillful hand can do and manage so as to make the work appear as if it were embossed. These water colors are best prepared by means of isinglass size, mixed with honey or sugar candy. These colors when laid on must receive a number of upper coats of the varnish we have described before.

Japanning Old Tea-Trays.--First clean them thoroughly with soap and water and a little rotten stone, then dry them by wiping and exposure at the fire. Now get some good copal varnish. mix it with some bronze powder, and apply with a brush to the denuded parts. After which set the tea-tray in an oven at a heat of 212 ° or 300 ° until the varnish is dry. Two coats will make it equal to new.

❯**Japan Finishing.**—The finishing part of japanning lies in laying on and polishing the outer coats of varnish. which is necessary in all painted or simply ground colored japan work. When brightness and clearness are wanted, the white kind of varnish is necessary, for seed lac varnish, which is the hardest and most tenacious, imparts a yellow tinge. A mixed varnish, we believe, is the best for this purpose, that is, for combining hardness and purity. Take then 3 ounces of seed lac, picked very carefully from all sticks and dirt, and washing it well with cold water, stirring it up, pouring it off, and continuing the process until the water runs off perfectly pure. Dry it and then reduce it to powder, and put it with a pint of pure alcohol into a bottle, of which it must occupy only two-thirds of its space. This mixture must be shaken well together and the bottle kept at a gentle heat (being corked) until the lac be dissolved. When this is the case, the clear must be poured off, and the remainder, strained through a cloth, and all the clear, strained and poured, must be kept in a well stopped bottle. The manner of using this seed lac varnish is the same as that before described. and a fine polishing varnish is made by mixing this with the pure white varnish. The pieces of work to be varnished for finishing should be placed near a stove, or in a warm, dry room, and one coat should be perfectly dry before the other is applied. The varnish is applied by proper brushes, beginning at the middle, passing the stroke to one end and with the other stroke from the middle to the other end. Great skill is displayed in laying on these coats of varnish. If possible the skill of hand should never cross, or twice pass over in giving one coat. When one coat is dry another must be laid over it, and so on successively for a number of coats. so that the coating should be sufficiently thick to stand fully all the polishing, so as not to bare the surface of the colored work. When a sufficient number of coats are thus laid on. the work is fit to be polished, which, in common cases, is commenced with a rag dipped in finely powdered rotten stone, and towards the end of the rubbing, a little oil should be used along with the powder, and when the work appears fine and glossy a little oil should be used alone to clean off the powder and give the work a still brighter hue. In very fine work, French whiting should be used, which should be washed in water to remove any sand that might be in it. Pumice stone ground to a very fine powder is used for the first part of polishing, and the finishing done with whiting. It is always best to dry the varnish of all japan work by heat. For wood work, heat must be sparingly used, but for metals the varnish should be dried in an oven, also for papier mache and leather. The metal will stand the greatest heat. and care must be taken not to darken by too high a temperature. When gold size is used in gilding for japan work. where it is desired not to have the gold shine, or appear burnished, the gold size should be used with a little of the spirits of turpentine and a little oil; but when a considerable degree of luster is wanted without burnishing ard the preparation necessary for it, a little of the size along with oil alone should be used.

Spirit Varnishes.—These varnishes may be readily colored Red by dragon's blood; yellow by gamboge. If a colored varnish is required, clearly no account need be taken of the color of the resins. Lac varnish may be bleached by Mr. Lemming's process: Dissolve 5 ounces of shellac in a quart of spirit of wine; boil for a few minutes with 10 ounces well-burnt and recently-heated animal charcoal, when a small quantity of the solution should be drawn off and filtered, if not colorless a little more charcoal should be added. When all tinge is removed press the liquor through silk, as linen absorbs more varnish, and afterward filter it through fine blotting-paper. Dr. Hare proceeds as follows: Dissolve in an iron kettle about 1 part of pearlash in about 8 parts of water, add 1 part of shell or seed lac and heat the whole to ebulition. When the lac has dissolved cool the solution and impregnate it with chlorine gas till the lac is all precipitated. The precipitate is white, but the color deepens by washing and consolidation. Dissolved in alcohol. lac bleached by this process yields a varnish which is as free from color as any copal varnish. One word in conclusion with reference to all spirit varnishes. A damp atmosphere is sufficient to occasion a milky deposit of resin, owing to the diluted spirit depositing a portion; in such case the varnish is said to be chilled.

Essence Varnishes.—They do not differ essentially in their manufacture from spirit varnishes. The polish produced by them is more durable, although they take a longer time to dry.

Oil Varnishes.—The most durable and lustrous of varnishes are composed of a mixture of resin, oil and spirits of turpentine. The oils most frequently employed are linseed and walnut; the resins chiefly copal and amber. The drying power of the oil having been increased by litharge, red lead, or by sulphate of lead, and a judicious selection of copal having been made, it is necessary, according to Booth, to bear in mind the following precautions before proceeding to the manufacture of varnish: 1. That oil varnish is not a solution, but an intimate mixture of resin in boiled oil and spirits of turpentine. 2. That the resin must be completely fused previous to the addition of the boiled or prepared oil. 3. That the oil must be heated from 250° to 300°. 4. That the spirits of turpentine must be added gradually, and in a thin stream, while the mixture of oil and resin is still hot. 5. That the varnish be made in dry weather, otherwise moisture is absorbed, and its transparency and drying quality impaired. The heating vessel must be of copper, with a riveted and not a soldered bottom. To promote the admixture of the copal with the hot oil, the copal—carefully selected, and of nearly uniform fusibility—is separately heated with continuous stirring over a charcoal fire. Good management is required to prevent the copal from burning or becoming even high colored, When completely fused, the heated oil should be gradually poured in with constant stirring. The exact amount of oil required must be determined by experiment. If a drop upon a plate, on cooling, assumes such a consistency as to be penetrated by the nail without cracking, the mixture is complete: but if it cracks, more oil must be added. The spirits of turpentine previously heated is added in a thin stream to the former mixture, care being taken to keep up the heat of all the parts. These are excellent varnishes.

Table Varnish.—Damma resin, 1 pound; spirits of turpentine, 2 pounds; camphor, 200 grains. Digest the mixture for 24 hours. The decanted portion is fit for immediate use.

Common Table Varnish. — Oil of turpentine, 1 pound; beeswax, 2 ounces; colophony, 1 dram.

Copal Varnish for Inside Work.—**1.** Pounded and oxidized copal, 24 parts; spirit of turpentine, 40 parts; camphor, 1 part. **2.** (Flexible Copal Varnish). Copal in powder, 16 parts; camphor, 2 parts; oil of lavender, 90 parts. Dissolve the camphor in the oil, heat the latter, and stir in the copal in successive portions until complete solution takes place. Thin with sufficient turpentine to make it of proper consistence.

Best Body Copal Varnish for Coach-makers, etc.—This is intended for the body parts of coaches and other similar vehicles, intended for polishing. Fuse 8 pounds of fine African gum copal, and 2 gallons of clarified oil, boil it very slowly for 4 or 5 hours, until quite stringy, mix with 3½ gallons of turpentine; strain off and pour it into a cistern. If this is too slow in drying, coach-makers, painters and varnish-makers have introduced to 2 pots of the preceding varnish, one made as follows: 8 pounds of fine pale gum-anime, 2 gallons of clarified oil and 3½ gallons of turpentine. To be boiled 4 hours.

Copal Polish.—Digest or shake finely powdered gum copal 4 parts, and gum camphor 1 part, with ether to form a semi-fluid mass, and then digest with a sufficient quantity of copal.

White Spirit Varnish.—Sandarach, 250 parts; mastic, in tears, 64; elemi resin, 32; turpentine, 64; alcohol of 85 per cent., 1,000 parts, by measure. The turpentine is to be added after the resins are dissolved. This is a brilliant varnish, but not so hard as to bear polishing.

White Hard Spirit Varnishes.—**1.** Gum sandarach 5 pounds, camphor 1 ounce, rectified spirit (65 over proof) 2 gallons, washed and dried coarsely-pounded glass 2 pounds; proceed as in making mastic varnish; when strained add 1 quart of very pale turpentine varnish. Very fine. **2.** Picked mastic and coarsely-ground glass, of each, 4 ounces, sandarach and pale clear venice turpentine, of each 3 ounces, alcohol 2 pounds; as last. **3.** Gum sandarach, 1 pound, clear Strasburgh turpentine 6 ounces, rectified spirit (65 over proof) 3 pints; dissolve. **4.** Mastic in tears 2 ounces, sandarach 8 ounces, gum elemi 1 ounce, strasburgh or scio turpentine (genuine) 4 ounces, rectified spirit (65 over proof) 1 quart. Used on metals, etc. Polishes well.

White Varnish.—**1.** Tender copal 7½ ounces, camphor 1 ounce, alcohol of 95 per cent, 1 quart; dissolve, then add mastic 2 ounces, venice turpentine 1 ounce; dissolve and strain. Very white, drying, and capable of being polished when hard.

Used for toys. **2.** Sandarach 8 ounces, mastic 2 ounces, Canada balsam 4 ounces, alcohol 1 quart. Used on paper, wood, or linen.

Soft Brilliant Varnish.—Sandarach 6 ounces, elemi (genuine) 4 ounces, anime 1 ounce, camphor ½ ounce, rectified spirit 1 quart; as before. The above spirit varnishes are chiefly applied to objects of the toilette, as work-boxes, card-cases, etc., but are also suitable to other articles, whether of paper, wood, linen, or metal, that require a brilliant and quick-drying varnish. They mostly dry almost as soon as applied, and are usually hard enough to polish in 24 hours. Spirit varnishes are less durable and more liable to crack than oil varnishes.

Brown Hard Spirit Varnishes.—**1.** Sandarach 4 ounces, pale seed lac 2 ounces, elemi (true) 1 ounce, alcohol 1 quart; digest with agitation till dissolved, then add venice turpentine 2 ounces. **2.** Gum sandarach 3 pounds, shellac 2 pounds, rectified spirits (65 over proof) 2 gallons; dissolve, add turpentine varnish 1 quart; agitate well and strain. Very fine. **3.** Seed lac and yellow resin, of each 1½ pounds, rectified spirits 2 gallons.

To Prepare a Varnish for Coating Metals.—Digest 1 part of bruised copal in 2 parts of absolute alcohol; but as this varnish dries too quickly it is preferable to take 1 part of copal, 1 part of oil of rosemary, and 2 or 3 parts of absolute alcohol. This gives a clear varnish as limpid as water. It should be applied hot, and when dry it will be found hard and durable.

To Varnish Articles of Iron and Steel.—Dissolve 10 parts of clear grains of mastic, 5 parts of camphor, 15 parts of sandarach, and 5 of elemi, in a sufficient quantity of alcohol, and apply this varnish without heat. The articles will not only be preserved from rust, but the varnish will retain its transparency and the metallic brillancy of the article will not be obscured.

Varnish for Iron Work.—Dissolve in about 2 pounds of tar oil, ½ pound asphaltum, and a like quantity of pounded resin, mix hot in an iron kettle, care being taken to prevent any contact with the flame. When cold the varnish is ready for use. This varnish is for outdoor wood and iron work, not for japanning leather or cloth.

Black Varnish for Iron Work.—Asphaltum 48 pounds, fuse, add boiled oil 10 gallons, red lead and litharge of each 7 pounds, dried and powdered white copperas 3 pounds; boil for 2 hours, then add dark gum amber (fused) 8 pounds, hot linseed oil 2 gallons, boil for 2 hours longer, or till a little of the mass, when cooled, may be rolled into pills, then withdraw the heat, and afterwards thin down with oil of turpentine 30 gallons. Used for the ironwork of carriages, and other nice purposes.

Bronze Varnish for Statuary.—Cut best hard soap 50 parts into shavings, dissolve in boiling water 2 parts, to which add the solution of blue vitriol 15 parts, in pure water 60 parts. Wash the copper soap with water, dry it at a very slow heat, and dissolve it in spirits of turpentine.

Amber Varnishes.—1. Amber 1 pound, pale boiled oil **10** ounces, turpentine 1 pint. Render the amber, placed in an iron pot, semi-liquid by heat; then add the oil, mix, remove it from the fire, and when cooled a little stir in the turpentine. **2.** To the amber, melted as above, add 2 ounces of shellac, and proceed as before. This varnish is rather dark, but remarkably tough. The first form is the best. It is used for the same purposes as copal varnish, and forms an excellent article for covering wood, or any other substance not of a white or very pale color. It dries well, and is very hard and durable.

Amber Varnish, Black.—Amber 1 pound, boiled oil ¼ pint, powdered asphaltum 6 ounces, oil of turpentine 1 pint. Melt the amber as before described, then add the asphaltum, previously mixed with the cold oil, and afterwards heated very hot, mix well, remove the vessel from the fire, and when cooled a little add the turpentine, also made warm. Each of the above varnishes should be reduced to a proper consistence with more turpentine if required. The last form produces the beautiful black varnish used by the coachmakers. Some of the manufacturers omit the whole or part of the asphaltum, and use the same quantity of clear black resin instead, in which case the color is brought up by lampblack reduced to an inpalpable powder, or previously ground very fine with a little boiled oil. The varnish made in this way, lacks, however, that richness, brilliancy and depth of blackness imparted by asphaltum.

Amber Varnishes.—1. (Pale.) Amber pale and transparent 6 pounds, fuse, add hot clarified linseed oil 2 gallons; boil till it strings strongly, cool a little and add oil of turpentine **4** gallons. Pale as copal varnish, soon becomes very hard, and is the most durable of oil varnishes; but requires time before it is fit for polishing. When wanted to dry and harden quicker, "drying" oil may be substituted for linseed, or "driers" may be added during the boiling. **2.** Amber 1 pound; melt, add scio turpentine ½ pound, transparent white resin 2 ounces, hot linseed oil 1 pint, and afterwards oil of turpentine as much as sufficient; as above. Very tough. **3.** (Hard.) Melted amber 4 ounces hot boiled oil 1 quart; as before. **4.** (Pale.) Very pale and transparent amber 4 ounces, clarified linseed oil and oil of turpentine, of each 1 pint; as before. Amber varnish is suited for all purposes, where a very hard and durable varnish is required. The paler kind is superior to copal varnish, and is often mixed with the latter to increase its hardness and durability.

Black Varnish.—Heat to boiling linseed oil varnish **10** parts, with burnt umber 2 parts, and powdered asphaltum **1** part, and when cooled dilute with spirits of turpentine to the required consistence.

Varnish for Certain Parts of Carriages.—Sandarach

190 parts, pale shellac 95, resin 125, turpentine 190, alcohol at 85 per cent, 1,000 parts, by measure.

Coach Varnish.—Mix shellac 16 parts, white turpentine 3 parts, lampblack sufficient quantity, and digest with alcohol 90 parts, oil of lavender 4 parts.

Mahogany Varnish.—Sorted gum anime 8 pounds, clarified oil 3 gallons, litharge and powdered dried sugar of lead of each ¼ pound; boil till it strings well, then cool a little, thin with oil of turpentine 5½ gallons, and strain.

Varnish for Cabinet Makers.—Pale shellac 750 parts, mastic 64, alcohol (of 90 per cent) 1,000 parts by measure. The solution is made in the cold with the aid of frequent stirring. It is always muddy, and is employed without being filtered. With the same resins and proof spirits a varnish is made for the bookbinders to do over their morocco leather.

Cement Varnish for Water-Tight Luting.—White turpentine 14 parts, shellac 18 parts, resin 6 parts; digest with alcohol 80 parts.

The Varnish of Watin for Gilded Articles.—Gum lac in grain 125 parts, gamboge 125 parts, dragon's blood 125, annotto 125, saffron 32. Each resin must be dissolved in 1,000 parts by measure, of alcohol of 90 per cent; two separate tinctures must be made with the dragon's blood and annotto in 1,000 parts of such alcohol; and a proper proportion of each should be added to the varnish, according to the shade of golden color wanted.

Cheap Oak Varnish.—Clear pale resin 3½ pounds, oil of turpentine 1 gallon; dissolve. It may be colored darker by adding a little fine lampblack.

Varnish for Woodwork.—Powdered gum sandarach 8 parts, gum mastic 2 parts, seed lac 8 parts, and digest in a warm place for some days with alcohol 24 parts, and finally, dilute with sufficient alcohol to the required consistence.

Dark Varnish for Light Woodwork.—Pound up and digest shellac 16 parts, gum sandarach 32 parts, gum mastic (juniper) 8 parts, gum elemi 8 parts, dragon's blood 4 parts, annotto 1 part, with white turpentine 16 parts, and alcohol 256. Dilute with alcohol if required.

Varnish for Instruments.—Digest seed lac 1 part, with alcohol 7 parts, and filter.

Varnish for Wood Toys.—Tender copal, 75 parts; mastic, 12·5; venice turpentine, 6.5; alcohol, of 95 per cent., 100 parts by measure; water ounces, for example, if the other parts be taken in ounces. The alcohol must be first made to act upon the copal, with the aid of a little oil of lavender or camphor, if thought fit; and the solution being passed through a linen cloth, the mastic must be introduced. After it is dissolved, the venice turpentine, previously melted in a water-bath, should be added;

the lower the temperature at which these operations are carried on, the more beautiful will the varnish be. This varnish ought to be very white, very drying, and capable of being smoothed with pumice stone and polished.

Varnishes for Furniture.—The simplest, and perhaps the best, is the solution of shellac only, but many add gums sandarach, mastic, copal, benjamin, etc., from the idea that they contribute to the effect. Gum arabic is certainly never required if the solvent be pure, because it is insoluble in either rectified spirit or rectified wood naphtha, the menstrua employed in dissolving the gums. As spirit is seldom used on account of its expense, most of the following are mentioned as solutions in naphtha, but spirit can be substituted when thought proper. **1.** Shellac 1½ pounds, naphtha 1 gallon; dissolve, and it is ready without filtering. **2.** Shellac 12 ounces, copal 3 ounces (or an equivalent of varnish); dissolve in 1 gallon of naphtha. **3.** Shellac 1½ pounds, seed lac and sandarach each 4 ounces, mastic 2 ounces, rectified spirit 1 gallon; dissolve. **4.** Shellac 2 pounds, benzoin 4 ounces, spirit 1 gallon. **5.** Shellac 10 ounces, seed lac, sandarach, and copal varnish of each, 6 ounces, benzoin 3 ounces, naphtha 1 gallon. To darken polish, benzoin and dragon's blood are used, turmeric and other coloring matters are also added; and to make it lighter it is necessary to use bleached lac, though some endeavor to give this effect by adding oxalic acid to the ingredients, it, like gum arabic, is insoluble in good spirit or naphtha. For all ordinary purposes the first form is best and least troublesome, while its appearance is equal to any other.

Furniture Polishes.—New wood is often French polished. Or the following may be tried: Melt 3 or 4 pieces of sandarach, each the size of a walnut, add 1 pint of boiled oil, and boil together for 1 hour. While cooling add 1 dram of venice turpentine, and if too thick a little oil of turpentine also. Apply this all over the furniture, and after some hours rub it off: rub the furniture daily, without applying fresh varnish, except about once in two months. Water does not injure this polish, and any stain or scratch may be again covered, which cannot be done with French polish.

Furniture Cream.—Beeswax 1 pound, soap 4 ounces, pearlash 2 ounces. soft water 1 gallon; boil together until mixed.

Furniture Oils.—**1.** Acetic acid 2 dram, oil of lavender ¼ dram, rectified spirits 1 dram, linseed oil 4 ounces. **2.** Linseed oil 1 pint, alkanet root 2 ounces; heat, strain and add lac varnish 1 ounce. **3.** Linseed oil 1 pint, rectified spirits 2 ounces, butter of antimony 4 ounces.

Furniture Pastes.—**1.** Beeswax, spirits of turpentine, and linseed oil, equal parts; melt and cool. **2.** Beeswax 4 ounces, turpentine 10 ounces, alkanet root to color; melt and strain. **3.** Beeswax 1 pound, linseed oil 5 ounces, alkanet root ½ ounce; melt, add 5 ounces of turpentine, strain and cool. **4.** Beeswax

4 ounces. resin 1 ounce, oil of turpentine 2 ounces, venetian red to color.

Etching Varnishes.—1. White wax 2 ounces, black and burgundy pitch of each ½ ounce; melt together, add by degrees powdered asphaltum 2 ounces, and boil till a drop taken out on a plate will break when cold by being bent double two or three times between the fingers; it must then be poured into warm water and made into small balls for use. **2.** (Hard Varnish.) Linseed oil and mastic of each 4 ounces; melt together. **3.** (Soft Varnish.) Soft linseed oil 4 ounces, gum benzoin and white wax of each ½ ounce; boil to two-thirds.

Varnish for Engravings, Maps, Etc.—Digest gum sandarach 20 parts, gum mastic 8 parts, camphor 1 part, with alcohol 48 parts. The map or engraving must previously receive one or two coats of gelatine.

Varnish to Fix Engravings or Lithographs on Wood. —For fixing engravings or lithographs upon wood, a varnish called mordant is used in France, which differs from others chiefly in containing more venice turpentine to make it sticky; it consists of sandarach 250 parts, mastic in tears 64, resin 125, venice turpentine 250, alcohol 1,000 parts by measure.

Varnishes for Oil Paintings and Lithographs.—1. Dextrine 2 parts, alcohol 1, water 6 parts. **2.** Varnish for drawings and lithographs: Dextrine 2 parts, alcohol ½ part, water 2 parts. These should be prepared previously with two or three coats of thin starch or rice boiled and strained through a cloth.

Varnish for Oil Paintings.—Digest at a slow heat gum sandarach 2 parts, gum mastic 4 parts, balsam copaiva 2 parts, white turpentine 3 parts, with spirits of turpentine 4 parts, alcohol (95 per cent) 50-56 parts.

Beautiful Varnish for Paintings and Pictures,—Honey 1 pint, the whites of 24 fresh eggs, 1 ounce of good clean isinglass, 20 grains of hydrate of potassium. ⅓ ounce of chloride of sodium; mix together over a gentle heat of 80 or 90 degrees Fahr.; be careful not to let the mixture remain long enough to coagulate the albumen of the eggs; stir the mixture thoroughly and then bottle. It is to be applied as follows: One tablespoonful of the varnish added to ½ tablespoonful of good oil of turpentine; then spread on the picture as soon as mixed.

Milk of Wax.—Milk of wax is a valuable varnish, which may be prepared as follows: Melt in a porcelain capsule a certain quantity of white wax, and add to it while in fusion, an equal quantity of spirits of wine, of specific gravity 0.830; stir the mixture and pour it upon a large porphyry slab. The granular mass is to be converted into a paste by the muller, with the addition, from time to time, of a little alcohol; and as soon as it appears to be smooth and homogeneous, water is to be introduced in small quantities successively, to the amount of four times the weight of the wax. This emulsion is to be then passed through canvas in order to separate such particles as may be imperfectly incorporated. The milk of wax, thus prepared, may be spread with a smooth brush upon the surface of a painting, allowed to dry, and then fused by passing a hot iron (salamander) over its surface. When cold, it is to be rubbed with a linen cloth to bring out the lustre. It is to the unchangeable quality of an encaustic of this nature, that the ancient paintings upon the walls of Herculaneum and Pompeii owe their freshness at the present day.

Crystal Varnishes.—1. Genuine pale Canada balsam and rectified oil of turpentine. equal parts; mix, place the bottle in warm water, agitate well, set it aside, in a moderately warm place, and in a week pour off the clear. Used for maps, prints, drawings, and other articles of paper, and also to prepare tracing paper, and to transfer engravings. **2.** Mastic 3 ounces, alcohol 1 pint; dissolve. Used to fix pencil drawings.

Italian Varnishes. —1. Boil scio turpentine till brittle, powder, and dissolve in oil of turpentine. **2.** Canada balsam and clear white resin, of each 6 ounces. oil of turpentine, 1 quart; dissolve. Used for prints, etc.

Water Varnish for Oil Paintings. — Boil bitter-apple, freed from the seeds and cut 5 parts, with rain water 50 parts, down to one-half. Strain and dissolve in the liquor gum arabic 8 parts, and rock-candy 4 parts, and lastly, add 1 part of alcohol. Let it stand for some days, and filter.

Varnish for Paper-Hangings.—Sandarach, 4 parts, mastic, seed lac, white turpentine, of each 2 parts, gum elemi, 1 part, alcohol 28 parts. Digest with frequent shaking, and filter. Before applying this varnish, the paper must be twice painted over with a solution of white gelatine, and dried.

Bookbinders' Varnish.—Shellac 8 parts. gum benzoin 3 parts, gum mastic 2 parts, bruise, and digest in alcohol 48 parts, oil of lavender ½ part. Or, digest shellac 4 parts. gum mastic 2 parts. gum dammar and white turpentine of each 1 part, with alcohol (95 per cent) 28 parts.

To Varnish Cardwork.—Before varnishing cardwork, it must receive 2 or 3 coats of size, to prevent the absorption of the varnish, and any injury to the design. The size may be made by dissolving a little isinglass in hot water. or by boiling some parchment cuttings until dissolved. In either case the solution must be strained through a piece of clean muslin, and for very nice purposes, should be clarified with a little white of egg. A small clean brush, called by painters a sash tool. is the best for applying the size, as well as the varnish. A light delicate touch must be adopted, especially for the first coat, lest the ink or colors be started, or smothered.

Size, or Varnish, for Printers, etc.—Best pale glue and white curd soap, of each 4 ounces, hot water 3 pints; dissolve, then add powdered alum 2 ounces. Used to size prints and pictures before coloring them.

Varnish for Brick Walls.—A varnish made with 1 pound of sulphur boiled for half an hour in an iron vessel is a perfect protection from damp to brick walls. It should be applied with a brush, while warm.

Mastic Varnishes.—1. (Fine). Very pale and picked gum mastic 5 pounds, glass pounded as small as barley, and well washed and dried. 2½ pounds, rectified turpentine 2 gallons; put them into a clean 4-gallon stone or tin bottle, bung down securely, and keep rolling it backwards and forwards pretty smartly on a counter or any other solid place for at least 4 hours; when, if the gum is all dissolved, the varnish may be decanted, strained through muslin into another bottle, and allowed to settle. It should be kept for 6 or 9 months before use, as it thereby gets both tougher and clearer. **2.** (Second Quality). Mastic 8 pounds. turpentine 4 gallons; dissolve by a gentle heat, and add pale turpentine varnish ½ gallon. **3.** Gum mastic 6 ounces, oil of turpentine 1 quart; dissolve. Mastic varnish is used for pictures, etc.; when good, it is tough, hard, brilliant and colorless. Should it get "chilled," 1 pound of well-washed silicious sand should be made moderately hot, and added to each gallon, which must then be well agitated for 5 minutes, and afterwards allowed to settle.

India Rubber Varnishes.—1. Cut up 1 pound of India rubber into small pieces and diffuse in ½ pound sulphuric ether, which is done by digesting in a glass flask on a sand bath. Then add 1 pound pale linseed oil varnish, previously heated, and after settling, 1 pound of oil of turpentine, also heated beforehand. Filter, while yet warm, into bottles. Dries slowly. **2.** Two ounces India rubber finely divided and digested in the same way, with a ¼ pound camphene, and ½ ounce naphtha or benzole. When dissolved add 1 ounce of copal varnish, which renders it more durable. Principally for gilding. **3.** In a wide-mouthed glass bottle. digest 2 ounces of India rubber in fine shavings, with 1 pound of oil of turpentine, during 2 days, without shaking, then stir up with a wooden spatula. Add another pound of oil of turpentine, and digest, with frequent agitation, until all is dissolved. Then mix 1½ pounds of this solution with 2 pounds of very white copal-oil varnish, and 1½ pounds of well boiled linseed oil, shake and digest in a sand bath, until they have united into a good varnish. For morocco leather. **4.** Four ounces India rubber in fine shavings are dissolved in a covered jar by means of a sand bath, in 2 pounds of crude benzole. and then mixed with 4 pounds of hot linseed oil varnish, and ½ pound oil of turpentine. Dries very well.

Flexible Varnish.—Melt 1 pound of resin, and add gradually ½ pound India rubber in very fine shavings, and stir until cold. Then heat again, slowly, add 1 pound of linseed oil varnish, heated, and filter.

Another Method.—1. Dissolve 1 pound of gum dammar, and ½ pound India rubber, in very small pieces, in 1 pound of oil of turpentine, by means of a water bath. Add 1 pound of hot oil varnish and filter. **2.** India rubber in small pieces, washed and dried, are fused for 3 hours in a close vessel, on a gradually heated sand bath. On removing from the sand bath, open the vessel and stir for 10 minutes, then close again, and repeat the fusion on the following day, until small globules appear on the surface. Strain through a wire sieve.

Varnish for Waterproof Goods. — Let ¼ pound India rubber, in small pieces, soften in ½ pound oil of turpentine, then add 2 pounds of boiled oil, and let the whole boil for 2 hours over a slow coal fire. When dissolved, add again 6 pounds of boiled linseed oil and 1 pound of litharge, and boil until an even liquid is obtained. It is applied warm.

Gutta Percha Varnish.—Clean ¼ pound gutta percha in warm water from adhering impurities, dry well, dissolve in 1 pound of rectified resin oil, and add 2 pounds of linseed oil varnish, boiling hot. Very suitable to prevent metals from oxidation.

Black Varnish for Harness. — Digest shellac 12 parts, white turpentine 5 parts, gum sandarach 2 parts, lampblack 1 part, with spirits of turpentine 4 parts, alcohol 96 parts.

Boiled Oil or Linseed Oil Varnish.—Boil linseed oil 60 parts, with litharge 2 parts, and white vitriol 1 part, each finely powdered, until all water is evaporated. Then set by. Or, rub up borate of manganese 4 parts, with some of the oil, then add linseed oil 3,000 parts, and heat to boiling.

Dammar Varnish.—Gum dammar 10 parts, gum sandarach 5 parts, gum mastic 1 part, digest at a low heat, occasionally shaking, with spirits of turpentine 20 parts. Finally add more spirits of turpentine to give the consistence of syrup.

Common Varnish.—Digest shellac 1 part, with alcohol 7 or 8 parts.

Waterproof Varnishes. — Take 1 pound of flowers of sulphur and 1 gallon of linseed oil, and boil them together until they are thoroughly combined. This forms a good varnish for waterproof textile fabrics. Another is made with 4 pounds oxide of lead, 2 pounds of lampblack, 5 ounces of sulphur, and 10 pounds of India rubber dissolved in turpentine. These substances, in such proportions, are boiled together until they are thoroughly combined. Coloring matters may be mixed with them. Twilled cotton may be rendered waterproof by the application of the oil sulphur varnish. It should be applied at 2 or 3 different times, and dried after each operation.

Varnishes for Balloons, Gas Bags, etc.—1. India rubber in shavings 1 ounce, mineral naphtha 2 pounds; digest at a gentle heat in a close vessel till dissolved, and strain. **2.** Digest 1 pound of India rubber, cut small, in 6 pounds oil of turpentine for 7 days, in a warm place. Put the mixture in a warm bath, heat until thoroughly mixed, add 1 gallon of warm boiled drying oil, mix, and strain when cold. **3.** Linseed oil 1 gallon, dried white copperas and sugar of lead, each 3 ounces, litharge 8 ounces, boil with constant agitation till it strings well, then cool slowly and decant the clear. If too thick, thin it with quicker drying linseed oil.

Gold Varnish.—Digest shellac 16 parts, gum sandarach, mastic, of each 3 parts, crocus 1 part, gum gamboge 2 parts. all bruised, with alcohol 144 parts. Or, digest seed lac, sandarach, mastic, of each 8 parts, gamboge 2 parts, dragon's blood 1 part, white turpentine 6 parts, turmeric 4 parts, bruised, with alcohol 120 parts.

Wainscot Varnish for House Painting and Japanning.—Anime 8 pounds, clarified linseed oil 3 gallons, litharge ¼ pound, acetate of lead ½ pound, sulphate of copper ¼ pound. All these materials must be carefully but thoroughly boiled together until the mixture becomes quite stringy, and then 5½ gallons of heated turpentine stirred in. It can be easily deepened in color by the addition of a little gold-size.

HOW TO MAKE COLORED VARNISHES.

Transparent Green.—To make the transparent green varnish, heat a quantity of copal varnish, and put into it, small quantities at a time, powdered verdigris (crystallized), until the liquid possesses the properties desired.

Blue Color.—Could indigo be incorporated with copal varnish, and communicate its color to it, persons would not be obliged to prepare this color from a substance which alters its limpidity. Prussian blue serves as the basis of this color. The best Prussian blue of the shops communicates to varnish a very transparent blue color; but it has not that richness of reflection and velvety appearance so agreeable to the eye when the extension of which it is capable without being weakened, has been given to it. When extended over a metallic plate, there are sometimes grains observed in it, which may be owing to its incomplete division, or to the separation of some earthy matter, which even the best Prussian blue of the shops usually contains. The blue when in a state of purity unites so completely with copal varnish that its transparency does not seem to be in the least affected by it.

Yellow.—Turmeric root and gamboge give very beautiful yellows, and readily communicate their color to copal varnish made with turpentine. Aloes gives a varied and orange tint.

Dark Red.—Dragon's blood, digested in warm varnish, gives reds, the intensity of which depends upon the quantity of the coloring resin which combines with varnish. The artist, therefore, has it in his power to vary the tones at pleasure.

Though cochineal, in a state of division, gives very little color to oil of turpentine in comparison to that which it communicates to water, carmine may be introduced into the composition of varnish, colored by dragon's blood. The result will be a purple red.

Violet. — A mixture of carminated varnish and dragon's blood, added to that colored by Prussian blue, produces violet. From these examples of the communication of colors to copal varnish, every person habituated to the operations of this art, and every amateur possessed of dexterity may readily prepare any color he desires.

Gold-colored Varnish for Wood or Metal. — Take 2 ounces of gum sandarac, 1 ounce of litharge of gold, 4 ounces of clarified linseed oil; boil them in a glazed earthen vessel till they appear of a transparent yellow, on a gas cooking-stove.

Gold Varnish for Wood or Metal.—One ounce of litharge of gold, 2 ounces of gum sandarach, 4 ounces of clarified linseed oil. Boil them together in a glazed earthen vessel to a transparent yellow; to be used with a soft brush.

Bright Varnish Green, for Inside Blinds, Fenders, etc.—The work must first be painted once over with a light lead color, and when dry, grind some white lead in spirits of turpentine; afterwards take about one-third in bulk of verdigris, which has been ground stiff in linseed oil; then mix them both together, and put into it a little resin varnish, sufficient only to bind the color. When this is hard, which will be the case in 15 minutes, pour into the color some resin varnish to give it a good gloss. Then go over the work a second time, and, if required, a third time. Thus you will have a cheap and beautiful green with a high polish. It possesses a very drying quality, as the work may be completed in a few hours. The tint may be varied according to taste, by substituting mineral green for verdigris; and if a bright grass-green is required, add a little Dutch pink to the mixture. This color must be used when quite warm, to give the varnish an uniform extension.

THE FARRIER.

Each and every recipe in this Department has been tested by the most eminent veterinary surgeons in the United States, and pronounced by them as the best.

Arabian Horse Tamer's Secret.—Take oil of cummin, oil of rhodium, and horse castor. Keep separate in air-tight bottles. Rub a little of the oil of cummin on your hand and approach the horse on the windward side, so that he can smell the cummin. The horse will then let you come up to him without trouble. Rub your hand gently on the horse's nose, getting a little oil on it. He will then follow you. Give him a little of the castor on a piece of loaf sugar or apple; get a few drops of the rhodium on his tongue, and he is your servant. He will follow you like a pet dog.

Best Condition Powders.—Fenugreek, cream of tartar, gentian, sulphur, saltpeter, resin, black antimony, and ginger, each 2 ounces, cayenne pepper 1 ounce. Pulverize and mix thoroughly. Dose, 2 teaspoonfuls once a day in feed.

Brittle and Contracted Hoofs.—Take castor oil, barbadoes tar, and soft soap, equal parts of each. Melt all together and stir while cooling, and apply a little to the hoof 3 or 4 times a week.

Bone Spavin.—Dog's lard ½ pint, best oil organum, 1½ ounces, oil cajeput, 2 ounces, pulverized cantharides, ½ ounce. Mix, and apply each morning for 4 mornings, heating it in with hot iron each time, then discontinue its use for 3 days, after which use as before for 5 mornings. Wait about 8 or 10 days, and if not gone repeat as before.

Bots.—Take new milk 2 quarts, syrup 1 quart. Mix and give the whole, and in 15 or 20 minutes after give 2 quarts of warm, strong sage tea; half an hour after the tea give 1 quart of raw linseed oil, or, if the oil can not be had, give lard instead.

Colic.—Gum camphor 1 ounce, cayenne 1 ounce, gum myrrh 1 ounce, powdered gum quaial 1 ounce, sassafras bark 1 ounce, spirits of turpentine 1 ounce, oil of organum ¼ ounce, oil of hemlock ½ ounce, pulverized opium ½ ounce, good alcohol 2 quarts. Mix, and let stand 10 or 12 days and filter. Dose, from 1 to 4 teaspoonfuls in a pint of milk. Keep this on hand. It is the best colic cure known.

Cure for Sweeney.—Alcohol and spirits of turpentine each 8 ounces; camphor gum, pulverized cantharides and capsicum, each 1 ounce; oil of spike 3 ounces. Mix; bathe with hot iron.

Cuts, Wounds and Sores.—Take of lard 4 ounces, beeswax 4 ounces, resin 2 ounces, carbolic acid ¼ ounce; mix the first three and melt; add carbolic acid, stirring until cool. This is excellent for man as well as beast.

Cure for Scratches.—Sweet oil 3 ounces, borax 1 ounce, sugar of lead 1 ounce. Mix and apply twice daily after washing thoroughly with castile soap, giving time for legs to dry.

Contracted Hoof and Sore Feet.—Take equal parts of soft fat, yellow wax, linseed oil, venice turpentine and Norway tar. First melt the wax, then add the others, mixing thoroughly. Apply to the edge of the hair once a day.

Cracked Heels.—Tar 8 ounces, beeswax 1 ounce, resin 1 ounce, alum 1 ounce, tallow 1 ounce, sulphate of iron 1 ounce, carbolic acid 1 dram. Mix, and boil over a slow fire. Skim off the filth and add 2 ounces of the scrapings of sweet elder.

Condition Powder.—Take crude antimony 1 ounce, ground lobelia 1 ounce, ginger 2 ounces, sulphur flour 3 ounces, ground berberry 1 ounce, cream of tartar 4 ounces, saltpeter flour 4 ounces; well mixed. Dose. 1 tablespoonful each day in wet feed. Best in the market; will sell well.

Diuretics.—Take balsam copaiba 2 ounces, sweet spirits of nitre 3 ounces, spirits of turpentine 2 ounces, oil of juniper 2 ounces, tincture of camphor 2 ounces. Mix; shake the bottle before pouring the medicine. Dose for adult horse, 2 tablespoonfuls in a pint of milk, repeated every 4 or 6 hours, if necessary. This is a reliable preparation for kidney difficulties.

Eye Water.—White vitriol and pure saltpeter of each 1 scruple, pure soft water 8 ounces; mix. This should be applied to to the inflamed lids three or four times a day, and if the inflammation does not lessen in one or two days it may be injected directly into the eye. The writer has used this for his own eyes, reduced ½ with water, and dropped directly into the eye, which would cause the eye to smart considerably for about five minutes, when he should bathe the eye in cold water for a few minutes, and by repeating this three or four times a day it has given the best of satisfaction. It does nicely, many times, to just close the eye and bathe the outside freely.

Farcy.—Nitrate of potash 4 ounces, black antimony 2 ounces, sulphite of soda, 1 ounce. elecampane 2 ounces; mix. Dose, 1 tablespoonful once or twice a day.

Farcy and Glanders.—Iodide of potassium, 1¼ drams, copperas ½ dram, ginger 1 dram, gentian 2 drams, powdered gum arabic and syrup to form a ball; or take ½ ounce sulphite soda, 5 grains powdered cantharides. Mix, and give at night in cut feed for several weeks; give at the same time every morning and noon 3 drams powdered gentian, 2 drams powdered blue vitriol; give the medicines for a long time; feed well. This is the best treatment that can be given for this disease.

Founder.—Vinegar 3 pints, capsicum ½ dram, tincture of aconite root 15 drops. Mix and boil down to 1 quart; when cool, give it as a drench. Blanket the horse well; after the horse has perspired for an hour or more, give 1 quart of raw linseed oil. This treatment will be found good for horses foundered by eating too much grain.

Great Arabian Heave Remedy.—Give your horse a teaspoonful of lobelia once a day for a week, and then once a week, and you will hardly know he ever had the heaves. Try it.

Jockey Tricks.—How to make a horse appear as though he was badly foundered: Take a fine wire and fasten it tightly around the fetlock, between the foot and the heel, and smoothe the hair over it. In 20 minutes the horse will show lameness. Do not leave it on over 9 hours. To make a horse lame: Take a single hair from its tail. put it through the eye of a needle, then lift the front leg and press the skin between the outer and middle tendon or cord, and shove the needle through, cut off the hair each side and let down the foot. The horse will go lame in 20 minutes. How to make a horse stand by his food and not take it: Grease the front teeth and the roof of the mouth with common beef tallow, and he will not eat until you wash it out. This in conjunction with the above will consummate a complete founder. How to cure a horse from the crib or sucking wind: Saw between the upper teeth to the gums. How to put a young countenance on a horse: Make a small incision in the sunken place over the eye, insert the point of a goose-quill and blow it up; close the external wound with a thread, and it is done. To cover up the heaves: Drench the horse with ¼ pound of common bird-shot, and he will not heave until they pass through him. To make a horse appear as if he had the glanders: Melt 4 ounces fresh butter and pour into his ear. To distinguish between glanders and distemper: The discharge from the nose in glanders will sink in water; in distemper it floats. How to make a true pulling horse balk: Take tincture of cantharides 1 ounce, and corrosive sublimate 1 dram; mix and bathe his shoulder at night. How to serve a horse that is lame: Make a small incision about half way from the knee to the joint on the outside of the leg, and at the back part of the shin bone you will find a small, white tendon or cord; cut it off and close the external wound with a stitch, and he will walk off on the hardest pavement and not limp a particle.

Liniment to Kill Pain.—One gallon alcohol, 1 ounce tincture cayenne, 2 ounces tincture gum camphor, 2 ounces tincture ammonia, ½ ounce chloroform. Mix well and let stand twelve hours.

Liniment, Wolf's.—One quart alcohol, 2 ounces tincture arnica, 1 ounce oil hemlock, 1 ounce oil of spike. Mix well, and let stand 24 hours. This will cure any burn, scald, bruise, sprain, or any like ailment, also aches and pains of all kinds. Apply by wetting a flannel cloth and wrapping it around the diseased parts.

Mange.—Oil tar, 1 ounce, lac sulphur 1½ ounces, whale oil 2 ounces. Mix. Rub a little on the skin wherever the disease appears, and continue daily for a week, then wash off with castile soap and warm water.

Poll-Evil.—1. Rock salt 1 ounce, blue vitriol 1 ounce, copperas ½ ounce. Pulverize and mix well. Fill a goose-quill with the powder and push to the bottom of the pipe. Have a stick at the top of the quill and push the powder out of the quill, leaving it at the bottom of the pipe. Repeat in 4 days, and in 2 or 3 days you can remove the pipe without any trouble. **2.** (Poll-Evil and Fistula). Tincture of opium 1 dram, potash 2 drams, water 1 ounce; mix, and when dissolved inject into the pipes with a small syringe, having cleansed the sore with soapsuds; repeat every 2 days until pipes are completely destroyed.

Spavin and Ringbone.—Cantharides 1 ounce, mercurial ointment ½ ounce, corrosive sublimate ½ dram, turpentine 1½ ounces, tincture iodine 1 ounce, gum euphorbium 4 ounces. Mix well with 1 pound of lard. For spavin or ringbone, cut the hair away and grease the part well with the ointment, rubbing it in well. In 2 days grease the parts with lard; wash it off in 2 days more, and again apply the ointment. So continue until a cure is effected, which will be in a short time. For bog spavin, wind gall, curb, or splint, apply the ointment every 6 days.

Wounds and Cuts.—Take 4 ounces lard, beeswax 4 ounces, resin 3 ounces, vaseline 4 to 6 ounces. Melt these together, and add carbolic acid ½ ounce. This is excellent.

OX, SHOWING THE MODE OF CUTTING UP THE VARIOUS JOINTS.

HIND-QUARTER.	FORE-QUARTER.
1. Sirloin.	10. Fore rib (5 ribs).
2. Rump.	11. Middle rib (4 ribs).
3. Aitchbone.	12. Chuck rib (3 ribs).
4. Buttock.	13. Leg of mutton piece.
5. Mouse-round.	14. Brisket
6. Veiny piece.	15. Clod.
7. Thick flank.	16. Neck.
8. Thin flank.	17. Shank.
9. Leg.	18. Cheek.

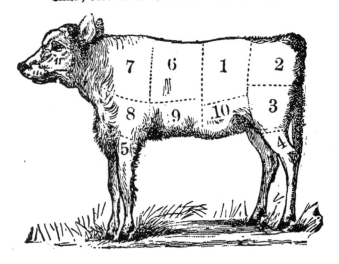

HIND-QUARTER.

1. Loin.
2. Chump end of loin.
3. Fillet.
4. Hind Knuckle.
10. Flank.

FORE-QUARTER.

5. Fore Knuckle.
6. Shoulder.
7. Neck, best end.
8. Bladebone.
9. Breast.

HIND-QUARTER.

1. Leg.
2. Loin.
3. Chump end of loin.

FORE-QUARTER.

4. Shoulder piece.
5. Scrag end of neck.
6 and 8. Shoulder and blade bone.
7. Breast.

PIG, SHOWING THE MODE OF CUTTING UP VARIOUS JOINTS.

FORE-QUARTER.	HIND-QUARTER.

FORE-QUARTER.

1. Neck piece.
2. Shoulder.
4. Fore-loin.

HIND-QUARTER.

3. Spring, or belly.
5. Loin.
6. Ham.

DEPARTMENT VI.

THE FARM AND DAIRY.

Axle Grease, To Make.—1. One pound tallow, ¼ pound castor oil, ¼ pound blacklead; melt the tallow and rub the whole together until cold and well mixed. **2.** Water 2 gallons. soda 1 pound, palm oil 20 pounds; mix well by heat. and stir until nearly cold. Just enough grease should be applied to the spindle of a wagon to give it a light coating. **3.** Tallow 8 pounds, palm oil 10 pounds, plumbago 1 pound.

NOTE.—To tighten tires to wheels, see same in last department. For Blackings and Enamels for harness, or the leather parts of buggies, etc., see "Leather."

Bins and Piles, To Measure.—So ascertain the number of bushels in a bin of any dimensions find the number of cubic feet by multiplying the three dimensions of the bin in feet, deduct 1·5 and the result will be the number of bushels. To find the cubic contents of a pile in the usual form of a cone, find the area of the base by the old arithmetical rule of multiplying the square of its diameter in feet by .7854, and this product multiplied by ⅓ the height of the cone will give the cubic feet.

Clearing Ground of Stones.—1. Heat the stone to a high degree by means of a fierce fire applied to one part of it only, which will cause it to expand; then pour water upon it to make it crack, the effect being increased by blows from a heavy sledge hammer. **2.** Pierce the stone in the direction of its veins and introduce into the hole a cleft cylinder of iron, then drive a wedge in between the two halves of the cylinder. **3.** A quantity of water placed in a hole made in a stone to a certain depth, and then stopped up, will during the winter season expand while freezing and break the strongest stone.

Clearing Stumps by Blasting.—Punch a hole in the stump with a crowbar, then insert a cartridge of giant powder 10 inches long by 1½ inches in diameter; pour in water around the cartridge and touch off the fuse. It will blow the stump into fragments.

Draining.—Tile draining, or by the means of pipes made of tiling. is by far the best method for drying wet land, although

287

the open ditch method is better than nothing. The following table gives the exact number of tiles required to the acre;

Distance Apart.	12-Inch Tiles.	13-Inch Tiles.	14-Inch Tiles.	15-Inch Tiles.
Drains 12 feet apart require..	3,630	3,351	3,111	2,934
Drains 15 feet apart require..	2,904	2,681	2,489	2,313
Drains 18 feet apart require..	2.420	3,234	2.074	1,936
Drains 21 feet apart require..	2,074	1,914	1,677	1,679
Drains 24 feet apart require..	1,815	1,065	1,556	1,452
Drains 27 feet apart require..	1,613	1,480	1,386	1,291
Drains 30 feet apart require..	1,452	1,340	1,245	1,162
Drains 33 feet apart require..	1,320	1,218	1,131	1,056
Drains 36 feet apart require..	1,210	1,117	1,037	968

Fertilizers, Artificial.—1. Sulphate of ammonia, common salt and oil of vitriol, of each 10 parts, chloride of potassium 15 parts, gypsum and sulphate of potassa, of each 17 parts, saltpeter 20 parts, crude epsom salts 25 parts, sulphate of soda 33 parts; for clover. **2.** Dry peat or marl 20 bushels, unbleached ashes 3 bushels, fine bone dust 3 bushels, calcined plaster 3 bush., nitrate of soda 40 pounds, sulphate of ammonia 33 pounds, sulphate of soda 40 pounds; mix the peat, ashes and bone dust, then mix the nitrate and sulphate of soda and the ammonia in 5 buckets of water; when dissolved add this to the first mixture; then add the calcined plaster and mix all thoroughly.

The following quantities of various fertilizers should be used to the acre: Barnyard manure 15 to 20 tons, bone dust 16 to 20 bushels, fresh fish 25 to 40 bushels (400 to 600 pounds), guano 300 to 800 pounds, night soil 20 bushels, tanner's refuse 500 to 800 pounds, wood ashes 20 to 40 bushels.

Fertilizers from Carcasses.—For a large animal draw 4 or 5 wagon loads of muck, sod or mold; roll the carcass on to this; sprinkle freely with quick lime—10 or 12 wagon loads will not be too much. In less than a year several wagon loads of excellent fertilizer will be made. Muck is the richness of upland soil washed by the rain down to the lowlands, where it accumulates.

Hay, To Measure.—Weighing is the only accurate method of measuring hay. As this is not always convenient, we give the following methods of approximating the amount in meadows, mows or stacks: About 25 cubic yards of average meadow hay in windrows makes a ton; 15 to 18 cubic yards make a ton when well settled in mows or stacks; 20 to 25 cubic yards make a ton when it is loaded on wagons from mows or stacks; 25 cubic yards of dry clover make a ton. **1.** The number of tons of meadow hay raked into windrows may be found as follows; Multiply the length, width and height of the windrow in yards, and divide by 25. **2.** To find the number of tons in a mow multiply the length, width and height in yards and divide the product by 15. **3.** To find the number of tons of hay in old stacks find the area in square yards of the base by the table of areas of circles given in this department; then multiply the area of the base by ½ the altitude of the stack in yards, and divide by 15. **4.** To ascertain the value of a given number of pounds of hay at a given price per ton of 2,000 pounds, multiply the number of pounds of hay, or any other article which is bought or sold by the ton, by one-half the price per ton, pointing off three figures from the right hand. The principle is the same as in interest; dividing the price by 2 gives the price of one-half ton, and pointing of three figures to the right is dividing by 1,000.

A truss of new hay is 60 pounds; old, 56 pounds; straw, 40 pounds; a load of hay is 36 trusses; a bale of hay is 300 pounds.

Parts of 1 acre.	Square feet.	Feet square.	Parts of 1 acre.	Square feet.	Feet square.
1-16	2,722½	52½	½	21,780	147½
⅛	5,445	73¾	1	43,560	208¼
¼	10,890	104½	2	87,120	295¼
⅓	14,520	120½			

Plants or Trees in Acre.

Distance Apart.	No.	Distance Apart.	No.
3 inches by 3 inches....	696,960	6½ feet by 6½ feet......	1,031
4 inches by 4 inches....	392,040	7 feet by 7 feet........	881
6 inches by 6 inches....	174,240	8 feet by 8 feet........	680
9 inches by 9 inches....	77,440	9 feet by 9 feet........	537
1 foot by 1 foot.........	43,560	10 feet by 10 feet.......	435
1½ feet by 1½ feet......	19,360	11 feet by 11 feet.......	360
2 feet by 1 foot.....	21,780	12 feet by 12 feet.......	302
2 feet by 2 feet......	10,890	13 feet by 13 feet.......	257
2½ feet by 2½ feet.....	6,960	14 feet by 14 feet.......	221
3 feet by 1 foot.....	14,520	15 feet by 15 feet........	193
3 feet by 2 feet......	7,260	16 feet by 16 feet........	170
3 feet by 3 feet......	4,840	17 feet by 17 feet........	150
3½ feet by 3½ feet......	3,555	18 feet by 18 feet........	134
4 feet by 1 foot.....	10,890	19 feet by 19 feet........	120
4 feet by 2 feet......	5,445	20 feet by 20 feet........	108
4 feet by 3 feet......	3,630	25 feet by 25 feet........	69
4 feet by 4 feet......	2,722	30 feet by 30 feet........	48
4½ feet by 4½ feet......	2,151	40 feet by 40 feet........	27
5 feet by 5 feet......	1,742	50 feet by 50 feet........	17
6 feet by 6 feet......	1,210		

Quantity of Seed Required for a Given Space.

Asparagus—One ounce produces 1,000 plants, and requires a bed 12 feet square.

Asparagus Roots—One thousand plants require a bed 4 feet wide and 225 feet long.

English Dwarf Beans—One quart plants 100 to 150 feet of row.

French Dwarf Beans—One quart plants 250 to 350 feet of row.

Beans, Pale, Large—One quart plants 100 hills.

Beans, Pale, Small—One quart plants 300 hills or 250 feet of row.

Beets—Ten pounds to 1 acre; 1 ounce plants 150 feet of row.

Cabbage—One ounce plants 2,500 plants, and requires 40 square feet of ground.

Cauliflower—The same as cabbage.

Carrots—One ounce to 150 feet of row.

Celery—One ounce gives 7,000 plants and requires 8 square feet of ground.

Cucumber—One ounce plants 150 hills.

Cress—One ounce sows a bed 16 feet square.

Egg Plant—One ounce gives 2,000 plants.

Leek—One ounce gives 2,000 plants; requires 60 feet of ground.

Lettuce—One ounce gives 7,000 plants; requires a bed of 120 feet.

Melon—One ounce plants 120 hills.

Onion—One ounce sows 200 feet of row.

Okra—One ounce sows 200 feet of row.

Parsley—One ounce sows 200 feet of row.

Parsnip—One ounce sows 250 feet of row.

Peppers—One ounce gives 2,500 plants.

Peas—One quart sows 120 feet of row.

Pumpkin—One ounce plants 50 hills.

Radish—One ounce sows 100 feet.

Salsify—One ounce sows 150 feet of row.

Spinach—One ounce sows 200 feet of row

Squash—One ounce plants 75 htlls.

Tomato—One ounce gives 2,200 plants; requires a bed of 80 feet.

Turnip—One ounce sows 2,000 feet.

Watermelon—One ounce plants 50 hills.

Quantity of Seed to the Acre.

Wheat	1¼ to 2 bush	Potatoes	5 to 10 bush
Barley	1½ to 2½ "	Timothy	12 to 24 qts
Oats	2 to 4 "	Mustard	8 to 20 "
Rye	1 to 2 "	Herd's Grass	12 to 16 "
Buckwheat	¾ to 1⅓ "	Flat Turnip	2 to 3 lbs
Millet	1 to 1½ "	Red Clover	10 to 16 "
Corn	¼ to 1 "	White Clover	3 to 4 "
Beans	1 to 2 "	Blue Grass	10 to 15 "
Peas	2½ to 3½ "	Orchard Grass	20 to 30 "
Hemp	1 to 1½ "	Carrots	4 to 5 "
Flax	1 to 1½ "	Parsnips	6 to 8 "
Rice	2 to 2½ "	Onions	4 to 5 "
Broom Corn	1 to 1½ "	Beets	5 to 6 "

WEATHER INDICATIONS.

Changes in Weather, How to Foretell.—Rain invariably follows when cattle sniff the air and herd together in a corner of the field with their heads to leeward, or take shelter in the sheds; when sheep leave the pasture unwillingly; when dogs lie about the fireside more than usual and appear drowsy; when cats turn their backs to the fire and wash their faces; when pigs cover themselves more than usual in litter: when cocks crow at unusual hours and flap their wings much; when hens chant; when ducks and geese are unusually noisy; when pigeons wash themselves; when peacocks squall loudly from trees; when the guinea fowl makes a continuous grating clamor; when sparrows chirp loudly and with much fuss congregate on the ground or elsewhere; when swallows fly low and skim their wings on account of the flies upon which they feed having descended toward the ground; when the carrion crow croaks solitarily; when wild water fowl dip and wash unusually; when moles throw up hills more industriously; when toads creep out in numbers; when frogs croak; when bats squeak and enter houses; when singing birds take shelter; when the robin approaches nearest the house; when tame swans fly against the wind; when bees leave their hives with caution and fly short distances; when ants carry their eggs busily; when flies bite severely and become troublesome in numbers; and when earth worms appear on the surface.

Chemical Barometer.—Put a small quantity of finely pulverized alum in a long ½-ounce vial and fill it with alcohol. When the atmosphere is dry and clear the spirits will be clear as crystal, but on the approach of rain or bad weather the alum will rise in the center in the form of a spiral cloud. This is a sure indication.

Catgut and Straw.—A simple hydrometer can be made of a piece of catgut and a straw. The catgut is twisted and put through a hole in a dial, in which a straw is also placed. In dry weather the catgut curls up; in damp it relaxes; and so the straw is turned either to one side or the other.

Color of Sky.—An intensely blue and serene sky indicates severe storms and heavy rains in from 12 to 48 hours. A gray, hazy sky indicates continuous dry, and usually hot weather. A bright sunset presages fair weather. A bright yellow in the evening indicates wind: a pale yellow, rain. A natural gray color constitutes a favorable sign in the evening; an unfavorable one in the morning.

Lunations of the Moon.—The following table, etc., is the result of many years' observation, and will seldom prove unavailing: **1.** The nearer the time of the moon's changes, first quarter, full. or last quarter, are to midnight, the fairer will the weather be the seven days following. The space for this calculation occupies from 10 p. m. to 2 a. m. **2.** The nearer to midday or noon the changes occur the more foul will the weather be during the seven days following. The space for this calculation occupies from 10 a. m. to 2 p. m. These observations refer principally to summer, though they affect spring and autumn in nearly the same ratio. Table is as follows:

Moon	Time of Change.	Summer.	In Winter.
If the new moon, the first quarter, full moon, or last quarter, happens	Between midnight and 2 a. m...	Fair.	Hard frost unless wind be S. or W.
	Between 2 and 4 a. m.	Cold, with frequent showers·	Snowy and stormy.
	Between 4 and 6 a. m.	Rain.	Rain.
	Between 6 and 8 a. m...............	Wind and Rain.	Stormy.
	Between 8 and 10 a. m.	Changeable	Cold rain if wind be W.; snow if E.
	Between 10 and 12 a. m.	Frequent showers.	Cold and high wind.
	At 12 o'clock noon and 2 p m........	Very rainy.	Snow or rain.
	Between 2 and 4 p. m.	Changeable.	Fair and mild.
	Between 4 and 6 p. m.	Fair.	Fair.
	Between 6 and 8 p. m.	Fair if wind is N.W. Rain if S. or S.W.	Fair and frosty if wind is N. or N.E. Rain or snow if S. or S. W.
	Between 8 and 10 p. m.	Rainy if wind is S. or S. W.	Rain or snow if the wind be S. or S.W.
	Between 10 p.m.and midnight.........	Fair.	Fair and frosty.

Smoke.—Dense smoke or haze in the early morning portend falling weather. If the smoke rises the weather will be clear; if it falls the weather will be rainy.

Wind.—Wind veering from north or west to south or southeast precedes falling weather. If the wind is in the southwest and rain sets in, the rain will be of short duration and light yield. As a rule if the wind touches northeast or east for two or three days it is a sure sign of rain. An immediate cessation of rain occurs as soon as a northwest wind sets in. The west wind brings three or four clear days.

STORING AND CURING.

FRUIT AND VEGETABLES.

Fruit which is to be kept beyond the natural period of ripening must be gathered before fully ripe. All sudden changes in temperature and moisture are productive of decay, and should be avoided. A dry, cool place, where the temperature is even is best calculated to retard decay and improve the keeping qualities. **1.** The following preparation is unequalled for preserving apples, pears, lemons, etc.: Rosin 2 pounds, tallow 2 ounces, beeswax 2 ounces; melt slowly in an iron pot, but don't boil; take the fruit separately and rub it over with pulverized chalk or whiting to prevent the coating adhering to the fruit, then dip it into the solution once and hold it up a moment to set the coating, then pack away carefully in barrels, boxes or on shelves in a cool place. **2.** Glycerine of the purest quality has been recommended for the preservation of fruits; previous to eating the fruit should be immersed in water to remove the glycerine. **3.** Using wheat bran for packing tender specimens of fruit to prevent bruising has been long practiced, but an improvement to this has been made by which, in addition to this protection, the fruit is preserved from decay. The bran is slightly charred by a patent process. **4.** Dry sand is one of the best articles in which to pack fruit; packed in this it will keep the year round. The fruit must be sound when stored, and the sand must be absolutely dry. The chief advantages of packing in sand are the exclusion of air currents, the preservation from changes of temperature and the absorption of moisture.

Apples, To Dry.—Pare and cut the apples in slices; then spread them on cloths, tables or boards and dry them outdoors. In clear dry weather this is the most expeditious plan. It is a good idea to use frames. These combine the most advantages with the least inconveniences in any way, and can be used either in drying in the house or out in the sun. In pleasant weather the frames can be set outdoors against the side of the building, and at night or in damp cloudy weather can be brought into the house and set near the stove or fireplace. After the apples are pared, quartered and cored, string them in lengths to reach twice across the frame; the ends of the twine are then tied together and the string hung on the nails across the frame. As fast as the apples are dry they can be taken from the string and others placed on to go through the same process. Dried apples are bleached by exposing to the fumes of burning sulphur.

Apples, To Keep.—1. The fruit must be free from bruise or blemish. and should be spread out on shelves or packed in barrels, and kept in a temperature of 40 to 45 degrees. Some cellars are just the thing, and preserve them beautifully; others are too moist. Where this is the case a few bushels of stone lime should be used. Sliding shelves, six inches apart, latticed bottom, with single layers of fruit, are extremely convenient, as they allow of frequent examination without disturbing the fruit. 2. Fall apples may be preserved in pits made as follows; Choose an elevated piece of ground in the orchard, and scoop out a shallow basin. in which heap the apples in quantities of not more than 10 or 12 bushels: cover them with straw laid lengthwise from top to bottom of the heap: leave them thus two or three days, during which time they will heat and sweat; after they have dried cover the straw with a light coating of earth except in three or four small places at the top and at the bottom, where a large wisp of straw should be inserted and bent over to make a water-shed.

Apples, To Pack.—1. Assort them so as to run uniform in size and quality. Pack in new sound barrels of the standard size, flat hoops preferred. only one variety in a barrel; turn the upper end of the barrel down, take out the lower head and commence packing by placing a tier of apples, stems down, upon the head, then fill up the barrel without bruising the fruit; shake down gently but thoroughly, and fill so full that the head must be pressed in with a level or barrel press. flattening the last tier of apples; then fastening the head turn the barrel over and mark plainly with a stencil or piece of red chalk. or ink, the variety contained. 2. Wrap each apple in manilla tissue paper; then pack as solidly as possible, putting a layer of soft chaff at the bottom of the barrel and sifting more over every layer. When the barrel is full place plenty of packing on top and press the head firmly down. In this condition apples will travel for months without injury.

Cherries, To Dry.—1. Stone, spread on a flat dish and dry in the sun or a warm oven: pour whatever juice may run from them over them, a little at a time. Stir them about that they may dry evenly. When perfectly dry line boxes or jars with white paper and pack close in layers; strew a little brown sugar over the cherries and fold the top of the paper over them and keep in a dry sweet place. 2. Take large cherries, not too ripe: remove the pits: take equal weights of cherries and sugar; make a thick syrup of the sugar; put in the cherries and boil them a minute and spread them on earthen platters till next day; strain the syrup and boil it down thick; put the cherries in and boil five minutes. Spread on platters as before; repeat the boiling two more days; then drain, lay them on wire sieves and dry in an oven nearly cold.

Cranberries, To Keep.—Cranberries will keep all winter in a firkin or tub of water in a cellar.

Currants, To Dry.—Beat up the whites of eggs or a little gum arabic in water, and after dipping in the bunches and letting them get a little dry, roll them in finely powdered loaf sugar; lay them on a sieve in an oven to dry, and keep turning them and adding sugar until they are perfectly dried. Not only red, white and black currants, but even grapes in bunches may be thus dried and preserved. They should be carefully kept dry in boxes lined with paper.

Figs, To Dry.—When ripe the figs are picked and laid out in the sun to dry, those of the better quality being much pulled and extended by hand during the process. Thus prepared the fruit is packed closely in barrels, rush baskets or wooden boxes.

Gooseberries, To Dry.—To 7 pounds of red gooseberries add 1½ pounds powdered white sugar, which must be strewed over them in the preserving pan. Let them remain at a good heat over a slow fire until they begin to break; then remove them. Repeat this process for two or three days; then take the berries from the syrup and place them in sieves near the fire to dry, spreading them out evenly. The syrup may be used for other preserves. When the gooseberries are quite dry store them in tin boxes or layers of paper.

Grapes, To Dry.—4. The grapes are allowed to remain on the vine until of a golden color and translucent; they are then picked and placed on wooden trays, 2 feet by 3 in size, between the rows, sloping to the sun; when half dried they are turned by placing an empty tray on top and turning over, thus transferring the contents from one tray to the other. When the grapes lose their ashy appearance, and after removing the green ones, the rest are put into large surat boxes with sheets of paper between every 25 pounds of raisins; they are left there for two weeks, when the stems are tough and the raisins soft. The packing follows, in which iron or steel packing frames are used, the raisins being assorted, weighed, inspected and made presentable. 2. The grapes are allowed to ripen and dry on the vines. After being plucked and cleaned, they are dipped for a few seconds into a boiling lye of wood ashes and quick lime of 12° or 15° Baume, to every 4 gallons of which a handful of common salt and 1 pint of sweet oil has been added. They are then exposed 12 or 14 days in the sun to dry. Lastly, they are carefully picked over to remove imperfect ones, and packed for shipping. The sweet, fleshy kinds of grapes are those selected for the above treatment.

Grapes, To Keep.—Grapes in bunches are preserved by

wrapping them in silver paper and packing them in dry bran. Each bunch is suspended by the stem with the fingers of one hand while the bran is poured around it with the other, the jar being occasionally shaken as the packing proceeds. Some paper is then tied over the mouth of the jar and a bladder over all to exclude moisture.

Lemons, To Keep.—1. Cover them with buttermilk or sour milk, changing once a week. Even lemons which are quite dry seem fresh if kept in this way. 2. Lemons can be kept for months by putting them in a clean tight cask or jar and covering them with cold water. The water must be changed as often as every other day, and the receptacle kept in a cool place.

Lemons and Oranges, To Pack.—Examine each one carefully to see that it is perfect; then wrap it in tissue paper and pack closely in boxes.

Peaches, To Dry.—Let the fruit get mellow enough to be in good eating condition; put them in boiling water for a minute or two and the skins will peel off readily; let them remain just long enough in the water to accomplish this; no longer; then quarter the fruit and place in the sun or near the stove to dry.

Peaches and Pears, To Keep.—Both peaches and pears can be kept several weeks by picking them just before ripening and wrapping them in tissue paper; pack in jars and keep in a temperature not above 60 degrees.

Raspberries, To Dry.—Black raspberries and blackberries are dried whole, and care must be taken that they are unbroken. Sun heat is the best method. Red raspberries do not dry well.

VEGETABLES.

To enjoy wholesome and palatable vegetables during the winter months proper care is essential in gathering and storing. As the cellars of most houses are too warm for proper preservation, the main stock should be kept in cool cellars, barns or pits dug outside. If it is not practicable to do this, select the vegetables to be kept with great care, and endeavor to keep them where the air is pure and cool, but free from moisture. A good plan is as follows: Sink a barrel, box or cask two-thirds its depth into the ground; heap the earth around the part projecting out of the ground with a slope on all sides; place the vegetables in the barrel, cover the top with a water-tight cover, and when winter sets in throw an armful of straw on the barrel. If the bottom is out of the barrel so much the better. Cabbage, celery and other vegetables will keep in this way as fresh as when taken out of the ground. Celery should stand nearly perpendicular; celery and earth alternating. Freedom from frost, ease of access, and especially freedom from rot, and freshness, are the advantages of this plan.

Beans, Lima, To Dry.—Gather while green and tender, and spread in the sun to dry.

Beans, String, To Dry.—Cut the beans up in the usual lengths; dry them and put in a bag. In winter soak them and cook in the usual way.

Beans, To Keep.—Take a wide-mouthed jar, lay on the bottom of it some freshly pulled snap beans, and over them put a layer of salt; fill the jar up in this manner with alternate layers of beans and salt. They will keep good for a year. When preparing for use soak in fresh water for several hours.

Cabbage, To Keep.—**1.** Gather them before the severe fall frosts; let the coarse outside leaves remain; fix a strong string around the stalk and suspend the cabbage from the timbers of ceiling, head downward. The cellar should be cool and dry. This method will preserve them with certainty. **2.** Pack in sawdust in the barn and allow the whole to freeze, the sawdust being such a non-conductor of heat that once it becomes frozen through it will not thaw out until well in April, and the cabbage will come out almost as nice as when put in. **3.** Cut the head from the stump; pack close in a cask and fill the vacancies with dry chaff or bran. Keep in a dry cellar.

Cauliflower, To Keep.—They can be kept in a cellar by covering the roots and stalks with earth till Feburary, or they may be placed in a trench in the garden, roots down, and covered with earth up close to the heads; then cover with hay or straw four or five inches thick, placing just enough earth on the straw to keep it in position.

Celery, To Keep.—About the last of October dig a trench 18 inches deep and 12 inches wide in some dry place where drainage is perfect, so that no water can stand in it; lift the celery with considerable soil about the roots; stand the branches upright, as they grow, in the trench; pack them as close as possible; draw the earth close against them; then cover them with a board, and on this place coarse straw or leaves, or both.

Corn, To Dry.—**1.** Clean the silk carefully from the corn; put the ears in a steamer over a kettle of hot water and steam 10 minutes; then draw a knife through each row of kernels and scrape out the pulp, leaving the hulls on the cob; spread on plates and carefully dry without scorching. **2.** Husk the corn and remove the silk; then cut off the kernels with a sharp knife. To 6 quarts of corn add 1 teacupful of sugar and stir well together; put on platters and set in the oven; let it remain 10 minutes; then remove it and place on a clean table, or other large cloth, and spread in the sun to dry; when dry put in a jar or box to keep.

Onions, To Keep.—Gather in the fall and remove the tops; then spread upon a barn floor or an open shed and allow them to remain there until perfectly dry; put in barrels, boxes or small bins and set in a cool place, and at the approach of cold weather cover with straw or chaff if there is danger of severe freezing

Onions are more frequently injured in winter by keeping them in too warm a place than by frost. It is the alternate freezing and thawing that injures and destroys them, and if placed in a position where they will remain frozen all winter and then thawed out slowly in a dark place, no considerable injury will be done them. Onions should always be stored in the coolest part of the cellar or put in chaff and set in the barn or some outhouse.

Parsley, To Dry.—To have bright crisp parsley for winter spread thinly, as soon as gathered, on a piece of paper, and place in a cool oven with the doors left open. As soon as dry powder it and put in a bottle, corking to exclude the air. Dried in this way it will retain its color and flavor.

Parsnips, To Keep.—The roots should be dug up late in fall, leaving all the tops on; then carefully heeled in thickly together in rows, after which they should be covered with a little coarse litter, and they can be reached whenever wanted during the winter.

Peas, To Dry.—Look the peas over, and remove any that are bad; then place them in the sun until they are dried.

Peas, Green, To Keep.—When full-grown pick and shell; lay them on dishes or tins in a cool oven or before a bright fire; do not heap the peas on the dish, but merely cover them; stir frequently and let them dry gradually; when hard let them cool; then pack in stone jars, cover close and keep in a very dry place. When required for use let them soak for some hours in cold water till they look plump before boiling. Excellent for soup.

Potatoes, To Keep.—1. A cave dug in the side of a hill, or a pit in a sand bank affords a excellent place for storing potatoes. If piled on top of the ground and covered with earth and straw, care should be taken that they are not exposed to the light. A dark cellar is preferable to a light one for keeping potatoes. **2.** To prevent potatoes from rotting dust the floor of the bin with lime and put in 6 or 7 inches of potatoes; then dust with lime as before and add more potatoes, using about 1 bushel of lime to 40 bushels of potatoes. The lime improves the flavor of the potatoes and effectually kills the fungi which cause the rot.

Pumpkins, To Dry.—Take ripe pumpkins, pare, cut into small pieces, stew soft, mash and strain through a colander as if for making pies; spread this pulp on plates in layers about $\frac{1}{2}$ inch thick; dry in an oven at a temperature sufficiently low as not to scorch it. In about a day it will become dry and crisp. The sheets thus made can be stored away in dry places, and are always ready for use for stewing or making pies.

Rhubarb, To Dry.—The best method is to strip it of its skin. This is a long operation, but both time and expense are spared in the end by the promptness and regularity of the drying.

Salsify, To Keep.—Salsify is kept best and improved by freezing.

Squashes, To Keep.—Squashes are injured by the slightest frosts and should be kept in a warm, dry storeroom rather than a cellar. If hung up by the stem in a moderately cool place they will keep for months.

Sweet Potatoes, To Keep.—There is no better way than to pack them in dry sand in boxes and keep the temperature of the place where they are stored between 45° and 60° Fahrenheit. Where one has but a few, dig when thoroughly ripe; handle carefully so as not to bruise; dry well and place them in the kitchen near the stove or some other warm place.

Tomatoes, To Keep.—Pick the green tomatoes before th vines freeze; put in a cool, dry place where air can be admitte and frost kept out.

Turnips, To Keep.—Turnips are very susceptible to hea They will sprout in a temperature of 40°. A little frost doe not hurt them. Place in small lots in stalls where the frost ca get at them and cover with straw.

THE DAIRY.

MILK AND MILKING.

Milk is a source of profit to the farmer when sold in its original state or made up into butter and cheese. To have good milk requires good food for the cows, for unless they are so fed it would be folly to expect any satisfactory returns. Then again, care should be taken to keep them perfectly clean and comfortably housed. Animals suffer from the inclemency of the weather, and a cow when distressed from any source shows it in the quality of her milk. To make good butter requires good milk, therefore the cows should be well fed and properly cared for. In milking observe the following rules:

Do not use a cow milking machine. They do not give good service, and in time injure the cow, besides causing them to run dry quicker. The hand method is the best. The milker should work both hands rapidly, keeping up a constant flow until the udder is empty, when (except in severely cold weather) the milk will be crested with a fleecy foam. Cleanliness is one great point to be kept in view. The best time to milk is either before or after feeding—never while the cow is eating. Do not draw the milk with a downward jerk; it irritates the cow and ofttimes works injury to the bag. Fill the teat, and with a firm pressure on the last three fingers empty it, drawing slightly on the teat and udder at the same time; so proceed alternately with each hand until the supply of milk is exhausted. The cow should be milked regularly and stripped quite clean. The milk will be quite thin in quality before calving, and should not be used for some days after calving, as at such times it is fit only for the use of the calf.

Before setting, the milk should be strained into cans and then set into cold water as fast as the cows are milked. Never mix the night's milk with the morning's. If cream is wanted for immediate use, enough will rise in 2 or 3 hours; for butter let it set at least 24 hours; 36 hours is the time in which all the cream will rise.

In skimming the cream should be taken off either early in the morning or in the evening after sunset. Take it off neatly and carefully with a skimmer; deposit it in clean stone crocks or a tin pail if for butter, or the cream jug if for immediate use. If the cream is for supper skim the morning's milk, if for breakfast that of the night before.

To prevent souring from thunder storms start a fire in the dairy; this should be done even in the hottest weather. Another good plan, which answers at all times, is to add to each quart 15 grains of bicarbonate of soda. A thin iron chain passed through the milk pans and the ends kept in cold water will prevent souring.

Butter, To Make.—Set the milk according to directions given; then skim; stir the cream every day; and the day before churning set the pot near the stove to allow the cream to warm and get sour. To sour the cream take the milk after it has stood 9 or 10 hours and place it over a clear slow fire, but do not boil it. In summer the process of scalding should be quicker than in winter, as in very hot weather, if the milk should be kept too long over a slow fire, it would be apt to run or curdle. Now turn all the cream into the churn. The coloring (if any is to be used) should be added now or worked into the butter after churning, but by adding it during the process or before churning, the color will be more evenly mixed with the butter. In churning care should be taken that the agitation is not too rapid or so violent as to injure the grain of the butter. Churning should occupy from ½ to ¾ of an hour; if the butter should be hard and granular, refusing to come together well, throw in a little warm water, churning all the while, and the butter will be gathered and ready to take up. Then work it until the buttermilk is worked out; this is an important feature. Buttermilk contains the sugar, caseine and salt of milk, and when it is procured from sweet cream is both delicious and nourishing, besides being easy of digestion. One ounce of fine purified dairy salt should be used for each pound of butter. The quality of the salt should be strong marine, free from the brine of mineral salt. The longer the butter is to be kept the greater the proportion of salt which should be used. Summer butter is the best for salting to keep.

Butter, To Make Come.—To 20 pounds of butter add 1 teaspoonful of bicarbonate of soda and 1 teaspoonful of powdered aluminate of sodium; put into the cream at the time of churning. It is claimed that the powder makes the butter come firm and solid and gives it a clean, sweet flavor, and that the yield of butter will be increased and the, labor of churning shortened; but this method is not advisable, as it adds to the butter a part of the curd that belongs to cheese-making properly.

Butter, To Color.—**1.** Annatto 1 ounce, curcuma 1 ounce, nice sweet lard 4 pounds; put 1 pound of lard in an iron kettle on the stove with the annatto; stir continually to prevent burning; put the curcuma and 1 pound of lard in another kettle; treat likewise; when the lard, which rises to the top, is of a bright clear amber color turn off the clear lard from both kettles into a jar, leaving the sediment at the bottom of the kettles: put the rest of the lard on this and heat and stir again until it is all dissolved: strain it after mixing together through toweling. **2.** Annatto 5 ounces, pulverized turmeric 6 ounces, saffron 1 ounce, lard oil 1 pint, butter 5 pounds. The butter is first melted in a pan over the water bath (which see in Department I.) and strained through a fine linen towel; the saffron is made into ¼ pint tincture, and together with the turmeric and the annatto is stirred into the butter and oil while hot, and boiled and stirred for about 15 minutes; it is then strained through a cloth as before and stirred until cool. **3.** Annatto 10 parts: caustic potassa 1½ parts, borax 1 part, water 100 parts, tincture of turmeric 20 parts; mix and filter. **4.** Take 2 large carrots, clean thoroughly, and then with a knife scrape off the yellow exterior, leaving the white pith; soak the yellow part in boiling milk 10 or 15 minutes; strain boiling hot into the cream. This gives the cream the desired temperature, colors it nicely, an` adds to the sweetness of the butter.

Butter, Rancid, To Purify.—**1.** Melt in twice its weight of boiling water and shake well; pour the melted butter into ice-water to regain its consistence. **2.** Wash in good new milk; wash afterward in cold spring water. **3.** First agitate the butter with hot water. On standing, it soon separates from the water, when it is again agitated for some time with an equal volume of fresh hot water and 2 ounces to the pound of fresh animal charcoal in coarse powder, free from dust. It is freed from charcoal by straining through a cloth while hot, and from the water by the difference in specific gravity. The butter when cold is well washed in sweet milk, to which a little sulphite of lime has been added; then reworked, salted and colored with a small quantity of annatto. An objection to this recipe is that so much working has a tendency to destroy the grain and make the butter oily.

Eggs, To Preserve.—**1.** Coat the eggs with lard or clean grease; pack them in bran. **2.** Wrap each egg in soft paper, twisting each end of the paper so that it cannot become loosened from the egg; take a bag of coarse muslin made in the shape of a pillow-slip, draw up one end in your hand, tie strong string around it tightly, leaving the ends long enough to tie a loop; place the eggs in this bag, ends down. It does not matter which end, but do not have them on the side. Put 50 in one bag; draw up the open end of the bag firmly against the eggs and tie it like the other end; suspend the bag where it will be free from injury from contact. **3.** As tne eggs are taken from the nest brush each one with a thin solution of gum arabic, being careful to leave no portion of the shell uncovered. One-half of each egg must first be done and left to dry before the remainder is touched, that the gum may not be rubbed off any part by contact while wet with the hand as it is held to be varnished, or with the table when laid down to harden.

Eggs, To Pack.—Eggs are best packed in boxes with divisions of stiff paper or pasteboard. so that they will not touch in transportation. Sometimes egg boxes are handled roughly by expressmen and others, and rough handling has a tendency to bruise the eggs.

DESTRUCTIVE INSECTS.

WORMS AND OTHER PESTS.

Apple Tree Louse.—This insect feeds on the leaves and twigs of apple trees. The female is without wings, of a pale green, with yellowish head and dark green stripes on the back. The winged ones have black heads, green abdomens and a row of black dots on either side. Tobacco juice and lime mixed will kill them.

Army Worm.—The army worm which causes such ravages among the small grains, corn and grass, is 1¾ inches in length when fully grown, and is striped lengthwise with black, dark green and yellowish lines intermingled with marginal white hair lines. The head is light or a yellowish brown, and has two blackish bent lines on the face. It has 16 feet, 6 small black ones in front, 8 fleshy ones along the middle part, and 2 at the hinder end. Its ravages begin about the last of May or 1st of June, great numbers travelling together, from which they got their name. They rarely touch clover or rye. timothy, blue grass and winter wheat being more to their liking, but when hard pressed they will eat the leaves of vegetables, fruit trees, and even each other. They are generally more destructive in a wet year following a dry one. Burning over a meadow or prairie or stubble field in winter or spring will effectually prevent the worms from breeding in such field. A ditch, with side toward the field to be protected, perpendicular or sloping under. will prevent them from invading such a field during their march from another region. When they are collecting in the ditch they can be destroyed by covering them with earth or by pouring some coal oil in the ditch, by burning straw over them, or by crushing them with rollers. Where the soil is sandy, so that a ditch cannot be made with a vertical side. dig it deeper and make the side as perpendicular as possible, so that when the worms attempt to crawl up the sand will crumble beneath their feet and they will fall back into the ditch.

Bark Lice.—Proper pruning of the branches, draining the land about the trees, manuring the soil and keeping it free from grass or weeds, have the effect of insuring vigorous growth, and are thus useful in preventing depredations. To kill the lice use strong lye made from wood ashes, a solution of caustic soda of potash, diluted soft soap, or a mixture of lime whitewash and kerosene oil. If the latter is employed, the proportions should be 1 pint of kerosene to 1 gallon of whitewash. Whatever substances are chosen they should be used thoroughly, and a second application should be made some days after the first to insure complete destruction of the insects.

Borers.—FLAT HEAD APPLE TREE.—The larva of a dark green beetle, and is pale yellow in color. The egg is deposited under the loose bark of the tree, from whence the young ones bore into the tree. The presence of the young borer is usually indicated by a discolored spot, a cracking of the bark, or the presence of sawdust on the outside of the tree. To destroy them wash the tree with strong soap suds during the spring or early summer.

BLACKBERRY BUSH.—A small, slender, red-necked beetle occasionally found eating out the pith of the blackberry stalks, but is not common. The beetle, which is the parent of the borer, is about half an inch long, black, rusty yellow on the breast and on top of the thorax. It lays its eggs early in August on the stems, generally at the base of a leaf. The grub penetrates the stem, eating out the pith, causing the young canes to wither. The infested canes should be pruned off in the fall and burned.

CURRANT—These are whitish with brown head and legs, and bore into the stems of currant bushes. The moth is blue-black with yellow on the tips of the fore wings. All infected stems should be cut and burned.

Ball Worm.—Color varying from pale green to light brown, striped longitudinally with darker stripes of the same color. It is from ¾ to 1½ inches in length. The moth is pale yellow or shining ash color. It feeds on green corn in the north, and in the south is found on the tips of cotton plants. The only remedy for corn is to plant it early enough so that it will begin to ripen upon the appearance of the worm. To destroy them in cotton fields: **1.** As the moth makes its excursions only after sunset, large numbers of them may be destroyed by building fires on the borders of the field. They will be attracted by the light and be burned. **2.** Take bottles filled with coal oil and supplied with wicks; place them on sticks higher than the growing cotton, with one end stuck in the ground at regular distances apart; light them, and the moths will be prevented from laying their eggs. The lamps should be used as long as it is deemed necessary.

Cinch Bug.—A small insect less than ¼ inch long; color

black and dirty white; body black, covered with a grayish down scarcely visible; legs, dark yellow. It attacks wheat, corn and oats. Irrigation is the most effective method of destroying them, but where this is not possible burn over the infested fields in winter. In timbered sections the leaves should be burned and the fence corners cleared out and burned. The practice of plowing land for spring grain the preceding autum, or if plowed in the spring, rolling it repeatedly with a heavy roller after seeding, is thought to possess advantages for fields invaded by them. The female bug has to work her way under ground in the spring to deposit her eggs at the roots, where she lays them, and the looser the soil the greater the facilities offered her for the operation. An emulsion of coal oil and milk will destoy them. The emulsion may be made with soap suds equally well; 1 pound of soap to 10 gallons of water, equal quantities of suds and coal oil being taken. If then this emulsion be diluted by an additional quantity of suds, or even of clear water, so that there will be 1 part oil to 19 parts water, the liquid will not injure grain.

Colorado Beetle or Potato Bug.—Body cream colored; 5 black stripes upon each wing case; wings rose color. Both the larva and the perfect beetle prey upon the potato plant. **1.** A few pounds of carbonate of lime, Paris green or London purple dusted from a dredging box, will kill them. **2.** Put ¼ bushel dry mandrake root in a barrel; fill with water and let it stand for two days, stirring now and then; strain the liquid through a cloth into a garden sprinkler; sprinkle toward sunset upon those plants on which the young brood hatch before they scatter to adjacent plants.

Corn Moth.—A moth injurious to grain laid up in bins. The perfect insect or moth measures from the head to the tip of the wing from 6 to 7 lines; the body is brown, with a little white on the back; the head has a thick tuft of whitish hairs; black eyes; upper wings more or less white with brownish and dusky dots, varying in size and form. This insect appears as a moth in May, June and July in buildings where grain is stored. It rests in the day time, flying only at night, when it attacks wheat, rye, barley and oats. To destroy them fill up the cracks and holes; sprinkle the floor with a mixture of strong white wine vinegar and salt before laying up the corn, sweeping the floor and walls well before storage, and if the moth has laid her eggs on the grain common salt may be mixed with it.

Cotton Army Worm.—Color, green; 2 black stripes on the back, and sprinkled with black dots along a yellowish sub-dorsal line. This worm is furnished with 6 fore, 8 middle and 2 hind legs or feet, the two first of the middle being imperfect, small and apparently useless for purposes of progression, which is effected by alternately stretching out the body and again contracting it in the form of an arch. When touched, the worms double themselves up and spring to a distance many times their length; but if undisturbed, when not feeding, they rest on the leaf with the forepart of the body elevated and slightly curved, sometimes varied by a sidelong swinging motion. They appear from June to September, and may be destroyed as follows: **1.** Dissolve ¾ of a pound of London purple in 40 gallons of water and apply to the under part of the foliage, where the poison will not be washed off by the rain. Paris green in like proportions will have the same effect, and if applied to the bottom of the leaves while the worms are in their infancy, will effectually destroy them. **2.** Add to 5 gallons of water 5 pounds of arsenic and 1 pound of soda; boil until the arsenic is dissolved. This makes a solution of arsenic that will keep for any length of time without depreciation. Put 1 quart of this in 40 gallons of water and sprinkle over an infested field. **3.** Kerosene and other oils mixed with fresh or spoiled milk, and applied to the leaves will effectually destroy the eggs. The emulsion should be diluted with water.

Caterpillars.—BUSH—The ordinary mode of disposing of this pest is to shake the bushes and collect the caterpillars. Hellebore powder and fox-glove are good destroyers. The latter is made into a strong tea by boiling it in water; water or syringe the bushes with this. As a preventative measure open a trench 1 foot in depth at the extremity of the roots, and then scrape or shovel the surface soil from over the roots for nearly 3 inches in depth into the trench in the hopes of burying and destroying the chyrsalis: the paring of soil should be well tramped down, and the occasion may be utilized for manuring the roots in the circle or line excavated; salt and soot might be used to cover the parings before tramping them down, or other strong materials which are at once fatal to insect life and a manure to the bushes.

APPLE TREE—Forms large cobweb-like nests in the forks of the limbs of apple and cherry trees during May. Destroy the nest and worms by pressing into the fork of the limb with a rough stick until the nest and worms are ground to pieces.

Grain Weevil.—The true wheat or grain weevil is a slender beetle about one-eighth of an inch long, and preys upon all kinds of grain in the bin and the corn crib. The insect being quite small is liable to be overlooked, particularly in a dark bin. Its mode of operation consists in piercing minute holes in the grain kernel and depositing its eggs therein; from these are hatched out small maggots that eat the heart out of the grain. In due time these grubs undergo transformation and come out of the hulls in the beetle state to lay their eggs for another brood. When possible avoid storing grain in bins that have been infected. When it is inconvenient to change the place of storage, fumigate the granary thoroughly with burning sulphur. Fumigation should not only be done before the grain is placed in bins, but repeated in the course of one or two months after it has been stored. The larva of the weevils that are in the grain may be destroyed by heating the grain when one has ovens or kilns at hand for the purpose. Scattering lime among stored grain may be practiced, if care is taken to remove it when the grain is taken out for use. Running it through a fanning mill will, if the grain is dry, blow out the dry lime. Grain that is stored in a cool place, if well ventilated and frequently moved, is said to be exempt from attacks.

Hessian Fly.—Tawny or black body, with pale brown or red eyes and black feet; wings blackish or tawny. It deposits its eggs on the young wheat plant at the first joint or crown; maggots are hatched, which work between the leaf and the stalk, live on the sap, and destroy the plant. If the fly is present burn over the stubble as soon as possible after the wheat is cut; thresh out the wheat before stacking and before it enters the sweating stage; then scatter the straw over the stubble and burn as thoroughly as possible, and follow after with the plow. Another way of destroying them is to turn the horses and cattle in on the young wheat when the ground is frozen and let them graze it close to the ground. Quicklime strewed over the field immediately after the grain is cut will destroy the pupæ. If an attack of the fly is threatening, delay the time of sowing.

Strawberry Worm.—A yellowish larva of a black fly. They feed on strawberry leaves and blossoms. **1.** Poultry will destroy them if turned into the patch before the berries are formed. **2.** Sprinkle the plants with 1 pound of white hellebore to 20 gallons of water.

Tobacco Worm.—The larva of a large moth which is very destructive to the leaf of the tobacco plant by eating holes in the leaves. thus spoiling them for wrappers for cigars, and when old by devouring the whole of the leaf. These worms appear in all sizes during late summer and autumn. The egg is deposited singly on the leaf of the tobacco or tomato plant, and the young worm when first hatched out by the heat of the sun, commences to eat holes in the leaf, and sheds its skin several times before attaining its full size; it then goes into the earth and the pupæ are formed in a subterranean cell, the late broods remaining as pupæ all winter and coming out as perfect moths the next spring. There are several parasites, and one in particular, that are very useful in destroying the potato and tobacco worms. It is a minute four-winged fly which deposits its eggs in the caterpillar and eventually kills it. The eggs of this parasite to the number of 100 or more are laid in the back and sides of the worm in small punctures made by the ovipositor of the fly. The simplest and best way of disposing of the tobacco worms is to pull their heads off as quickly as possible. This naturally necessitates search.

DEPARTMENT VII.

GENERAL MISCELLANY.

In this department will be found a little bit of everything—recipes and formulas unclassified, but of great value and usefulness. It will pay you to read through carefully.

A Gelatine Mold for Casting Plaster Paris Ornaments.—Allow 12 ounces of gelatine to soak for a few hours in water until it has absorbed as much as it can, then apply heat, by which it will liquify. If the mold is required to be elastic, add 3 ounces of treacle, and mix well with the gelatine. If a little chrome alum (precise proportions are immaterial) be added to the gelatine, it causes it to lose its property of being again dissolved in water. A saturated solution of bichromate of potash brushed over the surface of the mold, allowed to become dry and afterward exposed to sunlight for a few minutes, renders the surface so hard as to be unaffected by moisture

Art of Etching on Copper.—Having obtained a piece of fine copper, which will be well polished, make a mixture of beeswax and a small quantity of resin; melt these together, and when thoroughly incorporated by stirring, take a camel's hair brush and cover the plate, which must previously be warmed by the fire, with an even coating of the mixture. When the mixture becomes hardened upon the plate, sketch the desired object on the surface, then take an etching point—a large needle fixed in a handle will do—and cut through the wax to the surface of the copper, taking care to make the lines as distinct as possible. This being done, raise a border of wax all around the plate, then pour strong nitric acid on the plate to the depth of an inch. The acid will eat away the copper in those places which have been bared by the etching point. From time to time pour off the acid, and wash the plate to see how the work is going on. Stop up with wax those places that appear to be etched deep enough, pour acid upon the others, and let it remain until the process is completed. This done, melt off the wax, clean the plate, and the etching is ready for the press. This is an employment from which a good remuneration may be derived.

Celluloid, To Make.—A roll of paper is slowly unwound

307

and at the same time saturated with a mixture of 5 parts sulphuric acid and 2 of nitric, which falls upon the paper in a fine spray. This changes the cellulose of the paper into fine pyroxyline (gum cotton). The excess of acid having been expelled by pressure, the paper is washed with water until all traces of acid have been removed. it is then reduced to a pulp and placed into a bleaching trough. Most of the water having been got rid of by a strainer. the pulp is mixed with from 20 to 40 per cent of its weight of camphor and the mixture triturated under mill stones. Coloring matter having been added in the form of powder, a second mixture and grinding follows. The pulp is then laid out in layers and slabs. and from 20 to 25 layers are placed in a hydraulic press. separated from one another by sheets of blotting paper. and subjected to a pressure of 140 atmospheres until all traces of moisture have been got rid of. The plates obtained are broken up and soaked for 24 hours in alcohol, the matter then passed between rollers heated to from 140° to 150° Fahr., from whence it issues in the form of sheets. Celluloid is a most useful article. being made to imitate amber. tortoise shell and many other substances and is utilized for an almost innumerable number of purposes.

Copying Pad for Taking Transfers of Writing.—White gelatine 4 ounces, water 8 ounces, glycerine 8 ounces, gum dextrine 2 ounces. Always use these same proportions for any amount. Melt the gelatine in the water at a gentle heat, add to it the glycerine, in which the gum dextrine has been thoroughly incorporated, Now stir all together, until thoroughly mixed, and then pour into pans of the desired size, to the depth of ½ inch.

RECIPE FOR INK TO BE USED.—Violet analine 40 grains, gum arabic 12 grains, alcohol ¼ ounce, water ½ ounce; dissolve the gum in the water and alcohol, then add the analine. Shake in a bottle from time to time, until the analine is dissolved.

TO WORK THE COPYING PAD.—Write with the ink on any good paper, press the written surface on the pad, and allow it to remain two minutes; then take off and the writing will remain, from which impressions may be taken by laying on plain paper and smoothing with the hand. As soon as the last impression is taken, be sure and wash off with a wet sponge.

Cottolene, Cottosuet, Vegetole, etc., To Make.—This fine combination, known by many names. is coming into great favor among bakers, housekeepers. cooks, and all who use lard. It is purer, better and cheaper. This formula has never been printed before, and a trial will prove its intrinsic worth. Cotton oil 60 pounds, oleostearine 40 pounds, makes cottolene. 100 pounds. Do not bleach or refine stock; the color should be yellow. Melt together at about 180° Fahr.; do not go above that. No Fuller's earth or other refining stock must be used. After it is well mixed and heated, run through a filter, then into cans.

Cigars, To Flavor.—1. Ordinary cheap cigars may be

flavored or scented by moistening with a strong tincture of cascarilla to which a little gum benzoin and storax is added, or the leaves which are to form the cigars may be soaked for a short time in a strong infusion of cascarilla and then dried by a gentle heat. A small quantity of camphor together with oils of cassia and cloves is sometimes added to the above. **2.** Insert very small shreds of cascarilla bark between the leaves of the cigar, or in small slits made for the purpose. **3.** The poorest cigars can be finely flavored by standing them open end down in a vessel containing a sufficient quantity of port wine to cover them about 1 inch: 24 hours is the time they should be left in the wine. The tobacco absorbs the wine and imparts the flavor.

Cork, To Prepare for Bottles.—Before being made into stoppers the cork is charred on each side. It is readily cut, and is obtainable in sheets and squares, which can be flattened by the aid of moisture and pressure. or bent with that of heat and pressure. The knife for cutting should be broad in the blade, and kept sharp; cork dulls the sharpest knife very soon. There are two kinds of cork, the white which is smooth grained, and the darker or rough grained. If you have a batch of imperfect corks, dip them into a mixture of two-thirds virgin wax and one-third beef suet. Corks prepared with this mixture require no squeezing before putting in the mouth of the bottle. They are air-tight and durable.

Cotton Duck, To Make Mildew Proof.—Saturate the cloth in a hot solution of soap ¼ pound to 1 gallon of water; wring out and digest 12 hours or more in a solution of ½ pound alum to 1 gallon of water.

Everlasting Fence Posts.—I discovered many years ago that wood could be made to last longer than iron in the ground, but thought the process so simple and inexpensive that it was not worth while to make any stir about it. I would as soon have poplar, basswood, or quaking ash as any other timber for fence posts. I have taken out basswood posts after having been set seven years, which were as sound when taken out as when they were first put in the ground. Time and weather seem to have no effect on them. The posts can be prepared for less than two cents apiece. This is the recipe: Take boiled linseed oil and stir in it pulverized charcoal to the consistency of paint. Put a coat of this over the timber, and there is not a man that will live to see it rotten.

Eggs, To Preserve.—Get a water-tight barrel. To a pailful of water add 2 pints of fresh slacked lime and 1 pint of common salt. Fill the barrel half full of this fluid, place your eggs down in it any time after June, and they will keep two years if desired. This is reliable.

Glass, To Etch Upon.—Procure several thick, clear pieces of crown glass, and immerse them in melted wax, so that each may receive a complete coating, or pour over them a solution of wax in benzine When perfectly cold, draw on them with a fine steel point, flowers, trees, houses, portraits, etc. Whatever parts of the drawings are intended to be corroded with the acid should be perfectly free from the least particle of wax. When all these drawings are finished, the pieces of glass must be immersed one by one in a square leaden box or receiver, where they are to be submitted to the action of hydrochloric acid gas, made by acting on powdered flor-spar by concentrated sulphuric acid. When the glasses are sufficiently corroded, they are to be taken out, and the wax is to be removed by first dipping them in warm and then in hot water, or by washing with turpentine or benzine. Various colors may be applied to the corroded parts of the glass, whereby a fine painting may be executed. In the same manner sentences and initials of names may be etched on wine glasses, tumblers, etc.

Glass, To Cut or Break in Any Shape.—If you have no glazier's diamond or the common round steel wheel (which can be obtained at almost any first-class hardware store) the following methods may be adopted, and will be found effectual if carefully used: **1.** File a notch on the edge of the glass at the point you wish to start the break from; then put a suitably shaped red-hot iron upon the notch, and draw slowly in the direction you wish. A crack will follow the iron caused by the heat, if not drawn too fast. **2.** Glass may be easily cut with scissors by keeping it level under water while the scissors are being applied. To avoid risk, begin the cutting by taking off small pieces at the corners and along the edges, and so reduce the shape into that required, as if any attempt is made to cut the glass all at once into the shape it will most likely break just where it is not wanted. Some kinds of glass will cut much better than others, the softer glass being the best for this purpose. The scissors need not be sharp, as their action does not appear to depend on the state of the edge applied to the glass. When the operation goes on well, the glass breaks away from the scissors in small pieces in a straight line. **3.** To cut glass vessels in a neat manner heat a rod of iron to redness, and having filled the vessel the exact height you wish it to be cut, with oil of any kind, gradually dip the red-hot iron into the oil, which heating along the surface, the glass chips and cracks right around, when you can lift off the upper portion clean. **4.** (Bottles.) Turn the bottle as evenly as possible over a low gas or lamp light flame for about ten minutes, then place in water, and the sudden cooling will cause a regular crack to encircle the bottle at the heated place.

Glass, To Bore Holes In.—Any hard steel tool will cut glass with great facility when kept freely wet with camphor dissolved in turpentine. A drill bow may be used, or even the hand alone. A hole bored may be readily enlarged by a round file. The ragged edges of glass vessels may also be thus easily smoothed by a flat file. Flat window glass can readily be sawn by a watch spring saw by the aid of this solution. In short, the most brittle glass can be wrought almost as easily as brass by the use of cutting tools kept constantly moist with camphorized oil of turpentine.

Ground Glass, Imitation Of.—Paint the glass with the following varnishes; Sandarach 18 drams, mastic 4 drams, ether 24 drams, benzine 6 to 18 ounces. The more benzine the coarser the grain of imitation glass will be.

Glass, Pencils for Writing On.—The colors are mixed with the fats in warmed vessels, levigated with the same, and are then allowed to cool until they have acquired proper consistency for being transferred to the presses. In these the mass is treated and shaped similarly as the graphite in the presses for ordinary pencils. (See *Pencils, Blacklead.*)

BLACK.—Lampblack 10 parts, white wax 40 parts, tallow 10 parts.

BLUE, DARK.—Prussian blue 15 parts, gum arabic 5 parts, tallow 10 parts.

BLUE. LIGHT.—Prussian blue 10 parts, white wax 20 parts, tallow 10 parts.

WHITE.—Zinc white 40 parts, white wax 20 parts, tallow, 10 parts.

YELLOW.—Chrome yellow 10 parts, yellow wax 20 parts, tallow 10 parts.

Glass, To Powder.—Make a piece of glass red hot and plunge it into cold water; it will immediately break into powder. This must be sifted and dried; it is then fit for making sandpaper, for filtering varnishes and for other purposes.

Glass, Prince Rupert's Drops.—These are made by letting drops of melted glass fall into cold water. The drops assume an oval form, with the tail or neck resembling a retort. They possess this singular property, that if a small portion of the tail is broken off the whole bursts into powder, with an explosion, and a shock is communicated to the hand that grasps it.

Horn, To Weld.—Pieces of horn may be joined by heating the edges until they are soft, and pressing together until cold.

Ice, Artificial.—Take 4 parts nitric acid, 6 parts nitrate ammonia and 9 parts phosphate of soda. Having first prepared a vessel of galvanized iron 4 inches wide, 24 inches long and 12 inches deep, have it a little wider at the top than at the bottom. now make another vessel 8 inches wide, 28 inches long and 14 inches high. Put the small vessel inside the larger one, fill the small one nearly full of as cool water as you can procure, put the freezing mixture in the large vessel around the smaller one, set this in as cool a place as possible. If you will have a faucet at the lower edge of the large vessel and first fill the large vessel with the following it will greatly assist in freezing: Equal parts of sal ammonia and nitre dissolved in its own weight of water. In ten or fifteen minutes pour this off and put in the freezing mixture.

NOTE.—I have used the above description of a vessel gi

you an idea of how to operate. Any sized vessel made in the same proportion will work as well.

Ivory, Artificial.—1. Make a paste of isinglass, egg shell in powder and brandy. Give it the desired color and pour warm into oiled molds. Leave the paste in the molds until hard. 2. Dissolve 2 pounds of pure india rubber in 32 pounds of chloroform, and saturate the solution with purified ammoniacal gas, then distill off at a temperature of 185° Fahr., and mix the residue with pulverized phosphate of calcium or carbonate of zinc. Press into molds and cool.

Ivory Black.—Burn waste shavings and waste pieces of ivory from the ivory turners, in a covered crucible, till no smoke issues; cover close while cooling; then wash with diluted hydrochloric acid; then with water till no longer acid; dry and heat in a covered crucible. It is of a deeper color than bone black, and is used as a pigment, tooth powder and to decolorize syrups and other liquids.

Ivory, To Make Transparent.—Cut ivory in pieces, 1-20 inch. and place in phosphoric acid, specific gravity 1·131, until transparent; then take from the bath, wash in water and dry with a clean linen cloth; dry in the air without heat and soften under warm water.

Kustition's Metal for Tinning.—Malleable iron 1 pound, heat to whiteness; add 5 ounces regulus of antimony, and molucca tin 24 pounds.

TINNING PROCESS.—The articles to be tinned are first covered with dilute sulphuric acid, and when quite clean are placed in warm water, then dipped in a solution of muriatic acid, copper and zinc, and then plunged into a tin bath to which a small quantity of zinc has been added. When the tinning is finished, the articles are taken out and plunged into boiling water. The operation is completed by placing them in a very warm sand bath. This last process softens the iron.

Lard Compound.—Cotton oil 60 pounds, deodorized hog grease 20 pounds, tallow 10 pounds, oleostearine 10 pounds, for 100 pounds lard compound.

Leaf Photographs.—A very pretty amusement, especially for those who have just completed the study of botany, is the taking of leaf photographs. One very simple process is this: At any druggist's get an ounce of bichromate of potassium. Put this into a pint bottle of water. When the solution becomes saturated—that is, the water is dissolved as much as it will—pour off some of the clear liquid in a shallow dish; on this float a piece of ordinary writing paper till it is thoroughly moistened, let it dry in the dark. It should be a bright yellow.)n this put the leaf, under it a piece of of black soft cloth and several sheets of newspaper. Put these between two pieces of glass (all the pieces should be of the same size), and with spring clothespins fasten them together. Expose to ⅃ bright sun, placing the leaf so that the rays will fall upon it as nearly perpendicular as possible. In a few moments it will begin to turn brown; but it requires from half an hour to several hours to produce a perfect print. When it has become dark enough, take it from the frame and put it into clear water, which must be changed every few minutes until the yellow part becomes white. Sometimes the leaf veinings will be quite distinct. By following these directions, it is scarcely possible to fail, and a little practice will make perfect.

Making Blackboards.—The following directions for this work are given by an experienced superintendent: The first care must be to make the wall surface or boards to be blacked perfectly smooth. Fill all the holes and cracks with plaster of paris mixed with water; mix but little at a time: press in and smooth down with a case knife. The cracks between shrunken boards may be filled in the same way. Afterward use sandpaper. The ingredients needed for slating are liquid gum shellac, sometimes called shellac varnish, and lampblack or drop black. Gum shellac is cut in alcohol, and the liquid can be obtained of any druggist. Pour some shellac into an open dish, and stir in lampblack to make a heavy paint. With a clean brush, spread on any kind of surface but glass. Put on a little and test it. If it is glossy and the chalk slips over it reduce the mixture with alcohol. Alcohol can be bought of any druggist. If it rubs off, let the druggist put in more gum to make the liquid thicker. One quart of the liquid and a five-cent paper of lampblack are sufficient to slate all the blackboards in any country school with two coats.

Marble, Artificial.—Soak plaster of paris in a solution of alum, bake it in an oven, and then grind it to a powder. In using, mix it with water, and to produce the clouds and veins stir in any dry color you wish; this will become very hard, and is susceptible of a very high polish.

Molds and Dies.—Copper, zinc and silver in equal proportions, melt together under a coat of powdered charcoal, and mold into the form you desire. Bring them to nearly a white heat, and lay on the thing you would take an impression of, press with sufficient force, and you will get a perfect and beautiful impression.

Molds of Glue and Molasses.—These flexible molds are such as Rogers uses for making his statuettes, and are prepared as follows: Glue 8 pounds, molasses (New Orleans) 7 pounds; soak the glue over night in a small quantity of cold water, then melt it by heat over a salt water bath, stir until froth begins to rise, then add and stir in briskly the molasses previously heated. Continue to heat and stir the mixture for about half an hour and then pour. (See "A Gelatine Mold," *Department VI*.)

Muriate of Tin. Tin Liquor.—If druggists keep it, it is best to purchase of them already made, but if you prefer, proceed as follows: Get at a tinner's shop block tin, put it into a shovel and melt it. After it is melted, pour it from the height of 4 or 5 feet into a pail of clear water. The object of this is to have the tin in small particles, so that the acid can dissolve it. **Take** it out of the water and dry it; then pour it in a strong glass bottle. Pour over it muriatic acid 12 ounces, then slowly **add** sulphuric acid 8 ounces. The acid should be added about a tablespoonful at a time, at intervals of 5 or 8 minutes, for if you add it too rapidly you run the risk of breaking the bottle by heat. After you have all the acid in, let the bottle stand until the ebullition subsides; then stop it up with beeswax or a glass stopper, and set it away, and it will keep good for a year or more, or it will be fit for use in 24 hours.

Matches, Parlor.—Chlorate of potash (separately powdered) 6 drams, vermilion 1 dram, lycopodium 1 dram, fine flour 2 drams; mix carefully the chlorate with the flour and lycopodium, avoiding friction; then add the vermilion and mix the whole with a mucilage made with 1 dram powdered , um arabic, 10 grains gum tragacanth, 2 drams flour, 4 ounces hot water; mix, and add sufficient water to bring to a proper consistency and dip the sticks previously prepared by dipping in a solution of 1 ounce of gum thus, ½ ounce of camphor and 6 ounces oil of turpentine.

Matches, Safety.—Chloride of potash 4 to 6 parts, bichromate of potash 2 parts, ferric oxide 2 parts, strong glue 3 parts; mix thoroughly and use in the usual manner. Matches made by this method will not ignite on sandpaper or by ordinary means, but require a surface especially prepared for them as follows: Sulphide of antimony 20 parts, bichromate of potash 2 to 4 parts; oxide of iron, lead or manganese 4 to 6 parts; glass powder 2 parts, strong glue or gum 2 to 3 parts. This preparation is spread like paint in a warm condition on suitable paper, which is fastened on the boxes containing the matches.

Oleomargarine Manufacture.—The process by which suet is converted into the substance called oleomargarine, is as follows; The crude suet, after being washed in cold water, is "rendered" melted, and then drawn off into movable tanks. The hard substance is subjected to a hydraulic pressure of of 350 tons, and the oil extracted. The butter is made from the oil thus obtained, while the hard substance remaining is disposed of as stearine. The oil being carried off into churns, is mixed with milk and from 3 to 5 per cent of dairy butter. It is then drawn off into a consistent form, and cooled with broken ice. The latter is soon removed, and the butter worked up with a small portion of salt. When this is done, the article is ready for packing and consumption.

Pencils, Blacklead.—The easiest way of making not only black but all other pencils, is by the following process: Take white or pipe clay, put it into a tub of clean water, soak 12 hours, then agitate until it resembles milk; let it rest 2 or 3 minutes and pour off the supernatant milky liquor into a second vessel. Allow it to settle, pour off the clear, dry the residue on a filter; then add blacklead sufficient. Powder it and calcine it at a white neat in a loosely covered crucible, cool and carefully repulverize, then add prepared clay and prepared plumbago equal parts, water to mix. Make into a paste and put in oiled molds of the size required; dry gradually and apply sufficient heat to give the required hardness; then take from the molds (carefully) and place in the grooves of the wood prepared to receive it. The more clay and heat employed, the harder the crayon. The shade of black may be varied in the same way. Each mold must be made of 4 pieces of wood nicely fitted together.

Pencils, Indelible.—Buy a genuine No. 1 Faber pencil, prepare the label (cedar is the best material) and on the part you wish to write rub a little linseed oil, and write before it gets dry. This writing will remain indelible for years. If a little japan varnish is added to the oil it is better; a little white lead might be used in the oil, but is not absolutely necessary.

Pencil Writing, To Fix.—Pencil writing may be fixed almost as indelible as ink by passing the moistened tongue over it. Even breathing over the lines after writing will render them less liable to erasure. Brushing the writing or a drawing with skim milk will also act in the same manner.

Patent Lubricating Oil.—Water 1 gallon. clean tallow 3 pounds, palm oil 10 pounds, common soda ¼ pound; heat the mixture to about 210° Fahr.; stir well till it cools down to 70° Fahr.. when it is fit for use.

Powder for Cleaning and Polishing Tin, Brittania, and Brassware.—Take ½ pound ground pumice-stone and ¼ pound red chalk; mix them evenly together. This is for tin and brass. For silver and tinware, take ½ pound red chalk and ¼ pound pumice-stone. mix very evenly; use these articles dry with a piece of wash leather. It is one of the best cleaning powders ever invented and very valuable.

Rubber, Artificial.—A cheap and useful substitute for india rubber is prepared by mixing a thick solution of glue with tungstate of soda and hydrochloric acid. A compound of tungstic acid and glue is precipitated, which at a temperature of 86 to 104° Fahr. is sufficiently elastic to admit of being drawn out into very thin sheets. On cooling, this mass becomes solid and brittle, but on being heated is again soft and plastic. This new compound can be used for many of the purposes to which rubber is adapted.

Rubber Hand Stamps.—Set up the desired name and address in common type, oil the type, and place a guard about ½ inch high around the form. Now mix plaster of paris to the desired consistency. pour in and allow it to set. Have your vulcanized rubber all ready, as made in long strips 3 inches wide, and ⅛ of an inch thick, cut off the size of the intended stamp. Remove the plaster cast from the type, and place both the cast and the rubber in a screw press. applying sufficient heat to thoroughly soften the rubber, then turn down the screw hard, and let it remain until the rubber receives the exact impression of

the cast and becomes cold, when it is removed, neatly trimmed
with a sharp knife, and cemented to the handle, ready for use.

Rubber Stamps for Photographs.—Many photograph-
ers employ a rubber stamp for imprinting the backs of mounts,
and in these circumstances a good ink is very essential. Here
is the recipe for making one, quoted from the *Engineer*, and said
to yield an excellent ink, which, while not drying on the pad,
will yet not readily smear when impressed upon paper: Aniline
red (violet) 180 grains, distilled water 2 ounces, glycerine 1 teaspoonful, treacle ½ teaspoonful. The crystals of aniline are
powdered and dissolved in the boiling distilled water, and the
other ingredients then added.

Rubber, To Dissolve.—1. A mixture of 6 parts absolute
alcohol, with 110 parts sulphate of carbon; the latter is the real
solvent; the alcohol has an indirect action. The quantity of
solvent required depends on the consistency of solution required. If moderate heat is used and the mixture shaken, the
whole dissolves, but a better solution is obtained for adhesive
properties by using a large quantity of solvent, not shaking but
drawing off the clear, glazy liquid. 2. For a small quantity
place 1 fluid dram sulphuric acid and the same quantity of
water in a vial and shake together. Great heat is evolved. Allow to stand till cool, then add 2 fluid ounces spirits of turpentine, and shake well. Great heat will again be the result, and
the color changed to a deep cinnamon; allow to stand 24 hours,
after which a strong dark sediment will have formed at the bottom of the bottle; pour off the clear into another bottle, and add
1½ drams (apothicaries weight) common india rubber cut into
shreds and then place it, uncorked, over a gentle heat and boil
slowly 5 hours. At the end of that time the rubber should be
dissolved. It can be concentrated by longer boiling, or thinned
by the addition of turpentine. (See "Rubber Cements in *Glues,
Cements, etc.*)

Rubber, To Restore Elasticity Of.—Immerse the article
in a mixture of water of ammonia 1 part and water 2 parts for a
time varying from a few minutes to 1 hour, according to the
circumstances. When the mixture has acted on the rubber it
will be found to have recovered its elasticity, smoothness and
softness.

Rubber Hose, Composition For.—Grind together Java
rubber 20 pounds, para rubber 10 pounds, white lead 14 pounds,
red lead 14 pounds, yellow sulphur 1½ pounds; spread on flax
cloth which weighs 10-16 and 32 ounces to the square yard.

Rubber Hose, To Repair.—Cut the hose apart where it is
defective, obtain from any gasfitter a piece of iron pipe 2 or 3
inches long, twist the hose over it until the ends meet, wrap with
strong twine well waxed, and it will last a long time.

Rubber, To Preserve.—To keep rubber from cracking use
a mixture of 1 part water of ammonia and 2 parts water, in

which the articles should be immersed until they assume their former elasticity. smoothness and softness.

Stencil Cutting.—Take a thin copper or brass plate, lay flat on the side, then take a sharp edged steel, write thereon the same as common writing, but press sufficiently hard to cut through the plate. To mark, lay the plate thus cut upon the cloth, and apply ink by means of a brush to the back of the plate, and it will wet the cloth where the cut is made by the writing. A little practice will enable a person to cut beautifully. There is money to be made at this. Some make $10 a day.

Tobacco. To Flavor.—This is done by means of a mixture of 1 part each of lemon peel, orange peel, figs. coriander seed and sassafrass, ½ part each of elder flowers, elder berries and cinnamon, 2 parts saltpeter. 3 parts salt and· 4 parts sugar. This mixture must be digested in 50 parts water, and before applying it flavored with an alcoholic solution of gum benzoin, mastic and myrrh. This decoction gives a flavor to common leaves resembling Porto Rico, but to this end the leaves must be well dried, about 1 year old and well permeated with the preparation; keep in a pile for 8 days, turning daily, and finally dry.

Tobacco Pipes, To Clean.—Tobacco pipes may be thoroughly cleaned and made sweet by pouring alcohol in the bowl and permitting it to run out of the stem.

Tortoise Shell Imitation.—1. The appearance of tortoise shell may be given to horn by brushing it over with a paste of 2 parts lime, 1 part litharge and a little soap lye, which is allowed to dry. This acts by forming sulphuret of lead with the sulphur contained in the albumen of the horn producing dark spots which contrast with the brighter color of the horn. **2.** Mix an equal quantity of quick lime and red lead with soap lye, apply to the horn with a small brush in imitation of the mottle of tortoise shell; when it is dry, repeat it 2 or 3 times. **3.** Take a piece of lunar caustic, the size of a pea, grind with it water on a stone and mix with it sufficient gum arabic to make it of a proper consistency. Apply with a brush to the horn, in imitation of the veins of the shell. A little red lead mixed with it to give it a body is of advantage. It will stain the horn quite through without affecting its texture or body. Be careful when the horn is stained to let it soak some hours in water previous to finishing and polishing it. (*For Polishing, See "Household Recipes."*)

To Take Fac-similes of Signatures.—Write your name on a piece of paper, and while the ink is wet, sprinkle over it some finely powdered gum arabic, then make a rim around it, and pour on it some fusible alloy in a liquid state. Impressions may be taken from the plates formed in this way, by means of printing-ink and the copperplate press.

To Transfer Prints, etc., to Glass.—Take of gum sandarach 4 ounces. mastic 1 ounce, venice turpentine 1 ounce, alcohol 15 ounces. Digest in a bottle, frequently shaking, and it is ready for use. Directions: Use, if possible, good plate-glass of the size of the picture to be transferred, go over it with the above varnish, beginning at one side, press down the picture firmly and evenly as you proceed, so that no air can possibly lodge between; put aside, and let it dry perfectly, then moisten the paper cautiously with water, and remove it piecemeal by rubbing carefully with the fingers; if managed nicely, a complete transfer of the picture to the glass will be effected.

To Clean Oil Paintings if Smoked, Dull, or Dirty.—Dissolve a little common salt with stale urine and a grated potato mixed in them; rub them over with a woolen cloth till you think them clean, then with a sponge wash them over with clear water, then dry them, and rub them over with a clear cloth.

To Whiten Linseed Oil.—Shake up daily 2 ounces of litharge in a gallon of oil and 8 ounces of spirits of turpentine, for 15 days, afterwards let it settle 3 days. Pour off the clear part into a shallow vessel, and place it in the sun 3 days to whiten and clear it.

To Cure Damp Walls.—Boil 2 ounces of grease with 2 quarts of tar, for nearly 20 minutes, in an iron vessel, and having ready pounded glass 1 pound, slacked lime 2 pounds; well tied in an iron pot, and sifted through a flour sieve. Add some of the lime to the tar and glass, to make it the thickness of thin paste sufficient to cover a square foot at a time, as it hardens so quick. Apply it about ⅛ inch thick.

To Prepare Wood and Brick Work from Damp Weather.—Take 3 pecks of lime slacked in the air, 2 pecks of wood ashes, and 1 peck of fine sand. Sift them fine, and add linseed oil sufficient to use with a paint-brush; thin the first coat; use it as thick as it will work the second coat. Grind it fine or beat it in a trough, and it is a good composition.

To Transfer Printed Matter, and Print From it Again.—Take your picture or print and soak it for a short time in a weak solution of caustic potash, then remove it carefully, and let it dry on a sheet of clean paper. Then take a piece of copper, zinc or steel, which has previously been well cleaned, and dip it into hot white wax. Let the first coat set, then dip again. Having got the plate thoroughly coated and set, lay the matter to be transferred on the plate, and rub it gently all over on the back; now raise it up, and it will be transferred on to the wax on the plate. Now take needles of a different thickness, and scrawl all over the wax, following the lines of the engraving. Having got the picture all traced out, pour upon it some weak acid if you use zinc, which is too soft to print many from, therefore it is better to use copper or steel. If you use copper, make the following solution to pour over it: Verdigris 4 parts, salt 4 parts, sal ammoniac 4 parts, alum 1 part, water 16 parts, sour vinegar 12 parts; dissolve by heat. For steel use pyroligneous acid 5 parts, alcohol 1 part, nitric acid 1 part; **mix** the first two, then add the nitric acid. Pouring the preparations over the plates where the traces of the pictures are, it will eat into the metal plate without affecting the wax. Let it stand till it has eaten a sufficient depth, then wash the plate with cold water, dry it, and place it near the fire till all the wax is melted off. You can now print as many as you please from the plate by rubbing on it printers' ink, so as to fill all the fine spaces; which, when done, wipe it over smoothly with clean cloths to remove the superfluous ink which is on the face of the plate. Now take damp paper or card board, and press it on the plate, either with a copying press or the hand, and you get a fine impression, or as many as you want, by repeating the inking process. I would recommend beginners to try their skill with valueless prints before attempting to make transfers of fine engravings, as the picture to be transferred is destroyed by the process.

To Keep Tires Tight on Wheels.—Before putting on the tires fill the felloes with linseed oil, which is done by heating the oil in a trough to boiling heat, and keeping the wheel, with a stick through the hub, in the oil, for an hour. The wheel is turned round until every felloe is kept in the oil one hour.

Unshrinkable Patterns.—The best mixture for small patterns, that does not shrink in casting is 69 parts lead, 15-1 parts antimony, 15½ parts bismuth, by weight. A cheap kind for finished patterns can be made of 10 parts zinc, 1 part antimony, 1 part tin.

Vomiting, To Stop.—Drink hot water. Just as hot as can be borne.

Water Filter, To Make.—Take a deep flower pot and put a compressed sponge in the bottom; over the sponge put a layer of pebbles an inch thick; next an inch of coarse sand; next a layer of charcoal, and at the top another layer of pebbles. The water will filter pure and clear, through the hole in the bottom of the flower pot, into another vessel below, however impure previously. (See also "Apparatus," *Department I.*)

Wax Flowers, To Make.—The following articles will be required to commence wax work: Two pounds white wax, ¼ pound hair wire, 1 bottle carmine, 1 ultramarine blue, 1 bottle chrome yellow, 2 bottles chrome green (No. 1), 2 bottles chrome green (No. 2), 1 bottle each of rose, pink, royal purple, scarlet powder, and balsam fir, 2 dozen sheets white wax. This will do to begin with. Now have a clean tin dish, and pour therein a quart or two of water; then put in about 1 pound of the white wax, and let it boil. When cool enough, so the bubbles will not form on top, it is ready to sheet, which is done as follows:. Take half of a window pane, 7 x 9, and after having washed it clean, dip into a dish containing weak soap suds; then dip into the wax, and draw out steadily, and plunge it into the suds, when the sheet will readily come off. Lay it on a cloth or clean paper to dry. Proceed in like manner until you have enough of the white;

then add enough of the green powder to make a bright color. and heat and stir thoroughly until the color is evenly distributed, then proceed as for sheeting white wax. The other colors are rubbed into the leaves after they are cut, rubbing light or heavy according to shade.

NOTE.—For patterns you can use any natural leaf, forming the creases in wax with the thumb nail or a needle. To put the flowers together, or the leaves on the stem, hold in the hand until warm enough to stick. If the sheeted wax is to be used in summer put in a little balsam of fir to make it hard. If for winter, none will be required. You can make many flowers without a teacher, but one to assist in the commencement would be a great help, though the most particular thing about it is to get the wax sheeted. The materials I have suggested can be procured at any drug store, and will cost from $3 to $4.50.

Wood, To Petrify.—Gem salt, rock alum, white vinegar, chalk and peebles powder, equal parts; mix together. If after the ebullition is over, you throw into this any wood or porous substance, it will petrify it.

PECULIAR EXPERIMENTS.

1. To apparently burn water, fill a glass lamp with water, and put into it for a wick a piece of gum camphor. The lamp should not be quite full, and the camphor may be left to float upon the surface of the water. On touching a lighted match to the camphor. up shoots a clear, steady flame, and seems to sink below the surface of the water so that the flame is surrounded by the liquid. It will burn a long time. If the camphor be ignited in a large dish of water it will commonly float about while burning.

2. To change the faces of a group to a livid, deathly whiteness, and to destroy colors, wet a half teacupful of common salt in alcohol and burn it on a plate in a dark room. Let the salt soak a few minutes before igniting. The flame will deaden the brightest colors in the room, and the dresses of the company will seem to be changed. Let each one put his face behind the flame, and it will present a most ghastly spectacle to those who stand before it. This is serviceable in a tableau where terror of death is to be represented. The change wrought by the flame, when the materials are properly prepared, is very surprising.

3. Wet a piece of thick wrapping paper, then dry near the stove. While dry, lay it down upon a varnished table or dry woolen cloth, and rub it briskly with a piece of India rubber. It will soon become electrified, and if tossed against the wall or the looking-glass will stick some time. Tear tissue-paper into bits, ⅛ inch square, and this piece of electrified paper will draw them. Or take a tea-tray and put it on three tumblers. Lay the electric paper on it, and on touching the tray you will get a little spark. Let the paper lay on the tray, and on touching the tray again you will get another spark, but of the opposite kind of electricity. Replace the paper and you get another, and so on.

4. To produce a spectrum, burn magnesium wire in a dark room, and as soon as the flame is extinguished. let each one try to look into the others' faces. The spectrum of the extinguished light is clearly seen.

HINTS ON PATENTS AND INVENTIONS.

What to Invent.—Cheap, useful articles that will sell at sight. Something that every one needs, and the poorest can afford. Invent simple things for the benefit of the masses, and your fortune is made. Some years back a one-armed soldier amassed a fortune from a simple toy—a wooden ball attached to a rubber string. They cost scarcely anything, yet millions were sold at a good price. A German became enormously rich by patenting a simple wooden plug for beer barrels. What man has done, man can do."

How to Protect Your Invention.—Patent it. If you do not, others will reap the benefits that rightfully belong to you.

A Patent Is a Protection given to secure the inventor in the profits arising from the manufacture and sale of an article of his own creation.

To Whom Letters Patent are Granted.—Section 4886 of the Revised Statutes of the United States provides that;

"Any person who has invented or discovered any new and useful art, machine, manufacture or composition of matter, or any new and useful improvement thereof, not known or used by others in this country, and not patented or described in any printed publication in this or any foreign country, before his invention or discovery thereof. and not in public use, or on sale for more than two years prior to his application, unless the same is proved to have been abandoned, may, upon the payment of the fees required by law, and other due proceedings had, obtain a patent therefor."

And section 4888 of the same statute enacts:

Section 4888. "Before any inventor or discoverer shall receive a patent for his invention or discovery, he shall make application therefor, in writing, to the Commissioner of Patents, and shall file in the patent office a written description of the same, and of the manner and process of making, constructing, compounding and using it, in such full, clear, concise and exact terms, as to enable any person skilled in the art or science to which it appertains, or with which it is most nearly connected, to make, construct, compound, and use the same; and in case of a machine, he shall explain the principle thereof and the best mode in which he has contemplated applying that principle, so as to distinguish it from other inventions; and he shall particularly point out and distinctly claim the part, improvement and combination which he claims as his invention or discovery. The specification and claim shall be signed by the inventor, and attested by two witnesses."

It is also required by law that when "The case admits of drawings," it shall be properly illustrated; and also, if the Commissioner requires it, that a model shall be furnished in cases capable of such demonstration.

The cost of obtaining Letters Patent in ordinary cases is: First, Government fees, $15; counsel fees, including drawings, $25; second, or final Government fees, to be paid within six months from date of allowance, $20; total, $60.

Designs.—A design patent can be obtained for novelties in the shape or configuration of articles, or impressions by any means whatever. These patents are of great value to the trade. The government fees for a design patent are:

On filing every application for a design patent.............$10 00
On issuing a design patent for 3½ years no further charge.
On issuing a design patent for 7 years...................... 5 00
On issuing a design patent for 14 years..................... 20 00

Caveats.—A caveat is a confidential communication filed in the patent office, and it consists of a specification, drawings, oath and petition. The specification must contain a clear description of the intended invention.

How a Copyright is Secured.—The method by which a copyright is obtained under the revised acts of Congress is as simple and inexpensive as can be reasonably asked. All unnecessary red tape is dispensed with, and the cost to the author who is seeking thus to protect himself in the enjoyment of the profits of his work, is so small as to be scarcely appreciable. This is an example of cheapness and directness toward which all branches of public administration should tend, if a government is to fulfil its proper mission of serving the people without needlessly taxing them. Directions have lately been issued for the guidance of persons wishing to obtain copyrights; and as many of our readers may not be conversant with the subject, we give a brief abstract of the process.

The first thing necessary is to send a printed copy of the title of the work, plainly directed, to "Librarian of Congress, Washington, D. C." The copyright law applies not only to books, pamphlets and newspapers, but also to maps, charts, photographs, paintings, drawings, music, statuary, etc. If there is a title page, send that; if not, a title must be printed expressly for the purpose, and in both cases the name of the author or claimant of copyright must accompany the title. Use no smaller paper than commercial note.

The legal fee for recording each copyright claim is 50 cents, and for a copy of this record (or certificate of copyright under seal of the office) an additional 50 cents is required, making in all $1.00, if certificate is wanted, which will be mailed as soon as reached in the records. In cases of persons not residents of the United States, the fee for recording title is $1.00, and fee for copy 50c., making $1.50 in all.

Within 10 days after your book, or other article, is published, you are required to send two complete copies of the best edition to the Librarian, addressed as before, prepaying postage; or the Librarian will furnish "penalty labels," under which they can be sent free of postage. If this deposit of copies is neglected, the copyright is void, and you are liable to a fine of $25.

The law requires that on the title page of a copyrighted work, or some part of the drawing, painting, statue, or whatever it may be, there shall be printed these words: "Entered according to Act of Congress, in the year——, by——, in the office of the Librarian of Congress, at Washington;" or, if preferred, this briefer form may be used: "Copyright, 18—, by——." To this may be added, "Right of translation reserved," or "All rights reserved;" but in that case the Librarian must have been duly notified, so that he may include it in the record.

Any person who prints the copyright notice on his work without having obtained a copyright, is liable to a penalty of $100. The original term of a copyright runs for twenty-eight years, and it may then be renewed for a further term of fourteen years, either by the author or by his widow or children, application being made not less than six months before the expiration of the right. Trade marks and labels cannot be copyrighted under this law, but are provided for by a separate act, relating to matters of detail, which cannot here be recited, but in regard to which, the Librarian at Washington will give the needed information whenever required.

Trade Marks, Labels, Prints, etc.—Copyrights cannot be granted upon trade marks, nor upon mere names of companies or articles, nor upon prints or labels intended to be used with any article of manufacture. If protection for such names or labels is desired, application must be made to the Patent Office, where they are registered at a fee of $6.00 for labels, and $25.00 for trade marks.

By the word "label" is meant a slip of paper, or other material, to be attached to manufactured articles, or to packages containing them, and bearing the name of the manufacturer, directions for use, etc.

By the word "print" is meant any device, word, or figures (not a trade mark) impressed directly upon the article, to denote the name of the manufacturer, etc.

COMMON NAMES OF CHEMICAL SUBSTANCES

Aqua Fortis ....Nitric Acid
Aqua Regia...............Nitro-Muriatic Acid
Blue Vitriol..............Sulphate of Copper
Cream of Tartar.........Bitartrate of Potassium
Calomel..... ....Chloride of Mercury
Chalk ....Carbonate of Calcium
Salt of Tartar...........Carbonate of Potassa
Caustic Potassa..... . Hydrate of Potassium
Chloroform ....Chloride of Gormyle
Common Salt....... ....Chloride of Sodium
Copperas or Green Vitriol Sulphate of Iron
Corrosive Sublimate.....Bichloride of Mercury
Diamond........... ....Pure Carbon
Dry Alum................Sulphate Aluminum and Potassium
Epsom Salts..............Sulphate of Magnesia
Ethiops Mineral..........Black Sulphide of Mercury
Fire Damp................Light Carbureted Hydrogen
Galena ....Sulphide of Lead
Glucose...................Grape Sugar
Goulard Water..........Basic Acetate of Lead
Iron Pyrites..............Bisulphide of Iron
Jeweler's Putty..........Oxide of Tin
King Yellow.............Sulphide of Arsenic
Laughing Gas .... Protoxide of Nitrogen
Lime ....Oxide of Calcium
Lunar Caustic...........Nitrate of Silver
Mosaic Gold......... ....Bisulphide of Tin
Muriate of Lime.........Chloride of Calcium
Niter of Saltpeter........Nitrate of Potash
Oil of Vitriol............. Sulphuric Acid
Potash ....Oxide of Potassium
Red Lead.................Oxide of Lead
Rust of Iron........... ...Oxide of Iron
Sal Ammoniac...... ....Muriate of Ammonia
Slacked Lime............Hydrate of Calcium
Soda ....Oxide of Sodium
Spirits of Hartshorn. ...Ammonia
Spirit of Salt.............Hydrochloric or Muriatic Acid
Stucco, or Plaster Paris..Sulphate of Lime
Sugar of Lead...........Acetate of Lead
Verdigris.................Basic Acetate of Copper
Vermilion................Sulphide of Mercury
Vinegar...................Acetic Acid (diluted
Volatile Alkali........... Ammonia
Water...................Oxide of Hydrogen
White Precipitate........Ammoniated Mercury
White Vitriol.............Sulphate of Zinc

CLASSIFIED ALPHABETICAL INDEX

DEPARTMENT 1.—THE DRUGGIST.

Tables of Weights and Their Equivalents.... 10

Useful Table of Equivalents.......................... 10

Vermifuge Lozenges................................ 33

Wintergreen, Decoction of......................... 25

DEPARTMENT II.—THE CHEMIST.

DEPARTMENT III.—TOILET ARTICLES.

DEPARTMENT IV.—THE HOUSEHOLD.

DEPARTMENT V.—ALL TRADES.

DEPARTMENT VI.—THE FARM AND DAIRY.

DEPARTMENT VII.—GENERAL MISCELLANY.

––––––––

NOTE.—When there is more than one method given for performing the same thing, the form most in use is indexed, the others following it not being mentioned. Reference to the first will call attention to the others. The subject matter is for the greater part classified under the sub-heads alphabetically, but in some cases this rule has not been adhered to. Reference to the Table of Contents will show in what department any recipe can be found, while the index will indicate the page. If proper care is exercised it will not be found difficult to locate any formula in the book in a moment's time.